THE AUTHORISED WARTIME HISTORY
OF THE SPECIAL BOAT SERVICE
FROM THE SECRET SBS ARCHIVES

SBS
SILENT WARRIORS

SAUL DAVID

D0230631

WILLIAM
COLLINS

SAUL DAVID is a historian, broadcaster and the author of several critically acclaimed works of fiction and non-fiction including *Operation Thunderbolt*, which was turned into the movie *Entebbe*; *The Force*, described by Douglas Brinkley as 'a monumental achievement'; and most recently *Crucible of Hell*, which was picked as a Best Book of 2020 by *The Times* and *Telegraph*. David's histor the British Army Military Book of the Ye Military Literature and variously name Book of the Year and an Amazon Hist

THE *SUNDAY TIMES* BESTSELLER

'It is incredibly refreshing to read of these fabulously daring missions: of men of astonishing courage blowing up bridges, surveying invasion beaches, sinking ships in harbour and making clandestine rendezvous with secret agents – all by canoe and midget submarine . . . This is a terrific book, written with all the gusto, thrills and heady excitement these SBS operations richly deserve. It really is one of the most enjoyable histories I've read in many a year'   JAMES HOLLAND, *Daily Telegraph*

'It's an extraordinary trawl through the archives, backed up with diaries and interviews; an accomplished act of storytelling . . . This is a book about big personalities, adventurers and inventors . . . An authorised history of a secret unit has to record not only the bravery of its unacknowledged warriors – which David has done with style – but also make a case for its strategic importance . . . David has written a book that often gladdens the heart, but also makes you think about the nature of sacrifice'   *The Times*

'A brilliant account of how the SBS was born from wartime needs, and just how much the organisation and its affiliated units were able to achieve in those early years'   *Daily Mail*

'Riveting . . . Saul David has shown great skill in pulling the disparate threads of unit reports into a cohesive story. The knowledge of those involved, their bravery and jeopardy, will grip the general reader'   *Spectator*

'An absolute must-read if you are a fan of derring-do and Andy McNab. I am going to be telling everyone to buy it'   ROB RINDER, Talk Radio

Also by Saul David

NON-FICTION

Churchill's Sacrifice of the Highland Division: France 1940

Mutiny at Salerno, 1943: An Injustice Exposed

The Homicidal Earl: The Life of Lord Cardigan

Military Blunders

Prince of Pleasure: The Prince of Wales and the Making of the Regency

The Indian Mutiny: 1857

Zulu: The Heroism and Tragedy of the Zulu War of 1879

Victoria's Wars: The Rise of Empire

All the King's Men: The British Soldier in the Era of Sword and Musket

100 Days to Victory: How the Great War Was Fought and Won 1914–1918

Operation Thunderbolt

The Force: The Legendary Special Ops Unit and WWII's Mission Impossible

Crucible of Hell

FICTION

Zulu Hart

Hart of Empire

The Prince and the Whitechapel Murders

William Collins
An imprint of HarperCollins*Publishers*
1 London Bridge Street
London SE1 9GF

WilliamCollinsBooks.com

HarperCollins*Publishers*
1st Floor, Watermarque Building, Ringsend Road
Dublin 4, Ireland

First published in Great Britain in 2021 by William Collins
This William Collins paperback edition published in 2022

1

ISBN 978-0-00-839456-1

Maps by Martin Brown

Typeset in Sabon Lt Std by Palimpsest Book Production Ltd,
Falkirk, Stirlingshire

Printed and Bound in the UK using 100% Renewable Electricity at
CPI Group (UK) Ltd

MIX
Paper from
responsible sources
FSC C007454

This book is produced from independently certified FSC™ paper
to ensure responsible forest management.

For more information visit: www.harpercollins.co.uk/green

For Ollie

And in memory of Paddy Ashdown (1941–2018), ex-SBS

Contents

PART II: COCKLESHELL HEROES AND BEACHCOMBERS, 1942–4

PART III: ENDGAME, 1944–5

Illustrations

Integrated

Abbreviations

AJF	Anti-Japanese Force
AJCF	Anti-Japanese Civilian Force
BEF	British Expeditionary Force
CBE	Commander of the Order of the British Empire
CCO	Chief of Combined Operations
CODC	Combined Operations Development Centre
COHQ	Combined Operations Headquarters
COPP	Combined Operations Pilotage Parties
COSSAC	Chief of Staff to the Supreme Allied Commander
COTC	Combined Operations Training Centre
DCM	Distinguished Conduct Medal
DD	Duplex-drive
DFC	Distinguished Flying Cross
DSM	Distinguished Service Medal
DSO	Distinguished Service Order
DSC	Distinguished Service Cross
ETO	European Theater of Operations
HM	His Majesty's
HMS	His Majesty's Ship
LCP	Landing craft, personnel
LCT	Landing craft, tank
MBE	Member of the Order of the British Empire
MC	Military Cross
MGB	Motor gun boat
MiD	Mention in despatches
ML	Motor launch
MM	Military Medal
MV	Motor vessel

NID	Naval Intelligence Department
OBE	Officer of the Order of the British Empire
PT	Physical training
QWR	Queen's Westminster Rifles
RA	Royal Artillery
RAF	Royal Air Force
RAN	Royal Australian Navy
RASC	Royal Army Service Corps
RCN	Royal Canadian Navy
RCNVR	Royal Canadian Naval Volunteer Reserve
RE	Royal Engineers
RM	Royal Marines
RMBPD	Royal Marine Boom Patrol Detachment
RMFU	Royal Marine Fortress Unit
RN	Royal Navy
RNR	Royal Naval Reserve
RNVR	Royal Naval Volunteer Reserve ('Wavy Navy')
RV	Rendezvous
SAS	Special Air Service
SBS	Special Boat Section, Special Boat Squadron and, after 1987, Special Boat Service
SBSA	Special Boat Service Association
SEAC	South East Asia Command
SOE	Special Operations Executive
SOG	Small Operations Group
SRD	Special Reconnaissance Department
SS	Special Service
SSRF	Small Scale Raiding Force
TNT	Trinitrotoluene (explosive material)
VC	Victoria Cross

Maps

Western Europe and the Mediterranean

- Germany & German annexed territories after Sep. 1939
- German-occupied territory
- Pro-German neutral, or having a treaty of friendship with Germany
- - - - German blockade area, Aug. 1940
- Italy, Italian colonies & Italian annexed territory
- Vichy France & Vichy territories
- Soviet Union & Soviet Republics, from Aug. 1940
- Soviet occupied & annexed territories, 17 Sep. 1939–25 Mar. 1941
- Great Britain & British colonies and mandates
- Pro-British neutral
- Neutral

```
0                    500 miles
0          500 km
```

North Sea

IRELAND
Dublin

UNITED
Liverpool
KINGDOM
London
Amsterdam
Portsmouth
NETHERLAND
Brussels
BELGIUM
LU
Brest
Paris
F R A N C E
SW
Bordeaux
Toulon
PORTUGAL
S P A I N
Corsica
Lisbon
Madrid
Barcelona
Sardinia
Cadiz
Balearics
Gibraltar
(British)
Oran
Algiers
Casablanca
Tunis
F R E N C H
M O R O C C O
TUNIS
A L G E R I A

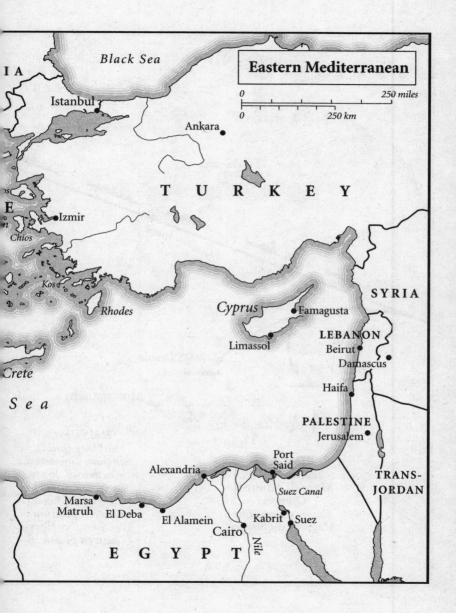

Black Sea

Eastern Mediterranean

0   250 *miles*

0   250 *km*

I A

Istanbul

Ankara

E

Izmir

Chios

T U R K E Y

Kos

Rhodes

Cyprus

Famagusta

SYRIA

Limassol

LEBANON

Beirut

Damascus

Crete

Haifa

Sea

PALESTINE

Jerusalem

Port
Said

**TRANS-
JORDAN**

Alexandria

Suez Canal

Marsa
Matruh

El Deba

El Alamein

Kabrit

Suez

Cairo

Nile

E G Y P T

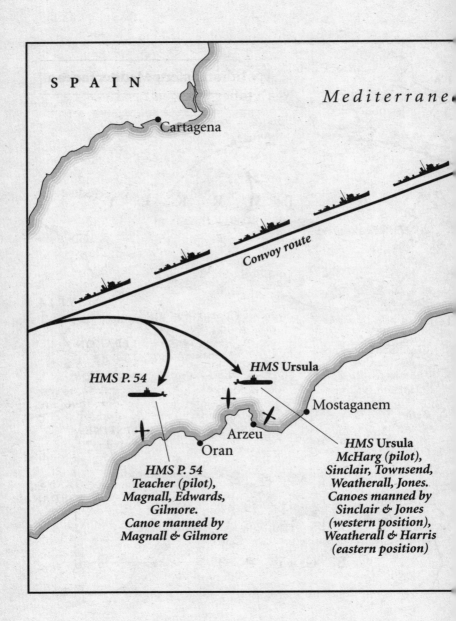

SPAIN

Cartagena

Mediterrane

Convoy route

HMS Ursula

HMS P. 54

Mostaganem

Arzeu

Oran

HMS P. 54
Teacher (pilot),
Magnall, Edwards,
Gilmore.
Canoe manned by
Magnall & Gilmore

HMS Ursula
McHarg (pilot),
Sinclair, Townsend,
Weatherall, Jones.
Canoes manned by
Sinclair & Jones
(western position),
Weatherall & Harris
(eastern position)

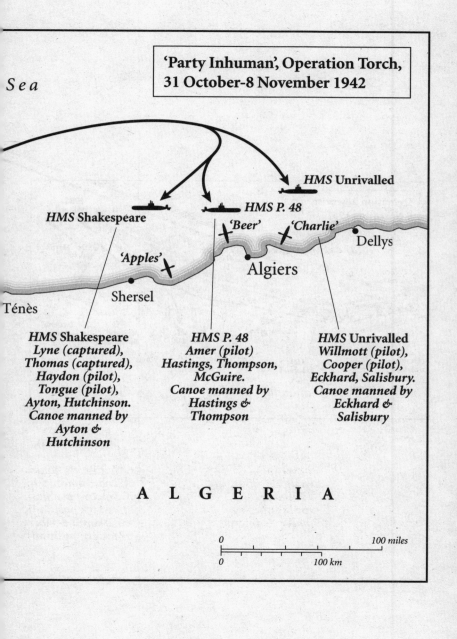

'Party Inhuman', Operation Torch, 31 October–8 November 1942

Sea

HMS Unrivalled

HMS Shakespeare

HMS P. 48

'Beer'

'Charlie'

Dellys

'Apples'

Algiers

Shersel

Ténès

HMS Shakespeare
*Lyne (captured),
Thomas (captured),
Haydon (pilot),
Tongue (pilot),
Ayton, Hutchinson.
Canoe manned by
Ayton &
Hutchinson*

*HMS P. 48
Amer (pilot)
Hastings, Thompson,
McGuire.
Canoe manned by
Hastings &
Thompson*

HMS Unrivalled
*Willmott (pilot),
Cooper (pilot),
Eckhard, Salisbury.
Canoe manned by
Eckhard &
Salisbury*

A L G E R I A

0   100 miles

0   100 km

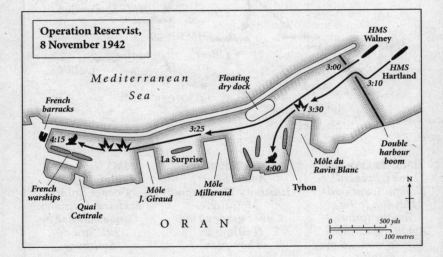

**Operation Reservist,
8 November 1942**

*Mediterranean
Sea*

Floating
dry dock

*HMS
Walney*

3:00

*HMS
Hartland*

3:10

French
barracks

4:15

3:25

3:30

4:00

**Double
harbour
boom**

La Surprise

*Môle du
Ravin Blanc*

N

French
warships

Quai
Centrale

*Môle
J. Giraud*

*Môle
Millerand*

Tyhon

O R A N

0   500 yds

0   100 metres

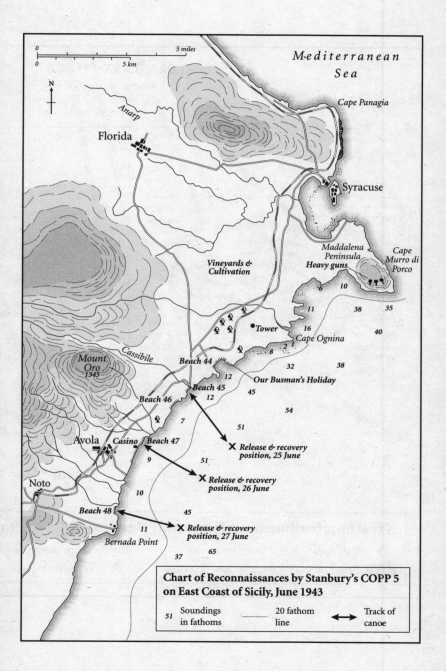

Chart of Reconnaissances by Stanbury's COPP 5 on East Coast of Sicily, June 1943

51 Soundings in fathoms · · · · · · 20 fathom line ⟵➤ Track of canoe

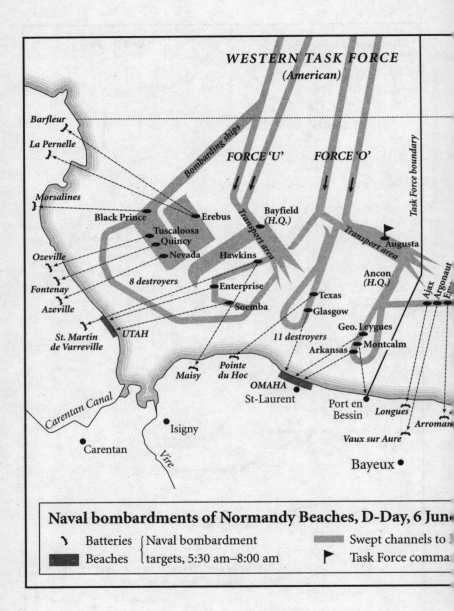

Naval bombardments of Normandy Beaches, D-Day, 6 Jun...

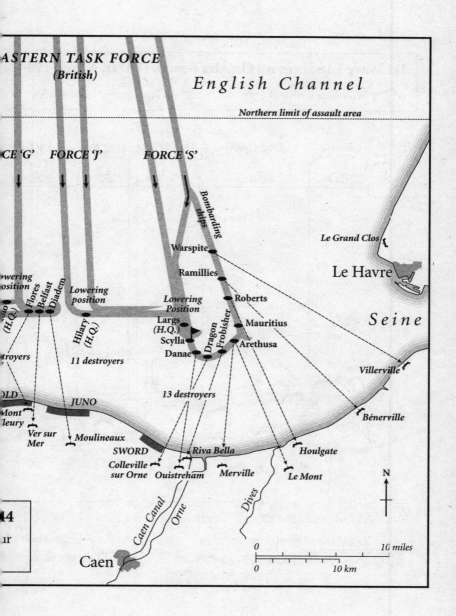

EASTERN TASK FORCE
(British)

English Channel

Northern limit of assault area

FORCE 'G'   FORCE 'J'   FORCE 'S'

Bombarding ships

Le Grand Clos

Le Havre

Warspite

Ramillies

Roberts

S e i n e

Lowering position

Lowering Position

Largs
(H.Q.)

Mauritius

Scylla   Dragon
Frobisher   Arethusa

Danae

Villerville

13 destroyers

Bénerville

Houlgate

Riva Bella

SWORD   Merville   *Le Mont*

Colleville
sur Orne   Ouistreham

Caen Canal   *Orne*   *Dives*

N

Caen

0   10 *miles*

0   10 *km*

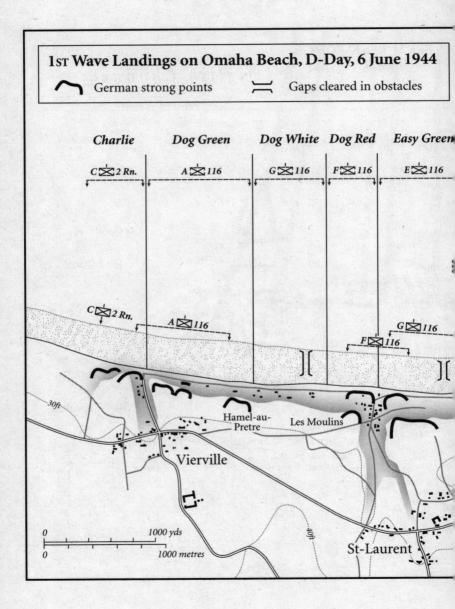

1ST Wave Landings on Omaha Beach, D-Day, 6 June 1944

German strong points

Gaps cleared in obstacles

Charlie

Dog Green

Dog White　**Dog Red**

Easy Green

C 2 Rn.

A 116

G 116

F 116

E 116

C 2 Rn.

A 116

G 116

F 116

30ft

Hamel-au-
Pretre

Les Moulins

Vierville

40ft

0   1000 yds

0   1000 metres

St-Laurent

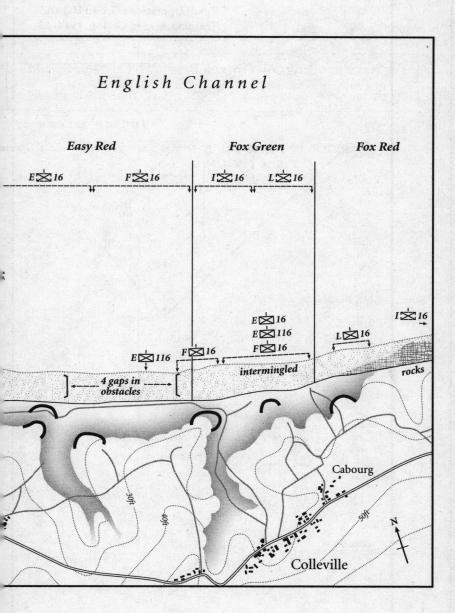

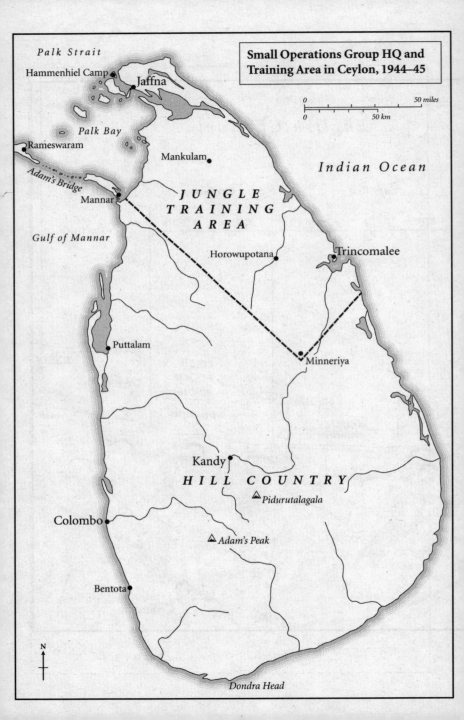

Small Operations Group HQ and Training Area in Ceylon, 1944–45

0   50 miles
0   50 km

Palk Strait

Hammenhiel Camp

Jaffna

Palk Bay

Rameswaram

Adam's Bridge

Mannar

Mankulam

Indian Ocean

*J U N G L E
T R A I N I N G
A R E A*

Gulf of Mannar

Horowupotana

Trincomalee

Puttalam

Minneriya

Kandy

H I L L   C O U N T R Y

△ Pidurutalagala

△ Adam's Peak

Colombo

Bentota

N

Dondra Head

INDIA

CHINA

Chittagong

Irrawaddy

Salween

Mekong

4

Mandalay

3

BURMA

5

Akyab

Ramree Island

Sandoway

Pegu

Bassein

Rangoon

SIAM

Bangkok

Andaman
Islands

*Mergui
Archipelago*

FRENCH

INDO-CHINA

Saigon

Mekong

*Andaman
Sea*

*Kra
Isthmus*

*Gulf
of
Siam*

*Nicobar
Islands*

6, 7, 8

*South China
Sea*

1   *2*

Kota Bharu

Penang I.

MALAYA

*Indian
Ocean*

Medan

Strait of Malacca

Kuala Lumpur

9

Singapore

N

0   250 miles

0   250 km

DUTCH   EAST   INDIES

**South-East Asia: Principal Raids
and Areas of Operations by Small
Operations Group, 1944-1945**

1 North Sumatra (Operation Frippery),
Aug. 1944

2 North Sumatra (Operations Spratt
Able and Spratt Baker), Sep. 1944

3 Akyab Island (Operation Lightning),
Dec. 1944/Jan. 1945

4 Irawaddy Crossings and Recces,
Feb.–May 1945

5 Elizabeth Island (Operations David
and Deputy), Oct./Nov. 1944

6, 7 & 8 Phuket (Operations Baboon
and Copyright), Mar. 1945

9 Morib Beaches, Malaya (Operation
Confidence), June 1945

Many operations by COPPs, SBS &
Detachment 385 were made in support of
local forces in the theatre and are not
included above.

Foreword

by the Colonel Commandant

It is a pleasure to have been asked to write a foreword for this authoritative book on the wartime exploits in the Second World War of units such as the obscurely named Combined Operations Pilotage Parties (COPP) and Royal Marine Boom Patrol Detachment (RMBPD) – some of the component parts of what was to become the Special Boat Service.

My first encounter with the SBS was in the 1960s when, as a young submariner in the Far East, I found myself working with the also young Paddy Ashdown and his SBS team; and I was very pleased to have been asked to collaborate with him to a small degree when he embarked on his vision to write an authorised history of the Service – a vision sadly never realised, as the author recognises in paying tribute to him in his Introduction.

From those early days and on through my submarine career, working with the SBS was a normal – albeit not frequent – practice and *SBS: Silent Warriors* subliminally draws out the very special relationship between these two silent services whose work is so invariably clandestine, and where both share a similar professional ethos.

This narrative of the formation of the units who would penetrate hostile territory from the sea to provide vital support to amphibious operations, create mayhem on enemy shoreside infrastructure, aid agents to land on hostile beaches and conduct other nefarious activities close to the coast, could not be more comprehensive. And the nature of those extraordinary men who made up these cadres – their common attributes of unobtrusiveness, independence of mind, determination and the harsh, rigorous training they underwent – is vividly painted. The reader is left with a clear image of the courageous and entrepreneurial forefathers of the modern-day SBS.

The operations carried out, mostly via canoes launched from submarines, are well laid out and the key roles played in, for example, the D-day landings is made very clear; and appropriate space is given to the legendary Operations Frankton and Sunbeam. Throughout the courage and selflessness of the men who took part in them and in other important but less iconic operations in the Mediterranean, Far East and Channel come across forcefully.

Insights into some of the operators themselves – such as 'Blondie' Hasler, Roger 'Jumbo' Courtney, Nigel Willmott and many others – are excellent and make the reader feel personally involved. And the politics and intrigues of getting these very independently minded people accepted by the more strait-laced and formal hierarchies are fascinatedly described.

It is an absorbing read that points to the beginning of the extraordinary journey taken by the much-expanded modern-day SBS. A detailed history of a group of outstanding men operating by 'Strength and Guile' at the limits of audacity, ingenuity, fitness and raw bravery in daring operations throughout the Second World War.

Having worked with the SBS on and off for sixty years it is clear to me that the legacy and spirit of those warriors of some eighty years ago lives on. Years in the Royal Navy have taught me that the water softens, dissolves and erodes. But it has the opposite effect on the SBS; they have been forged by the storms of the sea, they embrace its cruelty, and they exploit its freedom. The SBS's outputs are now much broader than they once were, but they are still made up of the select few; a special group of hardened professionals who operate by land, sea and air all over the globe. Collectively they make up one of the most feared and effective special forces units in the world; their heroic deeds and national endeavours are never told, shrouded in the utmost secrecy. They operate like no other, and by

'Strength and Guile' achieve outcomes that others simply cannot.

This book is the story of how it all began!

Mike Boyce

Admiral of the Fleet the Lord Boyce KG GCB OBE,
Colonel Commandant of the SBS
and Patron of the SBS Association

Introduction

Britain's SBS – or Special Boat Service – was the world's first maritime special operations unit. Founded by 38-year-old Lieutenant Roger 'Jumbo' Courtney, an amateur soldier with unconventional ideas,* in the dark days of 1940 as a country facing defeat looked for new ways to take the fight to a seemingly unbeatable enemy, it became – in its various guises – one of the most effective fighting forces of the Second World War and has served as a model for special forces ever since.

It preferred the subtle approach: arriving silently at night, on or below the sea, to gather intelligence, ferry agents or equipment, destroy enemy infrastructure or ships, and support advancing troops. 'The prime function of SBS,' wrote Major G. B. 'Gruff' Courtney, the brother of its founder and himself one of its early members, 'was to do maximum damage to the Axis war effort with a minimum of men and stores, by small-scale operations on hostile shores where the use of conventional means, such as aircraft or naval vessels, would have risked losses uneconomic in a long war of attrition. SBS was cost-effective.'[1]

Its first mission was a daring beach reconnaissance of Rhodes in the spring of 1941. Over the next four years, the SBS and its affiliates would carry out many more in the Mediterranean, the Atlantic, the Channel and the Far East: they included the destruction of enemy ships, railways and bridges; the rescue of fugitive Allied soldiers; the support of Commando operations (including the attempted assassination of Erwin Rommel and the ill-fated

---

* In much the same way that its sister service, the SAS, was founded by David Stirling a year later.

assault on Oran harbour); and the use of midget submarines to signpost the Normandy beaches on D-Day. During that time, Courtney's unit would grow in size and be called many different names. From 1942, its work was supplemented by Lieutenant Commander Nigel Willmott's Royal Navy Coppists, canoe-borne swimmers and beach surveyors who became the eyes and ears of every major Allied landing of the war; and also that year by the Royal Marine Boom Patrol Detachment (RMBPD), led by Major 'Blondie' Hasler, a unit directly under the then Chief of Combined Operations, Vice Admiral Lord Louis Mountbatten, whose role was to develop new ways of attacking ships in harbour. Hasler's finest hour, the raid on Bordeaux harbour by the 'Cockleshell Heroes', was arguably the toughest amphibious operation of the war.

Until now, there has been no authoritative history of the wartime SBS. Authors have concentrated instead on separate strands of the story. G. B. Courtney has written about the original Special Boat Section in *SBS in World War Two*. Others have focused on the confusingly titled Special Boat Squadron, the former marine branch of the SAS (created after the remnants of Courtney's original No. 1 SBS had been absorbed by David Stirling's raiding unit in 1942) that carried out a number of amphibious operations in the eastern Mediterranean from 1943 to 1945. They include John Lodwick's *The Filibusters: The Story of the Special Boat Service*, Barrie Pitt's *Special Boat Squadron: The Story of the SBS in the Mediterranean*, and Gavin Mortimer's *The SBS in World War II*. There are books about Coppists, notably Bill Strutton's and Michael Pearson's *The Secret Invaders* and Ian Trenowden's *Stealthily by Night*; and a few on Hasler's RMBPD, including C. E. Lucas Phillips' *Cockleshell Heroes*. John Parker's *SBS: The Inside Story of the Special Boat Service* covers the whole story of the SBS from 1940 to the present day – but not in any great detail.

The void should have been filled by the late Paddy Ashdown, himself a member of the SBS before becoming MP for Yeovil and Leader of the Liberal Democrats. Supported by the Special Boat Service Association (SBSA) – which has a charitable role in looking after both serving and former SBS operators and their dependants – Paddy was working on a book very similar to this one when he died suddenly, at the age of 77, in 2018. I was asked to step into Paddy's sizeable shoes. It was a daunting prospect: not least because Paddy understood the ethos of the SBS from personal experience; whereas I am very much an outsider. But I also felt that I could bring an objectivity to the project that would have its own advantages.

I decided to start from scratch, and do all my own research and writing. This was not a criticism of Paddy's work. I've read and enjoyed a number of his books, particularly *A Brilliant Little Operation* (the story of the Frankton Raid). But all authors have different writing styles, and the book would have read very strangely if I had completed what Paddy described in his introduction as both 'a homage and a history'.[2] It would also, I suspect, have been considerably longer.

Thanks to Paddy's initial work, I had one big advantage over previous authors: an introduction to the SBS Association. To gain the SBSA's backing I had, in effect, to undergo a vetting process: meet the relevant people and write a new proposal they were happy to endorse. In return they gave me the same access to previously unseen material in the secret SBSA's archives at Poole that had been granted to Paddy.

This book is the result. Using new material from multiple archives, published first-hand accounts and interviews, it tells for the first time the extraordinary intertwined stories of Courtney's SBS, Willmott's Coppists and Hasler's 'Cockleshell Heroes' (all acknowledged as forerunners of the modern SBS). Very much a human tale, it concentrates on the key personalities and the daredevil missions they undertook. It is an authorised history – the first time the SBSA has given its seal of approval to *any* book about the unit's past activities – but not an official one. The selection of material and opinions expressed are entirely my own, and not those of the unit or the Ministry of Defence. The narrative is not comprehensive, for reasons of word length and continuity. Not every mission is covered in detail, and the story of the Special Boat Squadron in the eastern Mediterranean from 1943 to 1945 is told only briefly because that unit had a different MO from the original SBS – undertaking sizeable inland raids rather than small canoe-borne missions – and is, in any case, the subject of a number of previous books.

What Courtney's SBS and its affiliated units – most notably Willmott's COPP and Hasler's RMBPD – were able to achieve in four years of warfare is nothing less than extraordinary. At no time did these units individually number more than a hundred officers and men. Yet these small 'Bands of Brothers' were able to take part in scores of planned operations from submarines, surface craft and other means of transport, as well as carry out numerous minor reconnaissance trips and fighting patrols. Their missions – as the following pages reveal – were some of the most audacious and legendary of the war.

The story is related chiefly from a British perspective, but there are strong Allied connections – particularly American – throughout. They include Operations Flagpole (dropping Major General Mark Clark and four US staff officers on the coast of Algiers for secret talks with the Vichy French), Torch (when canoeists guided US Rangers and other American troops on to their landing beaches in North Africa), Reservist (the assault on Oran harbour by the SBS and the US 6th Armored Infantry Regiment), and Overlord (where the American refusal to allow Coppists to mark their landing beaches on D-Day was a key factor in the huge casualties suffered by the US 1st and 29th Divisions on Omaha).

The 'silent warriors' who carried out these missions were singular men, and still are today. The SBS, wrote Paddy Ashdown, has always 'valued guile over size; technology and team work over brute force; silence over loud bangs and braggadocio. These are not qualities which have been arrived at by accident. They are derived and inherited from the separate, small and highly secret bodies, each with a different skill and discipline, which operated in the shadows of the Second World War and were incorporated into the modern-day SBS afterwards.'[3]

This book owes its existence to Paddy's vision. I hope it does him justice.

Part I
Beginnings, 1940–2

I
'A new style of warfare'

Expecting company, the armed sentries on the Commando ship HMS *Glengyle* were on full alert as the 10,000-ton former cargo ship sat at anchor off Inveraray, a small town at the head of Loch Fyne in the Scottish Highlands. Yet they failed to spot the low silhouette of a two-man collapsible canoe – known as a folbot – approaching through the inky darkness, propelled noiselessly by a single paddler.

Pausing briefly to chalk crosses 'along the hull to simulate limpet mines', the canoeist made for the ship's bows where, belying his 38 years, he slipped his thickset but immensely strong body into the icy water and began climbing up the anchor chain. Once on deck he carefully avoided the sentries until he found what he was looking for: the canvas cover for an Oerlikon 20 mm anti-aircraft cannon, one of twelve dotted around the *Glengyle*'s decks. Clutching his trophy, he retraced his steps, disappearing quietly over the guard rail and rejoining his canoe which he paddled back to shore. Barely half an hour later, still dripping water and shivering with cold, Second Lieutenant Roger 'Jumbo' Courtney – with his 'bashed-in kind of face' and 'blunt no-nonsense manner' – barged in to a high-level naval conference at the nearby Argyll Arms Hotel and placed his trophy on the table, as if to say: I told you so.[1]

The senior officers present – including the commander of the Combined Operations Training Centre (COTC) at Inveraray and the skipper of the *Glengyle* – were impressed, as was Courtney's ultimate boss Admiral of the Fleet Sir Roger Keyes who, as Director of Combined Operations, had the job of coordinating amphibious assaults against German-occupied Europe. Courtney had earlier tried to convince Keyes, a hero of the daring Zeebrugge Raid in 1918, that highly trained canoe teams could be used to great effect: scouting beaches, destroying shipping with limpet mines, landing secret agents, providing vital navigational information for landing forces and sabotaging enemy infrastructure like railway lines.[2] Keyes was interested, and for a time assigned Courtney to his headquarters in London for 'special duties'. But that project had come to nothing and in mid-October 1940 Courtney was ordered to rejoin his parent unit, 8th Commando, at the COTC at Inveraray.[3] He had not been there long when he set the navy a challenge: using his personal folbot *Buttercup*, he would 'board the Commando ship *Glengyle* unnoticed by night and depart again, leaving incontrovertible proof of his visit'; their job was to stop him.

The gun cover, not to mention the chalk crosses on the hull, were proof that they had failed. But Keyes needed to rule out luck, so he asked Courtney to perform the same feat against the nearest submarine depot-ship. Once again, Courtney was able to approach unobserved in his canoe and leave chalk marks above the waterline. He then overreached himself when he climbed up a conveniently placed rope ladder, and was met at the top by the master-at-arms and two Marines with fixed bayonets 'who had been lying in wait, presumably forewarned by the previous victim'.[4] But he had proved his point to Keyes that canoes could be a vital part of Britain's offensive strategy and, as a result, was authorised to raise a small cadre of men who would be trained in the use of folding boats 'for the purpose of carrying out raids upon enemy occupied territory'. Known initially as the Folbot Troop – later the Special Boat Section – it would be equipped with thirty canoes and, for the time being at least, remain part of 8th Commando.[5]

Thus was born, from Courtney's fertile imagination, 'a new style of warfare: a Special Force who came from the sea'. With

Courtney's 'simple act of invention and circumvention' at Inveraray, 'the extraordinary history of the Special Boat Service had begun'.[6]

*

Roger James Allen Courtney, the acknowledged 'father' of the modern SBS, was born in Fulham, London, on 30 July 1902. The eldest son of a wealthy manufacturer of machine tools – himself descended from West Yorkshire gentry stock – young Roger was educated at the minor public schools of Edinburgh House in Lee-on-Solent and Berkhamsted. Narrowly missing service in the Great War, he was commissioned a second lieutenant in the 7th West Yorkshires, a Territorial unit based in Leeds, in 1921. But peacetime soldiering – even part-time – was not for him and he gave up his commission two years later.[7]

Intended, as he put it, for a career in finance, Courtney worked for a time at a bank in Leeds, not far from his family's country home at Ben Rhydding, near Bradford. But the daily grind of a desk job in a provincial city held few attractions for him, and at the age of 19 he resigned to follow his dreams. 'I am,' he wrote later, 'a man whom no place or set of circumstances can satisfy for long.'[8]

Since childhood he had longed to live in the 'African wilds'. He would later recall placing his finger, as a 7-year-old, at the centre of a 'map of Equatorial Africa and declaring that some day I should go there'. Now was the opportunity to redeem that promise and, having overcome 'strenuous family opposition', he set off by steamer for the Kenyan port of Mombasa with £50 in his pocket.

Arriving in Nairobi, the Kenyan capital, Courtney took on a succession of poorly paid jobs, including store clerk and saw-miller. He finally got his first proper taste of Africa by becoming a ranger for a large timber concession. Forced to hunt for the bulk of his food, he quickly learned 'about bushcraft and big game', becoming skilled in 'trails, sign, stalking, habits of animals, range-finding – hundreds of things'. This gave him the confidence to try big-game hunting. He began with elephants (for their ivory),* moved on to buffalo (for their hides), and was eventually licensed as a 'White Hunter', the best of the best, and much in demand by 'untried people who want to go on *safari* in the bush – tourists, visiting scientists, big-game photographers, cinema people, rich men who have come to experience the thrills of big-game hunting'. He charged up to £50 a week for a safari that could last five months.

As well as making him a very good living, the job of White Hunter gave Courtney the material for a book, *Claws of Africa*, which he wrote in 1933 on one of his occasional visits back to England. It was published a year later to good reviews and solid sales, and was the first of four books on his adventures in Africa.[9]

Back in Kenya, he got 'gold fever' when he heard about a strike near the Tanganyika border and immediately quit his job to stake a claim with two co-prospectors. 'Evidence of gold in abundance', he recalled, caused the trio to work 'like beavers'. But when it became obvious that their limited resources were 'inadequate for the job in hand', and that 'modern machinery, proper organisation and capital on a considerable scale' were necessary, they sold out to a syndicate. Courtney decided to stay on as an employee, in case the mine came good. It was a mistake.[10]

Finding it hard to stomach the transition from partner to paid hand, he drank heavily and became, as he put it, 'mildly rebellious and strongly critical of authority', with a 'chip of discontent perched permanently' on his shoulder. The final straw was the news that a former sweetheart – the one woman who might have tamed his wanderlust – had agreed to 'marry the best-looking farmer in Kenya'. He decided to cut his losses and look for a new adventure.

As ever, he was short of money. 'Indeed,' he wrote, 'after spending my final pay-packet, I had to sell my rifle to pay my remaining debts. My only possessions after squaring up were a

---

* The origin of Courtney's nickname 'Jumbo'.

folding rubber canoe, a repair outfit for same, some camping and cooking gear, a miniature telescope and one pound in cash.' With these scant resources, he set off from the head-waters of the White Nile river to see how far he could get.[11]

His canoe, *Buttercup*, was a two-seater sports model he had bought for £22 from Selfridges department store in London on one of his trips home.[12] It was a 'seventeen-foot vessel, slim and speedy-looking, complete with mast and sail'. He stored his kit and stores, including three Oxo cubes and a bag of potatoes, and two petrol cans for buoyancy, 'fore and aft under the canvas decking'. Finally, after a mammoth drinking session with his fellow mine workers, during which one of them fell into the water and was almost eaten by a crocodile, he set off from the banks of Lake Victoria on an epic 4,000-mile journey down the fabled White Nile river to the Mediterranean Sea. The odyssey would take him more than six months to complete.[13]

There were two interruptions: first a spell working as a surveyor of a potential copper mine; then 'an interesting experiment to exist for a time as closely as possible in the manner of a N'dorobo hunter, eating native food, making fire by means of firesticks, and hunting with bow-and-arrow and spear for meat'. The latter experience toughened Courtney, turning his skin a 'deep coppery-brown' and leaving his bare feet insensitive to pain. It also taught him vital survival skills and the value of self-reliance. But with time moving on, he resumed his journey.

Hazards were many: he encountered leopards and lions, herds of hippos, and the chilling sight of thousands of crocodiles on either bank. In Egypt he almost succumbed to the cloying embrace of quicksand, but was saved when *Buttercup* floated towards him on a back-eddy. Only the last crowded stretch of the river, from Aswan to Isna in Egypt, did he find unrewarding. 'I have little affection for the human wharf-rats of the lower reaches of the Nile,' he wrote later, 'and I wanted to be rid of them as quickly as possible.' So he completed the final lap to Cairo in a third-class train compartment, packed with people and livestock whose pungent odours made him 'nauseous'.[14]

Penniless once again, Courtney headed for British-administered Palestine where Arab anger towards a rising tide of Jewish immigration had resulted in open revolt. 'It seemed to me,' Courtney recalled, 'that there was an opportunity here for honourable advancement.' Having entered the mandate illegally, he joined the Palestine Police and eventually rose to the rank of sergeant. His eighteen months of service, from July 1936 to early 1938, were full of incident and danger as he braved Arab snipers, rioters and bombs. He even worked for a time as bodyguard to the inspector general of police, and left during a lull in the violence, though the revolt rumbled on until the summer of 1939.[15]

By then, Courtney's wild ways had been partly tamed by a beautiful and spirited woman, Dorrise, whom he married in the summer of 1938. Well matched, they spent their honeymoon paddling *Buttercup* down the Danube river, before settling in a cottage in East Horsley, Surrey. In March 1939, in the wake of Nazi Germany's duplicitous annexation of Czechoslovakia, Courtney sensed that war was coming and rejoined the Territorial Army, this time as a private in the 1st Queen's Westminster Rifles.* In the section headed Trade on Enlistment, he wrote: 'Safari Manager'.[16]

When Britain responded to Germany's invasion of Poland by declaring war on 3 September 1939, and the British Expeditionary Force was sent to France, the 1st QWR remained at home with the bulk of the Territorial forces. Courtney was thus spared the humiliation of defeat the following spring as Germany's blitzkrieg sliced through the Allies' flimsy defences in Belgium and northern France, forcing the BEF's chaotic evacuation from Dunkirk. With France on the verge of surrender, and Britain left to fight alone, Prime Minister Winston Churchill told his military chiefs on 3 June 1940 that there was an urgent need to raise 'specially trained forces of the hunter class' to tie up enemy troops by raiding the German-held coastline of Europe.[17] Their response, on 9 June, was to ask all army commands to provide the names of up to

---

* Later the 11th Battalion, King's Royal Rifle Corps.

forty officers and 1,000 other ranks who were prepared to join a 'special force of volunteers for independent mobile operations'. Known as 'Commandos' – a nod to the Afrikaans horsemen who had given the British so much trouble during the Anglo-Boer War of 1899–1902 – they would be composed of fit young men who had seen action, could swim and, ideally, had knowledge of motor vehicles. Officers were expected to have 'personality, tactical ability and imagination', while the men sought were those of 'intelligence and independence', who could behave with minimal supervision.[18]

As the volunteers poured in, they were assigned to one of ten Commando units, each composed of a headquarters and ten troops of fifty men, led by a captain and two junior officers. Given his adventurous background, it was perhaps inevitable that Roger Courtney, now a second lieutenant,* would apply to join the Commando raised in London, No. 8. What is more surprising is that he was accepted and made a section leader of 8 Troop on 2 August. His age should have counted against him, but it was more than compensated for by his skill with a rifle, knowledge of field craft, linguistic ability and physical toughness. 'Although 38 years old,' noted the Commando selecting officer, 'he is extremely hard and fit.'[19]

The contrast with his fellow officers was marked. Most were wealthy aristocrats and landowners from the elite and socially exclusive Household Cavalry and Foot Guards, causing No. 8 to be dubbed the 'Guards' Commando. The commanding officer was the recently promoted Lieutenant Colonel Bob Laycock of the Royal Horse Guards, 33, an Old Etonian who had experience of sailing and navigation; while among the troop leaders were Baron Sudeley, viscounts Milton and Fitzclarence (heirs to the earldoms of Fitzwilliam and Munster respectively), and Dermot Daly, grandson of the 4th Baron Clanmorris. Daly's troop was exclusively Scots Guards, and included a young section

---

* In November 1939, five months after his promotion to corporal, Courtney had been granted an emergency commission.

leader from a Perthshire landed family, Lieutenant Archibald David Stirling, who would later create the SAS. Courtney's two colleagues in 8 Troop – the only composite unit in the Commandos – were both men with political connections: former MP Captain Godfrey Nicholson, 38, whose family owned a gin distillery; and 29-year-old Second Lieutenant Randolph Churchill, the prime minister's only son, who would shortly be elected Member of Parliament for Preston in an uncontested by-election.[20]

Randolph was not everyone's cup of tea. His father's secretary Jock Colville thought him 'one of the most objectionable people I have ever met: noisy, self-assertive, whining and frankly unpleasant'.[21] He had joined the Commandos to impress his father – who, as a young man, had fought in the Sudan and on the North-West Frontier – and what he lacked in physical ability, he made up for with bloody-minded determination. He was, remembered one of his men, 'very fat and unfit', yet he 'proved himself capable of taking anything we had to take'. On one speed march, for example, he 'must have lost a stone' in weight he was sweating so much. Yet Churchill refused to fall out and, as the camp came in sight, shouted gaily: 'Pick up the step!'

A voice from the ranks shouted back: 'Bugger off!'[22]

2

There was No Bluster or Swagger

Jim Sherwood, the son of an insurance broker, was just 16 when he left grammar school to work for a Stockport engineering company. 'I was the office boy,' he recalled, 'running messages, collecting mail, making tea, but at the same time being trained with a view to joining their technical staff.' When war broke out five years later, he possessed a City and Guilds diploma and had a promising career ahead of him. Yet he resigned immediately to join up, believing one volunteer 'was worth two conscripts'. He had been 'brought up on stories of excitement during the First World War, and none of the horror', and felt, in any event, that Hitler's regime needed to be stopped.

Failing the eye test for the RAF, he was enticed into the Royal Army Service Corps by the prospect of driving staff cars in France. Instead he spent the next eight months in charge of lorries and motorbikes in southern England, leaving him bored and frustrated. The call for Commando volunteers – 'to cross the Channel in fast motor launches, grabbing a German or two if possible, and generally creating mayhem on the coast of France' – came not a moment too soon, and he and three friends put their names forward. They were interviewed by an 'army lieutenant' they later discovered was Roger Courtney. He was, remembered Sherwood, 'a very tough, self-reliant sort of man, full of a love of adventure, rather like a grown-up boy, tremendously confident, confidence-inspiring, and very likeable as a person'. There was no bluster or swagger, just a 'straightforward man with an adventurous spirit that he wanted to put to good use'. Sherwood and his friends liked him instantly, and would have gone with him, then and there, if he had asked them to. 'He was that sort of chap,' said Sherwood. 'Full of enthusiasm for these raiding parties [and the need for an] aggressive spirit against the Germans.'

Courtney asked them if they could swim, or had any knowledge of demolitions or boat handling. Sherwood said yes to everything, thinking demolition work was similar to dismantling a house with a pickaxe. Only later did he realise that Courtney was referring to explosives. Not that it mattered. The questions, he suspected, were asked tongue in cheek. If Courtney 'saw some spark of adventure in the chap he was questioning, that was enough'. As the weeks passed with no decision, Sherwood and his friends assumed they had been rejected. Then one day they were called to the orderly room and told: 'You're off. Here's your rail pass to Windsor.' There they were assigned to Captain Nicholson's 8 Troop which was about to join the rest of 8th Commando at the Combined Operations Training Centre at Inveraray in Argyllshire.[1]

Courtney had gone ahead on detached duty. By the time Sherwood and the rest of 8 Troop reached Inveraray on 25 October, he had successfully demonstrated the potential use of canoes and was looking for suitable men for his Folbot Troop. But only limited training in *Buttercup* was possible until the arrival of the thirty canoes that had been ordered in mid-October from the east London firm of Folbot Folding Boats Ltd.[2]

An initial consignment of ten canoes reached Scotland in late November, by which time 8th Commando had moved to Largs in Ayrshire to prepare for its first mission, code-named Workshop: the capture of the small Italian island of Pantelleria, lying between Sicily and Tunisia, which would help to secure Britain's supply route to Malta and Egypt. Moreover, 8th Commando had now combined with 3rd (Southern) Commando to form the 4th Special Service Battalion, with Laycock as overall commander, and Major Dermot Daly running the 8th (now known as the 4th SS Battalion's B Company).[3]

Courtney was unhappy with the quality of the canoes when they arrived, noting that most of their 'struts, spars and ribs' were 'broken', and that 'the quality of the timber used was extremely cheap and inferior'.[4] But as there was nothing else available, he repaired them as best he could and got on with training. He himself had been slated to carry out a lone mission earlier that month. The exact details have never been revealed, and there is no mention of it in the official files. All we have is a brief reference to the mission in two memoranda that Courtney wrote in 1943. His unit's 'first job', he wrote, was against the 'coast of Holland' in 'November 1940'. They were taken close to their target in 'motor torpedo boats', but 'weather conditions made a landing impossible'. It was this experience that convinced Courtney 'that a submarine was a more suitable craft from which to operate folbotists'. With the Holland operation cancelled, Courtney was instructed to begin training his men for the 'recce [reconnaissance] of beaches in Pantelleria' prior to the assault by the Commandos.[5]

A particularly revealing portrait of his time with the Commandos at Largs was provided by the author and journalist Evelyn Waugh who, after a stint in the Royal Marines, had joined the 4th SS Battalion as a liaison officer. A well-known socialite and author – whose most famous novel *Brideshead Revisited* was loosely based on his own experiences at Oxford and during the war – he was friends with many of 8th Commando's 'smart set', some of whom, Randolph Churchill included, were living with their wives in Largs' Marine Hotel. They 'drink a very great deal', noted Waugh in his diary, 'play cards for high figures, dine nightly in Glasgow, and telephone to their [racehorse] trainers endlessly'. Such fast living was out of his league. Having dropped a rank to lieutenant, he had to be 'cautious about money' and found the hotel 'expensive and avaricious'. His bill for a fortnight was only a fifth of the £54 that Randolph and his wife were charged, 'but even so too high'.

Waugh was unimpressed by the 'standard of efficiency and devotion to duty' that he found in 8th Commando, noting that it was 'very much lower than in the Marines'. He added: 'There is no administration or discipline. The men are given 6s a day and told to find their own accommodation. If they behave badly they are simply sent back to their regiments. Officers have no scruples about seeing to their own comfort or getting all the leave they can.' Waugh thought such practices would not have worked with Royal Marines, 'but with the particular men Bob [Laycock] has chosen it is, with very few exceptions, a workable system'.[6]

There was very little contact with the officers of their sister unit, 3rd Commando, 'who live at the other and more squalid quarter of the town and are reputed to be a rough lot who drink with their men'. Waugh recorded: 'They regard us as "cissy" and beat us soundly in a boxing match. They have done one operation – a raid on the Channel Islands* – which proved a fiasco.'[7]

In a memorandum written later, Waugh elaborated on 8th Commando's unorthodox methods:

When formed they had been exceptionally zealous; discipline was already deteriorating when I joined . . . Two night operations in which I acted as umpire showed great incapacity in the simplest tactical ideas. One troop leader was unable to read a compass. The troops, however, had a smart appearance on inspection parades, arms drill was good, the officers were greatly liked and respected. The men had no guard duties. After parade they were free from all restraint and were often disorderly . . . [Yet] they had a gaiety and independence which I thought would prove valuable in action.[8]

On 9 December, the 4th SS Battalion left Largs for a 'brief period of intensive training' on the Isle of Arran, prior to its departure for Pantelleria. But when intelligence revealed the presence of German Stuka dive-bombers on Sicily, thus increasing the likelihood that the Commando ships would never reach their target, Operation Workshop was postponed (and later cancelled).[9]

---

* Waugh was referring to the 3rd's role in Operation Ambassador, one of the earliest Commando raids against German-occupied Guernsey during the night of 14/15 July 1940. Thanks to navigational errors and mechanical breakdown, only forty men of H Troop got ashore. They accomplished little and left behind four men, who were captured.

With the stay on Arran extended, the recently promoted Lieutenant Roger Courtney stepped up the recruitment drive for his Folbot Troop by holding interviews in the Lamlash Bay Hotel on the east of the island. Among the potential recruits was 29-year-old Lieutenant Robert 'Tug' Wilson, 'slim, slight of build, and no more than medium height, with fair hair, a neat military moustache, and gentle expressive blue eyes'. A pre-war draughtsman with the Bristol Aeroplane Company, Wilson was commissioned into a Territorial unit of the Royal Artillery in August 1939 and by the end of the year, though not long married, had volunteered for active service in France and was posted to the 3rd Survey Regiment. After Dunkirk he joined 8th Commando and was intrigued by Courtney's plans to use canoes to scout enemy shorelines and 'attack enemy shipping in harbour with delayed-action fuses'. Courtney, in turn, was impressed by Wilson's quiet but determined demeanour, and his apparent ability to hold his drink. 'Roger,' recalled his younger brother Godfrey ('Gruff'), 'liked to test a man's character by making him tiddly in the local pub and observing his behaviour. "Tug" survived by discreetly pouring much of his share into various flowerpots and helped a stricken Roger back to his billets at the end of the evening.' They formed an 'instant liking for each other' and, having passed Roger's character test 'with flying colours', Wilson was appointed his second in command.[10]

As well as Courtney and Wilson, the troop now totalled eleven men from a mix of regiments and corps, including Sergeant George Barnes of the Grenadier Guards, Corporal George Bremner of the London Scottish, and seven Royal Marines: Sergeant Reg Allen, Corporal John White, and Marines John Barlow, Wally Hughes, Miles, Duggan and Harris.[11] A late arrival to the troop was Lance Corporal Jim Sherwood, the former RASC man who had been so impressed by Courtney during his interview for the Commandos in August. Sherwood had been on Arran for only a couple of days when he and the rest of 8 Troop were called out on parade by Captain Nicholson and told that their 'standard of training' was not considered high enough by their CO, Major Daly, and they were being returned to their units. Desperate to avoid this, and hearing that Courtney was looking for recruits, Sherwood applied for an interview.

It helped his cause immeasurably that he had owned a two-seater folbot during a spell of work in Dublin in 1939. 'I knew about handling a canoe,' remembered Sherwood, 'was used to rough sea conditions, and confident in the water. I was a lousy swimmer, and could hardly swim a stroke, but this didn't bother me.' Nor did it bother Courtney. Hearing that Sherwood knew about folbots, and had experience of 'camping in the wilds in winter conditions', he said: 'You're in.'[12]

The men that Courtney had chosen for the Folbot Troop were, like him, tough, independent and problem solvers. Courtney's brother Gruff summed up the men who served in the early SBS:

They were ordinary Britons drawn from a wide range of routine peacetime occupations and, with few exceptions, had no exotic background. Nor were they undisciplined misfits and trouble-makers, for neither could exist in a unit where the most rigid self-discipline and loyalty were required for survival. Their moti-vation was as mixed as one would expect – the normal measure of undemonstrative patriotism, youthful adventure, self-reliance, independence of mind, and a liking for responsibility. Generally speaking, they were individualists, loners and survivors . . .

They were full of spirit, but quiet fellows, intent on getting on with the job [and] not boastful or belligerent and certainly not the bloodthirsty thugs that Commandos were made out to be by some irresponsible sections of the British Press.*[13]

Shortly after Sherwood joined the Folbot Troop, it was moved north from Lamlash to Sannox Bay so it could train in peace. Courtney and his men were billeted in the Ingledene Hotel, a former guest house. 'We were,' recalled Sherwood, 'out and about

---

* Similar qualities – not least the prevalence of brain over brawn – are still looked for in SBS recruits today.

folboting, doing field craft, compass work, map reading, night
and day exercises, night landings in folbots, until we were considered proficient. It was simply Roger Courtney making it up as
we went along.'

Discipline was almost non-existent because it was unnecessary
– we were the 'sort of people', commented Sherwood, 'who would
be self-disciplined anyway' – and they lived together in the guest
house like 'one big happy family'. They enjoyed venison for
Christmas dinner, having poached a stag from a nearby estate,
and trained hard in their folbots.[14] Known later as a 'Cockle'
Mark I, this civilian-designed canoe was 'made of rubberised
canvas on a wooden frame, weighed about fifty pounds, and
could carry two men'. It was sixteen feet long, with a fairly
narrow beam and a long bow. It was, moreover, 'very fragile,
very fast and silent, but prone to turn turtle'.[15] This is almost
certainly what happened to the folbot of two – unidentified –
members of the troop who were lost during a night exercise off
Corrie, a village south of Sannox. Their bodies were 'never found',
and nor was the canoe. The men had been wearing Mae West
life preservers,* but left uninflated so they could paddle. The
canoes were not fitted with flotation devices.[16]

In early January 1941, Courtney's troop took part in two large-
scale night landing exercises on Arran. Its task in the first was to
enter Lamlash harbour unseen; and in the second to mark one of
the landing places, scout another and penetrate Lochranza harbour
'for the purpose of destroying the Castle . . . and of reporting on
the suitability of the shores of the harbour for landing craft'. It
carried out these tasks with great efficiency, earning the praise of
Admiral Sir Roger Keyes who was present as an observer.
'Everybody,' recalled Sherwood, 'was enormously impressed.'[17]

The only hiccup was the continued absence of the other twenty
canoes that Courtney had ordered from Folbot Ltd in London.

---

* Named after the popular American film actress, who was renowned for her
generous bust, this inflatable life jacket was originally issued to RAF pilots
in 1939.

When the staff at Combined Operations HQ made enquiries, they were told by the makers that eight of the twenty folbots had been destroyed by German bombing, and the rest sent to HM Dockyard, Rosyth. Before Courtney could track them down, he and the rest of 8th Commando were given two weeks' leave and, on their return, told they were leaving the UK for operations in the Mediterranean.[18]

3

The Rhodes Reconnaissance

At 11:00 p.m. on 31 January 1941, the Commando ship HMS *Glenroy* weighed anchor at Brodick on the Isle of Arran and headed north-west into a strong headwind and rising seas. On board, crammed into every available space, were the 500 men of 8th Commando and half of 11th (Scottish) Commando. The rest of the 11th were with 7th (Eastern) Commando in *Glenroy*'s sister ship, the *Glengyle*. Collectively known as 'Force Z',* under the now Colonel Bob Laycock, the three Commandos were being sent to Egypt to prepare for a new operation: the capture of the Italian-held Dodecanese Islands in the eastern Mediterranean. The islands had been targeted in the wake of the crushing defeat of the main Italian field army in North Africa by Major General Sir Richard O'Connor's much smaller British and Commonwealth Desert Army which had, in just two months, captured 130,000 prisoners, 400 tanks and 1,290 guns, and conquered the whole of Cyrenaica (part of modern Libya).[1]

Before leaving, the men on *Glenroy* were given a pep talk by Admiral Keyes who wished them good luck and Godspeed. They would be 'put across the enemy' at the first opportunity, he promised, and so needed to keep their 'spearhead bright'.[2] The address made 'little impression' on the assembled Commandos, and was missed by Courtney and his troop who were hurriedly packing up their canoes and the rest of their kit in Sannox Bay.

---

* Since the cancellation of Operation Workshop, the 4th Special Service Battalion had ceased to exist, and 8th Commando reverted to its original name.

But they did return to the ship in time to hear Colonel Laycock's 'rousing send-off', and the news that they were heading for the Mediterranean, via the Cape.

Any high spirits were quickly dampened by overcrowding and the high seas, with *Glenroy* pitching and rolling in a force 9 gale. The Commandos had been assigned hammocks in the former cargo holds, with rows of makeshift toilets nearby, but most were so seasick they 'couldn't have cared where they sat or who with'.[3] After three days the weather had improved enough for training to begin. The Scottish Commandos – described by Evelyn Waugh, the Force Z adjutant, as 'very young and quiet, overdisciplined, unlike ourselves in every way' – completed every task with enthusiasm. The 8th, on the other hand, 'did very little except PT and one or two written exercises for the officers'. Off duty, its wealthy officers gambled heavily, playing 'poker, roulette, chemin-de-fer, every night'. The biggest loser was Randolph Churchill who forfeited the stupendous sum of £850 in two evenings.

Stopping briefly at Cape Town – where Randolph lunched with the South African prime minister, Jan Smuts, and Dermot Daly, commanding 8th Commando, 'got very drunk' – the *Glenroy* finally dropped anchor off Kabrit at the top of the Lower Bitter Lake, having passed through the southern part of the Suez Canal, on 10 March. Their first visitor was Major General John Evetts who announced that henceforth the three Commandos would be known as A, B and C Battalions of 'Layforce', under Colonel Laycock, and form an integral part of his 6th Infantry Division. They would soon be involved in 'important and hazardous operations against the enemy', he told them, for which 'a month's hard training would be required'.[4]

Based at Geneifa on the shores of the Great Bitter Lake – a transit camp of ramshackle tents and basic washing facilities – the Commandos began preparing for the invasion of Rhodes, the largest of the Dodecanese, code-named Operation Cordite. Jim Sherwood's chief memory was of 'flies, sand, heat' and 'great discomfort', nor did he warm to the locals who constantly pestered the Commandos to 'buy their rubbishy stuff'.[5] Courtney, meanwhile, was busy lobbying for the Folbot Troop to be used in conjunction with submarines, and was introduced by Laycock to Lieutenant Commander Nigel Willmott RN, one of the chief planners for Cordite, who was thinking on similar lines.

Born in Simla, India, in July 1910, Willmott was a career naval officer who specialised in navigation and hydrography. Tall, ungainly and good-looking, with an aquiline nose, full lips, a dimpled chin and 'dreamy grey eyes', he had long believed that beach reconnaissance was a vital prerequisite for all successful amphibious operations. The best example of how not to do it, he felt, was the hurried and unprepared landing at Anzac Cove on Gallipoli in April 1915, the details of which he had gleaned from his uncle Major Henry Clogstoun who had served there with the Australian Engineers.[6] Similar errors were made in Norway in the spring of 1940, a campaign that Willmott had witnessed at first hand from the deck of a heavily armed merchant vessel known as a Q-ship, and as a beach master at Narvik where his 'offensive spirit', initiative and 'persistence in devising methods of harrassing' the enemy had earned him a mention in despatches.[7]

Now tasked with the assault on the Dodecanese, Willmott knew little about the proposed landing zones in terms of landmarks, water gradients, obstacles, defences, beach bearing capacities and exits. So he had conducted his own reconnaissance, sailing in HMS *Rorqual*, a mine-laying submarine, in early March 1941, and learning much about the beaches of Kasos and Scarpantos by periscope observation. But Willmott knew that the fullest picture could only be obtained by landing on the beach itself. This became even more pressing when the chief target was confirmed as the island of Rhodes, a tough nut that would require armour to crack. Could the beaches support tanks? And was there a viable route off them and into the town? These were the questions that Willmott was seeking answers to as Roger Courtney and his Folbot Troop arrived in the Middle East. The timing was perfect.[8]

At first glance the two men had little in common. Willmott was 'meticulous over details with the mathematical approach of a navigator in facing problems'. Roger Courtney, on the other hand, was 'something of an adventurer with a flair for improvisation in a tight corner', a man who preferred to make it up as he went along.[9] Yet on meeting they 'formed an instant liking for each other which was to endure'.[10] They were kindred spirits who realised that, by working together, they could achieve their individual aims: Willmott needed a way to get on and off an enemy beach without being detected; Courtney was looking to prove his theory that folbots could revolutionise amphibious warfare, and that his unit deserved a permanent, and preferably independent, status. Both now seemed within reach.

Their proposed reconnaissance of Rhodes was the first to use a folbot transported by submarine. To prepare, Courtney, Willmott and two members of the Folbot Troop – one of whom was Jim Sherwood – moved down to the naval base at Kabrit to begin a fortnight of intensive training. The first thing Willmott learned was how to get in and out of a canoe without capsizing it. Courtney taught him 'the knack of hoisting himself aboard a canoe over the stern, and how to vault astride one steadied by a paddler'. He became 'adept at launching himself over the canoe's side': first 'leaning back with legs outstretched athwart the cockpit', then flipping over so that he was facing the water as he gently lowered himself into it. Next they practised 'swimming ashore at night, taking turns to act the part of a sentry while the other stalked around the acting guard until this could be done without the swimmer being detected'.[11] They quickly realised, recalled Sherwood, that any slight noise they made would be masked by the sound of waves breaking onto the beach, and that 'even with a calm sea' there was 'always some movement' onshore.[12]

After a few days at Kabrit, they moved up to HMS *Medway*, the depot ship for the 1st Submarine Flotilla in Alexandria harbour, where, with the assistance of the commanding officer, Captain Sydney Raw RN, they learned to launch and recover the canoes from submarines. They also tested from the island of Pharos, the site of the ruins of the ancient Alexandria Lighthouse, a top-secret infrared transmitter and receiving device that had been developed for the RAF. The transmitter was a hand-held Aldis-type lamp whose infrared signal appeared on the screen of the black box camera-sized receiver as a green dot. As its light was invisible to the naked eye, it enabled them to signal from a folbot to a submarine without being seen.[13]

It was during the repetitive training for the mission that their contrasting characters became apparent: Willmott, 'scholarly, leaning to erudite jokes, a "book" man', was the kind who liked to take notes on everything and leave absolutely nothing to chance; Courtney, on the other hand, was 'bluff and ruddy, careless of detail' and almost wanted 'to leave a certain sporting share of the venture to chance'. It was Willmott who kept insisting that they rehearse their drill one more time, while Courtney muttered in protest. He got the perfect excuse in the form of a bad chill, the result of too much time in the cold, late-winter sea. It put a stop to their last few days of training, much to Willmott's frustration.

'Look, Nigel!' responded Courtney. 'I can do the whole job in my sleep now.'[14]

Meanwhile the rest of the Folbot Troop had joined Courtney in Alexandria where they would 'work exclusively from HM ships', and come under navy rather than army control. It is from this date – mid-March 1941 – that the folbotists began to operate as an independent unit and, as confirmation of his enhanced status, Courtney was promoted to the rank of acting captain.[15]

*

Just after midnight on 31 March 1941, three miles off the northeast tip of Rhodes, Lieutenant Commander Wilfrid Woods RN[*] ordered his T-class submarine HMS *Triumph* to be 'trimmed

[*] Later Admiral Sir Wilfrid Woods, Commander-in-Chief of the Home Fleet.

down'* so that the torpedo loading hatch was a safe distance from the surface of the water. Then a partially assembled folbot was passed through the hatch and on to the casing where Jim Sherwood fitted its wooden cross struts. When that was done, the 35-year-old Woods moved his submarine by electric motor to within a mile and a half of a shingle beach – code-named A – just north of Rhodes' Mandraki harbour that Nigel Willmott and Roger Courtney had surveyed by periscope earlier that day.

Having departed HMS *Medway* during the morning of 24 March, the *Triumph* had reached this same location on the 26th. But as he was about to launch Willmott and Courtney in their canoe, Woods received an urgent message from Captain Raw, postponing the reconnaissance and ordering the *Triumph* to join a submarine patrol to the south in support of an Allied convoy. It took two days to complete, during which time Courtney and Sherwood got thoroughly acquainted with the cramped, nocturnal existence of a submariner.[16]

Space was very much at a premium in a vessel 'about the size of an underground-train coach, and very similar in length, width, and shape, except that the arch over one's head is far more pronounced'. In the centre of this compartment there was space to stand upright, but closer to the sides it was necessary 'to crouch to a great extent'. The only place where there was any real headroom was in the 'control room', directly below the conning tower. This was the 'brains' of the vessel, containing the periscopes – 'a big one for normal work, a thin one for attack' – the hydroplane wheels, and the valves to flood or 'blow' the ballast tanks.

Behind the control room were the engine and electric motor rooms, 'the former for driving the submarine on the surface, the latter underwater'. They occupied most of the rear half of the

---

* Submarines flood their ballast tanks to eliminate positive buoyancy and thus dive, then inject high-pressure air to re-surface. Once dived, they maintain neutral buoyancy or 'trim' by moving small amounts of water in and out of internal tanks by pumps or air. Submarines normally keep a level trim, adjusting depth through forward speed and their hydroplanes, but can use internal tanks to achieve a bow up or down angle.

vessel. Forward of the control room were the messes – officers' and petty officers', small compartments about seven feet square, 'with the passageway leading up the starboard side, through the many bulkheads'. In the submarine's bows was the torpedo compartment, about twenty-five feet long, 'which is shared by four "reload" torpedoes in racks, and about twenty ratings'.

Courtney and Willmott shared the officers' mess, or wardroom; Sherwood was billeted with the petty officers. The folboteers quickly got used to the rhythm of life on a submarine: sleeping by day in tiny bunks to conserve as much oxygen as possible; a breakfast of bacon, beans and coffee at 7:00 p.m.; and surfacing after dark to start the diesel engines and recharge the submarine batteries, and do any energetic work that was required.[17]

Having completed the convoy patrol by 28 March, Lieutenant Commander Woods continued with his original mission. Once HMS *Triumph* was in position off Rhodes' Mandraki harbour in the early hours of the 31st, Willmott and Courtney joined Sherwood on the casing.* With no specialised clothing and equipment available for this type of mission, the pair had had to improvise: they were wearing submarine sweaters and long johns, both covered in 'crab fat' (periscope grease) to keep out the cold, and a Gieves inflatable waistcoat for buoyancy. As the swimmer on this first mission, Willmott's kit included a .38 revolver – kept in a waterproof cellophane envelope – an army compass, also heavily greased, and a torch for signalling to the canoe. Courtney, who would remain in the canoe, had a Thompson sub-machine gun and the infrared transmitter. They had both taken Benzedrine tablets† to keep themselves alert, and darkened their faces with tan boot polish. Their cover story, in case they were captured, was that they were conducting a reconnaissance from a motor torpedo boat, prior to a raid on the south-east coast.[18]

---

* A light metal structure, perforated with holes, that is built over the upper surface of the vessel's pressure hull, and that acts as a deck.

† An amphetamine-based stimulant that was widely taken by combat soldiers in the Second World War. First introduced as a decongestant in 1933, it was later used in pill form to treat narcolepsy, obesity and low blood pressure.

Once Sherwood had launched the folbot from the starboard fore hydroplane (or foreplane),* which was lowered to provide a stable platform, the pair clambered in, taking care not to capsize. It was a delicate manoeuvre. 'If there was any kind of sea running,' recalled Sherwood, 'you had a hell of a job to hold on to the cable on the foreplane with one hand, while you held on to the canoe with the other while the chap tried to get into it with all his gear.'

This launch technique was soon superseded by a simpler method: the two paddlers would get into the canoe on the casing, at which point 'the sub trimmed down, and you floated off'.[19] This was much safer than using the foreplane, and it was fortunate that on this initial mission the sea was 'flat calm, sky clear, slight westerly breeze'. Such conditions were perfect for canoeing, and Courtney and Willmott got aboard without incident.

It was a velvety-dark night and not a light was visible from the distant shoreline. Cast off by Sherwood, they paused briefly to check the compass bearing before heading in at a steady pace of three knots. Though not a long paddle, it was into a slight headwind and both men were soon breathing heavily and sweating from the exertion. At one point a patch of heavy swell caused the canoe to corkscrew and slither 'sideways into the hollows with the waves clapping aginst the canvas sides and blowing cold spray over them'. It eventually took them just over twenty-five minutes of hard paddling to reach a point 150 yards short of 'A' Beach where, with aching shoulder muscles and heightened senses, they scanned the shore for any sign of life. Satisfied that all was quiet, Willmott slipped noiselessly over the side of the canoe as he had been taught. He gasped at the shock of the cold water, and clung for a moment to the folbot's stern. Once his body had adjusted, he struck out for the shore, using a powerful breaststroke that he had perfected during hours of

---

* Submarines had two pairs of hydroplanes, horizontal fins like aircraft elevators, to control upward and downward movement. The foreplanes were located near the bow and the after-planes adjacent to the rudder.

practice at Cairo. The closer he got, the slower he swam, keeping as low a profile as possible. Feeling firm ground beneath his feet, he moved forward, a foot at a time, until a rocky promontory loomed up in front of him. Aware it would prevent the landing of tanks, he decided to swim further along the bay, using a chinograph pencil to note the depth of the water and the suitability of the beach for landing craft and vehicles on a slate that was attached to his wrist. At one point, his chin resting on pebbles at the water's edge, he could hear sentries talking Italian a short distance away. Convinced they were looking directly at him, he clenched his teeth tightly to stop them chattering. It worked, and eventually the sentries moved away.

Over the next hour or so Willmott made four separate landings at different points on A Beach, collecting rock samples and moving inland a short way to survey exit points and road communications. He got to within sixty yards of an Italian military headquarters in the Grande Albergo delle Rose,* where he heard a sentry yawn, but again was not discovered. Checking his watch, he realised it was time to go and, re-entering the freezing water, began swimming to the point where Courtney should have been waiting 400 yards offshore, the canoe nose pointed at the beach so that it would present the smallest possible silhouette. It was now, with the effect of the Benzedrine tablets wearing off, and his brain dulled by cold and exhaustion, that Willmott felt a mounting dread: would Courtney see the flashes from his torch before the enemy did or, worse, he succumbed to the cold and drowned? There was only one way to find out. Lifting his tired arm out of the water, he flicked the torch on briefly three times to spell out in Morse the letter 'R'. When nothing happened, he did it a second time, then a third. There was still no response. Was he in the right place? he wondered. Had Courtney drifted out of position, or been spotted by a patrol boat? Surely it could not end like this?

Just when he was beginning to lose hope, he heard the faint

* Grand Hotel of Roses, so named because of its famous rose garden.

rhythmic sound of a series of fast paddle strokes and, in no time at all, the canoe was beside him. Courtney leaned out and, taking advantage of his powerful upper body, hauled the exhausted Willmott into the rear seat of the canoe and gave him a thermos of coffee laced with brandy. This revived Willmott a little, and together they paddled out to sea in a thickening mist that soon cleared enough for them to use the infrared transmitter.[20] The signal was picked up by an officer on the conning tower of the *Triumph* at 3:50 a.m. and within twelves minutes the canoe and its occupants had been recovered. The mission had lasted just under four hours, and was judged a complete success.[21]

During the next three days they carried out a periscope examination of five more beaches: B, C, D, E and F. Two were examined in person: B by Willmott in the early hours of 1 April, and E by Courtney, twenty miles to the south, two days later. Courtney's recce was almost a disaster. First, he attracted the attention of a dog which followed him up and down a stretch of wire fence, the dog on one side and him on the other. 'He growled at me,' recalled Courtney, 'but did not bark.'[22]

Then, as he tried to swim back to the canoe, he got cramp and his torch failed. In desperation he used his sound signal and Willmott responded by paddling close in to the beach and hauling the stricken Courtney into the canoe. 'Cramp!' gasped the army captain. 'Damn near did for me! Sodding cramp!'

'Quiet,' murmured Willmott.[23]

By 3:27 a.m. they were back on the submarine. They had been due to carry out one more night reconnaissance. But when the *Triumph* was forced to surface in daylight after grounding near C Beach that afternoon, Lieutenant Commander Woods chose discretion over valour and called off the operation. Setting a course for Alexandria at lunchtime on 3 April, they arrived back at HMS *Medway* in the morning of the 5th. They had not encountered a single enemy surface patrol, and spotted only the occasional Axis aircraft.[24]

Courtney was delighted with the result of the Folbot Troop's first mission. 'We reconnoitred three beaches,' he recorded. 'One of them in front of the main hotel. We brought back sketches, tested the wire defences and the main lesson we learnt was that people not expecting an attack keep very poor watch.'[25] It had taken extraordinary courage and fortitude to survey a closely guarded hostile shore with improvised equipment and at a time of year when the weather was inclement and unpredictable. The attempt might easily have ended in the canoeists' death or capture. It was a risk these bold forerunners of maritime special operations were only too happy to take.

The official report of the mission showered Courtney and Willmott with praise. Despite undergoing 'a period of considerable physical and mental stress', wrote Lieutenant Commander Woods, both had maintained a 'cheerful and determined bearing' at all times. The operation as a whole, added Captain Sydney Raw, 'was carried out in a most efficient manner and much useful information obtained'. The folbot canoe had 'served its purpose admirably and the infrared signalling was most satisfactory'.[26]

For successfully completing such a hazardous operation, Willmott and Courtney were awarded the Distinguished Service Order (DSO) and Military Cross (MC) respectively.* Courtney's medal citation noted that he had 'carried out a daring recce in enemy territory'. It added: 'He swam ashore from a submarine and carefully recced about half a mile of enemy defences and strong points. He experienced difficulty in returning to the submarine and exposed himself voluntarily to considerable danger and physical hardship for a period of four hours.'[27]

In the event, the vital information that they brought back from Rhodes was never used because Operation Cordite was cancelled soon after their return as all available shipping was

---

* The DSO was, after the Victoria Cross, the second-highest award for gallantry that could be given to British and Commonwealth officers. Willmott's was awarded jointly for the Rhodes operation and for 'distinguished services' during the later withdrawal of Allied troops from Greece in late April 1941. The Military Cross was the third-highest award for gallantry for army officers. Its navy and air force equivalents were the Distinguished Service Cross (DSC) and the Distinguished Flying Cross (DFC) respectively.

needed to evacuate Allied troops from Greece. But both had
been vindicated, particularly Courtney who now had proof that
his folbots could make a difference. Together they had pioneered
a new technique of warfare – close beach reconnaissance – that
would save thousands of lives as the Allies launched a succession
of major amphibious operations in the years to come.

4

'Are you a professional "tough guy"?'

Shortly after 9:00 p.m. on 19 April 1941, HMS *Triumph* surfaced a mile off Bardia, a port just inside Italian Cyrenaica that a week earlier had been recaptured from the Allies by Axis troops commanded by Generalleutnant Erwin Rommel.* Sharing the cramped interior of the 275-feet submarine with Lieutenant Commander Wood and his fifty-eight crew were Captain Roger Courtney and three other folbotists, including Corporal George Bremner and Lance Corporal Jim Sherwood. Their task was to land by canoe on an islet just off the entrance to Bardia's harbour and place a green navigation light to guide in landing craft from the Commando ship HMS *Glengyle*. The raid was to be carried out by 500 men from 7ᵗʰ (Eastern) Commando 'with the object of harassing the enemy's lines of communication and inflicting as much damage as possible to supplies and materials'.¹

Originally scheduled for the night of 16/17 April, the raid had been postponed because of bad weather. But as Sherwood completed the assembly of the first folbot on the submarine's casing, the wind continued to stiffen to force 3, or 12 mph. As this was already close to the safety limit, Courtney decided to use both folbots 'to make certain of establishing the light'. The first one was 'launched satisfactorily' into the water, but as soon

---

* Rommel and the vanguard of two German divisions – the 5ᵗʰ Light and 15ᵗʰ Panzer – were sent to Libya in mid-February 1941 to support their Italian allies who had been driven out of Cyrenaica and were in danger of collapse. The effect was immediate and by 12 April Rommel's Afrika Korps had reconquered all of Cyrenaica, bar the port of Tobruk which was under siege.

as Courtney got in it capsized and was wrecked against the submarine's hull. Pulled from the water, Courtney was all for trying again with the second folbot. But he was overruled by Lieutenant Commander Wood on the grounds that the sea conditions were too dangerous and, already delayed by a mistaken attack by RAF planes, the submarine was running out of time to reach its own signalling position two and a half miles from Bardia. Even then it arrived fifteen minutes late.[2]

Despite these and other mishaps – such as one landing craft never leaving the *Glengyle* because of a jammed hoist, another arriving at the wrong place, and one beach being so 'narrow and difficult' that the men had to 'wade ashore in water up to their waists' – the landing was unopposed.[3] But thereafter the raid was a flop. 'Our information,' remembered Evelyn Waugh, 'was that 2,000 enemy troops held the town and that there were large concentrations of transport there; also one or more coast defence guns. All this proved to be entirely false. The town was deserted, the only vehicles were abandoned trucks, the guns had been destroyed some weeks before when we evacuated the town. The only enemy seen were a motorcycle patrol. No other use was made of the road, which had been reported as frequented, during our three hours' occupation.'

In fact, the only shots fired were at a Commando officer who had failed to give the correct countersign and paid with his life. To add insult to injury, one troop returned to the wrong beach and were left behind to became prisoners of war. Waugh was not happy with the navy, noting that '*Glengyle* lay four miles out and would not approach closer even when it was clear that there was no opposition; their reluctance caused the loss of sixty men.'[4]

While 'not a little disappointed with the general conduct of the raid', the first by his Commandos in the Middle East, Colonel Laycock thought that 'many valuable lessons were learned', and that in future his men should be capable of 'operating with success on the darkest nights over considerable distances in difficult country'. Although the folbot component of the raid had not been a success, this was down to bad luck and adverse weather. Laycock simply stated the facts: 'The FOLBOT detachment failed to exhibit the green light on the islet.'[5]

*

Just a day after returning from the Bardia raid, HMS *Triumph* sailed from Alexandria on its third Mediterranean war patrol. It was carrying a new folbot team of Lieutenant Robert 'Tug' Wilson and his paddler Marine Wally Hughes. The pair would, over the course of the next eight months, execute a succession of extraordinarily daring and successful operations that made them the scourge of the Italian military. Yet both were quiet and unassuming types. According to Gruff Courtney, Wilson was 'the complete opposite of the Commando of fiction, usually portrayed by post-war journalist-authors as rip-roaring, bloodthirsty thugs ever ready to slit a throat'. Wilson described his paddler as 'short, lean, tough and ready to tackle anything'. He might have been talking about himself. Where they differed was in their manner: Hughes was a man of few words; Wilson his 'suave, sophisticated opposite'.[6]

They took with them on this first patrol along the coast of Italian Cyrenaica a stock of limpet mines and TNT explosives in case 'night attack on small craft anchored near the beach should prove possible'. As hoped, three suitable merchant ships were spotted by periscope in Benghazi's outer harbour, and a folbot attack was scheduled for the night of 28 April. But it was cancelled when the ships were found to have departed, 'leaving no remaining targets'. They had to make do, instead, with sinking an Italian motor coaster, the 279-ton MV *Tugnin F*, after Wilson and one of the submarine's officers had boarded her and returned with charts and papers, a sample of the ship's cargo of macaroni, and pictures of Adolf Hitler and Benito Mussolini. The crew were cast adrift in a lifeboat.

The one real scare was after the *Triumph* had failed to torpedo the rear ship of an Italian convoy and was counter-attacked by the escorting destroyer. Three depth charges were dropped, but none within 2,000 yards of the British submarine. 'Carried out evading tactics at 45 ft [depth],' reported Lieutenant Commander Woods, 'coming to periscope depth at short intervals to look. Destroyer disappeared after the convoy.' After a long and eventful, if largely unsuccessful, eighteen-day patrol, the *Triumph* arrived back in Alexandria on 12 May.[7]

*

Roger Courtney's chief concern during these early months with the 1ˢᵗ Submarine Flotilla at Alexandria was how to maintain the Folbot Troop's independence. Layforce was already being split into penny packets – with 11ᵗʰ Commando sent to Cyprus and part of the 8ᵗʰ to the besieged port of Tobruk – and, as the German paratroop attack on Crete developed in late May, 7ᵗʰ Commando was sent to that island with the locally raised 50ᵗʰ/52ⁿᵈ Middle East Commando to act as rearguard during the Allied evacuation. They did a good job in difficult circumstances, but most arrived at the beach after the last boats had sailed and were among 8,000 Allied troops who were taken prisoner.[8]

With the very existence of Layforce under threat – it would eventually be disbanded in late July 1941 – there was a strong likelihood that the Folbot Troop would not survive. It was 'touch and go', recalled Jim Sherwood, 'because it was difficult for Courtney to get people to use the [troop] for the kind of work we had trained for: reconnaissance work, putting people ashore, agents and that sort of thing'. But thanks to Courtney's 'persistence and enthusiasm', the troop not only survived, it expanded in size.[9]

It had quickly become apparent to Courtney that there was more enthusiasm for his fledgling unit among senior naval officers than their army counterparts. Yet when it was suggested in late April that, for administrative reasons, all folbotists should be transferred to the Royal Marines, both he and Colonel Laycock protested. Courtney's preference, Laycock told the British High Command in Cairo, was to be 'permanently attached either to the Royal Navy or the Royal Marines'. That way the Commandos 'could exercise first call on the activities of the Folbotists'.[10] This was sanctioned, and the Folbot Troop became an independent unit attached to the Royal Navy.

Already, on 1 April 1941, the Folbot Troop had been granted a slightly expanded war establishment of eighteen men: two officers, two sergeants, four corporals, two lance corporals, eight privates or Marines, and twelve canoes.[11] In late August 1941, the nominal size of Courtney's unit – now known as the Folbot Section (and soon to become the Special Boat Section*) – was increased further to twenty-three officers and thirty-one other ranks, though it was typically under strength because Courtney wanted only the best people. Its chief function, according to an official memorandum of August 1941, was 'to provide submarine [commands] with an auxiliary weapon for the express purpose of carrying out sabotage and small-scale anti-personnel raids as and when the opportunity occurs while the submarines are out on patrol'. Potential folbotists needed to have: a willingness to undertake work that was 'more than usually hazardous'; 'extreme patience' and 'personal courage'; the ability to spend many days cooped up in a submarine that was 'neither comfortable nor healthy'; and lungs and a heart that were healthy.[12]

Courtney's own paper on the ideal recruit – entitled 'The Compleat Folbotist' – asked:

Are you a professional 'tough guy'? i.e. Do you imitate the film stars, wear funny hats, or walk around carrying more weapons than a Mexican bandit, get truculent after a few drinks and proceed to beat up the town?

Or have you got the true conception of 'tough guy'? Are you the quiet type of man who would not be 'picked out' in a crowd,

---

* Some authors, Gruff Courtney among them, date the renaming of the unit to 'Special Boat Section' from its attachment to the 1st Submarine Flotilla at Alexandria in March 1941. But I found no mention of this renaming in official papers until 22 October 1941 when a paper on the 'Future Organisation of SS Troops in MEF [Middle East Force]' referred to Courtney's unit as the 'Special Boat Section' (LHCMA, Laycock Papers, 3/16).

the unassuming type who would be expected to be employed in professional business and never in the 'thugeree' you might be engaged in?

He wanted men who got satisfaction from 'a job well done', and not those 'prepared to take a spectacular risk – just for the gallery'. Men who were discreet, even when drunk, with a keen sense of responsibility and the knowledge that 'any unconsidered act' of theirs 'might risk a valuable submarine and the lives of 52 trained men'. Men who could 'get along well' with, and earn the 'good opinion' of, their navy hosts. Such men, if accepted, would 'get many interesting jobs, mostly of a secret nature', including scouting for the army and navy, demolitions, wrecking and sabotage, and assisting secret agents.

His tips on how to survive life in a submarine were to 'take plenty to read', but also to volunteer to help with 'cyphering' and 'lookout watches' at night; for heavy smokers to take along chewing gum and sweets; and to have a good range of old clothing as submarines were 'very hot below but often bitterly cold at night on deck'. If folbotists were unfortunate enough to be depth-charged, his advice was to 'pay no attention, read an improving book (it might be held upside down but it doesn't matter, it is the impression that counts), everyone else is just as tense as you are and nothing can be done about it'. He added: 'So why worry, it may never happen?'[13]

Courtney's ideal folbot crew was an officer as commander/ swimmer and another rank as the paddler, hence the high proportion of officers in the war establishment set for the Folbot Section in August. But during the early missions in the Mediterranean – before he could recruit more officers – he often sent out two other ranks from his Sannox Bay 'originals'. The pair he trusted most was George Bremner and Jim Sherwood who had been on earlier missions. 'When we went on spec,' noted Sherwood, 'it was up to the commander of the submarine to see some opportunity to use us.' This meant a lot of downtime, and the constant threat of being depth-charged, which was 'very frightening' as a submarine could 'only creep about at 1 or 2 knots on electric motors' while a destroyer hunted it from above. Fortunately, the pair had taken Courtney's advice. Sherwood recalled: 'We were stuck with this, and made the best of it. We volunteered to be on the bridge at night, we'd take a turn on the fore or aft plane controls, in the main control room, and sometimes helped with the decoding in the wireless office, and anything else we were asked to do. This relieved the boredom, and made us more acceptable to the sailors on board.'[14]

Their first mission without an officer was, once again, in Lieutenant Commander Woods' HMS *Triumph*. Arriving off Benghazi in the early evening of 30 May, Woods identified two 'good folbot targets' in the outer harbour: a 5,000-ton cargo steamer and a fast armed merchant ship.[15] Told to try and sink one or both of them, the two folbotists got their kit together, including limpet mines 'shaped like a service tin hat with the brim cut off, stuffed full of explosives, and with magnetic feet underneath'. They were 'supposed to place these below the water-line, set the fuse for however much time you needed, and escape'. But Sherwood was anything but confident: 'We'd had no experience of handling these bloody things. It was terribly amateurish. Anyway, we'd said we'd have a go, with some trepidation, I have to say . . . But by dusk the skipper had changed his mind, so he fired a torpedo instead. This was just as well because it was a hairy operation and I doubt we would have come back.'[16]

Woods fired two torpedoes at the armed merchantman because 'both ships presented a clear target' through the harbour entrance, and seemed to be on the point of leaving. One 'hit the target, which was seen a few minutes later with the forecastle awash', and Woods hastily withdrew to the north.

A few days later, patrolling off Burat to the west of Benghazi, they surfaced in mid-afternoon to engage three schooners* and their escort – an anti-submarine trawler – with the four-inch

---

* A type of sailing ship with two or more masts, the foremast being slightly smaller than the mainmast.

deck gun. Firing more than forty rounds, the gun crew sank the escort and two schooners, with the third escaping 'into shallow water'. It was now time to return to Alexandria, but en route they were diverted north to Gavdos Island, just south of Crete, where Allied fugitives from the earlier battle were said to be hiding out. Reaching Gavdos during the evening of 8 June, with a west-north-westerly wind strengthening to force 6, Woods asked the folbotists to take in one of his officers to a beach on the more protected eastern side of the island. 'We tossed a coin to see who should go,' remembered Sherwood, 'and I lost. I was very frustrated.'

Bremner and the officer, a young sub lieutenant, left the submarine in the folbot at 11:30 p.m. and paddled 500 yards into the shore at Korphi Bay. They returned three hours later, having discovered 'several empty huts' and heard a challenge that might have come from a sentry. Further inland they spoke to a peasant family 'with the aid of pictures', but got no information 'about troops of any nationality'.

Later that morning, just to make certain, Woods moved the *Triumph* to the more populated north-east of the island and surfaced in a cove with a 'good beach on which were several large boats'. Running up a large ensign to identify the submarine as 'friendly', Woods soon drew a large crowd of peasants and four unarmed soldiers to the beach. To find out who they were, Sherwood was told to paddle across alone and bring one back in the canoe. He set off 'full of excitement', but soon realised there was 'a stiff breeze blowing' and ended up 'crabbing across the bay, paddling desperately'. When he finally reached the shore, the canoe was grabbed by some of the men and hauled up onto the beach. 'I stepped out of it,' said Sherwood, '[my] .45 pistol came adrift and fell in the sand, so whoever these people were I was defenceless. None of them seemed to be able to speak English.'

One could speak a little French, however, so Sherwood took him back to the submarine. He explained there were 'no British soldiers on the island, but that a few Germans with a machine

gun were at the southern end'. He and three friends were Greek
Communists who had been exiled from the mainland. Told he
could not be taken to Athens, the Greek elected to stay on
Gavdos and urged the submarine to leave before it was spotted
by enemy aircraft. He was taken back to the beach by Sherwood
with an offer to evacuate any Greek soldiers who wanted to
leave. This prompted a heated argument which was cut short
by several blasts from *Triumph*'s siren. Sherwood 'returned immediately, and alone, bringing with him a note from one of the
[Greek] soldiers saying that eighteen British sailors had been
removed from the island' by Germans on the 8th and flown to
Athens.

The *Triumph* had arrived a day too late.[17]

*

'It was obvious,' recalled Roger Courtney, 'that no one was aware
of our presence. The village and harbour of Mersa Brega lay
shimmering and cooking under a blazing summer sun. It almost
hurt the eye to look out through the periscope onto this airy
sunlit world, then to turn away from the eyepieces to the old
familiar scene of our dark little world below. The dim electric
lights shining on the bodies of shipmates who lay or squatted
in the various corners of our steel prison. Or the phosphorescent
glow of the compass card reflected from the face of the peering
steersman.'[18]

It was the afternoon of 8 June 1941. A week earlier, with
HMS *Triumph* still at sea, Courtney and Sergeant George Barnes
had sailed from Alexandria on HMS *Taku*, another T-class
submarine skippered by 34-year-old Lieutenant Commander
Edward Nicolay RN. The *Taku* was also sent to patrol the coast
of Cyrenaica where, on the 7th, it had engaged an Italian convoy
with its four-inch deck gun but was forced to break off the
engagement because of numerous misfires. That evening, Courtney
and Barnes examined the island of Gharah, but found no sign
of life.[19] The view through the periscope on the 8th, however,

offered real possibilities. Courtney could see plenty of Italian troops – some of whom were being 'marched down' to the beach to bathe like a herd of 'depressed and apprehensive sheep' – but also a nearby fort and 'a signal station onshore with a multitude of telegraphs running from it' that looked 'easy to sabotage'.

Sitting round the table in the submarine's wardroom, Courtney persuaded Nicolay to let him and Barnes land that night and try to blow up the signal station with explosives. Ignoring the fact that it was a full moon, Courtney stressed that the coast appeared to be 'unwatched' and that the weather was calm. Another imperative, which he did not mention, was that he and Barnes were fed up with their 'stuffy prison' and were 'dying for a run around if it is only for fresh air'.

At 11:00 p.m. that evening, the *Taku* surfaced 'in bright moonlight' three miles off the coast. Using the new technique of floating the folbot off the casing by trimming down the submarine, Courtney and Barnes paddled towards shore, armed with 'tommy guns and knives, and about fifty pounds of explosive apiece'. The latter had been made into 'pack loads' with the fuses and detonators inserted and ready for action. Courtney recalled:

We landed in white sand-dune country to the west of [Mersa Brega]. It was nearly as light as day, and therefore concealment was impossible in such bare country. So we decided to bluff it out and march up towards the fort, which was our first objective, in the hope that if any person did spot us from a distance, they would take us for 'locals', arguing to themselves, no doubt, that no enemy would have the cheek to wander about in such a brazen fashion.

It worked, in that they reached the fort unchallenged. Yet they quickly discovered that while the structure 'looked quite sound from the front', the rest had long since been 'blown to smithereens'. They moved on to the signal station, re-embarking in their canoe so they could approach it from the point beyond the harbour. 'We hoped the shadow of the low bluffs, and our own scouting ability would get us through,' remembered Courtney. 'If only we had stuck to the brazen-bluff method instead of the cunning-scout one on such a night, we might indeed have reached our objective. To the unseen watchers, however, our methods of approach were obviously suspicious.'

No sooner had they landed on the point than they spotted several 'dark, armed shadowy figures creeping down through the rocks' above them. With the enemy barely a hundred yards away, and still uncertain whether the folbotists were 'friend or foe', they barely had time to push the bows of the canoe out to sea 'before the first shot rang out and a bullet spat viciously into the sand' at their feet. Remembering some Italian from a book he had read in the wardroom, Courtney shouted: 'Basta! Basta!'

This caused the soldiers to pause, wondering if they had nearly 'made a ghastly mistake'. When they realised they had been fooled, the canoe was a hundred yards out to sea and moving at pace. They responded with a 'perfect fusillade of shots'. Courtney recalled: 'How they managed to miss us I don't know, because I could have sworn that I felt the wind of those bullets fanning my neck. And so we did get away with it and we were lucky.'

Two hours early for their pick-up, they 'hung about miserably waiting for the sound of Italian E-boats'.* Luckily none appeared, and at 2:15 a.m. they were picked up by the submarine. An hour later, to punish the Italians for 'being beastly' to the folbotists, Nicolay sailed close inshore and used his deck gun to fire seven rounds into a nearby Italian gun battery. One was a direct hit.[20]

Commenting on the lessons learned, Lieutenant Commander Nicolay[†] noted that the stretch of coast along the Gulf of Sirte was closely watched, and that similar folbot missions were 'most

---

* The Allied name for a fast-attack craft, the E-boat was typically 105 feet long, heavily armed with torpedoes and cannon, and capable of speeds of up to forty-four knots (fifty miles per hour).

† In early August 1941, after Taku was sent back to the UK to refit, Nicolay took command of HMS Perseus. Awarded the DSO, he perished when Perseus struck a mine and went down with all hands on 6 December 1941.

hazardous' during a full moon. Yet the two landings had been of 'great value to the submarine yielding useful information', and in future all submarines patrolling near coasts should carry 'a folbot with trained crew' to gather intelligence and attack coastal targets.[21]

5

The Maltese Connection

On 17 June 1941, five days after Courtney and Barnes had arrived back in Alexandria from their near fatal patrol, the small U-class* submarine HMS *Utmost* set off from Lazaretto, the former leper hospital in Valletta's Marsamxett harbour that served as the depot ship for Malta's 10th Submarine Flotilla. Commanded by Lieutenant Commander Richard 'Deadeye Dick' Cayley RN, the 33-year-old grandson of an honorary surgeon to Queen Victoria, *Utmost* was also carrying a canoe and two folbotists: Lieutenant Dudley Schofield, 'not long from school', and his paddler Lance Corporal Francis Morgan. They were not, however, part of Courtney's Folbot Troop. 'Schofield and his men,' noted Courtney, 'were working independent of my Unit, and had embarked into coastal reconnaissance without any advice from older hands at the game or any specialised training.'[1]

This was not entirely accurate. Originally with the Royal Fusiliers, Schofield and Morgan had arrived in Malta in January 1941 as part of Force X, a sixty-four-strong contingent raised from 2nd Commando† (then part of the 1st Special Service Battalion) for a 'secret operation of a hazardous nature'. Trained

---

* A class of small 540-ton submarines built just before and during the Second World War, they were 191 feet long, armed with four external torpedo tubes and a three-inch deck gun, and had a crew of forty-nine.

† The original 2nd Commando, raised in June 1940, was airborne-trained and became, in late 1941, the 1st Parachute Battalion. Its successor took part in the famous and costly Saint-Nazaire Raid of March 1942, for which its commander, Lieutenant Colonel August Charles Newman, was awarded the Victoria Cross.

in Scotland in the use of folbots – a specialisation that Courtney wanted for all Commando units – Force X had been sent to Malta with a 'ton of special stores', including canoes and explosives, to carry out raids on the coast of North Africa and Italy. One of its first missions was to land on Sicily and kill a senior Luftwaffe commander* who, according to intelligence, had established his headquarters at the Mirimar Hotel in Taormina. But it was postponed the day before the submarine was due to sail to await a more 'suitable moon', and later cancelled when it became clear the German general had 'left Taormina'.

Instead Force X was used to target 'the vulnerable railways which hug the Italian coastline'. The man who came up with the idea was Captain George 'Shrimp' Simpson RN, commanding the 10th Submarine Flotilla at Malta to which Force X was attached. Shortly before Schofield and Morgan left Malta in HMS *Utmost*, they were joined on the island by Lieutenant 'Tug' Wilson and Marine Wally Hughes, two of Courtney's best men, as part of the new strategy to use folbots to strike targets on Sicily and the Italian mainland. But, much to Courtney's consternation, it was the unattached Schofield and Morgan who were given the first opportunity.[2]

Just after midnight on 24 June, their canoe was launched 400 yards off the toe of Italy. Their target was a tunnel on the Rome–Messina railway line and, having landed, they 'laid the explosives and pressure fuses without difficulty, just after a train had passed'. They then returned to the submarine and waited for the next train. It arrived at 2:00 a.m. but passed through the tunnel without incident. The pressure switch had failed. Schofield and Morgan went back a second time with twenty-one feet of slow-burning fuse which, with dawn approaching, they ignited. The charge blew as they reached the submarine. 'There

---

* In his autobiography, Captain 'Shrimp' Simpson identified the German commander as Albert Kesselring. In fact, Kesselring did not arrive in the Mediterranean theatre as Commander-in-Chief, South until the autumn of 1941 (Simpson, *Periscope View*, p. 128, and *The Memoirs of Field Marshal Kesselring*, p. 103).

was a loud report from the tunnel,' wrote Lieutenant Commander Cayley, 'and there is no doubt that a section of the line was blown up, and traffic dislocated for at least a day. Up till the explosion steam and electric trains had been running about once every ¼ of an hour.'

Four days later, a few hours after the *Utmost* had sunk a 6,000-ton merchant ship en route to Palermo, Schofield and Morgan made a second attempt at blowing up a train on the north coast of Sicily. In the event, a strong westerly current made it hard to find the prearranged landing place, and either the canoe or the submarine was spotted by a sentry who raised the alarm. 'Very sensibly,' noted Captain Simpson, Schofield made the decision to return to the submarine 'at once, and the rail sabotage was then abandoned'. Yet the folbotists had gained 'useful experience,' and Simpson 'felt confident' that with 'better equipment' they would, in the future, 'blow up the trains as well as the railway'.[3]

The honour of achieving that feat went instead to Courtney's men, Lieutenant 'Tug' Wilson and Marine Wally Hughes. They left Malta on 23 June in HMS *Urge*, another U-class submarine, and four days later were patrolling off the east coast of Sicily when they identified through the periscope a suitable target: a railway tunnel lying between Taormina and Catania, almost at the foot of Mount Etna. Their folbot was launched shortly before midnight in near perfect conditions: a calm sea, slight mist and no moon.

Steering by compass, they covered the three-quarters of a mile to the shore with 'great caution' as 'voices could be heard' and the occasional light observed. Closer in they saw several local fishing boats. Landing on a shingle beach, they hid the canoe among the rocks and climbed some steeply rising ground towards a telegraph pole. It marked the edge of the railway line and, not far away, they found the entrance to the tunnel which was unguarded. 'It was decided,' wrote Wilson, 'to place the charge just inside the tunnel, and work was commenced. After a few minutes the signal turned to green, heralding the arrival of a train, so work was speeded up to ensure the charge would be in position in time.'

They placed it between two sleepers, using their hands to dig out the dry soil beneath the line. Wilson reported:

The means of ignition mounted on a Fifty Players cigarette tin (filled with gelignite to destroy the evidence) was carefully packed so that the dual pressure studs were bearing flush with the underside of the rail, and then connected up to the main charge.

Finally the detonators were placed in position and the whole layout left invisible lest a failure should occur. The whole operation on the line took approximately twenty-five minutes.

A cautious return was made to the beach. Voices were heard and it was necessary to lie low for some little time – more fishermen and their boats just off the beach. The canoe was floated and the compass bearing set. Half a mile out the prearranged signal was made. After continuing for approximately ten minutes, the submarine was sighted off the starboard bow.

A quarter of an hour after reboarding the submarine, Wilson was called to the bridge on the conning tower from where *Urge*'s skipper, Lieutenant Edward Tomkinson RN, had just seen a train entering the southern or 'safe' end of the tunnel, the 'light shining brightly' out of its firebox as its crew tried to get up a good head of steam for the steep uphill climb. A minute later, there was a 'brilliant flash as the engine reached the charge at the north end'. It had been blown up in the tunnel, and it would take more than three days to clear the wreckage.

Tomkinson praised Wilson and Hughes for carrying out their duties 'quietly, efficiently and expeditiously'. Hughes, according to Wilson, had displayed 'extreme keenness, calmness and efficiency throughout the operation'. So too had Tomkinson and his crew in tackling a fleet of six Italian warships – two cruisers armed with eight-inch guns and four destroyers – close to the Straits of Messina on 29 June. Tomkinson fired four torpedoes at the leading cruiser, using a ten-second interval and a range of 5,000 yards. Two hit their target, badly damaging but not sinking the 10,000-ton *Bolzano* which was put out of action for three months.

The response of the destroyer escort was immediate, and over the next two hours it dropped no fewer than eighty-four depth charges in an attempt to sink *Urge*. 'The noise of the attack was appalling,' recalled Wilson, and, as he tucked himself 'out of the way', he remembered Roger Courtney's advice for such a situation: 'Be seated, say nothing, hold an open book and look at it. It does not matter if it is upside down – they will not notice it.' Eventually, the attack ended and he and Hughes could breathe again.

A few days later, as *Urge* approached the safe haven of Valletta harbour, Tomkinson ordered the hoisting of the Jolly Roger, the skull-and-crossbones pirate symbol used by British submarines in the First World War. It carried a bar, to denote the attack on the Italian cruiser, and 'in a corner the bosun had embroidered a dagger to celebrate the first pinprick inflicted on the Italians' by Courtney's folbotists.*⁴

*

Thus began a summer of mayhem as the two competing folbot crews at Malta carried out a succession of attacks on Italian trains, railways and bridges. In mid-July, Lieutenant Schofield and Lance Corporal Morgan went out again in *Utmost* – whose skipper Lieutenant Commander Cayley had just been decorated with the DSO – and succeeded in derailing a train near the Calabrian town of Pizzo in southern Italy. Almost spotted by a nude bathing party during their first attempt to land, they moved to 'an adjacent secluded spot' where they got ashore safely. They

---

* Tomkinson and *Urge* assisted a similar special operation in March 1942 when two other folboteers – Lieutenant Walker and Sergeant Penn of the Special Service Detachment – landed and destroyed a train on the north Sicilian coast. During the same patrol, *Urge* sank an Italian cruiser. The submarine was lost with Tomkinson and all hands a month later after striking a mine near Malta.

had just got back in their canoe, and were making for *Utmost*, when a southbound train triggered the explosive and brought down overhead power cables. 'The engine carried on for 200 yards,' reported Captain Simpson, 'the rest of the train piling up and being set on fire by the electrical leads. Much debris fell in the sea, and among the surprised bathing party.' It even came close to the canoe, which by then was 400 yards away.[5]

Wilson and Hughes went on *Utmost*'s next patrol. Departing Malta on 19 August, they made for the east coast of Calabria where their target was a double-span railway bridge over the Seracino river. The attack was scheduled for the night of the 27th, but with a 'short, choppy sea' and a folbot loaded with two men and 250 pounds of plastic high explosives, Cayley tried to reduce the risk by taking the submarine to within 300 yards of the shore. It was just as well because the folbot, though 'expertly handled', shipped a lot of water on the short stretch to the beach. Having unloaded and hidden the gear, Wilson and Hughes moved inland, crossing '250 yards of rough scrub, a barbed-wire fence and a short steep embankment to the railway line'. A short distance away was the bridge, 'unguarded and a most attractive target', with its seaward side camouflaged by tree branches.

It took two trips to fetch all the explosives – made up of eight thirty-pound charges – from the beach. These were placed 'cross-section-wise where the two spans joined' so the 'damage would not be confined to one half of the bridge only'. Wilson climbed over the landward side of the bridge to place one charge 'between the two main horizontal girders'. The other seven were put nearby and 'connected up in circuit'. When all was ready, Wilson pulled the igniter pin from the safety fuse and they 'ran like hell along the track, crashed down through the bushes and flung themselves prone on the beach'. They were just in time. A 'violent explosion' sent a huge 'column of fire and debris' rising into the night sky.

A couple of minutes later, lookouts on *Utmost* heard a short burst of tommy-gun fire and, fearing the worst, manned the Lewis gun on the bridge 'in case covering fire should be required'. They later discovered that 'Marine Hughes had a very light trigger finger' and had 'loosed off by mistake'. By 2:30 a.m. the folbotists had been recovered and the submarine was heading seaward.

Though Wilson's decision to place all the charges at the junction of the two girder spans was not the 'approved method', reported Captain Simpson, it was assumed that the bridge had 'been wrecked due to the amount of explosive used'. The whole operation, he added, reflected 'great credit on Lieutenant Wilson and Marine Hughes, both for boatmanship and quick execution of the considerable task of transporting this large weight of explosive and successful laying and detonating of the charges'.[6] Such feats were not only a test of nerve and skill, but also physical endurance: it required considerable strength and fitness to paddle the overloaded and unstable canoe to shore, unload and hide the gear, scout the target and then return twice to collect all 250lbs of explosives, before finally making their escape with just seconds to spare. Wilson and Hughes had the requisite qualities in abundance.

With each successful attack, the Malta folbotists looked for ever more ambitious targets; meanwhile the Italians were stepping up security on their coastal railway network. A disaster was waiting to happen, and it would come as no surprise to Courtney that its chief protagonist was, in his eyes, the comparatively untrained Lieutenant Schofield of Force X (or No. 1 Section Middle East, as it had become known). On 19 August – the day that Wilson and Hughes left in *Utmost* – Schofield sailed from Malta in Lieutenant Commander Woods' HMS *Triumph*. The larger T-class submarine was necessary because accompanying Schofield was Lance Corporal Morgan and ten other men from Force X, nine folbots, 2,015 pounds of 'TNT plastic explosive, and other demolition stores'. To accommodate the extra weight, all spare torpedoes had to be left behind. Their mission was to destroy the huge seven-arch railway bridge, carrying the Messina–Palermo track, at Torrente Furiano on the north coast of Sicily.

After a delay of a few days as *Triumph* was diverted to attack the Italian Fleet 'which was known to be at sea' – one of two torpedoes fired struck the cruiser *Gorizia* but failed to sink it – the submarine reached its dropping-off point, half a mile off

Torrente Furiano, during the evening of 27 August. An earlier periscope reconnaissance had spotted nothing unusual. But no sooner had all the canoes been placed on the casing, surrounded by their crews and gear, than a 'boat was sighted on the port beam' at the distance of 500 yards. Convinced it was a patrol boat, Woods ordered the submarine full astern and all personnel below. 'As he had not apparently seen us,' noted Woods, '[I] decided to stalk and ram him.'

Having missed the first attempt to ram 'by inches', Woods told his crew to open fire with Lewis guns and pistols. 'I bitterly regretted this immediately afterwards,' wrote Woods, 'when I saw that the boat was an open fishing [vessel], for I now considered it was no longer justifiable to land the demolition party. To avoid further compromise I decided to take the fishermen prisoner and sink their boat.' After much toing and froing, with the occupants of the boat 'shouting continuously', four men and two boys – the majority wounded, some seriously – were taken on board the already packed submarine.

Consulting with Schofield, Woods decided to withdraw out to sea for two days 'to allow any suspicion ashore to die down'. They would try again during the night of 29/30 August, and the operation would be abandoned if it could not be completed by dawn on the 31st 'as, after this, the moonless part of the night would be too short'.

As planned, all nine canoes were launched half a mile from shore at 12:50 a.m. on 30 August: Schofield and Morgan went ahead to scout the beach, leaving the remaining canoes – four manned, each towing an unmanned canoe loaded with explosives – to remain 200 yards offshore until they received the signal to land. There was 'a slight swell, otherwise conditions were ideal'.

Once the canoes had departed, Woods took *Triumph* to sea where it completed the charge of its electric batteries while it waited. At 3:30 a.m. the submarine was returning to its pick-up position, one mile from the beach, when a large explosion was heard from the direction of the bridge. Woods increased speed to twelve knots and noted a blue light flash from the shore soon after. He stopped a mile from shore and drifted to half a mile, knowing the canoeists had explicit orders not to paddle further to seaward than their dropping position. Instead they were to stay there, flashing 'longs'. On seeing this signal, *Triumph* would move towards them until the signal changed to '2 longs', 'indicating that the canoes had sighted her and were closing'.

As time wore on, and there were no signals, Woods became 'increasingly afraid' that the canoes were further out to sea and so began to flash the recall signal in that direction. Still there was no response. The minutes ticked agonisingly by to 4:30 a.m., the 'latest time for the canoes to reach the submarine'. Still 'there was no sign of them, and dawn was just beginning to break'. Knowing it was suicidal to remain on the surface so close to shore, Woods reluctantly gave the order to withdraw. Half an hour later, he saw two blue flashes to seaward – the signal that the canoes were further out than the submarine – and shortly after a canoe was spotted with three men in it. 'They had been told by Lieutenant Schofield not to land,' recalled Woods, 'but to return to the submarine, as the first boats in had capsized in the surf. They had scuttled their tow, and were on the point of returning ashore to give themselves up. They reported that one other canoe (and tow) had also been sent back with them, but had parted company.'

Woods continued searching to seaward and, twenty minutes later, sighted the second canoe with two men almost five miles from land. They had also scuttled their tow and were determined to remain at sea until they were either picked up or ran out of food. They confirmed that no canoes left the beach after the explosion and no signals were seen. Contrary to Woods' instructions, they had paddled to sea 'without making any signals and, in consequence, missed *Triumph*'.

It was now light so Woods abandoned the search and dived. Closing with the beach he could see through the periscope that one and a half of the bridge's spans had been wrecked and two piers partly demolished, and that two trains were stopped to the west, and another to the east. Schofield's intention had been to destroy two piers if possible, but that was using all the explosive. As only half of it had been landed, he had done his best.

The fallback plan, in case the folbotists missed the original rendezvous, was to meet at the same place the following night. In position at 3:45 a.m. on 31 August, *Triumph* flashed the recall signal towards the beach for forty-five minutes. But with the wind freshening, and the sea rising, Woods thought it doubtful the party 'could have reached the submarine either by canoe or swimming'. He wrote later: 'No signals had been seen. Lieutenant Schofield's party had 48 hours iron rations but no water. I considered that the chance of recovering them, even had the weather held, was too slight to justify my remaining any longer, and reluctantly began the return passage.'

Of the six Sicilian fishermen prisoners he took with him, two had serious leg wounds that were smelling 'so bad' they had to be moved from their wardroom bunks 'into the fore-ends'. They left behind Schofield, Morgan and five other members of Force X, as well as Petty Officer Telfer, a member of Woods' crew, who had volunteered to join the mission. Woods reported:

It is my opinion that, his boats having been smashed while landing, Lieutenant Schofield abandoned any idea of returning to the *Triumph*, and turned his entire attention to demolishing the bridge. This is borne out by the fact that he sent four canoes back to the submarine instead of ordering them to lie off outside the surf and ferry the remainder back after the demolition had been completed. He sent no message with these four canoes.

Woods' chief regret was that Schofield had failed to mention in his operation orders – a copy of which he found later – two key details: that the submarine 'would withdraw to seaward to charge [batteries] after landing the party'; and that 'any boats withdrawing should keep together and should in no circumstances go further to seaward than the original dropping position until they actually sighted the *Triumph*'. By not passing these instructions on to his men, Schofield had risked not only his own liberty, but also that of the two crews who were picked up, their rescue owing more to luck than judgement.[7]

Having received Woods' report, 'Shrimp' Simpson added criticism of his own. 'It would appear,' he wrote, 'that the failure to return [to the submarine] was due to lack of training and boat sense.' Yet Simpson himself had made 'a trip of 500 miles down the Danube and experienced rapids and rough water conditions', and was 'of the opinion that parties can land from FOLBOTS and return with a reasonably heavy surf running, because it is possible to get into a FOLBOT from the sea without upsetting it, nor will it break its back if the occupants get out . . . before landing on the beach.' He was, however, impressed by Schofield's 'determination to succeed' and thought it only right that the lieutenant, having now undertaken four special operations behind enemy lines, should be recommended for a gallantry award.[3]

Simpson was as good as his word. He put not only Schofield up for a medal, but the other seven missing men as well. The awards were finally made in 1946 after the eight men – all taken prisoner by the Italians and eventually sent to prison camps in Germany – were repatriated to Britain at the end of the war. Schofield got the DSO, Petty Officer Telfer a bar to his Distinguished Service Medal, Sergeant Derrick de Nobriga a Distinguished Conduct Medal, and Morgan and the others Military Medals. This granting of so many gallantry medals for a single operation was unprecedented, but richly deserved given the difficulty of the operation and the fact that it was carried to its conclusion with no hope of rescue.[9]

Roger Courtney, however, thought that lessons could be learned. Soon after hearing about Schofield's capture, he wrote a personal letter from HMS *Medway* in Alexandria to Colonel Bob Laycock, now commanding all Special Service units in the Middle East. An 'untrained Folbotist', wrote Courtney,

not only imperils his own life, but he endangers the life of a trained Submarine crew and gambles with the safety of the Submarine itself. Above this, if he is captured with his craft it is unlikely that a successful operation would ever be carried out in that area again. A perfect example of this, was Schofield's last operation [in which] he and seven men were captured with their canoes, and demolition materials of the latest type.

On reading through the Submarine's report, it is quite clear to me that Schofield and his men, although extremely plucky, were quite untrained and that the mistake they made was totally unnecessary and would never have arisen had this particular operation been performed by trained Folbotists.[10]

6

'I will never forgive him'

Peering through his periscope at the picturesque harbour of Syros in the Cyclades Islands, the skipper of HMS *Torbay* was disappointed to see only a single fishing trawler on the southern shore. Fortunately, there were other tempting targets, including 'a power station, a foundry, a number of workshops and warehouses'. It was, he decided, an ideal opportunity 'for a Folbot operation', with a strong 'element of surprise' and the 'presence of the moon more likely to be a help than a hindrance'.[1]

It was 7:00 a.m. on Saturday 5 July 1941. Having left Alexandria a week earlier on its third Mediterranean war patrol, the T-class submarine had already torpedoed an Italian merchant ship, and sunk with its deck gun two laden caiques* and a schooner. But that was not enough to satisfy a skipper as hard-driving and ambitious as 34-year-old Lieutenant Commander Tony Miers. Born in Scotland, the son of a regular army officer killed in the First World War, Miers was raised by his formidable mother Margaret who arranged for him to attend Wellington College, 'the school for the sons of heroes', for a nominal sum. A talented athlete who was later given a trial for the Scotland rugby team, Miers had a win-at-all-costs attitude towards sport that he also applied to war. By 1939, having entered the Royal Navy as a regular officer eleven years earlier, he had gained a reputation as 'totally loyal, outstandingly keen, fearless, hot-tempered and incautiously outspoken'.

---

* A traditional fishing or trading boat found in the Aegean and Ionian seas.

Short and stocky, with a penetrating glare, he had a presence that, noted *The Times*, 'no one could be indifferent to'. The newspaper added: 'He was not always easy to deal with and he was not always right in his judgements or decisions. But his impulses were so often warm and generous that while his energies might raise the temperature of the affairs that he was engaged in, they also created wide tolerance and great loyalties.' Nicknamed 'Gamp' by his subordinates – after the dissolute and incompetent Charles Dickens character Mrs Gamp in *Martin Chuzzlewit* – while his fellow officers knew him as 'Crap',* he set incredibly high professional standards and worked his crew ferociously. But he was not infallible, and almost sank *Torbay* when his impatient recklessness caused her to strike a tanker in Loch Long during her sea trials in late 1940. He was lucky to keep his command.[2]

His aggressive temperament, however, was perfectly suited to war where risk was rewarded, and caution scorned. Having identified targets in Syros harbour on 5 July, he asked the two folbotists on board to prepare a plan of attack for that evening. But as the day wore on, and the weather kept deteriorating, Miers was forced to cancel the mission. He was almost relieved. 'I am bound to confess,' he reported with typical frankness, 'that, though their keenness was beyond question, I doubted whether the [folbotists] had sufficient experience to ensure success in other than a plain *ship* demolition operation.'

This was a little harsh, as was Miers' comment that he regretted not having 'two Folbots so that an officer could have accompanied the expedition'. For the men in question were two of Courtney's best: Corporal George Bremner and Lance Corporal Jim Sherwood. Accompanying their first submarine patrol since the eventful if largely fruitless trip to Benghazi and Gavdos in early June, and only their second without an officer, they were

---

* 'The origin of the name is not clear,' wrote Miers' biographer. 'It may have been a play on one of his names, Capel, or "because he gave out a lot of crap".' (Izzard, *Gamp VC*, p. 30)

eager to do their bit. Despite the cancellation of the Syros mission, they would soon get their chance.

But before that, in the evening of 5 July, the officer of the watch spotted through the periscope the conning tower of a surfaced enemy submarine* off the southern coast of Mykonos. Miers closed to within a mile and fired six torpedoes to make certain of the kill. 'Heard one fairly loud explosion,' wrote Miers, 'followed ten seconds later by a tremendous double explosion which shook the submarine considerably, breaking the glass in both navigation lights.'[3]

One of Miers' crew remembered hearing 'things hitting the water' and 'wondered what the devil it was'. He assumed it 'must be mines or something, but it was pieces of submarine hitting the water'.[4] With an enemy plane fast approaching, Miers ordered *Torbay* to dive, but not before glancing in the direction of the hostile submarine where all he could see was 'an enormous upheaval of dirty-coloured water and no sign of the enemy'.

Three days later, while patrolling off Cape Malea in the Peloponnese, *Torbay* surfaced to attack a 200-ton schooner 'full of troops and stores' and flying 'the German flag', bound for Crete. Interrupted by a plane, Miers broke off the initial attack and dived. Twenty minutes later, with the coast clear, he surfaced and resumed the attack, using a Lewis light machine gun. With most of the enemy troops 'destroyed by Lewis gun fire', reported Miers, the schooner was finally sunk by shells from the four-inch deck gun.

In the early hours of the following morning, 9 July, *Torbay* could see by the light of a full moon four caiques heading from Crete to the mainland, about two miles apart. Running low on four-inch ammunition, Miers decided to stop each one in turn with a well-aimed shot of high-explosive, 'clear the decks with Lewis gun [fire], go alongside and blow them up with TNT charges.'

---

* It was, in fact, the Italian submarine *Jantina*, a 600-ton Argonauta-class vessel with a crew of fifty.

These were the tactics used on the leading caique, which was 'about 100 tons', carrying 'troops and stores (including petrol)', and flying the German flag. But the initial shots started such a 'blazing fire' on the vessel that it was 'not possible to go alongside'. Instead the Lewis guns were used 'until the occupants had all been either killed or forced to abandon ship and she was left to burn'.[5]

Torbay then moved on to the second caique, also flying a Nazi flag, which was attacked twenty minutes later. 'We engaged the vessels with our 4-in[ch] gun, and the sub's Lewis gun,' remembered Corporal George Bremner, 'and I fired tracer with my Bren gun from the bridge. They returned fire but they were no match for the 4-inch gun.'

As the submarine closed with the caique, the latter's crew 'jumped overboard with some of the [German] troops and cried for help in the water'. Those remaining on board 'made signals of surrender, shouting "Captain is Greek"'. The first man on to the enemy vessel was George Bremner. 'Whilst leading the explosive party aboard the caique,' he remembered, 'I spotted a German soldier about to throw a grenade into the bridge of the *Torbay* and I shot him. I then continued to capture and disarm seven Bavarian Alpine troops whom I shepherded aboard the casing of the submarine *Torbay* whilst the explosive crew prepared the charges.'

Meanwhile Lieutenant David Vershoyle-Campbell RN, commanding the explosive party, had used his pistol to kill a German 'who had pointed his rifle at him'. He was about to shoot another at 'point-blank range' when Bremner, noticing the German was unarmed, stopped him.[6] Having set the explosive charge, Vershoyle-Campbell and the rest of the boarding party returned to the submarine. The caique, he told Miers, was 'filled with ammunition, oil and petrol', and equipped with a wireless transmitter.[7]

There was still the issue of what to do with the prisoners. 'During the time I was on the casing,' wrote Bremner, 'I removed some of their headgear, insignias and badges of rank for identification purposes in Alexandria. I then asked Miers' permission to take the Germans inboard, which he furiously refused, shouting that submarines never took any prisoners.'[8]

Miers' version of events – contained in his official report – is that the remaining Germans on the boat 'were all forced to launch and jump into a large rubber float (which was the only form of lifeboat)'.[9] Bremner claims that, after Miers refused to take the Germans below, he 'looked everywhere for a lifeboat or raft for the prisoners, but there was no sign of any such craft'.[10]

Either way, it was what Miers did next that broke the unwritten rules of submarine warfare and stirred up a controversy that still rages today. Miers ordered the cold-blooded machine-gunning of the soldiers who had been cast adrift in the rubber raft to, as he put it in his report, 'prevent them regaining their ship'. This was, of course, nonsense. Miers knew that an explosive charge had been set on the ship. It went off a few minutes later, starting a 'fierce blaze which continued until the ship sank, ammunition exploding at frequent intervals'.[11] His decision to kill the soldiers was simply a continuation of his earlier ruthless actions in sinking enemy shipping and leaving the survivors to drown. But it was one thing not to help the enemy adrift in the water, quite another to shoot them in a life raft.

Bremner had gone below by the time the Germans were killed. When he later asked the deck crew 'about the fate of the prisoners', he was told they had been 'shot in the water and no mention was made of a rubber raft'. If Bremner is correct, Miers deliberately murdered unarmed prisoners – an obvious war crime.[12] But even if Miers' version of events is accurate – and the German soldiers were never formally taken prisoner and herded on to the submarine casing – his decision to use the Lewis gun to shoot them in 'the rubber raft' is still unforgiveable. Miers' apologists – his 21-year-old first lieutenant Paul Chapman RN among them* – argue that his actions need to be

---

* Chapman wrote in his memoirs: 'We shot the lot. Fanatical Nazis make treacherous companions . . . They gave no quarter and *Torbay* was likeminded in respect of them.' (Chapman, *Submarine Torbay*, p. 65.)

seen in the context of a naval war in the Mediterranean that was particularly savage, that the Germans had committed far worse atrocities during the evacuation of Crete (which was true), and that, as Miers' son put it: 'Here were men who were the enemy, with guns, in uniform. The shore was two miles away, they could swim let alone go in a boat. They could go and kill some of our soldiers. That's war.'[13]

There was, in truth, no justification for shooting German soldiers who were powerless to defend themselves. They were almost certainly unarmed – despite claims by Miers' deputy to the contrary – and no threat to Torbay or its crew. But Miers had a score to settle: the death of his father in the First World War. 'He hated the Germans,' recalled one of his stokers, 'he had no love for them at all.' Yet by killing them in cold blood, Miers was setting a dangerous precedent. That was the gist of the letter that Admiral Sir Max Horton, Flag Officer (Submarines), wrote to the Admiralty after reading the report of Torbay's third patrol:

There is reason to believe that the incidents referred to have become known to the enemy and that his propaganda has made much of them. The possibility of reprisals clearly exists and such reprisals may not only affect submarines but also the crews and passengers of any ship sunk by enemy action. As far as I am aware, the enemy has not up to now made a habit of firing on personnel in the water, on rafts, or in open boats, even when such personnel were members of the fighting services; since the incidents referred to in Torbay's report, he may feel he is justified in doing so. In my opinion it would be wise for the Admiralty to issue a clear statement of the policy to be followed in this matter and, in this connection, looking at it from the material as opposed to the ethical point of view, it appears that we have more to lose than the enemy by following the policy adopted by Torbay.

The German propaganda ministry had indeed mentioned the so-called 'outrage' in a number of radio broadcasts, noting that survivors from one Greek sailing craft were ordered into a rubber boat and then fired on at a distance of 'only twenty yards'. It added: 'Four sailors were killed and two severely wounded. The bullet-ridden rubber boat sank. The submarine machine-gunned the swimming men. By skilfully dodging the machine-gun fire, none of the survivors were hurt. After a time the submarine disappeared.'

M Branch, the Admiralty's secretariat, responded to Horton's letter by pointing out that 'the enemy have much more to answer for in this respect than we have', and, as a result, they did not propose 'to take any further action'. The Lords of the Admiralty agreed. They were satisfied, they told Horton, 'that commanding officers of HM submarines can be trusted to follow the dictates of humanity and the traditions of the service in matters of this kind and that it is unnecessary to promulgate general rules'.[14]

In truth, Britain was facing a life-or-death struggle in the Mediterranean in the summer of 1941, and ruthless and daring submarine commanders like 'Crap' Miers were needed to help turn the tide against the Axis powers. Which is why, after *Torbay* had returned safely to Alexandria in mid-July, Miers' immediate superiors commended his actions, rather than censured them. '*Torbay*'s patrol was again brilliantly carried out,' wrote Captain Sydney Raw of the 1st Submarine Flotilla. 'The results achieved were – one U-boat [*sic*], the tanker STROMBO, one transport . . . and seven sailing vessels all laden with German troops and military stores. Great credit is due to Lieutenant Commander Miers for his offensive spirit, careful planning, accurate appreciation and happy quality of being in the right place at the right time. The operation against the caiques was a model of efficient destruction.'[15]

Admiral Sir Andrew 'ABC' Cunningham, commander-in-chief of the Mediterranean Fleet, agreed. 'This was,' he informed the Admiralty, 'a brilliantly conducted offensive patrol which inflicted severe damage on the enemy. These results are not obtained by chance, but by sound appreciation and careful planning, which together with his offensive spirit, render Lieutenant Commander A. C. C. Miers, Royal Navy, an outstanding submarine commander.'[16]

George Bremner, on the other hand, had witnessed at first hand Miers' brutality and was not impressed. Shortly after the killings, Miers made Bremner hand over the insignias and badges of rank that he had taken from the German Alpine troops, using the excuse that he would 'hand them over to the Intelligence in Alex[andria]'. Yet there is no mention of them in Miers' report, and Bremner was unsure whether 'they were ever delivered'. He wrote in 1989: 'Miers was brave and deserved all his honours and awards,* but I will never forgive him for his actions in the shooting incident, which I have had to live with on my conscience for the past 47 years.'[17]

*

Despite the bad blood between Miers and Bremner, the folbotist was assigned to *Torbay*'s next patrol which left Alexandria on 2 August 1941. With Sherwood absent this time, the newly promoted Sergeant Bremner went alone. He kicked his heels for much of the time as Miers searched for targets along the Libyan coast, eventually torpedoing a merchant ship near Benghazi on the 12th.

This was Bremner's fourth submarine patrol, but even for the regular crew it was an unpleasant and disorientating experience. '*Torbay* was closely packed with 60-odd men,' wrote one new arrival, 'and you were very close to one another in bunks . . . Even the officers weren't very comfortable.' After a few days, everybody 'reeked of diesel and bilge water and exhaust fumes', and there was no opportunity to wash. 'Body odour didn't mean a thing to you,' noted the sailor, 'because so many of us smelt. It took a long while for it to work out of your pores.' Food was stacked in every available space, and there was little room for personal effects. Each submariner took

---

* Miers would become one of the most highly decorated submarine commanders of the war, winning the Victoria Cross, DSO and bar, the American Legion of Merit, and a mention in despatches. After the war he rose to the rank of rear admiral and was knighted.

only some writing materials, toothpaste and his 'steaming kit – several pairs of overalls and clean underwear and a cap and jacket, in case you had to go ashore'. Once out at sea, the normal circadian rhythm of sleeping when it was dark was reversed: because a submarine stayed underwater by day, and surfaced at night to recharge its batteries, circulate fresh air, and allow any heavy work to be carried out, its crew 'classed midnight as being midday' and ate when they were hungry.[18]

Having put up with this troglodyte existence for more than two weeks, Bremner was finally called into action after *Torbay* had been ordered north on a special mission to pick up a British SOE* operative – Lieutenant Commander Francis Pool, who was liaising with resistance groups and arranging escape routes for fugitive Allied soldiers† – from a beach on the south-west coast of Crete.

During the morning of 18 August, Miers carried out a periscope reconnaissance of the 'easily recognised' beach and found it 'deserted'. Of more concern was the 'extremely unfavourable' weather, with wind 'blowing strongly from the north' and the sea 'rough and confused'. Well aware that Bremner would have difficulty paddling his folbot in such dangerous conditions, he decided to try at dusk 'while there was sufficient light to observe its progress rather than to await total darkness and send the Folbot in at the ordered time'.

They surfaced at 9:00 p.m., but the wind was, if anything, even stronger than it had been. Stationed with Bremner in the conning tower, Miers was 'hesitating on the wisdom of the enterprise when the correct signal was received from the beach'.

---

* The Special Operations Executive was set up in July 1940, under the Ministry for Economic Warfare, to conduct espionage, sabotage and reconnaissance in occupied Europe (and later the Far East), and to aid local resistance movements.

† Pool had been taken to Crete in the submarine *Thrasher* at the end of July and dropped off in a folbot paddled by a Corporal M. Durand, one of Courtney's newer recruits. Durand and his fellow folbotist, Trooper Keith Edsall, had then helped to evacuate seventy-three Allied soldiers and five Greek civilians durng the night of 27/28 July. (TNA, ADM 236/30.)

This made up his mind, and he told Bremner to set off in his folbot.[19]

Despite serious reservations, Bremner did so and immediately got into difficulties. 'As we watched him paddling frantically,' remembered Lieutenant Paul Chapman, 'we saw the wind catch him so that he disappeared into the murk travelling in a direction not intended. Of course to us, hardened submariners, one soldier here or there made no difference – they were expendable. But our captain was a Scot. He thought that Scottish soldiers were precious. So we stopped everything and went off to look for him.'[20]

Having re-embarked Bremner and his canoe, Miers told him to try again. Bremner was horrified. 'Miers tried to insist,' he recalled, 'that I paddle ashore in a force 8 gale. I knew from past experience that I could not survive in such stormy water and I refused to embark in my canoe.'

Bremner's stand infuriated Miers who threatened to shoot him 'for mutiny', and even went so far as to call 'through the voice-pipe for his revolver'. But after it had been brought to him he 'seemed to calm down' and agreed to Bremner's suggestion that they should 'go below and study the local charts for a more sheltered position for embarkation'. They soon found one.[21] Miers, needless to say, made no mention of the pistol and the threat to shoot Bremner in his report. He wrote instead: 'The Folbot was launched and after being carried out to sea quite out of control was eventually guided into more sheltered water on the far side of the bay and lost to view under the land.' He added, with no little understatement, that Bremner undertook the mission 'rather against his better judgement and fully under-standing the considerable risk to himself'.

Miers waited anxiously for an hour with no message from Bremner that he had reached his objective. Fearing the worst, he sent a short signal to the beach: 'Report when boat arrives.' This was a mistake – as Miers himself acknowledged – because it caused Lieutenant Commander Pool 'to suspect treachery and leave'. When Bremner finally reached the beach he found only an Australian sergeant, a New Zealand private and a few Greeks waiting for him. Bremner ferried both Allied soldiers to the submarine and re-embarked himself at around 1:30 a.m. The New Zealander, it turned out, was Maurice 'Morrie' McHugh, a talented boxer who had won the New Zealand amateur heavy-weight championship in 1938.*

When they tried to re-establish contact with Pool the following night, Miers found that the 'weather had deteriorated to such an extent' that there was no hope of sending in Bremner and the folbot unless the submarine was so close to the shore it was almost aground. Despite the risk, the manoeuvre was accomplished successfully, bar some slight damage to the 'ASDIC' sonar dome† which was put out of action. This enabled Bremner to get ashore and bring back Pool with the news that twenty-six Allied and two Cypriot soldiers were on the beach hoping to be rescued, while a further hundred or so were hiding in nearby villages. With Bremner already exhausted, 'the gusty wind making even this short trip both dangerous and difficult', Miers decided that 'the men must be swum off with the aid of lifebelts and a lifeline'.²² He even adjusted the position of *Torbay* 'to make the journey as short and as sheltered as possible and to ensure that if anyone was caught by the stream he would be swept towards the submarine'.

The man sent to supervise the operation was the engineer officer, Lieutenant Tono Kidd, who was ferried in by Bremner. Kidd was followed in by a New Zealand stoker called Philip Le Gros whose job was to fix a line known as a 'grass' or coir hawser to the shore. 'Some of them got so excited knowing a submarine was coming,' recalled Le Gros, 'they slipped down a cliff and had bits and pieces knocked off them.' But one by one, he got them to pull themselves along the hawser and through the choppy water to the submarine, while Bremner transported

---

* McHugh survived the war and went on to play rugby for the famed All Blacks.
† Located on the hulls of submarines and surface ships, the domes housed electronic equipment that was used for detection and navigation.

the wounded in his folbot. Miers was waiting in the conning tower to welcome them. 'Who are you?' he asked one. 'Do you like rum?'

'Too bloody right!' the man replied.[23]

As well as all twenty-eight soldiers, the submarine took on board twelve Greeks who had swum from the shore. Before heading out to sea to recharge *Torbay*'s batteries, Miers arranged for Pool's Greek guide to tour the nearby villages and inform as many Allied soldiers as he could find that the submarine would be waiting to pick them up the following night at dusk. 'I felt confident,' wrote Miers, 'that I should be acting in accordance with the wishes of the Commander-in-Chief if I made every effort to rescue as many . . . trained British troops [as possible].'

When *Torbay* returned to the beach at 9 p.m. the following night, 20 August, the weather was much improved and 'conditions for the operation were perfect'. This allowed Bremner to use the folbot to ferry in Lieutenant Kidd who would once again take charge. They were met by the alarming spectacle of literally hundreds of local Cretans, including children and even dogs, who had come to see the submarine and wave goodbye to the fugitives. 'The noise,' wrote Miers, 'was such as to fill one with utmost alarm for the success of the operation.'

Among the locals were no fewer than twelve Allied officers and eighty men. While some used the fixed line to swim to the submarine, others were ferried across by Bremner who made, according to Miers, 'as many as thirty trips to and from the beach mostly with unskilled passengers without sustaining damage to his craft'. The trouble began when Miers insisted that the twelve Greek civilians were removed from the submarine. When some refused to go, 'considerable force' was used in a violent struggle that almost cost one Greek his life when he fell into the water and nearly drowned. Luckily, he was rescued by an 'extremely gallant' able seaman who got him ashore and resuscitated him on the beach.

By this time some of the Greeks onshore were hoping to get on the submarine, and 'there was a tense, almost threatening attitude, amongst the crowd (most of whom were armed with sticks) which caused considerable misgiving to Lieutenant Kidd for the safety of the Folbot and the last few men to come off'.[24] Lieutenant Chapman had to hit one man's hands with a paddle as he tried to scrabble onto the casing, forcing him to 'let go and swim away'.[25] Fortunately most of the other locals were distracted by the plight of the 'half-drowned Greek', and the operation was completed without losing a single man.

In all, twelve officers and 118 Allied soldiers were rescued over the course of three nights: sixty-two New Zealanders, forty-two Australians, eleven British, one RAF man, five Cypriots, one Yugoslav, three Greek guides and five Greek 'stowaways'. With the submarine full to bursting, it was a hot and uncomfortable voyage back to Alexandria. Yet the crew behaved impeccably at a time when 'fresh food and water were running low and when the general stamina was at its lowest, [and] they were suddenly faced with the influx of more than double their total number, all requiring to be fed and looked after'.

It was a remarkable rescue operation and Miers gave fulsome praise in his report to Lieutenant Commander Pool's 'energies', Lieutenant Kidd's 'efficient handling of the beach operations', Lieutenant Chapman's skilful work on the casing where 'many exhausted and several injured men' were received, and Corporal Bremner's courage in risking his life 'on several specific occasions in very unfavourable weather'.[26] For this and other gallant acts that autumn – displaying 'coolness and courage' while engaged in 'three dangerous operations' from British submarines – Bremner was awarded the Military Medal.*[27]

---

* Many years later, Bremner would complain that 'Miers was always very generous with bravery awards to his officers and crew' – including Lieutenant Kidd who was 'awarded the DSO for holding a hemp line whilst I paddled him ashore' – whereas 'none of the Folbot Section who sailed with him were recommended for bravery'. (Letter to *Sunday Telegraph*, 26 February 1989.) Bremner's recommendation came from his CO, Roger Courtney.

7

'The initiative on all enemy coastlines has passed into our hands'

'During the six months that [my] Unit has been operating out here,' wrote Roger Courtney to Colonel Bob Laycock on 18 September 1941, 'it has had many successes, as you can well see from our War Diary. But it has also made many mistakes. It is from the many mistakes that we have learned the possibilities, and above all the limitations of this kind of work. In fact, we have accumulated a vast amount of experience, which will become invaluable to all who partake in coastline reconnaissance.'

Written from the submarine base HMS *Medway* in Alexandria, this private letter to Laycock was Courtney's attempt to secure not only his own role as the undisputed leader of Britain's fledgling maritime special operations capability, but also the independence of his Folbot Section (soon to become the Special Boat Section), and preferably its expansion into a much larger unit. A number of recent events had given Courtney cause for concern: his close brush with capture and death during the botched sabotage mission at Mersa Brega in early June; the capture of two of his men, Corporal R. Halloran and Marine Miles (one of the Sannox Bay 'originals'), after the attempted sinking of a freighter with limpet mines in Benghazi harbour in late July;* and the even more disastrous loss of Lieutenant

---

* Though explosions were seen from the submarine *Taku*, it was later concluded from an examination of aerial photos that 'no success was achieved' because the folbotists 'mistook their target and further damaged the sunken hulk GEORGE'. (TNA, ADM 236/24.)

Schofield and seven men, mostly members of Force X, in Sicily at the end of August.

What had worried Courtney most, however, was the news in late July that Layforce was to be disbanded and its personnel either returned to their units or sent as volunteers to other Special Service units in the Middle East. This was a blow because, while Courtney and his men had been exempted the fate of the rest of Layforce, their long-term future was still far from certain. As a temporary measure, the Folbot Section had been assigned with other Special Service units – such as the Long Range Desert Group and the recently-created 'L' Detachment, Special Air Service Brigade* – to form part of the Middle East Headquarters General Reserve. But Courtney knew that he needed friends in high places to ensure his unit's survival, and so was hugely relieved when he learned, as he put it in his letter, that Laycock had been given command 'of all the Special Service units in the Middle East, including the Folbot Section'.

The letter, therefore, was Courtney's pitch for future employment. In it he stressed the need for folbotists to be properly trained 'under the light of my own experiences, or under those who have already been trained by me'. If they were not – as Schofield and his men, 'working independent from my unit', had not been – they endangered their own lives, the lives of a 'trained submarine crew', and gambled with 'the safety of the submarine itself'. Yet the opportunities for folbotists, continued Courtney, had never been greater. He wrote: 'Now that the Germans are entangled in the depth of Russia' – having invaded the Soviet Union in a surprise attack, Operation Barbarossa, in late June 1941 – 'the initiative on all enemy coastlines has passed into our hands'. Careful reconnaissance was, in his opinion, 'an

---

* 'L' Detachment, SAS – a name dreamt up by Colonel Dudley Clarke, head of strategic deception in the Middle East, to make the new unit seem larger than it actually was – was formed in July 1941 by another former 8th Commando officer, Captain David Stirling, to carry out deep penetration raids against Axis airfields and lines of communication. It was the forerunner of the modern SAS.

absolute necessity before any type of landing operation' could be planned. 'I believe,' he added,

> that this work should be done by a highly trained Folbot Corps, which should extend its branches of specialised offices to every important naval base. For this reason, I should like to return to England, where I am certain that I could start a new branch which, within a very short time, would be doing invaluable work. It would then be possible to join the branches in England, Malta, and Alexandria into a Folbot Corps. This corps could have its own Military and Naval Staff who could look after the intricate details that such Special operations desperately need.[1]

Courtney was right to stress that, thus far, he and his men had been on a steep learning curve. They had, after all, started out as little more than a band of willing volunteers with no experience of maritime special operations. Yet they had learned from their mistakes and now had invaluable knowledge that would stand them in good stead for the future. What they still needed, he realised, was a proper structure – in the form of a UK-based headquarters – that would allow them to refine their tactics, training and procedures. This, in turn, would produce a highly trained and professional force that could be deployed in any theatre; and one that focused on the collective, not the individual, and was willing to adapt, learn and develop.

Courtney would later insist that he was 'ordered home' in December 1941 to 'form a new [Special Boat] section, leaving behind him a greatly increased Section under the command of Major Kealy, who carried on with many successful operations', including the 'destruction of numerous aircraft on the island of Crete and cooperation with the Long Range Desert Group and the newly formed SAS Reg[iment] who were composed of parachutists'.[2] This was mostly true, but what Courtney failed to mention was that the move was his idea. Even as early as September 1941, he worried that his folbotists would soon be absorbed by one of the other 'private' armies that were springing up in the Middle East, and it was not an idle fear.

Laycock's preference, as outlined in his memorandum of 16 September 1941, was to combine all Special Service troops in the Middle East into a 'force capable of waging amphibious warfare'. It would include one 'General Service Commando' of 250 men, one 'SAS Commando (Parachutists)' of seventy men, and Courtney's 'Folbot Troop (attached Royal Navy)' of thirty men. He envisaged these units being kept up to establishment strength from Commando drafts from the UK. Working in conjunction with the navy and RAF, they would carry out the vital tasks of 'reconnaissance, security of beach-heads, sea or airborne attacks on the flank and rear of the enemy, and seizure or sabotage of important installations in the rear of the main battle'. The force would also be available, during periods when no major operations were in progress, for 'harassing raids' on the enemy's lines of communication.[3]

If Laycock had had his way, Courtney's folbotists – now known as the Special Boat Section – would have retained their independent status on attachment to the Royal Navy. But he was overruled by other senior officers at General Headquarters in Cairo who insisted that, as of 11 October, all Special Service troops were grouped into a single 'ME Commando', consisting of a headquarters troop (No. 1), an 'L' Detachment SAS troop (No. 2), three Commando troops (Nos 3–5), and an SBS troop (No. 6). Headed by Laycock, the Commando would come under GHQ control and, subject to accommodation, be based at Kabrit on the Lower Bitter Lake.[4] With the writing clearly on the wall, Courtney continued to push for a posting back to the UK so that he could raise a new home-based Special Boat Section. Permission was finally given in December 1941. 'Behind him,' wrote his brother Gruff,

he left fifteen officers and forty-five other ranks under Major [Mike] Kealy (Devonshire Regiment). After his departure the long battle of attrition for the independence of No. 1 SBS was lost, and it was attached to No. 1 Special Air Service (SAS), raised and commanded by the expansionist, influential but very effective Lieutenant Colonel A. D. ('David') Stirling (Scots Guards) of desert raiding fame. The role of [No. 1] SBS was changed from beach reconnaissance and shoreside sabotage to small-scale assault raiding, with a consequent sharp increase in casualties.[5]

Among those casualties was Lieutenant Eric Newby, the travel writer who would go on to pen the celebrated *A Short Walk in the Hindu Kush*. Educated at St Paul's School in London, Newby had worked for an advertising agency before crewing a Finnish yacht in the Grain Race from Australia to Europe, via Cape Horn (an adventure he wrote his first book about). When war broke out, he joined a battalion of the London Scottish as a private and later trained as an officer, serving in both India and the Middle East. It was shortly after arriving in Egypt, in the autumn of 1941, that he volunteered for the SBS. Thirsting for adventure, he very much liked the sound of a unit whose job was 'to land from submarines on hostile coasts in order to carry out acts of sabotage against railway systems, attack enemy airfields, and put ashore and take off secret agents'.

The interview on board HMS *Medway* was his first meeting with Roger Courtney, 'an astonishing officer who had been a white hunter in East Africa and had canoed down the Nile'. On Courtney's desk was a sign that read in block capitals:

ARE YOU TOUGH? IF SO GET OUT. I NEED BUGGERS WITH INTELLIGENCE.

Alarmed by the sign, Newby thought he would be rejected. He was, in fact, precisely the type of clever, adventurous and unshowy recruit that Courtney was looking for. He spent the next few weeks at the Combined Operations Centre at Kabrit on the Suez Canal, 'learning to handle folbots and explosives, how to sink shipping, and how to blow up aircraft and trains or otherwise render them inoperative'. The training for ship attacks meant 'swimming at night in the Bitter Lakes – which lived up to their name in the depths of winter – covered with grease and wearing long woollen naval issue underwear, and pushing a limpet towards whichever merchant ship lying at anchor had been chosen as the target, the limpet being supported by an inflated car inner tube with a net inside it'.

Sent first to Beirut in Syria to prepare the ground for sabotage operations in the event of a German invasion from the north (which never materialised), Newby was captured with seven other members of 'M' (Malta) Detachment of the SBS on only his second mission – to destroy German Ju-88 bombers on an airfield in Sicily – in August 1942. Intercepted by sentries on the edge of the airfield, they aborted the mission but missed their rendezvous with the submarine *Una* and were saved from drowning by Sicilian fishermen who promptly handed them over to the military. After a brief period of freedom following the Italian armistice in late 1943, Newby spent the rest of the war in German POW camps.[6]

*

While Roger Courtney was fighting to secure the SBS's future, 'Tug' Wilson and Wally Hughes continued their two-man war on the Italian railway network from their submarine base in Malta. Their next mission was their most ambitious yet: to make a 'permanent breach' in the Naples–Messina railway. Transported once again in Lieutenant Commander Cayley's HMS *Utmost*, they reached the target area on the Calabrian coast on 22 September 1941 and were launched in two folbots loaded with explosives at 10:00 p.m. Hughes then returned for more TNT while Wilson reconnoitred the railway tunnel they were hoping to block. Their plan was to plant 750 pounds of high explosives at the entrance to the tunnel. The resultant explosion, triggered by a passing train, would hopefully prevent the use of the line 'for some months'.

All went as hoped for the first two and a half hours. The

explosives had been piled at the tunnel entrance and their remaining task – to put the TNT in its 'executive position' and connect the fuses – was barely fifteen minutes from completion when they were interrupted by a patrol of Italian militiamen who immediately opened fire. Wilson and Hughes fired back, before beating a hasty retreat to the beach. They were safely aboard the submarine by 2:00 a.m., but 'great disappointment was felt by all at the failure of the operation and as all the Plastic HE [high explosives] had been left ashore'. A further attempt to destroy a railway bridge was made by Wilson and Hughes the following night, but it was also abandoned when they were intercepted by a guard and gave the wrong reply to his challenge. Amidst 'a certain amount of acrimony', reported Captain 'Shrimp' Simpson, 'an exchange of gunfire took place in the darkness, after which Lieutenant Wilson and Marine Hughes made a well-judged retirement' to *Utmost*.

What disappointed Simpson most was the revelation that Wilson had wasted valuable time during the first attempt by 'plastering the tunnel with subversive propaganda before laying the charge'.[7] He had also come to realise that, stung by Wilson and Schofield's previous raids, the Italians had increased the number of guards on their railway tunnels and bridges. When Wilson returned to Malta in *Utmost* in early October, therefore, he was told by Simpson that the Combined Operations staff in Egypt were concerned that his operations had become too dangerous and were to 'cease forthwith'. Desperate to continue, Wilson made two suggestions: that henceforth he would avoid tunnels and bridges, and target only the 'long stretches of unguarded railway line'; and he would take with him an explosive charge that had been 'tailored for the job and made up beforehand, ready for placement at short notice when a train was approaching, with no patrol in sight'.

Simpson agreed, and Wilson and Hughes' next foray from Malta was in late October on the T-class HMS *Truant*, commanded by Lieutenant Commander Hugh Haggard DSC (the great-nephew of the novelist Sir Henry Rider Haggard) who, at six feet five inches, was one of the tallest submarine officers in the navy. Targeting a section of electrified train line between Ancona and Senigallia in the upper Adriatic, that was both close to the shore and just twelve feet above sea level, Wilson and Hughes left *Truant* with their equipment and explosives in a single folbot at 1:00 a.m. on 27 October. Despite medium-sized waves, they landed safely but found, to their surprise, that it was a built-up area with a house just a few yards away. After lying low for a few minutes, they crawled 'cautiously on bellies in the direction of the railway, over [a] heavy shingle beach, marsh, a farm-track and a cultivated field'. They found the line – a double railway track with overhead power cables – 150 yards from the beach. Two trains passed, one in either direction, before they had time to place their charge under the seaward line. Hearing a third train, they headed back to the beach and were just getting underway in the folbot, having set the compass for the rendezvous, when they heard a 'violent explosion' as the 'train detonated the charge'.

The only hiccup was a slight swell which caused the canoe to capsize as they attempted to board the submarine. But, 'after a little swimming about', they were able 'to regain the boat and, with the aid of those on the casing, to salvage the canoe' which had only suffered minor damage. The success of the mission prompted Wilson to conclude that, while bridges, tunnels and other vulnerable points were 'adequately guarded', long straight runs of line could 'still be attacked with success even though they are patrolled, since a charge sufficiently large to crater the line and to derail a train can be effectively laid in under one minute'. The precautionary measures taken by the Italians to counter these attacks were, he wrote, 'inadequate, and by no means warrant an even temporary cessation of landings'.[8]

Returning to Alexandria on 8 November – their first visit since April – Wilson and Hughes were met by Roger Courtney who congratulated them on the havoc they had been causing. He also gave Wilson the welcome news of his promotion to acting captain, and the drinking spree to celebrate went long into the night.

Having recovered from their hangovers, Courtney and Wilson began devising 'a new method of placing limpet mines on enemy ships, consisting of a frame holding three linked limpets which could be attached to the side of a vessel in one motion'. The existing limpet mine, which had only come into use in the middle of 1941, was a 'two-pound charge of plastic explosive which was held to a ship's side by six magnets'. It was attached below the waterline by means of a pole and, once its delayed action fuse had been activated by tightening a butterfly nut, 'could blow a six-foot diameter hole in the plate of most merchant ships'. Yet it was 'not thought to be really effective against naval vessels of any size', which is why Courtney and Wilson wanted to make it more powerful.[9]

Wilson would soon get the opportunity to try out the new device. But before that, with a major British offensive in the Western Desert – Operation Crusader – planned for 18 November, Courtney's SBS was tasked with helping Colonel Bob Laycock and No. 3 Troop of the Middle East Commando (composed of men from 11th Scottish Commando, all that remained of the original Layforce), to land on the coast of Cyrenaica, 250 miles behind enemy lines, and capture or kill General der Panzertruppe Erwin Rommel, the wily German commander known as the 'Desert Fox'.

8

Get Rommel!

'There was a moment none of us will ever forget,' recalled Lieutenant Tommy 'Tubby' Langton of the SBS. 'It was as we were closing the beach in *Torbay*. We were on the forward casing of the submarine, blowing up the dinghies and generally preparing. We could just see the dark coastline ahead. We had been told that [Captain] Hasleden [an SOE agent] would be there to meet us, but I think no one really believed that he would. He had left Cairo quite three weeks before, and during the interval there had been several changes of plan.'

Suddenly there was a 'gasp of amazement and relief from everyone' as a torch on the shore flashed the prearranged signal. In any other circumstances, thought Langton, it would have been met by a 'spontaneous cheer'. But this was a highly dangerous, clandestine mission and stealth was essential.[1]

It was 7:30 p.m. on 14 November 1941 and, having left Alexandria four days earlier, *Torbay* was lying a mile off the beach at Zaviet-el-Hamama on the coast of Cyrenaica. On board were four SBS men – Langton, his second in command Lieutenant Bob Ingles, and corporals Clive Severn and Cyril Feeberry – and three officers and twenty-five men of 11th (Scottish) Commando, led by Lieutenant Colonel Geoffrey Keyes, the 24-year-old son of Admiral Sir Roger Keyes.* The younger Keyes had taken command of 11th Commando after the death of his predecessor, Richard Pedder, in

---

* Admiral Keyes had recently been replaced as the head of Combined Operations by Commodore Lord Louis Mountbatten, a cousin of the king.

a successful action against the Vichy French* on the Litani river in Syria. Self-motivated and ambitious, Keyes had joined the Royal Scots Greys as a regular before volunteering for the Commandos. Regarded by some of his officers as overzealous and the beneficiary of nepotism – he was once knocked unconscious by a hulking subaltern, Blair 'Paddy' Mayne, who later found fame in the SAS – Keyes was undoubtedly brave, and was awarded the Military Cross for his leadership on the Litani.

His task was to land his troop of Commandos – the other half of which, another two officers and twenty-five men, were being transported with Colonel Laycock in a second submarine, HMS *Talisman* – on the beach and then deploy it against four assigned targets: General Rommel's house and the main German headquarters which was 'believed to be at Beda Littoria', a distance of about eighteen miles inland; an Italian headquarters at nearby Cyrene; the Italian Intelligence Centre at Apollonia; and a communications hub at a crossroads between El Faidia and Lamluda.[2]

Keyes would lead the group assigned to kill or capture Rommel. 'If he comes quietly,' he told his men, 'we'll bring him along. If he doesn't, we'll knock him off.' According to his sister, Keyes' job was to 'get Rommel' and he 'never expected to get back'.[3]

The job of the SBS men was to get the Commandos safely ashore and then wait on the beach, with a covering party, to re-embark them. This was 24-year-old Langton's first mission and he was understandably nervous. Educated at Radley public school and Jesus College, Cambridge, he had recently completed his Bar exams and was returning from a tour of South Africa with the university Boat Club when war broke out in September 1939. As their liner took evasive action from U-boats by zigzagging, Langton and his fellow oarsmen helped to camouflage the

---

* After the defeat of France by Germany in June 1940, the northern half of the country was occupied, while the southern half and the colonies were left under French control. The seat of government of this new pro-German and authoritarian French state, led by Marshal Philippe Pétain, was the spa town of Vichy.

ship and act as emergency lookouts. Back in Britain, Langton volunteered for the Royal Navy and for a time patrolled the Irish Sea as a crew member of an armed yacht. But boredom prompted him to switch to the army as an officer cadet, joining first the Irish Guards and then Major Daly's troop in 8th Commando in 1940. When Layforce was disbanded in the summer of 1941, he applied for and was accepted into Courtney's Folbot Section.[4] Though at home in the water – he was a strong swimmer and had twice rowed for Cambridge in losing Boat Races in the late 1930s (the second as president of the Boat Club) – Langton was dismayed to see 'sea and swell rolling in from the north-east' as they closed with the beach. But with the start of Operation Crusader just four days away, there was no time to postpone. 'They knew it,' wrote Miers' second in command, Lieutenant Paul Chapman, 'we knew it, the attempt had to be made.'

While Lieutenant Ingles, formerly of the Argyll & Sutherland Highlanders, and 22-year-old Corporal Severn paddled ashore to make contact with Captain John 'Jock' Hasleden MC – a fluent Arabic-speaker who had been dropped off from the *Torbay* in the same location by Severn five weeks earlier – Keyes and the Commandos prepared to launch from the submarine in two-man rubber dinghies. The original plan was for *Torbay* to use a line ashore to recover the dinghies after the men had landed. But Miers decided that the wind and heavy swell made this impractical, so he got Keyes to agree to hide the boats near the 'HQ dump ashore'.

It was a bitterly cold night, and the Commandos were wearing extra layers under their battledress and two Mae West life vests. This was to counteract the extra weight of their packs, weapons and reserve ammunition. Once all fourteen dinghies had been inflated and lined up along the submarine's casing, Lieutenant Chapman instructed Keyes and his men to sit in them and, when the sea came over, 'to grind their arses into the boat's bottom whilst bearing up with their arms against the wire jackstay, which ran at a suitable height from *Torbay*'s bow to the gun tower'.

Not everyone listened, because four boats and one Commando were washed overboard during the preparations. They were rescued by two sailors – able seamen James Vine and Bill Hammond – and the remaining SBS men, Langton and his paddler Corporal Cyril Feeberry, a fourteen-stone former boxing champion – who dived in to help. It was just as well because the Commando in the water could not swim. But it still took more than an hour to recover the waterlogged dinghies. Fortunately, the extra kit, rations and explosives, were in sealed four-gallon petrol cans and nothing was lost.

At 9:30 p.m. they began to launch the dinghies. 'Torbay's casing party lowered the boats to the water,' remembered Chapman, 'and towed them, one at a time, to the forward hyrdoplanes, whence the Commandos had been shown how to board. But that was in the calm waters of a remote, for secrecy, part of Alexandria. On the night, in the sea and swell, it was much more difficult, and boat after boat capsized as rather inexperienced soldiers tried to board.' Once again, they were rescued by the two sailors, though some equipment, including 'boots, blanket, shirt and rations wrapped up in an anti-gas cape', was lost. What had taken an hour in rehearsal, now extended to four as the swell worsened and the operation was paused while Torbay regained position.

Most of the dinghies were guided to shore by a light shone by Ingles and Severn in the folbot. The SBS men came to investigate, during one of the lengthy hiatuses, and Miers ordered them back on board. 'Unfortunately,' wrote Miers, 'the [canoe] shipped so much water alongside that, although she was handled extremely efficiently, and both crew and gear were successfully disembarked, when the boat itself was lifted out the water ran to one end causing the boat to break its back and become a total loss.' That left just one folbot – Langton and Feeberry's.

By midnight, twelve dinghies had got safely away. The next one 'gave more trouble than all its predecessors, capsizing three times and turning its occupants into the sea'. Realising that time was running out, and that the stricken pair were 'obviously clumsy and unfitted for such difficult conditions', Miers sent them a personal message 'to do their very best not to delay (and therefore jeopardise) the operation any further'. They replied that 'they would do their utmost', and a few minutes later could be seen 'pulling for the shore in splendid style, drenched but in good spirits'.

They were the last to be put ashore. Two Commandos remained, but as one had suffered a recurrence of 'old cartilage trouble' when his knee was crushed between his dinghy and the submarine, and could not march, they were ordered down below. Overall, Miers was delighted with the success of the evening's work. 'It had been accomplished,' he wrote, 'in spite of the weather conditions by the determination, grit and courage of all concerned on the casing, some of whom received a very severe buffeting while handling the boats alongside in the swell, and nearly all were completely exhausted at the finish. No less splendid was the spirit of the soldiers under strange and even frightening conditions. They were quite undaunted by the setbacks experienced and remained quietly determined to "get on with the job".'[5]

At 12:30 a.m. on 15 November, shortly after the thirteenth and last dinghy had been launched, Miers signalled HMS *Talisman*: 'Operation completed.' He then took *Torbay* out to sea at full speed to recharge its batteries, while the other submarine took its place. A little earlier, frustrated by the delay, Lieutenant Commander Michael Willmott of the *Talisman* had sent two of his four SBS men – Lieutenant John 'Farmer' Pryor of the Beds & Herts Regiment, a Territorial officer who had been commissioned only the previous January, and Bombardier John Brittlebank of the Royal Artillery – in a folbot to find out what was going on. But they had difficulty launching, with the folbot capsizing four times, and when they did get away they failed to locate *Torbay* in the dark and 'returned without news'. Realising he needed 'to proceed to sea at least 2 hrs before dawn' to recharge *Talisman*'s batteries, Willmott had just got Bob Laycock to agree to postpone their own drop-off for twenty-four hours when he learned that Miers had completed his disembarkation. He 'therefore closed the beach with all dispatch, took station and trimmed down' so that his dinghies could be launched.[6]

To guide them in, Pryor and Brittlebank were sent ahead in their folbot. They made for the only light they could see – a bonfire just behind the beach that had been lit by Hasleden to dry the wet and cold Commandos from *Torbay* – but were capsized in the heavy swell before they could land. Desperate to save the canoe, they clung to its hull as it was repeatedly driven on to rocks, and then off again by the undertow. 'I don't think this canoe is much more use, sir,' said Brittlebank, at last.

'No,' Pryor replied, 'damn the thing.'

They let go and stumbled ashore. While Brittlebank joined the others round the fire, Pryor, shivering with cold, signalled back to *Talisman* for the embarkation to continue. Aware that time was short, Willmott decided to take *Talisman* as close to the shore as possible by running her bow aground. This had unfortunate consequences. 'With the heavily flooded bow firmly aground,' wrote Chapman, 'the stern rose to the sea and swell, whereas the bow did not. Thus a surge of sea over the forward casing swept away half the Commandos, plus boats.'[7]

With seven dinghies and eleven men in the water, and the submarine in danger of 'broaching to',* Willmott ordered the main tanks to be blown so that *Talisman* could 'go astern and get clear'. As this left the men in the water 'to fend for themselves', he asked his remaining two SBS men to assist. But their folbot was 'wrecked while being launched'. As a last resort, Willmott told the Commandos to throw the remaining dinghies over the side and then jump in after them. 'The men very pluckily carried out this order,' noted Willmott, 'but only one boat got away the right way up with the men on board.' The others

---

* A nautical term to denote a craft being turned sideways by a wave or swell so that it was out of control. In this case, it would have resulted in grounding fore and aft.

turned turtle or 'got into difficulties with the current'. The end result was that only Laycock and seven Commandos reached the shore, where they joined Pryor and Brittlebank.[8]

Of the remaining twenty Commandos on *Talisman*, one drowned and the rest swam back to the submarine. It did not help that, unlike the Commandos on *Torbay*, they were wearing only a single Mae West, which did not have enough buoyancy to keep afloat men weighed down with 'extra ammunition, grenades and personals arms'. The end result, noted Chapman, was that '*Torbay*'s soldiers who went overboard floated; *Talisman*'s sank.'[9]

With both of *Talisman*'s folbots now out of action, Laycock knew he had to keep the dinghies. 'We will hide boats ashore,' he signalled the *Talisman*, using an electric torch. 'Please try and collect those adrift.' Laycock sent the message because, incredibly, he was the only person on the beach who knew Morse code. There were no signallers or sappers with the raiding party because, since the disbandment of Layforce, all specialist ranks had been transferred to other units. Laycock had warned higher command that such a state of affairs 'might prove prejudicial to the success of the operation', but nothing was done.[10]

At 4:00 a.m., having recovered all the men and boats it could find, *Talisman* headed out to sea. Willmott's intention was to land the remaining Commandos that night. But when bad weather prevented this, he was ordered to return to Alexandria and leave *Torbay* to recover any Commandos that survived the operation.[11]

Laycock, Keyes and the other thirty-two Commandos onshore, meanwhile, had hidden the dinghies in a cave and spent the 15th lying up in a deep wadi about a mile from the shore, leaving Lieutenant Pryor and Bombarder Brittlebank to keep watch on the beach. With the weather deteriorating, and a high likelihood that no more men could be landed, Laycock decided to press on that night with a modified plan that would concentrate on the two main objectives: Lieutenant Colonel Keyes, Captain Robin Campbell and twenty-one men would attack the German headquarters and Rommel's house at Beda Littoria; Lieutenant

Roy Cooke and six men were tasked with sabotaging the communications hub south of Cyrene. In addition, Captain Haselden and his party agreed to cut a vital road nearby. Laycock decided to stay at the deep wadi, the rendezvous point, with the remaining three Commandos and guard the dump of reserve ammunition and rations.

The raiding parties left in torrential rain at dusk on the 15th. 'The condition of the troops,' noted Laycock, 'left much to be desired.'

That night, and the next two, Laycock visited the beach in the hope that the missing Commandos would be dropped off by *Talisman*.* But each time a heavy surf 'precluded any possibility of landing' and there was no sign of either submarine. By the third night, he had 'abandoned all hope' of his reserve getting ashore as the next one, 18/19 November, 'had been fixed as the first on which evacuation might be possible'.[12]

---

* Lieutenant Commander Michael Willmott DSO perished with his crew when *Talisman* sank near Sicily in mid-September 1942. The cause is unknown.

9

'Do you think they'll shoot us, sir?'

With no word from the raiding parties, Laycock was beginning to fear they had all been killed or captured when
Sergeant Jack Terry and twenty men from the first detachment
appeared at the rendezvous. Tired, hungry and cold, they were
otherwise unhurt. But they brought bad news: they had attacked
the German headquarters in Beda Littoria, killing at least two
German staff officers and wounding others, but there was no
sign of Rommel.* Worse still, Lieutenant Colonel Keyes, who
led the assault on the house, had been shot and killed as he
opened the door to a room full of armed Germans so that
Captain Campbell could throw in a grenade. Soon after, Campbell
was shot in the leg by one of his own men as he checked the
rear of the house. 'Realising that a superhuman effort would be
required to carry him back over 18 miles of a precipitous country,'
wrote Laycock, 'entailing a descent of some 2,000 ft, [he] ordered
himself to be abandoned.'

Of Lieutenant Cooke and his six men there was no sign.

With one hour of daylight remaining, Laycock went down to
the beach to keep an eye out for a submarine. He was met there
by Lieutenant Pryor who reported that 'friendly Arabs had

---

* Rommel was in Rome, discussing his own plans for an offensive. According
to one of his senior officers, Fritz Bayerlein, the building that Keyes attacked
had been Rommel's headquarters. 'He himself had had the first floor,' wrote
Bayerlein, 'and his ADCs the ground floor.' But at the time of the attack it
was occupied by 'the Quartermaster staff, who lost two officers and two
other ranks'. (*The Rommel Papers*, p. 156.)

returned and, considering that the cave in which we had hidden our boats was unsuitable, had moved them but had departed without showing us the new hiding place'. As the boats might be needed that night, it was news that Laycock found 'most aggravating'.

His spirits were raised a little, however, by the marginal improvement in the weather. The wind was still strong, but there was 'less swell', and he thought there was a 'fairish chance of evacuation provided that the submarine could launch a folbot and get a line ashore'. Without boats, however, he would need 'to ask for a number of life jackets to be sent ashore'.

Laycock's plans were interrupted by the arrival of a message from Sergeant Terry at the wadi. Their hiding place had been spotted by an Arab who then made off 'at a great pace, keeping to cover as much as possible'. Though worried the Arab would report them to the enemy, Terry did not open fire because he had 'no desire to start a local battle with the Arabs'. Thinking he had 'acted wisely', Laycock ordered Terry and most of the other Commandos to move to caves near the beach where they would be available for re-embarkation and hidden from any enemy soldiers who came to look for them. He left just one sergeant and two men with the reserve rations and water at the far end of the wadi to keep a lookout for Lieutenant Cooke's party.*

Just as it was getting dark, Laycock spotted *Torbay* through his field glasses, 'fully surfaced' about a quarter of a mile offshore. He at once signalled her with a torch, requesting a folbot to come in 'with a grass-line and life jackets'.[1]

Watching from *Torbay*'s conning tower, Miers was suspicious. He knew the Commandos had landed with two Mae Wests each, as well as rubber dinghies. So where were they? Deciding not to respond by signal, Miers preferred to send in two of the SBS

---

* Despite struggling to ignite their explosive charge with wet matches, Cooke and his men had managed to destroy the communications pylon at the cross-roads. But they were intercepted by enemy troops as they withdrew to the coast and, after a brief gun battle, were all taken prisoner.

men, Lieutenant Ingles and Corporal Severn, in a dinghy with twenty-three lifebelts, twelve water bottles and some food. They were to inform the Commandos 'that the weather was unsuitable for boat work but that, as the weather was improving rapidly, and in order not to delay the re-embarkation if there was a large proportion of the force present', Miers would 'close to within 100 yards of the spit of land at the western end of the beach at dawn for them to swim off'.

But it proved impossible to embark the SBS men safely in the heavy swell, and once the dinghy had 'broken adrift' without a crew, Miers let it take its chance, calculating that the tide would land it on the beach. He then signalled to the shore: 'Too rough tonight, have floated in boat with Mae Wests, food and drink. How many of you and what luck, where are your boats and Mae Wests?'

The reply came back: 'Twenty-two here, have not found boats and Mae Wests. Goodnight.'

It was followed up, a few minutes later, by an acknowledgement that the dinghy had arrived safely.

Knowing the importance of the mission, and the need to get word of its result to General Headquarters in Cairo, Miers was surprised and angry that there was no response to his question: 'What luck?'

He repeated it, and got a garbled response that appeared to say: 'Goodness only knows. Some killed in camp and missing from HQ.'

Laycock later insisted that his messages were misread. Having just received word from Pryor that the friendly Arabs had returned and revealed the dinghies' hiding place, his previous message had meant to say 'have *now found* boats and Mae Wests'. But it had been incorrectly deciphered as '*not found*'. As for the latest message, he had tried to say: 'Good work – messed up their HQ but sad casualties – Keyes killed – Campbell, Cooke and 6 ORs missing.' That, too, had been misinterpreted.

At least Miers' overall impression that the Commandos were in 'considerable danger' was accurate. He therefore sent another signal, offering to 'close the spit west of the bay at dawn so that you can swim, otherwise try again tomorrow night'.

This was, Laycock admitted later, a 'tempting offer, but after due consideration' he 'came to the conclusion that the troops in their exhausted condition would almost certainly be drowned in attempting to swim from a rocky foreshore against surf, wind and sea'. The other option, of course, was to use the dinghies. Why Laycock did not consider this, when he suspected that an unfriendly Arab had reported the Commandos' hiding place and time was running out, was never explained. Miers, for his part, was under the impression that Laycock no longer had the dinghies. The end result was Laycock's lame reply: 'Try tomorrow night.'[2]

Next morning (19 November), an hour before dawn, Laycock ordered the men to adopt all-round defensive positions. 'The main body,' he wrote, 'remained in the vicinity of the caves covering our northern front whilst 2 smaller detachments were placed so as to protect the eastern and western flanks with sentry posts pushed well forward commanding an extensive field of view.' The small party of three was left in the wadi.[3]

Around midday, Laycock heard shots from the direction of the wadi and the small detachment on the western flank. From his position with the main body, manning a ruined house above the beach, Lieutenant Pryor could see away to the west 'some Arabs in red turbans crawling towards us'. He recalled: 'Everybody fired and they fired back, there were a few bigger bangs that I imagined were from a mortar, and I remember thinking "our old wall doesn't look a bit bulletproof". There didn't appear to be many of these native troops as enemy, so we . . . thought if we could mop them up, we might still get away in the *Torbay* that night.'

He said to Laycock: 'Give me a Scotsman with a gun and I'll go and try and get round the seaward side.'

Laycock ordered a Commando with a tommy gun to accompany Pryor. He also sent a separate party to outflank the enemy from the east. He was convinced that the Arabs were *carabinieri*, working for the Italians, and would not put up much resistance.

Pryor and the Commando worked their way forward under heavy fire, pausing first in the dead ground of a stream, and then behind a stone trough, as bullets pinged all around them. 'Very bad shots they are,' muttered Pryor. 'They'll never hit us.' He pointed ahead. 'On to those rocks next.'

As he ran, he could see six tin-helmeted Italian soldiers lying behind the red-turbaned Arabs, leisurely shooting at him and the Commando. Fortunately, they missed, allowing the pair to reach the safety of the rocks. They were now just 200 yards from the Italians. Turning, Pryor saw the Commando poking and banging his tommy gun as he tried to remove a jammed cartridge. But it would not budge. Losing patience, Pryor said crossly: 'Well try and clear it for God's sake. I'm going on.'

Armed only with a revolver and a grenade, Pryor got as far as the next patch of rocks, fifty yards on, when he noticed even more Italian soldiers on a hill further west. He had two options: charge towards the nearer group of Italians in a suicidal dash; or head back. He knew the former was the 'brave thing to do'. But as it was a 'long uphill rush' with no more rocks to hide behind, and his chances of survival were zero, he decided to head back to Laycock and report what he had seen.

Leaping up, he had gone only a few yards when a piece of shrapnel struck his right foot. 'Damn!' he cursed, running even faster and missing his next piece of cover. Suddenly he heard a bang and his leg buckled under him. He had been shot in the thigh, a pain he likened to a kick from a horse. 'I was covered with sand,' he remembered, 'the bullets kicked up all around me, and "Hell," I thought, "that's hardly the game."' Crawling to a flat stone nearby, he raised it as a shield. Chips flew off it, and he realised that if the snipers moved position he was done for. So he set off, once again, and found to his suprise that his injured leg could support his weight. Stumbling and crawling, he somehow made his way back to the main position.

He got there just as the enemy – a combination of *carabinieri*, Italian and now German troops – was closing in. Aware that it

'would be impossible to hold the beach until dark against superior forces', and that their 'only remaining line of retreat to the
eastward would soon be cut off', Laycock ordered the main
body 'to split into parties of not more than 3 men each' and
'make a dash across the open' and 'retire through' the eastern
picket. Once hidden by the vastness of the desert – or jebel –
they had three options: return to the alternative beach off which
a submarine would be lying until just before first light on 21
November; head for 'area of Slonia' where the Arabs were known
to be friendly and there was a chance of being picked up by the
Long Range Desert Group; hide in the wadis north of the Cyrene
escarpment and hope the Allied offensive got that far.

To Pryor, Laycock said: 'We'd better bugger off. Can you
walk?'

The answer, of course, was no, though Pryor felt his leg wound
looked worse than it was, 'with a lot of blood about'. Worried
that Pryor 'might otherwise bleed to death', Laycock left a 'very
reluctant' medic from Manchester to look after him, and ordered
both to surrender at the first opportunity. He then made his own
getaway, writing later:

> On reaching the position originally held by our eastern detach-
> ment I found Sgt Terry waiting for me and we set off together.
> The first ½ mile of the withdrawal was unpleasant owing to the
> open nature of the country but the enemy's marksmanship seems
> to have been particularly poor and, though we had some close
> shaves, I do not believe that we suffered a single casualty since
> Sgt Terry and myself would almost certainly have observed any
> which had occurred.

Pryor, meanwhile, was lying 'cold and miserable', waiting for
the Italians to approach, when the medic piped up: 'Do you
think they'll shoot us, sir?'

It seemed, he thought, an unfortunate way to speak to a
wounded man. Yet it cheered him up. 'Yes,' he responded in a
deadpan manner, 'I'm sure they will.'

The horrified look on the medic's face was quite a 'picture'.

Eventually the Italians arrived and, after a lot of shouting and exclaiming, orders and counter-orders, Pryor was put on a mule and taken to their 'dirty old HQ' which lay twelve miles to the west. En route they passed a 'lovely great red-backed shrike sat on a juniper bush' watching them intently. The sight of the bird made Pryor's day.[4]

*

Lieutenant 'Tubby' Langton was observing from the conning tower as *Torbay* returned to the beach at dusk. 'The sea', he wrote later, 'was considerably calmer, though a long swell was running in from the NW, i.e. straight on to the beach. We were dismayed to see no signals from the beach.'

Fearing the worst, Miers waited patiently for more than an hour and a half. Still there was no signal. As a last resort he asked Langton and Feeberry to take the folbot in to investigate. The SBS men had trouble launching the folbot from the fore-planes, and by the time they got away they had 'shipped a lot of water'. Langton had 'hoped to approach the beach slowly and turn the boat around to face seawards before getting out'. But the 'long swell prevented this' and – in spite of their combined twenty-eight stone – Langton and Feeberry 'rode into the beach on the crest of a wave like a couple of mermaids'.

There was no sign of life. After draining the folbot of water, they began to move stealthily along the beach towards a light which had appeared on the hillside. It was the right colour – blue – but not giving the correct recognition signal, and Langton was 'most suspicious'. Walking on a little, Langton thought he saw a movement inland, so they crept towards it 'but saw nothing further'. Then they both heard a shout and, as they were some distance from their canoe and 'liable to be cut off', Langton decided to head back.

Reaching the canoe, they paused for ten minutes. Still no one approached. So they relaunched the folbot through the line of breakers and headed along the shore in the direction of the blue light. Langton used his torch to flash 'T's – denoted by a single dash – but there was no signal in response. Only a shout. Soon after they were swamped by a wave and, as they tried to run in again, the folbot capsized. They lost a paddle but saved the tommy gun and all their gear. As they righted and drained the boat, Langton could see the glow from what he took to be a lighted cigarette in the undergrowth. But no one challenged them and, though the boat was holed, they had no option but to clamber in and hope they got to the submarine before they sank.

It was a close-run thing, made even more hazardous by their single paddle and reduced speed. Fortunately, Feeberry was a strong man and, thanks to his brute strength, they reached *Torbay* just before their waterlogged craft went under. 'Everything possible had been done,' reported Miers, 'and both folbotists deserve credit for their good work in far from favourable conditions.'

Having drawn a blank at the first rendezvous, Miers moved *Torbay* along the coast to the alternative beach, three miles to the west, in case the Commandos were there. Again, no luck. Next day, 20 November, he saw through the periscope enemy troops 'moving up and down the beaches in extended order apparently searching'. He closed with the beaches after dark but, again, there were no signals from shore. On the 21st, he saw guns being dragged into position above the original beach. With a rescue operation now out of the question, Miers reluctantly gave orders to leave the area that afternoon and, having shot up a lone enemy aircraft on an airstrip near Ras Aameer ('our contribution to the Libyan offensive'), *Torbay* arrived back in Alexandria on 24 November.

Miers later praised the four SBS men on *Torbay* for 'displaying marked skill in overcoming the adverse conditions under which they had to operate'. Both officers had used their initiative when things did not go to plan, and 'all took their full share in the arduous tasks on the casing and in the general work of the submarine'.[5]

*

Most accounts of Operation Flipper conclude with Colonel Laycock and Sergeant Terry's incredible forty-one-day trek through the Libyan desert, dodging enemy patrols and living off berries and food provided by friendly Senussi tribesmen, before finally reaching British lines near Cyrene on Christmas Day 1941.[6] Terry was especially grateful to be rescued. Laycock had killed time by reading aloud to him from a copy of *The Wind in the Willows*. 'Safe at last!' muttered Terry. 'And now, thank God, I shan't have to hear any more of that bloody Mr Toad!'[7]

Their escape was made possible by the hard-fought success of the 8th Army's Operation Crusader which, by the end of the year, had relieved Tobruk, captured Benghazi and driven Rommel's troops back more than 300 miles to El Agheila in western Cyrenaica, inflicting more than 33,000 casualties and destroying 300 tanks in the process. Allied losses were just under 18,000 men and 278 tanks.[8]

What accounts of Flipper fail to mention, however, is that Laycock and Terry were not the only escapees to avoid capture or death. In fact, one other soldier got away: Lieutenant Pryor's paddler, Bombardier John Brittlebank. He was later awarded the Distinguished Conduct Medal for a separate piece of gallantry. The citation by Bob Laycock, then Chief of Combined Operations, added: 'This non-commissioned officer previously had taken an active part in the raid on . . . Rommel's Headquarters and had succeeded in finding his way back to his unit after being 40 days in the desert behind enemy lines.'*[9]

---

* Other awards included the DCM for Sergeant Jack Terry and a posthumous Victoria Cross for Lieutenant Colonel Geoffrey Keyes. The British casualties included two dead and twenty-eight captured (three of them wounded, including Captain Campbell whose leg was so badly injured it had to be amputated). Only three men escaped. German losses were four dead and three wounded.

No. 2 SBS

'Gentlemen,' said Brigadier Charles Haydon, glancing round the long conference table at the thirteen naval and army officers present, 'we are here to discuss the setting up of a Military Special Boat Section in this country on lines similar to those that have been operating from submarines and seaplanes in the Middle East against objectives in Libya and elsewhere. It is recommended that Major Roger Courtney, who sits among us, and who has been in command of these formations in the Middle East, should take charge of them in this country. I should add that these Boat Sections would operate with folbots of all types and would be controlled by the Chief of Combined Operations.'[1]

The 42-year-old speaker was a legendary figure in the Commando story. Chief of the Special Service Brigade – composed of up to ten Commandos – since 1940, he had recently been awarded a bar to his DSO for personally leading Operation Archery, a raid on the Norwegian island of Vågsøy that succeeded in overpowering the German garrisons and destroying vital infrastructure. Highly regarded by his boss Commodore Lord Louis Mountbatten, the Chief of Combined Operations, who was about to make him his deputy (with Bob Laycock, just back in the country, taking over the SS Brigade), Haydon had called this meeting in the Combined Operations Headquarters at 1a Richmond Terrace in Whitehall on 25 February 1942 to thrash out once and for all the future of the SBS.

The officers round the table read like a *Who's Who* of maritime special operations. They included, of course, Roger Courtney

who had recently returned to Britain in the submarine *Utmost*,*
having been ordered back by the Commander-in-Chief,
Mediterranean Fleet, 'to take command of the Special Boat
Section in this country';[2] Lieutenant Commander 'Deadeye Dick'
Cayley, the skipper of *Utmost*, who had as much experience as
any submariner of folbot operations, having carried out successful
missions with both lieutenants Schofield and Wilson; Captain
Gerald Montanaro, a 27-year-old Cambridge University graduate
and Royal Engineer, who had been commanding 6th Commando's
folbot section, known as 101 Troop, since the spring of 1941;
and Major H. G. 'Blondie' Hasler of the Royal Marines, also
27, a veteran of the campaign at Narvik in Norway who, in
May 1941, had urged Combined Operations to use canoes and
underwater swimmers to attack enemy ships in harbour. His
suggestion had been rejected on the grounds that the necessary
equipment did not exist. But in January 1942 – a month after
the successful raid on Alexandria, when Italian frogmen of the
Decima Flottiglia MAS had used manned torpedoes known as
maiali (pigs) to cripple two Royal Navy battleships – Hasler had
been tasked by Mountbatten with developing 'a British version
of the explosive motor boat' with 'particular attention to methods
of attacking ships in harbour'. Working out of the Combined
Operations Development Centre (CODC) in Southsea, he quickly
came up with the idea for the boom patrol boat, but his preferred
method of attack was by canoe and swimmers, and using limpet
mines, hence his presence at this meeting.[3]

The first item of business was Haydon's proposal to set up a
'Military Special Boat Section' in the UK. This was passed unan-
imously, with the recommendation that the War Establishment
for the new unit should be the same as the SBS in the Middle
East. It was further agreed that the main body should be trained
at Fort William and on the Clyde before being distributed to the

---

* Courtney had left Alexandria in *Utmost* on 29 December 1941 and, after
brief stops in Malta and Gibraltar, finally reached the UK on 1 February
1942. Granted leave, he was reunited with his wife Dorrise for the first time
in a year. (SBSAA, R. J. A. Courtney's Service Records and Documents.)

vice admiral, Dover, and 'other commanders who were likely to require them'. The first three weeks would be spent learning how to manage folbots, use explosives and carry out reconnaissance, and a further week 'training with submarines' on the Clyde. The details would be worked out by Courtney and Commander Taylor RN on the staff of Admiral Sir Max Horton, the Flag Officer, Submarines.

As for the development of technique and equipment, it made sense to ask submarine commanders to contribute ideas and suggestions arising from their own experiences. 'In this respect,' said Lieutenant Commander Cayley,* 'I should mention that my only complaint against the folbot is that it is two inches too broad.'

Courtney replied: 'I'm well aware of this, and the solution is in hand. The boat is being modified by adding an expanding rib, which will permit it to be mounted at a breadth of 21 inches, passed through the hatch and then straightened out to full width afterwards.'

Moving on to equipment, Haydon mentioned that the SS Brigade had about thirty folbots in service, most with Montanaro's 101 Troop, and any held in store were to be kept in reserve. Finally, the meeting agreed that suggestions for future operations would come from the staffs of both Admiral Horton and Mountbatten, and that 'the fullest collaboration should be arranged so as to prevent clashes'. SOE would be kept in the loop as a matter of course.

Courtney's one quibble was the insistence by the naval officers present that submarines be used for SBS operations only 'if the objective were really important'. He responded: 'During operations

---

* Cayley returned to the Mediterranean in the summer of 1942 to take command of a new T-class submarine, HMS *P311*. In early January 1943, *P311* (about to be renamed *Tutankhamen*) was heading for the port of La Maddalena in Sardinia to attack two Italian cruisers with 'Chariot' manned torpedoes – as part of Operation Principal – when she was sunk by mines. The wreck was found by Italian divers in 2016. With a DSO and two bars, Cayley was one of Britain's most decorated submariners.

in the Middle East, my men were often taken on patrols on the chance of finding a land target or a harbour target. This worked very well, and I would suggest that Special Boat Section personnel might normally be included in submarine patrols from home ports with the same possibilities in mind.'

Commander Taylor was unconvinced. 'I'm not sure that would work,' he said. 'From May onwards, as the days get longer, we will be severely restricting the activities of submarines off the Norway, Dutch and Belgian coasts. Only the west coast of France will offer possibilities for onshore and harbour operations from submarines. In the Channel, only surface craft are suitable for carrying folbots because of the particular conditions there with regard to weather, tide and depth.'

But, overall, Courtney had got what he wanted: a new, independent and home-based SBS that would in the future, he hoped, supply the trained personnel for maritime special operations around the globe.[4]

*

Not everyone was happy with the result of the meeting. 'Much talk & little done,' Captain Montanaro noted sourly in his diary.[5] Until Courtney's return from the Mediterranean, Montanaro had assumed that his unit – 101 Troop – would carry out all folbot operations from home waters. Born in Kent, the scion of a distinguished Maltese military family on his father's side, he entered the Royal Military Academy, Woolwich from Bedford School and, having received a commission in the Royal Engineers, continued his studies at Cambridge University where he graduated with a Master's in 1938. After a spell as garrison engineer in Corsham, he accompanied the BEF to France as forward engineer with the 1st Division. On returning to Britain from Dunkirk, he volunteered for 6th Commando and in early 1941 helped set up its 101 (Special Canoe) Troop with Captain John Woollett.

Montanaro was, in many ways, the antithesis of Courtney: a professional soldier, academically clever and ruthlessly ambitious.

He had taken command of 101 Troop in March 1941 after Captain Woollett, its original boss, fell and badly injured himself in a night exercise. Since then, he had pushed the men hard in training and was proud of their record time for a thirty-six-mile march through the Highlands made famous by the Marquess of Montrose's army in the seventeenth century. But operational opportunities were hard to come by and an early example, a beach reconnaissance near Calais in November 1941, had ended badly when one of the two canoes – containing Montanaro's second in command, Lieutenant Keith Smith, and his paddler Lance Corporal Woodhouse – failed to return. It was assumed that the folbot never relaunched in heavy surf and the pair were taken prisoner.[6] 'I feel considerable personal regret in the matter,' wrote Montanaro to Brigadier Haydon,

> particularly since it was only with the greatest difficulty that Keith persuaded me to let him carry on at Dover & 'finish the job' which he had began so well under Vice Admiral Ramsay. It was against my better judgement that he did so, since although he was a good canoeist as regards balance, navigation & in other ways, his bulk would have made an operation involving embarkation in surf necessarily difficult. I suggest that his canoe never left the shore.[7]

Montanaro was already in bad odour with his superiors, having been reprimanded by his commanding officer, Lieutenant Colonel Timothy Featherstonhaugh, for ignoring instructions to rejoin the main Commando in the summer. His response was to appeal directly to Brigadier Haydon. 'The CO [Featherstonhaugh],' he wrote, 'has put into writing his resolve to be rid of me. He has . . . ordered me to do a road survey for Home Guard defence scheme when I should be training the troop . . . He distrusts Lt Smith and thinks that he is a bad influence and inefficient. My own opinion is the reverse.'[8]

Desperate to escape Featherstonhaugh's authority in Scotland, Montanaro was granted a measure of autonomy when he was

permitted to join Smith and a detachment of 101 Troop at Dover
in November. But Smith's subsequent capture did not reflect well
on the competency of the troop, and Montanaro made matters
worse in early 1942 when he breached protocol by trying to
gain the support of Vice Admiral Bertram Ramsay, in charge of
operations at Dover, for a scheme he had already submitted to
Combined Operations HQ in London. Rapped on the knuckles
by a 'very angry' Brigadier Haydon, his hopes were further
dashed when Roger Courtney arrived back in London from the
Mediterranean. After meeting Courtney and Haydon, Montanaro
knew his hopes of an independent command were over. 'All is
practically lost,' he noted in his diary on 18 February, '& best
hope is to accept position under Courtney, keeping as many men
as one can. Retired defeated . . . Future looks very doubtful.'[9]

A day later, trying to make the best of a bad situation,
Montanaro submitted a paper on the SBS's future structure that,
by and large, was accepted. 'Results were rather better than I
expected,' he wrote. 'Most of it was approved.' But his 'wangle'
to have himself and Courtney promoted to major and lieutenant
colonel respectively did not succeed.[10]

On 9 March, Montanaro was back at the Combined Operations
HQ in London to discuss folbot design with Courtney and
'Blondie' Hasler. Courtney spoke first, pointing out that when
he received the first delivery of ten folbots in Scotland in
November 1940, 'most of the struts, spars and ribs' arrived
'broken' and the 'quality of the timber used was extremely cheap
and inferior'. Little had improved by the time the next batch of
eighteen folbots were delivered to Alexandria in August 1941,
and Montanaro confirmed that the boats he had been sent in
early 1941 were no better. Particularly galling for Courtney was
the knowledge that the 'peacetime quality of the boats as made
by the same firm' – Folbot Ltd of Golden Lane – was 'excellent'.[11]

The trio then discussed their ideal requirements for a military
folbot, and came up with the following list: to take a maximum
load of two thirteen-stone men and one hundredweight of cargo
(total 476 pounds); to weigh between seventy and a hundred

pounds; to travel at speeds of three to five knots, depending on load and weather; to be able to withstand a wind of force 4 in the open sea and to be beached through surf; to have a skin that could withstand constant grounding on shingle and working alongside other vessels; to measure around sixteen feet; and to have a width that could satisfy both stability and the ability to get out of a submarine's forward torpedo hatch.

They also agreed that the boat needed to be 'partially collapsible', but with 'no loose parts' and 'capable of complete assembly in thirty seconds in the dark'. Its draft was to be not less than four inches or more than six inches when loaded.[12]

While 'Blondie' Hasler looked for a suitable designer to build the perfect folbot – eventually settling on Fred Goatley of the Isle of Wight – Roger Courtney travelled north to Scotland to set up his new unit, first known simply as the Special Boat Section (Home), and later No. 2 SBS (to distinguish it from his original No. 1 SBS, the remnants of which were now operating in the eastern Mediterranean as Lord Jellicoe's Special Boat Squadron).* It was officially formed on 2 April 1942, sharing its headquarters with that of Bob Laycock's Special Service Brigade at Seafield House in Ardrossan on the Ayrshire coast. Major Courtney was in command, with Captain Montanaro as his deputy and chief instructor. The war establishment was fixed at fifteen officers and thirty-two men, with the nucleus provided by volunteers from Montanaro's 101 Troop which had since been disbanded.[13]

As well as Section Headquarters, the unit was subdivided into four operational groups: each was composed of a captain, a subaltern, two sergeants and two corporals. These groups were 'easily detachable' and could be sent to operate under the

---

* In late 1942, wrote G. B. Courtney, 'a much-depleted No. 1 Special Boat Section was . . . finally absorbed into No. 1 SAS and became part of the Special Boat Squadron under the command of Major the Earl Jellicoe . . . The unit operated with great distinction in the Aegean, mainly in caiques (small Levantine sailing coasters) after the capture of Colonel Stirling in January 1943 . . . It had ceased to have any connection with the original Commando Special Boat Section.' (Courtney, SBS, p. 55.)

commanders of submarine flotillas in various parts of the world. Transporting their folbots in various vessels – including submarines and motor torpedo boats – they would have the capability to destroy shipping, carry out the reconnaissance of beaches, sabotage shore installations and communications, and supply navigational aids to landing forces.[14]

Among the new arrivals from 101 Troop was 29-year-old Corporal Stamford 'Stan' Weatherall,* a pre-war regular with the 1st Duke of Wellington's Regiment. Born into the hardy coal mining community of Bulwell, Nottinghamshire, Weatherall was taught how to use a gun by his father so he could put down his neighbours' unwanted pets. He joined the army a few days after his eighteenth birthday, and saw service on India's North-West Frontier. He also became a crack shot with a rifle, winning numerous competitions at Bisley (including the 1937 Whittingham Medal) before joining the Reserve List in 1938. Two months into his new job as a labourer at Bestwood Pit, he was charged with manslaughter for his part in a drunken brawl. He pleaded guilty, but the case was dismissed.[15]

Called back to the Colours in September 1939, Weatherall served with the Transport Section of 1st Battalion in France and Belgium. After evacuation from Dunkirk in June 1940, Weatherall and two friends volunteered for parachute training for the extra pay, and then switched to the Commandos when they were told it was their best chance of staying together. The initial pep talk by their troop commander in 6th Commando, John Woollett, was as follows: 'You will do some very hard training, and you will be made to suffer all manner of discomforts, and anyone who feels he is not up to it can return to his unit without loss of face. Any idle ones, shirkers and such like will be RTU'd [returned to unit] as undesirables.'

These were not hollow words. 'The training was tough,'

---

* His full name was Stamford Tarlton-Weatherall, the result of his grandfather Robert Hodgkinson's unofficial adoption by his employers Robert Tarlton and Mrs Weatherall. Having squandered his inheritance, Robert resumed work as a miner. His son Bill, Stamford's father, was also a miner.

recalled Weatherall, 'and at times certainly tested every one's stamina to the limit'. But no one asked to go back to their unit or was sent as an undesirable. There were demotions and accidents, however. First his friend Harry 'Curly' Tunstall was reduced from lance corporal to private for shooting a deer without permission on the Isle of Arran. Then he disappeared during a folbot exercise in Loch Shiel on the mainland, and was probably 'drowned when the canoe capsized in the turbulent waters at Black Rocks'. The folbot and paddles were recovered, but 'no sign of Tunstall'. His body, wrote Weatherall, 'never came to the surface and was never found'.

They were billeted in Corrie on Arran at the same time that 'Lieut Roger Courtney and his canoeists were in digs in Upper Sannox, just above Corrie'. Weatherall recalled: 'We often met them in the bar of the hotel. Our main role here was mountaineering, and [we] climbed all the mountains and high hills in the region . . . Herds of deer roamed about the lower part of the hills which were green with grass and heather, and even came down into people's gardens for a feed of garden produce.'

It was after the troop had been moved to Salen on the Scottish mainland in early 1941 that it received its first consignment of canoes, each one packed in two rubberised bags. 'We soon learnt how to assemble them,' noted Weatherall, 'and take them to pieces to repack them. They were just a plain canoe made for river cruising, and were named folbot. We hadn't had the canoes [for more than] a few days, when the first long canoe trip was made.' To make the folbots safer, Montanaro – who had recently taken over as CO – got hold of some 'proper triangular buoyancy bags', which 'could be blown up by mouth and stowed for'ard and aft, also some netted bags of ping pong balls, which served the same purpose'.

Montanaro also tried firing a two-inch mortar from a folbot, instructing Weatherall 'to make a wooden base for it' in front of the seat. The corporal used it to lob high-explosive shells onto two deserted islands, and only later discovered from locals that the blasts had damaged 'some of the headstones of the MacDonald clan who were killed in The Massacre of Glencoe'.

Weatherall was part of the detachment that accompanied Lieutenant Smith to Dover in May 1941. After Smith was captured in November, Montanaro took charge and made Weatherall his pay clerk. A few months later, shortly before they joined the newly formed UK-based SBS in Scotland, Roger Courtney paid Montanaro's men a visit in Dover. The previous night, Montanaro had conducted an arduous exercise that involved his men 'swimming in the icy waters of the harbour', with limpet mines strapped to the back of their kapok suits, ready to attach to a sunken vessel. As the men were introduced to Courtney, their commander said: 'Oh Roger, we had such jolly fun swimming in the harbour last night!'

The men looked at each other, nonplussed. 'Just hark at the twat,' mumbled a voice from the back. Montanaro 'may have thought it was fun', noted Weatherall, 'but we didn't'.[16]

II

'First-rate show!!'

Shortly after midnight on 12 April 1942, a single folbot was dropped by motor launch three miles from its target in the English Channel: a 4,000-ton tanker, believed to be filled with copper ore, that was moored in Boulogne's outer harbour. The folbot contained Gerald Montanaro and his paddler, Sergeant Freddie Preece. A week earlier, Montanaro had received orders from Vice Admiral Bertram Ramsay to carry out Operation JV, the sinking of the tanker with limpet mines. Montanaro was overjoyed: here, at last, was the opportunity to prove his unit's worth before he and the bulk of his men travelled north to join Courtney's SBS at Ardrossan.[1]

Utilising his sapper training, Montanaro had helped to design the 'special camouflage' for both craft and crew. In the case of the former, it consisted of 'longitudinal flaps, which could be flicked over, changing the colour of the canoe from white to black when at an angle of sight to the enemy lookouts of 15°'. The crew, meanwhile, wore 'octopus suits, which could be flicked inside out to change colour in five seconds, at the same time as the canoe changed'. They were equipped with eight limpet mines, each fitted with a chemical fuse that activated after a four-hour delay at 50°F. Thanks to a 'sensitive device', if one went off, they all would, thus avoiding the possibility that they might be blown from the ship's side.[2]

Despite a calm sea and excellent visibility from bright starlight, Montanaro and Preece found the going tough as they battled against a strong tide and a light headwind. They paddled for more than an hour to reach the outer harbour entrance where, physically drained, they found two detached 'forts' and two anchored E-boats guarding the northern approach. Passing cautiously between the northern fort and an E-boat, and 'in full view of both', they could see torches flashing from the former. It did not help when the wind freshened, recalled Montanaro, 'making silent progress here difficult, and drifting the canoe fast towards the forts, since paddling was being done almost in the prone position'.

As they passed the southern fort, they noticed brightly lit doorways opening and men 'moving about noisily as though a drinking party were in progress'. This was confirmed when a reveller threw a beer bottle over the rampart, the missile narrowly missing the folbot and splashing its crew. Even more alarming was the sudden roar of engines and the arc of bright headlights from three E-boats, moored just inside the entrance to the inner harbour, who were preparing for a patrol. They paddled quickly away, leaving the entrance to the inner harbour behind them.

Scanning for the tanker using night field glasses, they finally located it at the far end of the outer harbour, 'nearly invisible against the background of the breakwater and lighthouse'. Approaching stealthily, lying almost flat but still using both paddles, they were within ten feet of the breakwater when the bow suddenly struck a concrete ledge covered by two inches of water and held fast. They 'relaunched with difficulty and immediately struck in succession three . . . large boulders' lying just out from the ledge. Here was the moment of crisis. 'The canoe was holed and leaking fast,' noted Montanaro, 'and was forced out from the shelter of the wall, to be silhouetted from the forts in the occulting light.'

Under the circumstances, Montanaro might easily have chosen discretion over valour and aborted the mission. Instead, in a show of extraordinary determination and courage, he ordered Preece to stem the leak by ramming his cap-comforter* into the

* A cylindrical woollen hat favoured by British Commandos.

hole, and then to start all the chemical time-delay fuses on the limpet mines. This gave them just four hours to get clear, and committed them to the attack. Splitting their paddles, they moved by single blades as quietly as they could, but 'still forced fully into the open until opposite the [tanker's] stern'. There they executed a sharp right-angled turn until they were under the stern's exaggerated down-sweep. The intention was to use a magnetic placing rod to fix the mines six feet below the surface so they would not be detected. But the stern's 'great curvature' made this impossible, and the first mine was placed by hand at a depth of just two feet six inches.

It became easier to use the rod as they moved up the shadowy port side of the tanker. 'It was,' recorded Montanaro, 'extremely successful, but it requires great practice to use it silently. Twice a loud clang was produced against the ship's sides in spite of great care being taken.' Both men held their breath. They could hear a small motor running, and knew that some of the crew were awake. After reaching 'the foremost point to be attacked on the port side', the canoe slid astern into a large hole – fifteen feet wide and eight high – that had been made by a torpedo. Paddling inside one of the ship's large tanks, in complete darkness, they sang 'extremely quietly' to raise their spirits.

Risking the more exposed starboard side, they placed a single mine next to the engine room, opposite one on the port side. When it slid down, and 'may have dropped off', they fixed another, the last of the eight they had brought with them, and this time it 'held well'. Spotting a possible 'flak ship' moored off the tanker's starboard bow, Montanaro checked his wristwatch – 2:35 a.m. – and knew it was time to leave, as they were due at their rendezvous at 3:00 a.m. Still using single blades, and lying as flat as possible, they moved back along the breakwater, careful to avoid the rocks, and then out 'across the harbour to circle the forts'.

The quickest route to the open sea was through a gap in the mole near the southern fort. Montanaro later claimed he and Preece went through it, ignoring surf and heavy swell, and

ABOVE: Major Roger James Allen ('Jumbo') Courtney MC, Late King's Royal Rifle Corps. Awarded the Military Cross on 21 October 1941 after his reconnaissance of Rhodes. Original caption states 'Jumbo Courtney and Friend'.

ABOVE: Jumbo Courtney and his wife.

LEFT: Lt Cdr Nigel Wilmott DSO* RN. Awarded Distinguished Service Cross on 16 March 1943 and awarded a Bar to it on 4 April 1944.

RIGHT: Lt Robert Wilson DSO* RA. Awarded the Distinguished Service Order on 24 February 1942 for service in the Middle East along with a Mention in Dispatches. Awarded a Bar to his DSO on 20 December 1945.

BELOW: HMS *Triumph*, the T-class submarine that transported Courtney and Willmott to Rhodes for the first maritime special operations mission of the war.

ABOVE: Crew in the mess room of a British T-class submarine.

LEFT: Lt Cdr A. C. Miers VC DSO*.

BELOW: HMS *Torbay* (Miers) in 1943.

ABOVE: HMS *Urge* (Wilson and Hughes, on first destruction of railway, June 1941).

RIGHT: Brig Bob 'Lucky' Laycock, CCO, 1943.

ABOVE: Lt Col Geoffrey Keyes VC,
KIA November 1941.

RIGHT: Grave of Lt Col Keyes.

BELOW: General der Panzertruppe Erwin Rommel and officers of the Afrika Korps.
The target of Keyes' mission, Rommel (the 'Desert Fox'), was in fact in Rome when
Operation Flipper was launched.

ABOVE: Stamford 'Stan' Weatherall, Sgt Arthur Embelin (X – killed at Oran) and two other members of 101 Troop bringing back a stag, Inveraray, Scotland, 1941.

BELOW: Major General Mark Clark.

ABOVE LEFT: General Henri Giraud, Operation Kingpin, October 1942.

ABOVE: Captain (Acting Major) Herbert George 'Blondie' Hasler DSO OBE RM.

FAR LEFT: Bill Sparks.

LEFT: Lts George Sinclair and Neville McHarg.

ABOVE: Captain (Acting Major) Herbert George 'Blondie' Hasler with Captain James Donald 'Jock' Stewart RM behind him, aboard a two-man Klepper also referred to as a Cockle Mark II.

BELOW: A still from *The Cockleshell Heroes*, showing canoe being lowered from sub.

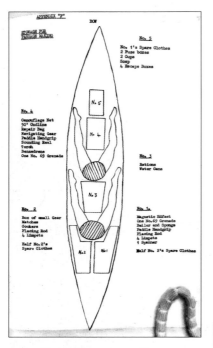

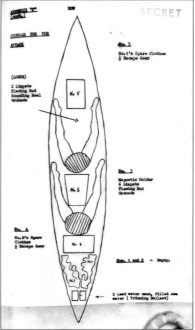

ABOVE: Figure of canoe stowage for passage during Operation Frankton from Hasler's report. And (RIGHT) the figure showing the stowage for attack.

TOP: COPP personnel on a training exercise at Hammenhiel Camp, Ceylon.

ABOVE: Yacht Club on Hayling Island.

LEFT: Captain George Burbridge, COPP 3, KIA February 1943.

ABOVE: COPP personnel on a training exercise.

BELOW: Sergeant V. Allen and Captain Edward Dacre Stroud RM (Detachment 385) practising assembling a canoe on top of a Catalina flying boat of 240 Squadron RAF in the Far East.

'escaped seaward'. But his official report says otherwise. 'It was,' he wrote, 'not considered advisable to try the passage round the end of the fallen breakwater near the southern fort owing to rocks and surf, and the danger of silhouetting against the occ[ulting] light. This could have been done, however.'

Though well behind schedule Montanaro chose to go back the way he had come, passing between the anchored E-boat and the northern fort. They were paddling as fast as they could, but the water in the canoe was now at four inches and 'a following wind across the tide' made the bow 'yaw heavily'.

Once past the southern fort, Montanaro set a course of 'N 60°W'. Before they had gone half a mile, they saw lights come on at the outer harbour entrance and heard loud engine noises. Fearing German boats were about to emerge, and seeing heavy bursts of flak to the north, they pressed on. But by now the canoe was filling rapidly, and while Preece bailed with naval cigarette tins, Montanaro paddled and navigated at the same time. To make it easier for Preece to bail, he had moved stores from the bow to the stern, thus sending the water to the back of the boat. The sea, meanwhile, 'was rising and the following wind growing stronger, making control very difficult'.

At 3:55 a.m., nearly an hour after the rendezvous, they heard the faint sound of engines. Though their reserve pick-up time was not for another five minues, Montanaro risked using the infrared torch because he knew the folbot would not stay afloat for much longer and, if the approaching craft was hostile, they would soon be captured anyway. Having signalled to seaward, they prepared their weapons – Luger pistols and knives – but did not need them because, to their great relief, the boat proved to be their motor launch, escorted by two motor gun boats.

They were picked up at 4:01 a.m., having paddled in excess of nine miles. Despite a strong tidal stream and other deviations, Montanaro's fine navigation – assisted by his determination to keep to an average speed of 2.5 knots – had brought them close to the precise pick-up point. So cold and exhausted were both men, after sitting in freezing water for so long, they had to be hoisted aboard the motor launch. Their rescue was not a moment too soon. They would have sunk, Montanaro estimated, 'within fifteen minutes of the rendezvous'.

Thanks to inaccurate fuses, the limpet mines did not explode until six hours after initiation, sinking the tanker. The first air photo reconnaissance reported the tanker as 'unharmed'. But a later flight confirmed the mission's 'complete success', and Montanaro and Preece's extraordinary achievement – battling tides, wind and inclement weather in a flimsy and ultimately holed canoe to breach the defences of a major enemy port, set explosive charges on a tanker, and then evade capture and drowning by the narrowest of margins – was a major blow to German morale. If the British could strike at ships in the heavily defended harbour of Boulogne, they could strike anywhere.[3]

Though details of the mission were kept from the press for reasons of operational security – thereby denying the British military and government an obvious propaganda coup – the effect was still considerable in that the Germans were forced to strengthen their coastal security by the deployment of ever greater numbers of troops and armaments that might have been used elsewhere. The knock-on effect of the Boulogne raid, and the reconnaissance in force of beaches south of the port by Lord Lovat's No. 4 Commando ten days later, was a 'tightening up of measures in the coastal districts' as far north as Holland.[4]

Montanaro's diary entry for 12 April was typically understated: 'Attacked Boulogne. 7 limpets on Tanker! Sailed w[ith] Preece and nearly sank. Picked up ML very successfully. First-rate show!!'[5]

He and Preece were later awarded the DSO and DCM respectively for their 'high degree of courage, resolution, and indifference to danger, as well as skill in successfully carrying out this operation'.[6] It was the least they deserved.

*

Roger Courtney was quick to claim Montanaro's success as his own, noting that among the new SBS's 'numerous projects' was the 'destruction of shipping in Boulogne harbour'. In truth, Montanaro did not leave for Scotland with his remaining men, including Preece, until 22 April, and he would always insist that he was still commanding 101 Troop when he sunk the tanker.[7]

Montanaro arrived at Ardrossan on the 23rd in pouring rain and, having billeted his men, took up residence in the Kilmeny Hotel where living conditions were fairly spartan. A day later, he noted in his diary: 'Hard day at paperwork for the new SBS. Set up office in Staff Captain's room at [Brigade] HQ. Got everything going.'[8]

Among the new recruits was Courtney's youngest brother Gruff, 27, who had joined the Royal West Kent regiment as a regular officer in 1935 and served for a time in Palestine during the Arab Revolt. 'Gruff too,' noted one account, 'was burly, florid, full of fight and with the same rip-roaring confidence [as his brother]. He spoke in a kind of clipped shorthand.'[9]

According to Lieutenant Eric 'Sally' Lunn, who joined the SBS from the Commando depot later in the year, Gruff was in 'disfavour' with his regiment when his elder brother took him into the SBS 'as a brotherly gesture'. True or not, Roger was worried he would be accused of nepotism when he appointed his brother, a former adjutant, to take over the 'administrative side' of the SBS while he sat on the selection boards.[10] His fears were allayed by Bob Laycock, who told him: 'If you think that your little brother is good enough . . . take him on; after all he is a regular and knows more about Army procedure than you do.'

Laycock then gave him his own six rules for 'Special Service':

1. Select the right man for the right job and let him get on with it.
2. Let him abuse you to your face if he thinks that things are going wrong, and that it is your fault and not his.
3. Tolerate no creepers.
4. Choose your other ranks more carefully than you would choose a wife, and trust them; also keep them in the picture as much as you dare.

5. Bring no petty charges; if a man is not up to scratch, return him to his original unit by the first available train.
6. Above all, you must be accessible at all times to your officers and men; you must be Daddy.

This was all excellent advice which Courtney never forgot. Less welcome was Laycock's insistence that 'majors at forty and over were to be considered fit only for office chairs or training centres'. Which meant, Courtney wrote later, 'no more active operations for old ducks like me . . . I was later to have greater frights in training than I ever had in war.'

From 101 Troop, Courtney had chosen Montanaro and fifteen experienced other ranks. He added to them by selecting 'the pick of the Commandos'. He recalled: 'I only wanted about thirty men to begin with and, in spite of some opposition, skimmed the cream.'

His first choice, he admitted, was 'any boy scout (especially ex Rover Scouts) – they need no explanation'. He also favoured 'ex-bandsmen in the Army' because their ability to march, read music and play their instrument was the same as firing a weapon. 'This makes them excellent marksmen,' noted Courtney, 'because they have to do three things at once – aligning foresight, backsight and target at any range with any weapon.' The third category he looked for was 'studious and artistic types' whose super-sensitivity would be vital 'when approaching an enemy coast because every nerve had to be a prickling antenna, and every pore an ear'. The 'swaggering, tough type', on the other hand, he 'rejected unreservedly' as 'most of their toughness' was 'displayed in pubs'.

His final method of selection had not changed from the early days on Arran. It was, recalled Gruff, 'simple and highly unorthodox, being based upon the ancient truth "*In vino veritas*" – that very strong drink loosens the tongue and bares the soul'. He would 'visit the nearest pub with the new recruit and fill him full of favourite liquors until all was revealed or he became speechless'. The only interviewee to get the better of him in this ordeal was 'Tug' Wilson who poured his drinks away. For the others, it was a reliable test of character.[11]

Among the new arrivals was Second Lieutenant Harry Holden-White, 24, a tall upper-class Englishman with striking turquoise eyes in a tanned, handsome face. Passionate about the natural world and a keen fly fisher, Holden-White had transferred from a battalion of the Royal Sussex Regiment that was about to be converted to anti-aircraft duties. 'Eighteen months on the Suffolk coast,' he recalled, 'waiting for an invasion that never came, had become increasingly tedious, and I had been living for the day when the battalion would be sent to an operational area overseas. But, with the change in its role, this now seemed unlikely to happen in the near future.'

Anxious to get to grips with the enemy, he volunteered for the Commandos and was interviewed at Seafield Towers, the headquarters of the Special Service Brigade, where questions were fired at him 'with such rapidity and venom' that a rational response was impossible. He remembered: 'I just stood there, shaking with fright and trying to ward off the verbal blows with the first thing that came into my head, in the vain hope that this would satisfy them. In all this bedlam, only two questions made any sense – did I have experience of small boats? And of navigation? I did – on both counts – and managed to say so.'

A month later, Holden-White received a 'signal from Seafield Towers, announcing my attachment to No. 2 (Commando) Special Boat Section, which was stationed there'. It 'marked a red-letter day' in his life and, almost unable to believe his luck, he 'threw himself on to the grass outside our company office, and rolled about on it, whooping with joy'.

Arriving at Ardrossan in April 1942, he was given an initial pep talk by Gerald Montanaro, the chief instructor, who described the unit's tasks as 'sabotage of bridges, ships and railway lines, together with reconnaissance missions of enemy beaches and coastal defences, and the landing of agents in enemy occupied territories – all to be carried out by canoeists taken to the scene of action in small surface vessels, such as motor launches, or, for long journeys, in submarines'. Montanaro then took him on a quick tour of the unit's equipment, including 'a number of canoes stacked higgledy-piggledy against the side of a hut and looking at first sight unprepossessing objects in which to go to war'.

Holden-White was impressed by Montanaro, the holder of the DSO, who 'exuded great intelligence and vitality, and, except when furious at some stupidity, had an attractively boyish expression that hinted at a predilection for unconventional behaviour'. Referring to the Scottish weather, the chief instructor would often exclaim, 'God, isn't it vile?' Yet he would never let its vagaries affect his actions 'in any way'.

When Holden-White first joined the SBS, Courtney was lobbying for future operations in London, using 'honeyed words' to sell to Mountbatten and his staff what must have seemed 'impossibly hare-brained enterprises'. He laid much of the groundwork in the bar at Combined Operations Headquarters, assisted by his 'delightful wife' Dorrise. On first meeting the CO, Holden-White was slightly intimidated by Courtney's 'prize-fighter' appearance. Yet, noted the younger officer, 'beneath all the toughness and cunning, lurked a softie with a heart of gold'. Courtney and his wife treated the officers and men of the SBS with great consideration and care. 'In a sense,' wrote Holden-White, 'we were their children.'

First they were taught how to assemble and dismantle the canoes, and then how to paddle them at a steady two and a half knots, the speed on which their navigation was based. Montanaro guided their 'faltering footsteps into the strange new world of Admiralty charts, and moon and tide tables'. Many hours were spent puzzling over Vector triangles, and plotting wildy inaccurate courses, which caused 'fury and gloom' to those with only an elementary understanding of mathematics.

'Demolitions we practised in the grounds of Seafield Towers,' remembered Holden-White, 'making up systems of fuse and detonator, primer and explosive, to cope with the types of problem we could expect to encounter on operations – the most likely being the blowing up of bridges, and the cutting of railway lines'. It was 'play, rather than work, combining as it did the pleasures of a toy construction set with the touch of danger of Guy Fawkes' night, and the resulting bangs were loud enough to satisfy the need for noise of even the most demanding child'. They were particularly fascinated by the limpet mines that Montanaro had used at Boulogne: fifteen inches long, with an oblong body filled with TNT, and on either side a line of magnets 'jutted out in a manner that suggested a crouching crustacean'. Being magnetic, they 'caused violent oscillations in the needles of the compasses in the canoes, which would have made naviga-tion impossible had they not been corrected with a key provided'.[12]

With the intention of getting the unit operational in under three months, Montanaro pushed the new men hard in training. 'Extremely windy,' he noted in his diary on 28 April. 'Good sun. Took out in canoes 14 men & new officer (Lt Kerr), Went 2 [miles north] along coast. *Very* heavy pulling returning against wind. Lost Sgt Embelin & Kerr. Sent out naval drifter with Courtney & found them on Horse Island. *Everyone* seems to end up on Horse Island.' Next, he attended a 'surprisingly good' lecture by Courtney on 'our aims & objects'.[13]

The furious training, recalled Courtney, involved the 'usual canoe stuff, which meant paddling and tumbling over in the icy waters of a Scottish loch'. He also had the bright idea of getting his men used to firing a submarine's four-inch gun, so that if a gun crew was knocked out, his 'merry men' could take over. With permission from the local 'naval officer in command', he soon had his boys 'banging away' at 'targets which were being towed well out to sea'.

Even more unorthodox was his plan to train his men to live off the land in case they were ever stranded ashore in enemy territory. To show the men how to do this, he invited up to Scotland an elderly eccentric called Jim Branson* who, having parcelled up his Hampshire estate among his tenants, had gone

---

* The great-uncle of the entrepreneur and Virgin founder Richard Branson.

to live in Balham where he survived mainly on grass. Laycock had received a letter from Branson, offering to teach Commandos how to survive on plants, and it was Courtney who wrote back, promising to pay his rail fare to Scotland 'and as much grass as he wanted, so that he might come and give us a demonstration'.[14]

There was no reply to the letter, but a week later 'a gnome-like old gentleman' arrived at Ardrossan on an ancient bicycle. 'He must have been about seventy years old,' recalled Courtney, 'and had a brown leathery wiriness remarkable in a man of that age. He had come about 500 miles in a week, but he apologised mildly for being late; he stated that he had stopped once or twice along the coast to sample the seaweed.'

With the whole unit gathered outside to hear him talk, Branson began by extolling 'the Japanese method of gathering their food from the countryside through which they walked'. He explained: 'Most hedge weeds are safe provided they do not sport gaudy flowers; you must find them in the cool shade. Croquet lawns and bowling greens are not to be recommended unless you like the taste of mowing-machine oil. To mix your salad you need a little oatmeal, a little sugar, a little vinegar or a little milk if you have no vinegar.'

He then did a demonstration, plucking a bunch of chickweed from the ground and dousing it with vinegar and bran that he had brought with him. While the SBS men watched in amazement, he ate some with no ill effects and offered the rest to the audience. To Courtney, the mixture looked utterly revolting, yet there was no doubt it was filling. 'I stopped all our normal rations,' he recalled, 'and in three days the boys were screaming for steak. [Branson] offered to initiate us into the mysteries of seaweed, but we shook him by the hand and thanked him fervently, and he pedalled away back to London.'[15]

As well as survival, Courtney needed his men to be able to 'find a point on an enemy coast on a dark night by use of calculation and instruments alone, and it was just as important for them to find the dark shape of their submarine again'. As the latter might be lying up to two miles off the coast, this required a 'high degree of skill in tidal navigation', for the teaching of which he brought in many experts.[16]

They were also sent on long-distance survival trips up the coast, an ordeal that was not unlike 'selection' for the modern SBS. One punishing exercise lasted for three days and nights, remembered Stan Weatherall, as they paddled folbots across the Firth of Clyde, up through the Crinan Canal, and across to Craignish Point – a total sea distance of more than eighty miles – where they 'effected a landing, and went to a cottage in Aird, to seek a phone'. Mistaken for Germans by the old lady who answered the door – on account of their unfamiliar waterproof kapok suits – they were welcomed in nonetheless and given a cup of tea and a biscuit. The nearest phone, they were told, was in Craignish Castle, 'not too far up the road'. Weatherall went over to make a call back to Ardrossan, and was told his wife had arrived on a visit. They then set off on the final leg, paddling a further twenty miles up the Sound of Scarba to the Isle of Kerrera, and, 'after making a panorama sketch of the seaplane base', they headed for Clachan, where Courtney was waiting with trucks to take them back to Ardrossan.[17] Weatherall described the 140-mile canoe exercise from Ardrossan to Clachan, via the Isle of Kerrera, in typically understated prose. Yet that should not obscure the fact that he and the other SBS men had completed a gruelling physical and mental challenge of which only very few people, then and now, are capable.

On another occasion, folbot teams were sent by submarine to carry out a reconnaissance of beaches north of Troon in Ayrshire. One was composed of 20-year-old Lieutenant Jimmy Foot, only recently commissioned in the Devonshire Regiment, and Company Sergeant Major Arthur Embelin of 101 Troop. Having launched from their submarine in excellent conditions, they navigated perfectly to the correct beach where they made 'soundings to seaward from the water's edge [for] some two to three hundred yards'. Barely fifty yards from the coast, they were surprised to discover a sandbank at a depth of just two feet, with a 'nice shelving run up on the seaward side' and deeper water beyond.

They then checked beach gradients, sand consistency and beach exits, before heading back to their pick-up point. Thanks to a stiff offshore wind and choppy sea, they failed to make contact with their own submarine, but were later rescued by another one when conditions had improved.

In their reports they were careful to mention the sandbank, concluding that the beach was not suitable for tank landing. But the reports were ignored by senior naval officers planning for the invasion of Vichy territory in North Africa – Operation Torch – who insisted that no barrier was visible on Admiralty charts. When a practice landing was made, the first three tanks toppled over the sandbank and sank in deeper water up to their turrets. 'They were still there in mid-1944,' wrote Gruff Courtney, 'as far as Foot can remember.'

Once ready to be sent on operations, the SBS men were given 'Passing Out Instructions' by Roger Courtney to be 'kept and looked at occasionally'. A mix of solid advice and quirky hints, they sum up Courtney's idiosyncratic approach to soldiering:

1. You are now considered fit to operate on your own, and should be proficient in Navigation, Demolition, and Scoutcraft. You have been selected on your character qualifications as much as anything else and, as far as we can judge, you can be trusted to take responsibility and can be trusted on your own. We are jealous of our good name, and our reputation is in your hands.

2. If you go abroad you will very largely have to administer yourselves . . . Remember, if you have to deal with the military establishment ashore, that the personal touch will get you more than a mass of paperwork.

3. If you find any way that our system can be improved, put it into practice and let us know the results, and we will do the same for you. The SBS Depot is your servant. Let us know what you want and we will let you have it by the quickest possible means.

4. Keep in touch. Good luck and good hunting.

'This splendidly offensive-spirited little cove'

'Captain Wilson returns from disembarkation leave,' noted the SBS War Diary on 25 May 1942. 'He is attached to the unit pending receipt of posting orders.'[1]

The arrival of 'Tug' Wilson at Ardrossan should have been a cause for celebration. After all, his exploits in the Mediterranean, mostly with Marine Wally Hughes, had already earned him a DSO, a mention in despatches and almost legendary status among his fellow folbotists.* But things were not quite that simple. First there was the issue of where he, as Courtney's former second in command, would fit into the new unit's command structure; second, the question of whether he was in a fit state of mind to go on further operations. Not surprisingly, given that he had the most to lose from Wilson's presence, it was Gerald Montanaro who flagged up the second concern. 'Suggested to Courtney,' noted Montanaro in his diary on 30 May, 'how awful Wilson is & how far his nerve is gone.'[2]

Was Montanaro stirring up trouble in the hope of sidelining an officer with far more operational experience than he had? It is possible. Certainly, the younger man saw himself as Courtney's annointed successor, and was encouraged to do so. In June, for example, he was told by Courtney that he would soon be in 'full command' of the SBS. Wilson was, therefore, an obvious threat

---

* The DSO – for carrying out six raids in the Mediterranean between June and December 1941 – and the mention in despatches were announced in late February 1942.

to Montanaro's advancement. But there is also good reason to believe that Wilson was not himself when he reached Scotland in the late spring of 1942.[3]

He had carried out a number of missions since he and Hughes had derailed a train on Italy's Adriatic coast in late November 1941. Not all had been successful, however. Transported on Miers' *Torbay* in December, for example, the pair tried to sink a ship in Navarino harbour on the south-west coast of the Peloponnese using the more powerful triple limpet mine that Wilson and Courtney had designed. But their first approach in the folbot was abandoned after they were detected and shot at; and a second almost cost Wilson his life when he tried to swim the final 150 yards to the target – an Italian destroyer – pushing the triple mine on a makeshift raft, and nearly drowned in the freezing water. 'The operation would, I feel certain, have been successful,' wrote Wilson, 'had I been able to withstand the cold.'[4]

Paul Chapman, the submarine's first lieutenant, remembered Wilson returning 'with his teeth chattering like castanets'. He noted cruelly: 'Wetsuits were in the future, and Wilson was a skinny man; a plumper operator might have managed.'*[5]

Wilson's next two missions, in early 1942, involved ferrying secret agents to beaches in Tunisia: done without his regular partner Wally Hughes, they were both successful. Prior to the second mission, Wilson had been given permission to return to the UK on leave to visit his wife and receive his DSO from King George VI at Buckingham Palace. The plan, therefore, was for him to complete the mission and then transfer from his host submarine *Upholder* – a U-class vessel commanded by Lieutenant Commander David Wanklyn VC, DSO and two bars, the most

---

* The failed attempt to sink a ship in Navarino harbour in December 1941 was Wilson's and Hughes' last joint mission. 'They made an unlikely pair,' notes the modern SBS, 'yet they blew up more bridges and de-railed more trains than any other commando raiders in the early years of the war.' (*By Strength and Guile*, p. 137)

highly decorated submarine captain of the war* – to *Unbeaten* which was damaged and heading back to Britain, via Gibraltar, for a refit. But when the rendezvous took place after dark on 10 April, a 'bad sea was running' and Wilson had to decide if the transfer was worth it.[6]

As he assessed the risk, a voice from *Unbeaten* shouted: 'Piss off Tug. We've got two feet of water in the fore-ends and aft. We'll never make it to Gib.'[7]

Undeterred, Wilson got safely across and into Gibraltar, and finally arrived back in the UK in early May. It was, in hindsight, a fateful and fortunate decision to transfer to a damaged submarine in a rough sea. A few days later, *Upholder* was lost at sea with all hands. She was 'probably successfully hunted', concluded the naval commander-in-chief, 'and sunk on 14th April . . . Loss of this valuable submarine and her outstanding commanding officer after a long and brilliant career in the Mediterranean is much to be regretted.'[8]

Wilson was, therefore, the last man still living to have spoken to Wanklyn, 'the acknowledged ace submariner of the Second World War'. He probably felt survivor's guilt and this, on top of almost a year of dangerous special operations, might explain why he was so off-colour when he arrived at Ardrossan in late May 1942, following an all-too-brief reunion with his wife Marjorie in Bristol. Montanaro equated Wilson's distressed state of mind with a loss of nerve. A more likely explanation is that he was suffering from combat stress – or post-traumatic stress disorder (PTSD) as we diagnose it today – but it did not last.

In August – by which time Courtney's SBS was operational and had moved its headquarters from Ardrossan to Tichfield Haven in Hampshire – Wilson flew back to Malta, via Lisbon, Lagos, Khartoum and Egypt, with four miniature hand-operated torpedoes 'marked as auto spare parts or something equally

---

* During the previous sixteen months, *Upholder* had sunk 122,000 tons of enemy shipping, making it by far the deadliest British submarine in the Mediterranean. Her victims included three enemy submarines, a destroyer and an armed trawler. She also sank fifteen enemy transports and supply ships.

innocuous'. Just developed and top secret, the torpedoes 'were 21 inches long and powered by twin opposed screws, with a 7½ pound cavity charge in the nose'. They offered the potential of sinking ships in harbour at a distance, as long as the aim was accurate, and Wilson had been tasked with trying them out in the Mediterranean.[9] The downside to using torpedoes, of course, was the absence of a time-delay fuse, making a successful escape much less likely. But despite the risks – and possibly because of them – Wilson was determined to give it a go.

Pausing in Alexandria to consult with Vice Admiral Sir Henry Harwood, the new commander-in-chief of the Mediterranean Fleet, Wilson suggested Navarino harbour as a possible target because he 'had been there twice before, and being a natural harbour, it was surrounded by rough ground which made shore movement by Infantry very difficult'. Harwood issued the necessary orders. A string of recent victories by Rommel's Panzerarmee Afrika had brought Axis troops as far as El Alamein in Egypt, just seventy miles from Harwood's headquarters in Alexandria. If they broke through the Allied defences there, the Suez Canal, Britain's lifeline to India, would have been under threat, not to mention the oil fields of the Middle East. Any offensive operation that struck at Rommel's marine supply line, therefore, was to be encouraged.

But in discussions with 'Shrimp' Simpson in Malta, Wilson acknowledged that Navarino was 'particularly strongly defended' and he was prepared to look elsewhere if the target was worthwhile. Simpson knew from talks with Miers after Wilson's first crack at Navarino – with the submarine forced to wait for more than four and a half hours outside a port with a minefield, shore batteries and anti-submarine craft, an ordeal Miers described as the 'most objectionable' of his time in the theatre – that the location 'presented unnecessary hazards for the submarine and little chance of success for Wilson'. In his opinion, a smaller port which had not previously been attacked by a submarine was a better bet. Wilson agreed, as did Harwood, and they selected Crotone, on the sole of Italy's Calabrian coast – where aerial reconnaissance 'showed shipping always present' – in Navarino's place.[10]

Wilson left Malta in the U-class submarine *Unbroken*, commanded by 27-year-old Lieutenant Alastair Mars, on 31 August.* He took with him a new paddler: Bombardier John Brittlebank, the lone SBS man amongst the three escapees from the Rommel raid. Arriving off Crotone in the early hours of 5 September, they remained submerged until dusk. Shortly before surfacing, Mars saw through the periscope a heavily laden ship of about 1,500 tons leaving the harbour and heading north, escorted by 'a craft similar to a small E-boat'. He was unconcerned because an even larger ship, of around 2,500 tons, was still visible inside the harbour.

They surfaced seven miles off Crotone at 9:00 p.m., and charged the batteries before moving closer to the harbour. At 11:30 p.m. they were in position: bows to the shore, the Crotone breakwater visible through binoculars at a distance of 2,500 yards. A clear moonless sky and a light offshore wind meant that conditions were ideal.

With the folbot assembled and packed with equipment – including the torpedoes, personal weapons, two deflated dinghies and eight days' water and provisions – Wilson and Brittlebank got in and launched off the submarine's casing at 11:40 p.m. 'I expect to be back alongside,' Wilson told Mars, 'in one hour and twenty minutes.'

They paddled on a compass bearing for the harbour entrance, making rapid progress in a sea that, but for a slight breeze and a faint swell, was almost a flat calm. Spotting the seaward end of the south mole from a distance of 250 yards, they paused to split paddles so they would make less noise. Approaching the entrance head-on, to present the smallest possible silhouette,

---

* Two weeks earlier, Mars and *Unbroken* had exacted some retribution for grievous British naval losses during Operation Pedestal – the attempt to resupply Malta – by torpedoing the Italian heavy cruiser *Bolzano* and the light cruiser *Muzio Attendolo* off Sicily. Both warships were crippled and written off. Mars was rewarded with the DSO.

Wilson realised that even a folbot would be detected by a lookout at the end of either mole. He decided, therefore, to investigate the south mole in the hope that the breach made by an earlier bomb – and identified from aerial photos – was large enough to allow the folbot to pass through. This proved to be the case and, having folded back some makeshift barbed wire, they were able 'to ease the canoe through into the harbour proper by hand'.

All was quiet, the stillness almost 'intense and the sky clearly reflected on the water'. Directly opposite, lying distinctly visible alongside the northern mole, was their target ship, its 'funnel, bridge and mast silhouetted against the sky'. On a line roughly parallel to the target, anchored in the middle of the harbour, was a large schooner.

Estimating the ship to be a hundred yards in length, Wilson felt 'the ideal position of attack would be at a point where the target length would subtend an angle of between 46 degrees and 50 degrees, affording a good angle of error and necessitating only 25 per cent of the torpedo's maximum range (i.e. 400 yards) whilst the chances of being observed at that distance would not be great'.

To reach that position, part of the way across the harbour, he decided to take a circuitous route to keep the maximum distance between the folbot and the schooner until the last possible moment. Then he would approach the schooner 'bow on until the final turn to deliver the attack'.

Sitting up front and using a single split paddle, Brittlebank moved the folbot silently forward while Wilson was 'aft with torpedoes ready for immediate action, excepting that the nose caps were still in the "safe" screwed-on position'. The final approach was made at a slow crawl to avoid disturbing the glassy surface of the water and stirring up phosphoresence.

Once in position, Wilson checked the angle of attack. But before he could complete his calculations, the stillness was 'exploded' by a challenge from the schooner. It was 'followed immediately by a shout from the target, then by the noise of people running about and shouting' in Italian.

Spotted from two directions, and acutely vulnerable to gunfire,

Wilson might have aborted the mission then and there. But hoping the seamen would not open fire immediately, he felt there was still time to launch one torpedo. He quickly removed its nose cap, 'made certain that the split collar fell from its groove in the striker head, placed it in the water and pressed the starter button'. Nothing happened, so he made a quarter-turn of the propellor and tried the button a second time. The motor started, 'sounding extremely healthy'.

Telling Brittlebank to stand by with the double paddle for a speedy departure, he placed the torpedo just under the surface of the water and took careful aim at the target. He then gave the missile a gentle push and let go. Grabbing his own paddle, he stole a last glance at the torpedo and was relieved to see the white line along its back was 'pointing directly at the centre of the target's length'. It was running steadily at a depth of about five feet, and with no suggestion of 'porpoising'.

As they raced for the breach in the mole, both using double paddles, there was 'plenty of commotion' and lights kept coming on. But no shots were fired. Equally, there was no sound of an explosion and Wilson could not be certain of a hit.

Once through the breach, Wilson set the compass bearing for the rendezvous – ninety degrees (due east) from the end of the breakwater – and they tore out to sea at speed. Having covered three-quarters of the 3,000 yards, and with no sign of the submarine, Wilson began to flash an 'S' signal (dot-dot-dot) with his blue torch, as per his instructions. But nothing came into view and, with a swell 'increasing very noticeably', they carried on, signalling at 'specified intervals'.

Half an hour after sending the first signal, Wilson saw what he thought was 'the familiar looking blob of a submarine' off his port bow and headed towards it. Soon a similar object appeared to the left of the first one. He quickly realised this was 'no submarine, but two surface craft approaching line abreast'.

With no time to change course, and hopeful the craft would pass on either side of them, thus minimising their silhouette until the last possible moment, they crouched as low as they could.

Wilson estimated the speed of the approaching boats at 'ten knots, the bow waves now being very marked and about sixty yards apart'.

All of a sudden, self-preservation went out the window as Wilson 'quickly made ready and launched one of the torpedoes over the port side'. Why he did this when the chances of hitting a moving target were small, and the risk of capture high, is a mystery. In any event, the torpedo missed its mark – a 'dark and light grey camouflaged craft' with 'knife edge bows and low waist' – probably a light destroyer which, seconds later, appeared on the folbot's port beam. Then they were between both vessels, and at such close quarters that Wilson expected a challenge. He held the remaining two torpedoes in readiness, just in case. Luckily the enemy boats failed to spot them and continued on their course, while Wilson and Brittlebank moved at a 'steady speed' in the opposite direction. There was a nervous moment as they crossed the boats' wake, 'but the canoe withstood the test without capsizing'.

It was now 1:45 a.m. and moonrise – the latest time for the rendezvous – was not for another hour and a quarter. But with enemy vessels patrolling the harbour area, Wilson knew that any hope of being picked up by *Unbroken* that night had ended. There was, however, an alternative rendezvous at dawn: on the same compass bearing from the harbour entrance – ninety degrees – but at a much longer (and therefore safer for the submarine) distance of five miles. The problem the folbotists now faced was deteriorating weather, with a 'considerable swell' and occasional white horses running diagonally across their course, conditions that make it extremely difficult to maintain 'an accurate course and position in an open canoe'.

Their best option was to patrol up and down, doing their best to ship a minimum of water. 'The avoidance of capsizing,' recalled Wilson, 'required such concentrated attention that the accuracy of my position for the rendezvous at dawn was a little doubtful. The canoe was heavy with water and did not feel too stable after her recent buffeting.'

Everything was soaked, and it was impossible to wipe the compass and binoculars effectively. But Crotone could be seen in the distance, roughly in the right direction, and Wilson concluded that they were close to the rendezvous. They stayed there for two hours, either side of dawn, with no sign of *Unbroken*. Eventually, as a last resort, Wilson threw two hand grenades over the stern, hoping the underwater explosion would be picked up by the submarine. No periscope was sighted.

Worried that the folbot might sink if they did not reach land and make repairs, they headed south-south-east towards Capo Calonne and, having rounded the point, Wilson selected a beach that was hemmed in by steep cliffs and could only be approached from the sea. Before landing there, he flooded the last two torpedoes and chucked them overboard in deep water.

Once on land, they drained the folbot and spent twenty minutes on running repairs. They relaunched at noon, intending 'to make a bid for Malta some two hundred and fifty miles away'. The plan was to get there in stages, hopping along the southern coasts of Italy and Sicily, before heading out into open water. But with a damaged canoe, and the 'absolute necessity of frequent landings', they both knew the odds of success were low.

Heading for the Golfo di Squillace, they passed a few fishing boats who hailed them. They waved in response. By 6:00 p.m. the folbot was leaking so badly they were forced ashore with no time to select a suitable beach. They had been there twenty minutes, and were working as quickly as they could, when armed Italians appeared from all sides. Their landing had been observed and they were prisoners of war.[11]

Only after the war would Wilson and Brittlebank discover the main reason why they had missed *Unbroken* at both rendezvous. The first issue was smoke from a nearby chemical factory that reduced visibility from the submarine to a mile. This was compounded by the approach of a motor vessel on the starboard quarter at 1:20 a.m., forcing Lieutenant Mars to dive *Unbroken* to sixty feet and zigzag away from the rendezvous point. The skipper soon realised he was being hunted by two vessels, 'both equipped with ASDICs [sonar equipment]'. By 2:00 a.m., he had shaken them off, but as the 'hunting craft appeared to be working a line 090 [degrees] from the harbour, it was decided to keep to the southward for a while'.

More fatal for the folbotists' chance of rescue was Mars' decision to station himself ten miles due east of the harbour entrance for the second rendezvous at dawn, and not the five miles agreed with Wilson. He also arrived an hour late and chose not to surface, preferring to use his high-power periscope 'in view of good visibility'. By 8:20 a.m., having scanned the horizon without success for fifty minutes, Mars was seven and a half miles from Crotone when he spotted two naval schooners approaching. He immediately altered course to the south-east. The schooners responded by dropping a series of small depth charges, five at a time. But they were off target and, after an hour, they gave up and moved away.

The last chance to recover the folbotists was gone. Having failed in both attempts, Mars obeyed orders and continued his patrol. 'The loss of this brave officer and his companion,' he wrote in the submarine's log, 'is very much regretted and it is hoped that the submarine did all that was possible for their recovery.'[12]

His boss, 'Shrimp' Simpson, felt that it had. 'The Narrative [by Mars],' he wrote, 'gives full details of the steps taken to recover Wilson and in my opinion [Unbroken] was handled very properly . . . In discussing the operation with Lieutenant Mars and Captain Wilson, I had stressed that [Unbroken] must be handled with great caution and no risk with modern enemy ASDIC-fitted craft was acceptable. Wilson appreciated and had fully expected this.'

The failure of the mission and the loss of the folbotists was, in Simpson's view, the fault of an overambitious plan whose 'object' – the sinking of a minor enemy supply ship – 'never justified its means'. He expanded on this point in an appendix to Mars' report. He agreed in principle, he said, with attempting 'every possible step' to harass the enemy. But a mini torpedo –

or 'mobile limpet', as he called it – seemed to him to be a downgrade from an ordinary limpet mine 'since having no delay action [gave] the Operator less than a minute from release to explosion', and made his escape highly unlikely. He continued:

> Enemy ports are now well guarded and have auxiliaries fitted with ASDIC available, therefore if the risk is to be taken of endeavouring to penetrate the defences and retire and re-embark on a submarine, then results should be of some corresponding value to the risks run . . . I do not feel that such results can be obtained with a 7½ lb explosive charge.

The ideal environment to use a mini torpedo was, in Simpson's opinion, against enemy shipping in neutral ports. In well-defended enemy harbours, on the other hand, it was little more than a suicide weapon. He particularly regretted Wilson's loss because he 'was a man of much experience in train wrecking' who could have continued to operate 'safely and successfully in that enterprise', and much 'to the great discomfort of the enemy', had he not been assigned to such a high-risk, low-reward mission.[13]

Lessons were learned, and no more attempts to sink shipping in enemy harbours with mini torpedoes were made. This was small consolation to Roger Courtney who had lost, at a stroke, his most experienced officer and one of his best young NCOs. Wilson, one of Courtney's originals, was particularly hard to replace. He was the ideal folbotist and a model for SBS soldiers ever since: quiet and unassuming, small-framed but deceptively strong, a team player but capable of independent action, an intelligent problem solver, eager to embrace new technology and as brave as a lion.

It might have cheered Courtney to know, however, that both would continue to be thorns in the enemy's side. 'Throughout the operation,' wrote Wilson later, 'Bombardier Brittlebank's conduct and reactions to the varying circumstances left nothing to be desired and also during the subsequent interrogations after capture. He proved to be the model soldier. When told by the

Italian general at Catanzaro, where we were interrogated, that he was to be shot at dawn he merely requested permission to write a letter to his next of kin.'[14]

They were both sent to a prison camp in Sulmona, central Italy, from where Wilson, with Brittlebank's assistance, absconded with another officer. Soon recaptured by *carabinieri*, Wilson was sent to a second camp near Bologna where he remained until Italy withdrew from the war in September 1943. With the Germans now in control, the prisoners were loaded into cattle trucks for transport north to Germany. But Wilson jumped from the moving train and, helped by Italian partisans, made his way to Rome where he was lodged with other British escapees. He even attended a performance of the opera *Il Trovatore* and, having spotted the German commander Generalfeldmarschall Albert Kesselring in a private box, persuaded his attractive Italian date to ask for an autograph. Wilson was later picked up by the Gestapo and sent to Oflag 79, a prison camp in northern Germany, from where he was finally liberated by US troops on 12 April 1945.

Later that year, the gallantry exhibited by 'this splendidly offensive-spirited little cove' at Crotone was recognised by the award of a bar to his DSO.[15] Brittlebank was given a DCM. 'I consider,' wrote Bob Laycock, 'that his determination and devotion to duty on this occasion were well worth the award for which I recommend him.'[16]

13

Special Boat Squadron

A week after 'Tug' Wilson's capture in Italy, another of the originals, Jim Sherwood, was almost snared when he took part in Operation Bigamy, an ill-fated SAS-led mission to Benghazi 'to divert the attention of the Germans and Italians before Alamein'. The intention was to destroy the harbour and storage facilities at Benghazi, and raid the airfield at nearby Benina. The troops involved were a mix of David Stirling's SAS, Long Range Desert Group, SBS, Royal Navy and even French. 'Our role,' remembered Sherwood, 'was to assemble our canoes on the side of [Benghazi] harbour, paddle out with limpet mines and try and sink enemy ships there. Nobody was enthusiastic about this . . . and a great deal of moaning and grumbling went on.'[1]

He and the other SBS men never got to use their folbots because, having completed a gruelling journey around the southern end of the Great Sand Sea to the oasis of Kufra, the main raiding party of 200 men in forty jeeps and trucks, headlights blazing, was ambushed by Italian troops at a roadblock on the outskirts of Benghazi.

Under heavy fire, and with the element of surprise lost, Stirling told his driver: 'Get the convoy turned round and we'll have a go another day.'

The vehicles were forced to perform laborious three-point turns as tracer lit up the night sky and, amazingly, only one jeep was hit and burst into flames. The rest fled in disorder towards the escarpment, 'racing to reach cover before the sunrise'.[2]

Sherwood remembered: 'The extraordinary thing was, they scored very few hits. Which was just as well because, sitting on top of our explosives, one wrong hit and the SBS would have disappeared in a big bang. We were told to get out of it, every man for himself, in jeep or lorry as best we could . . . We [left], having achieved nothing at all. It was a complete fiasco, the whole operation.'[3]

They reached the escarpment south of Benghazi as the sun came up and hastily hid their vehicles in the many ravines, using camouflage nets to prevent their identification from the air. The Axis pilots responded by indiscriminately machine-gunning and bombing the ravines, hitting the odd vehicle more by luck than judgement. Sherwood's truck escaped damage and, at dusk, set off with the others for the desert, twenty-five miles to the south. The night drive was a 'wretched affair', remembered an SAS medical officer, as the injured groaned in the back of the trucks, 'amid the stench of blood, burned flesh and singed clothing'.

Next morning, in the desert, the air attacks continued. Convinced their hiding place had been spotted, Stirling ordered the remaining vehicles to move, abandoning the more seriously wounded. 'I'm sorry,' said one SAS man to a casualty, 'you've had it. You're just numbers.' He pointed to the others preparing to leave. 'They're fit. They're ready to fight another day. You can't. I'm sorry.'

Unfortunately, Sherwood's truck refused to start and, in attempting to prime the carburettor with petrol, the driver caused an explosion and was badly burned. Leaving one man to take care of the driver, the others set off on foot, covering twenty-five miles the first night. Their unguarded supplies were stolen by Arabs as they searched for water, however, and they would certainly have perished in the open scrub desert had not Stirling happened upon them in his jeep. He directed them to an abandoned lorry which they used to get back to Kufra oasis, picking up an SAS officer en route. They finally got back to Cairo, via Wadi Halfa, in their tattered clothing in late September.

The operation had been a fiasco. 'We were too big,' admitted one of Stirling's men. 'They knew we were coming.' More than a quarter of the raiding force had been killed, wounded or captured, and half the vehicles destroyed. Apart from diverting a few troops to defend Benghazi, the impact of the operation was nil. 'A few months earlier,' wrote Ben Macintyre in *SAS: Rogue Heroes*, 'such a failure might have spelled doom for the SAS. Yet, instead of recrimination, Stirling was rewarded. On his return to Cairo, while his bedraggled force licked its wounds, he was promoted to the rank of lieutenant colonel and told that his unit was being granted full regimental status.'[4]

Stirling owed his promotion to Major General Richard McCreery, chief of staff to General Sir Harold Alexander who had succeeded Claude Auchinleck as Commander-in-Chief, Middle East Command, a month earlier. There was a small special forces unit operating in North Africa, McCreery told his boss, that has had 'conspicuous success and its morale is high'. He added:

The personality of the present commander, L Detachment SAS Brigade, is such that he could be given command of the whole force with appropriate rank. In view of this I make the following suggestion. That L Detachment SAS Brigade, 1 SS [Special Service] Regiment, Special Boat Section should all be amalgamated under L Detachment SAS Brigade and commanded by Major D. Stirling with the rank of lieutenant colonel.

Alexander approved the recommendation and, in late September 1942, Stirling's unit became the 1st SAS Regiment with twenty-nine officers and 572 other ranks, and its base at Kabrit in Egypt. Its four operational squadrons included A (Paddy Mayne), B (Stirling), C (the French squadron) and D (Major Kealy's No. 1 SBS). Stirling would write of the latter: 'This unit had had a separate existence up until August 1942 and had carried out many brilliant operations. My intention was to absorb them into the 1st SAS Regiment as a squadron but I was in the meantime giving them the full SAS training, including a parachute course. They had about 15 officers and about 40 OR [other ranks].'[5]

The news was a crushing blow to Mike Kealy's No. 1 SBS, much-depleted since Roger Courtney's departure and the change of tactics from 'beach reconnaissance and shoreside sabotage to small-scale assault raiding'.[6] Even before the Benghazi debacle, Kealy's men had joined the SAS in raids on a number of enemy airfields in the eastern Mediterranean, including targets on Crete and Sicily in June and August 1942. It was during the latter operation that Eric Newby and seven other members of M (Malta) Detachment were captured. Losses such as these 'crippled the unit', wrote John Lodwick, 'and led to its temporary incorporation in the Special Air Service'.[7]

Old hands like Jim Sherwood and George Barnes were horrified. 'We didn't want anything to do with the SAS,' remembered Sherwood. 'We wanted to remain our own independent force. However, in the end their greater strength prevailed and we were absorbed into the SAS, while still known as the SBS.' The pair refused, however, to do the parachute training that was mandatory for the new regiment, telling Kealy that they would prefer to return to their units. He decided to let the matter lie, and they were the only SBS men not to earn their wings while part of the SAS. The reprieve, however, was temporary. Having returned to England to join No. 2 SBS in the spring of 1943, Sherwood and Barnes were later 'made to do a parachute course at Roger Courtney's request'.[8]

Back in the Middle East, meanwhile, the capture of David Stirling on a mission to Tunisia in January 1943 left the SAS ship 'without a rudder' and led inexorably to the break-up of the regiment. Given the mercurial character of Stirling's replacement Paddy Mayne, an 'unexploded ordnance' who was 'baffled and bored by paperwork', the outcome might have been disbandment. But Middle East HQ compromised by splitting the 1st SAS Regiment into two parts: a Special Boat Squadron, under the dashing 24-year-old Major the Earl (George) Jellicoe DSO (son of the famous admiral and yet another former member of 8th

Commando, who had joined Stirling's L Detachment in April 1942), to carry out amphibious operations in the eastern Mediterranean; and the Special Raiding Squadron under Mayne, to be used as assault troops in the coming invasion of Europe.[9]

Jellicoe's 250-strong Special Boat Squadron would operate with 'great distinction' in the Aegean and the Adriatic for the rest of the war.[10] Based near Haifa, it took part in raids on airfields in Sardinia and Crete, parachuted into Rhodes to discuss an armistice with Italian troops, and fought in the lost battles for Kos and Leros in the Dodecanese Islands in late 1943. The following July, Jellicoe's men and the Greek Sacred Band raided the island of Symi in the Aegean, taking all their objectives, and killing twenty-one German and Italian defenders and capturing another 151 in the process. From August 1944, the Special Boat Squadron joined the Long Range Desert Group in operations in the Adriatic, Greece, Albania and Istria. So successful were they that, by the end of the year, these relatively small forces of a few hundred men were keeping no fewer than six German divisions occupied.[11]

The unit's last operation was a diversionary raid on German positions on the shores of Lake Comacchio, a stone's throw from the Adriatic in northern Italy. Advancing up a narrow spit of land in the early hours of 9 April 1945, the eleven-man SBS patrol was engaged by fire from multiple enemy machine guns. In response the patrol leader, 24-year-old Danish-born Major Anders Lassen, blew on his whistle and shouted to his men, 'Forward you bastards!'[12] Throwing grenades as he ran, he 'annihilated the first position containing four Germans and two machine guns'. He then moved on to the second position and silenced that. By this time, the patrol had taken casualties – two killed and two wounded – and its firepower was 'very considerably reduced'. Lassen continued to advance, however, and engaged the third position. Hearing a cry of 'Kamerad', he was moving forward to order the enemy outside and take their surrender when he was 'hit by a burst of Spandau fire from the left'. He fell mortally wounded, but not before throwing a final grenade.

Lassen was later awarded a posthumous VC. His citation noted that he 'refused to be evacuated as he said it would impede the withdrawal and endanger further lives, and as ammunition was nearly exhausted the force had to withdraw.' It added:

By his magnificent leadership and complete disregard for his personal safely, Major Lassen had, in the face of overwhelming superiority, achieved his objects. Three positions were wiped out, accounting for six machine guns, killing eight and wounding others of the enemy, and two prisoners were taken. The high sense of devotion to duty and the esteem in which he was held by the men he led, added to his own magnificent courage, enabled Major Lassen to carry out all the tasks he had been given with complete success.[13]

14

Operation Flagpole

At 10:00 a.m. on Sunday 18 October 1942, Major General Mark Clark strolled into Norfolk House, the redbrick building in St James's Square, London, that was serving as Allied Force Headquarters, and found it deserted but for Brigadier General Al Gruenther, the deputy chief of staff. 'I've got a message for you,' said Gruenther. 'It's red hot.'

Tall and loose-limbed, with a long beaky nose, thick lower lip and prominent Adam's apple, the 46-year-old Clark was a brilliant planner and trainer of troops who had arrived in Britain in the summer as deputy to Lieutenant General Dwight D. 'Ike' Eisenhower, commanding general of the US Army's European Theater of Operations. Ike had recently been appointed commander-in-chief of the Allied Expeditionary Force for Operation Torch, the invasion of French North Africa that was scheduled for 8 November, exactly three weeks away.

Taking the cable from Gruenther, Clark saw it was addressed to Ike from General George S. Marshall, the US Army's chief of staff in Washington. Before he could read it, the telephone on his desk – a direct line to Ike's office at 20 Grosvenor Square – started ringing. He picked up the handset.

'Come up,' said Ike, in his Kansas drawl. 'Come right away.'

On the short drive to Ike's headquarters, Clark read the cable. It contained a message from Bob Murphy, President Roosevelt's special envoy in North Africa, suggesting an 'almost unbelievable' mission that, if successful, would give the whole Torch operation a much better chance of success. Murphy's suggestion was for an American delegation to land on the Algerian coast for a secret meeting with General Charles-Emmanuel Mast, the military commander in Algiers, to discuss French cooperation instead of resistance at the time of the Allied landings. Mast had suggested a meeting in a deserted house, sixty miles west of Algiers, during the night of 21 October, only three days away. Travelling by submarine, the delegation would ideally include a senior general, an officer thoroughly familiar with the Torch plans, a supply officer, a naval expert and a political expert who could speak French. Clark knew all too well what was at stake. If it succeeded, a bloodless occupation of French North Africa was a very real possibility. If it failed – well that did not bear thinking about. Either way, he was determined to be involved.

On entering Ike's office, he asked: 'When do I go?'

They were discussing details when a call came through from General 'Pug' Ismay, Winston Churchill's chief military assistant, who was with the prime minister at his Chequers country retreat at the foot of the Chiltern Hills. 'What's the problem?' said Ismay.

'Pug,' replied Clark, 'we've got a hot message here.'

'How hot?'

'Well it's too hot for the telephone.'

After a pause, Churchill came on the line. 'What have you got?' he asked. 'This phone is secret.'

Clark handed the receiver to Ike who told Churchill that the message was so secret it needed to be discussed in person.

'Then come to Chequers.'

'Sir,' said Ike, 'there isn't time.'

'Very well. Should I come back to London?'

'Yes, sir.'

'All right,' Churchill said. 'I'll meet you at Number 10 late this afternoon.'

They arrived at Downing Street to find Churchill and most of his senior political and military advisors, including Anthony Eden, Admiral Sir Dudley Pound, General Sir Alan Brooke and Vice Admiral Lord Louis Mountbatten, a member of the Chiefs of Staff Committee. Churchill was, Clark remembered, 'as enthusiastic as a boy with a new electric train'. After Eisenhower had read out Marshall's cable, the prime minister broke into a huge grin between puffs of his giant cigar. 'This is great,' he kept saying.

Once Churchill and his advisors had approved the mission – on which the 'fate of thousands of British, American, and French soldiers and sailors might hang' – Clark asked if they should wear civilian clothes or uniforms.

'Have you got civvies?' asked the prime minister. 'If you have, take them with you.'

As they were leaving, he added: 'The entire resources of the British Commonwealth are at your disposal. I want to assure you once more how important it will be to get this information and to cut down French resistance. You have my genuine support. Keep in mind that we'll back you up in whatever you do.'[1]

*

Churchill was as good as his word. A day later, having replaced his general stars with the insignia of a lieutenant colonel, Clark and his delegation of four officers were flown to Gibraltar.* They took with them copies of the Torch plans, 'none of which divulged the imminence of the operation', and money belts containing a total of $1,000 in Canadian gold coins and the same in US currency in case they 'got stuck' and had to buy their way out of a jam, or simply hold on 'until the invasion troops arrived'.

At Gibraltar they were introduced to Lieutenant Norman 'Bill' Jewell, the skipper of HMS *Seraph*, the brand-new S-class submarine that would take them to Algeria. He was, recalled Clark, 'a handsome young man with plenty of self-confidence' who knew very little about the mission.

'All they told me,' confided Jewell to Clark, 'was that I was to take some Americans someplace and land them at night on

---

* They departed Polebrook air base, north of London, in two B-17 USAAF bombers. Clark's plane, *Red Gremlin*, was flown by Major Paul Tibbets who, in August 1945, would pilot the B-29 bomber *Enola Gay* that dropped the 'Little Boy' atomic bomb on Hiroshima.

the African coast.' After Clark had filled in the details, Jewell seemed unconcerned. 'I am sure we can get you in there and get you off again.'

Clark was relieved. Previous conversations with senior navy officers at Gibraltar had offered little prospect of success, given the prevalence of shore patrols, spotting planes, and a French navy and air force 'bolder than it had been before'. Jewell's confidence was a breath of fresh air. He went on to explain that Clark and his party would be taken ashore by three SBS officers using folbots, 'little collapsible, wood-framed canvas canoes'. If they were to arrive at the rendezvous in daylight and submerged, they would need to get going immediately.[2]

It was in the *Seraph*'s tiny wardroom – generously given over to the submarine's passengers – that Clark and his officers met the men they would trust with their lives: captains Gruff Courtney and Dickie Livingstone, and Lieutenant Jimmy Foot. The trio were part of a ten-strong contingent of SBS men that had arrived in Gibraltar by sea in mid-October to assist Lieutenant Commander Nigel Willmott, Roger Courtney's partner during the Rhodes reconnaissance, with preparations for Operation Torch. Desperate to see more action, Roger had asked to be involved. But Mountbatten was adamant: Roger was needed in England to train more SBS men; his brother Gruff would go in his place.* The contingent had arrived at HMS *Maidstone*, the depot ship for Gibraltar's 8th Submarine Flotilla, on 13 October and immediately began training for the invasion. 'We were woken at 0530,' recalled Gruff, 'given cocoa and a ship's biscuit at 0600 and made to run up the Rock (altitude twelve hundred feet) before breakfast. Being portly and short of breath, I did not take too kindly to this over-enthusiasm by our clean-living naval commander and was happy to disappear on [the Clark mission] . . . a week later.'[3]

---

* Gerald Montanaro would almost certainly have got the nod, had he not recently taken up a new appointment as commander of the Mobile Flotation Unit – a long-range vessel which could be submerged while its crew carried out a mission in their canoes – with the naval rank of lieutenant commander (equivalent to an army major).

Code-named Operation Flagpole, their mission was to put Clark and his party – composed of Brigadier General Lyman Lemnitzer, Eisenhower's principal planning officer, Colonel Arch Hamblen, a logistics expert, Captain Jerauld Wright of the US Navy, and Colonel Julius Holmes, formerly of the State Department – 'safely ashore at a spot where a white light would be shining from a large house with white walls and a red-tiled roof at a small place called Messelmoun about sixty miles west of Algiers'. There the Americans would meet with General Mast. Also present would be Roosevelt's envoy Bob Murphy, and Ridgeway Knight, the US consul at Oran. 'They hoped,' wrote Courtney, 'to persuade Mast to cooperate in making the imminent landings peaceful and unopposed by the forces under his command. They would emphasise the whole Torch operation would be under American control because of the deep hostility felt by the Vichy French towards the British. Meanwhile we were to look after the Americans ashore and bring them safely and secretly back to the submarine.'[4]

Escorted by a Royal Navy destroyer, *Seraph* ran for most of 20 October on the surface to save time. After nightfall, Jewell stopped the submarine to allow the SBS officers to practise embarking in folbots with Clark and his officers. Lemnitzer got 'pretty wet' with Jimmy Foot, noted Clark, but otherwise all went to plan.[5] That was not how Foot remembered the exercise. 'To a canoe,' he wrote later, 'we lost the submarine. We were only supposed to go round it – not very far away – but it's surprising how easy it is [to lose contact], even at a distance of a few hundred yards . . . [Eventually] they gathered us unto them once again and we went merrily on our way.'[6]

At 4:00 a.m. the following morning, *Seraph* closed to within half a mile of the coast where a light shining from a house matched the description of the rendezvous. But it was too near dawn to risk a landing, so Jewell took the submarine back out to sea and dived. The Americans spent 'another day of discomfort in the overcrowded undersea craft', while Dickie Livingstone – a 27-year-old graduate of Corpus Christi College, Oxford, and former member of the Royal Ulster Rifles and 6th Commando – drew panorama sketches of the landing beach and hinterland through the periscope. That evening, at dusk, *Seraph* surfaced again and moved inland to wait for the light signal from the house. It finally came on at midnight, prompting Courtney to order the landings by folbot. He recalled:

> Holmes, who knew some of the men ashore, went first with Livingstone. Lemnitzer and Jimmy Foot were next, then Wright and Hamblen. General Clark and I were to embark next but, as I stepped into the canoe, a wave overturned it, and it drifted under the foreplanes of the submarine, with some damage to the frame. I recalled Wright's boat, and Hamblen gave up his place to Clark. Although my boat was cracked in several places, Hamblen and I decided to risk it, and we were able to catch up with the rest of the party before they hit the beach.

Livingstone and Holmes were the first to reach dry land, followed by Clark and the others. 'We touched the beach,' noted the SBS man, 'leaped out, and with the unease of all special boatmen on an open shore, prepared to get the boat up into the black shadows among the bushes at the foot of the bluff. Then a man appeared out of the trees to our left.'[7]

It was Bob Murphy, accompanied by his French associates. 'Welcome to North Africa,' said Murphy.

'I'm damn glad we made it,' replied Clark, puffing with exertion.

Still carrying the folbots, they climbed up a steep and stony path over the bluff to the house. It was a 'typical French colonial villa of red-roofed white stone built round a courtyard, with the main highway to Algiers only thirty yards away'. M. Teissier, the owner, had sent his servants away so that the meeting could take place in secret.

Informed that General Mast and his staff were coming by car from Algiers and would not arrive before 5:00 a.m., Clark ordered Courtney and his officers to stow the folbots in a room off the courtyard, and keep well out of sight. The French, he knew, were not well disposed to the British 'after the naval attacks at Dakar and Mers-el-Kébir'.*[8]

The SBS men did as they were told, adjourning to a small brightly lit room where, Livingstone recalled, 'glasses of whisky were forced upon us – not much force was required – and we were able to take stock of our fellow conspirators'. When told that 'practically all local authority except the police and Navy were in on the plot', they felt much more relaxed. Led upstairs to a 'good-sized bare room, unfurnished with an enormous double bed covered with gaudy rugs and a skeleton bed', the SBS trio 'peeled off their damp clothes, rolled up in the blankets, put our heads on our haversacks, and went to sleep'.

Meanwhile, Clark enjoyed a short rest in a separate room and was woken at 5:00 a.m. to meet General Mast who spoke little English, but said in greeting: 'Welcome to my country.'

Clark, Murphy and Mast ate a traditional French *petit déjeuner* of coffee, bread and jam while they discussed military strategy and North Africa in the living room. Taking care not to admit the Torch operation was underway – with the advance elements from the United States already at sea – Clark sounded out Mast as to the possible French response to the Allied landings. 'I was very impressed with Mast's sincerity,' recalled Clark. 'He certainly convinced me that he was entirely at our disposal and would do everything possible to help us carry out an operation that to him was only a hope.'

A couple of hours later, by which time their respective staffs had joined the conference, Mast asked Clark how many Allied soldiers might be involved. Trying to keep a straight face, Clark said: 'At least half a million, as well as 2,000 planes and many US ships.'

---

* On 3 July 1940, Royal Navy ships and planes attacked the French fleet at Mers-el-Kébir, Algeria, after its commander had refused an ultimatum to give up his ships. One French battleship was sunk and two more damaged (as well as three other warships). Nearly 1,300 French sailors were killed. Two months later, a British naval assault on the strategic port of Dakar in French West Africa in September 1940 was repulsed by pro-Nazi Vichy forces.

This was a gross exaggeration: only 112,000 American and British troops would participate in Operation Torch. But if his intention was to impress Mast, Clark achieved his purpose. The French general suggested, in turn, that an American submarine was sent to the coast of Vichy France to pick up General Henri Giroud as soon as possible. Fiercely anti-Nazi, Giroud would help to prevent bloodshed in North Africa, said Mast, if he was appointed supreme commander of Allied troops. 'I will,' said Clark, non-committally, 'do what I can.'

Worried he might be missed, Mast returned to Algiers while his officers continued to supply the Americans with information as to the 'positions and strengths of troops and naval units', the location of supplies like petrol and ammunition, and the places where resistance would be stiffest, particularly Oran and Casablanca where pro-Vichy sentiment was most pronounced.

It was late afternoon when Teissier received a phone call that the police were on their way. Cue a major panic as French officers fled in every direction until only Teissier, Murphy and Knight were left. Ushering the American officers and the SBS men into a wine cellar, Murphy and the others pretended to be drunk when the police arrived. 'They clanked bottles about,' wrote Clark, 'sang a little and were very jovial indeed.'

Having identified himself as the American consul in Algiers, Murphy told the police a party was in progress and there were women in the room upstairs. He urged the police not to embarrass him. They responded that they were bound to search the house, as the owner's Arab servants had reported suspicious footprints on the beach.

Listening from the cellar, Clark knelt at the foot of the stairs with a carbine in his hands, fully intending to shoot his way out if the police opened the trapdoor. But not familiar with the carbine's mechanism, he kept muttering, 'How does this thing work?'

Eventually someone snapped: 'For heaven's sake, put it down!'

Then Courtney was seized with a coughing fit and, as he

choked and spluttered in the darkness, he whispered to Clark, 'General, I'm afraid I'll choke.'

Clark answered, 'I'm afraid you won't!' He handed Courtney a piece of chewing gum and it seemed to do the trick.

Not long after, the trapdoor swung open and the eight men inside cocked their weapons. Fortunately, it was Murphy with news that the police had left but would soon be back. They needed to leave.

Retrieving the folbots, they headed for the beach where the surf was 'curling thunderously' onto the beach. It looked too rough to paddle through, but they were determined to try. After Courtney had called in the submarine by wireless radio, Livingstone and Clark made the first attempt to reach it, with the American general stripping down to his underwear to keep the rest of his clothes dry. 'We floated the boat, waist-deep,' recalled Livingstone, 'waited for the lull with the undertow tearing at our legs, and at a favourable moment made a dash for it; but just as we were almost clear an extra large wave crashed down on top of us, she rolled over, and in an instant we were struggling to free ourselves in a boiling turmoil of foam.'

The others rushed to help, pulling free both occupants and saving the paddles. But they were unable to rescue Clark's rolled up trousers, inside which he had placed his money belt – containing several hundred dollars in gold – in case the weight caused him to drown. The money was never recovered.

They sent someone to hire a fishing boat from a local. But that plan failed and, as it was close to midnight, and Clark was cold, wet and hungry, he went up to the house to see what he could find. He was intercepted by Teissier who was 'very upset' and wanted him gone. But Clark 'held out for some bread and wine, a pair of trousers, and two of Teissier's sweaters, all uncomfortably tight'. He had just finished dressing when the police returned. 'Please, for God's sake,' Teissier implored Clark, 'get out of my house!'

Still barefoot, Clark jumped over a cement wall and dropped painfully onto the path that led to the sea. At the beach there was more indecision until Clark decided to make a second attempt to reach the submarine, this time with Captain Wright. Their task was made easier when Courtney, remembering the technique used by inhabitants of the Gold Coast, instructed the others to carry the loaded boat through the first line of surf. It worked. 'Paddling furiously,' wrote Livingstone, 'they surmounted a series of waves by the skin of their teeth, while the rest of us watched. Twice they swerved, then they were through, rising and falling on the smoother waves beyond.'

The others did the same and, after more setbacks, got safely away. 'We seemed to be paddling for hours,' remembered Clark, 'without seeing anything before we spotted the loom of the *Seraph* in the blackness. The others finally arrived, the last being [Livingstone] and Holmes' boat. A big wave knocked it against the side of the submarine and broke the framework of the folbot. Holmes just barely climbed up the side as the boat filled and disappeared.' It went down with a number of items of kit, as well as Holmes' papers, and there was 'some anxiety' as to whether the latter would be 'washed ashore'.

As Livingstone climbed the conning tower, he looked towards the shore and saw headlights approaching the house. The police were back in force and they had got away just in time.

Soaked and exhausted, they celebrated with a glass of whisky, while Jewell's crew were given, on Clark's authorisation, a double ration of rum. 'Our feat,' noted Livingstone, 'in getting our valuable charges off that death trap of a beach was something of a personal triumph for Courtney, as we should never have managed it without his determination and experience.'

A day later, 24 October, the *Seraph* surfaced in daylight to allow Clark and his party to be transferred by folbot to a Catalina flying boat. 'We ferried the generals and their luggage across to her, little by little,' noted Livingstone, 'leaving them with mutually cordial farewells, and the promise of future meetings.' Before leaving, Clark had handed a gold coin to each of the officers who had taken part in Operation Flagpole – five Americans, five Royal Navy, and three SBS – and declared that henceforth they were members of the newly founded North African Canoe Club (NACC). There was one rule: if at any future meetings a member was found not to be in possession of his coin, he would buy the drinks.*

As the lumbering Catalina rose into the sky and turned towards Gibraltar, the SBS officers felt relieved that a 'considerable responsibility had been discharged, in spite of some extremely anxious moments'.

After a brief stop in Gibraltar for a hot bath and a decent meal, the Americans continued on to England in the B-17s. On arrival, Clark went straight to Ike's country retreat, Telegraph Cottage, where he gave a full account of the mission. Ike was delighted and phoned Churchill to tell him Clark was back. They were both asked for supper at 10 Downing Street, but Clark was 'too tired to accept'.

A couple of days later, invited to Buckingham Palace, Clark was introduced to George VI. 'I know all about you,' said the king. 'You're the one who took that fabulous trip. Didn't you, by the way, get stranded on the beach without your trousers?'[9]

Clark was quick to praise the role played by the SBS men, telling Mountbatten that the success of his mission was 'in large measure due to the three Commando officers' who accompanied him. 'Without their wholehearted assistance,' he wrote, 'and skillful use of the fine specialised equipment furnished them, I am sure that we could not have overcome the physical obstacles encountered in getting ashore and re-embarking through a heavy surf.'[10]

---

* This 'coining' tradition is still used by the SBS today. The first reunion of the NACC – limited to those who had taken part in Operations Flagpole and Kingpin – was a boozy dinner in the Hotel de France in Algiers in early December 1942. It was attended by the Americans Clark, Wright, Lemnitzer, Holmes, Hamblen and Gaylord, and Jewell and three of his officers. Courtney, Livingstone and Foot missed the dinner because they were on a mission to Corsica. Clark said to those present: 'I told you at Gib that I hoped the conference would save lots of lives. Well, you can take it from me it saved thousands, and you chaps carry just as much of the responsibility for it as we do.' (Terence Robertson, *The Ship with Two Captains* (London: Evans Brothers Ltd, 1957; repr. 1974), pp. 99–100.)

'Sit down, you silly old fool!'

In the evening of 27 October 1942, just two days after returning from the Algerian coast, *Seraph* left Gibraltar on another top-secret mission. This time, however, it sailed under the flag of the US Navy and with an American skipper, Captain Jerauld Wright. 'It was, I think, unique in the history of the two nations,' wrote Captain Fawkes, commanding the 8th Submarine Flotilla at Gibraltar, 'that a United States naval officer should be placed in nominal command of a British submarine thereby making her the only warship on active duty to be commanded by two captains'.[1]

This extraordinary anomaly had come about because General Henri Giraud (code-named 'Kingpin'), the man *Seraph* was being sent to collect from the coast of Vichy France, had flatly refused to be rescued by the British and there were no US Navy submarines within 3,000 miles. The solution was to put Captain Wright in nominal charge – though he had no experience of submarines and would leave day-to-day control in the hands of Lieutenant Jewell – and hope that Giraud was fooled by the subterfuge.

Also on board, to assist Wright, were Colonel Bradley Gaylord of the 12th US Army Air Force who 'spoke fluent French and was a cheerful character who could mix a mean martini'; and the three SBS officers who had taken part in Operation Flagpole – Gruff Courtney, Dick Livingstone and Jimmy Foot – and whose task was to supervise Giraud's rescue and, once it was successful, transfer the French general to a flying boat.

Arriving off the French coast after dark on 31 October, they waited anxiously for instructions. None arrived until the evening of 4 November when – with fewer than four days until the invasion and time running out – the radio operator handed Jewell a coded message. It read:

'Kingpin' with three others will be ready to embark in shoreboat at La Fosette 1,000 yards east of Le Lavandou tomorrow Thursday night November 5th . . . if weather permits Catalina aircraft will subsequently rendezvous with you to take off passengers.

They set off at once for La Fosette, motoring on the surface through the night, and diving just before dawn. *Seraph* spent the day submerged, moving at one point to within 500 yards of the shore so that Courtney and his officers could familiarise themselves with various distinguishing marks in case they had to land.

Seraph surfaced at dusk in an uncomfortable swell, and was soon forced to dive to avoid a line of fishing boats. Once on the surface again, the foredeck reception party changed into bathing trunks and plimsolls. With the weather expected to deteriorate, all eyes were looking landwards when a light started flashing from a house on the shore. It was Morse code, translated by a signalman on the bridge as: 'O-n-e h-o-u-r'.

Suddenly a lookout spotted a boat to seaward, three miles away but closing fast. Using his binoculars, Jewell saw what he thought was an E-boat, a mortal threat to the submarine. His instinct was to dive, yet he knew that would mean abandoning the mission. Fortunately, it was not his decision. Feeling a tap on his shoulder, he turned to see Wright shaking his head, as if to say, *Don't even think about it*.

The E-boat drew nearer and it seemed impossible that it could miss the submarine's distinctive silhouette. The men on deck held their breath and prayed that Giraud's party did not start signalling again. Their prayers were answered. After slowing down, the E-boat changed course and moved away, 'the faint sound of her powerful motors subsiding until there was only the slap of the angry sea at *Seraph*'s sides'.

Jewell restarted the submarine's engines so that her bow was facing the beach. It was 1:00 a.m. and he had, he estimated, about an hour before the sea got so unruly a rescue was impossible. 'Sir,' said one of the lookouts, pointing ahead, 'a boat is pulling away from the jetty.'

It was a small white rowing boat that, buffeted by a strong crosswind, was struggling to make headway. A hundred yards from shore, it began signalling with a dim light. The recognition signal was correct, but Wright chose not to reply in case the light was spotted by others. But when it became obvious that the boat was heading in the wrong direction, Wright ordered the reply to be given. The boat responded by changing direction.

To greet its occupants, Wright and Gaylord joined the SBS officers and crew on the casing, but not before lifelines had been attached to them just in case. As the rowing boat approached, its outline clearly visible in the bright moonlight, the crew threw it a line so they could pull it alongside. It had just made contact, and was drifting away, when a tall man stood up, put one foot on the gunwale and jumped. He misjudged the distance and fell between the casing and the rowing boat. Happily he landed on the submarine's ballast tanks, just below the surface, and was quickly grabbed and hauled to safety before the rowing boat came thudding into *Seraph*'s flank a second time.

Getting to his feet, the tall man announced: '*Je m'appelle général Henri Giraud.*'

Giraud, 63, was a legend in the French Army. Awarded the Légion d'honneur for gallant service against Rif tribesmen in Morocco in the 1920s, he had escaped from German captivity in both world wars. On the first occasion, he got away by pretending to be a circus worker and was assisted by the Brussels-based British nurse Edith Cavell, who was later shot for helping Giraud and other fugitives. More recently, after two years of meticulous planning, he had absconded from the high-security POW camp at Königstein Castle near Dresden by using a makeshift rope to climb down a steep cliff. Wearing a disguise and using fake identity papers, he eventually reached the Swiss border and from there slipped into Vichy France.

His rescue by submarine was child's play in comparison, and he seemed quite unconcerned by almost falling into the sea. He shook hands with Captain Wright as Gaylord, acting as interpreter, welcomed him aboard the USS *Seraph*. He was joined a couple of minutes later by three other men from the boat: his son Léon, his chief of staff, and an aide. Once all were safely on board, the ropes were cast off and the rowing boat disappeared into the blackness.

Wright's priority, now, was to get Giraud and his party to Gibraltar as quickly as possible. The plan was stay submerged during the day, and travel on the surface at night, on a fixed line, while waiting for the Catalina to make a rendezvous. But this became increasingly unlikely when the submarine's transmitter broke down and there was no way to signal its position. As dawn rose on 7 November, Jewell was in a quandary. If he ordered the submarine to dive, the last opportunity to get Giraud to Gibraltar in time for the invasion was lost. If he stayed on the surface, they would be sitting ducks for both enemy and Allied aircraft, with the latter ordered to sink submarines on sight. He took the second option, 'despite all orders to the contrary, because it seemed important to me to get Kingpin or a message through to Gibraltar as soon as possible.'

Shortly before 9:00 a.m., a lookout shouted: 'Aircraft on the port quarter, up sun, elevation thirty degrees.'

The men on the conning tower held their breath as they watched the tiny black speck grow larger. Was it friendly? Or hostile? Jewell exhaled in relief as he recognised the outline of a Catalina flying boat. It came in low, dipped its wings and circled the submarine. As it did so, Jewell flashed a message that his radio transmitter was out of action, and that the flying boat was to land and pick up passengers. It did so, landing 400 yards downwind of the submarine. By that time the SBS officers had prepared their folbots for the transfer, and Giraud and his party were on the foredeck with Wright and Gaylord, waiting to say farewell to Jewell.

Then a lookout shouted: 'Aircraft dead astern coming this way. Elevation ten degrees, distance about 8,000 yards.'

It was very low – 200 feet – and approaching at speed. 'Looks like a Ju-88, sir,' added the lookout.

If it was a Junkers Ju-88, the Luftwaffe's fast and versatile twin-engined bomber, Jewell knew that both flying boat and submarine were sitting ducks. He tensed in anticipation of the explosions that were bound to come if the Junkers dropped its bombs. But at the last minute the plane turned away and Jewell recognised the twin tail of an RAF Hudson light bomber. It was friendly and must have been aware of the mission. While the Hudson circled overhead, the transfer got underway. Jimmy Foot had been given the honour of taking General Giraud. 'He was an old man,' recalled Foot. 'The canoe's not a very stable thing at the best of times, and the old boy wouldn't get down into it.'

Instead he 'perched himself on the stern with his legs inside the rear cockpit'. This made the canoe very top-heavy, difficult to paddle and liable to capsize. Foot's problems were exacerbated by a rough sea and the fact that the Catalina, with its propellors still turning, was moving away from the submarine at a speed of about a knot. As he struggled to close the gap, Foot would paddle for two strokes, and then turn the blade flat to the water to stabilise the folbot. He had been threatened with a court martial if Giraud went into the water, and vented his frustration by yelling, 'Sit down, you silly old fool!'

After much shouting and struggling, they finally reached the Catalina. 'Watch the old bugger,' said Foot to the flying boat's navigator. 'He doesn't speak a word of English and he's nearly had me over the side about four times!'

The crew grabbed Giraud and hauled him into the plane, saying: 'We've got him in here – he's all in one piece.'

At which point, Giraud turned to Foot and said in perfect English: 'Thank you very much, Lieutenant, that was very pleasant. I'm sorry I've been such a nuisance to you.'

Years later, Foot was told by Giraud's son that the general never forgot their verbal exchange as it 'tickled his sense of humour'.

Once the other Frenchmen and Americans had been transferred, the SBS men returned to *Seraph* where they joined Jewell on the bridge and waved as the Catalina surged across the water and lifted into the sky. They had all played their part in one of the riskiest rescue operations of the war.[2]

*

That afternoon, having landed at Gibraltar, General Giraud was taken to meet Ike Eisenhower in his grim underground headquarters below the Rock where the air was damp and cold, and the 'eternal darkness of the tunnels' was only 'partially pierced by feeble electric bulbs'.

It would be, for Ike, one of the 'most distressing' interviews of the conflict. Though clad in civilian clothes, Giraud looked every inch a soldier. 'He was,' noted Ike, 'well over six feet, erect, almost stiff in carriage, and abrupt in speech and mannerisms. He was a gallant if bedraggled figure, and his experience of war, including a long term of imprisonment and a dramatic escape, had not daunted his fighting spirit.'

Yet it quickly became apparent to Ike that Giraud had 'come out of France laboring under the grave misapprehension that he was immediately to assume command of the whole Allied expedition'. He and Clark, on the other hand, had been led to believe that Giraud would be satisfied with the command of French troops in North Africa, and that he would lead them into the Allied camp.

When Giraud offered his services as Allied commander, Ike was unable to accept. That role, after all, was his. 'I wanted him,' wrote Ike, 'to proceed to Africa, as soon as we could guarantee his safety, and there take over command of such French forces as would voluntarily rally to him. Above all things, we were anxious to have him on our side because of the constant fear at the back of our minds of becoming engaged in a prolonged and serious battle against Frenchmen.'

Giraud, however, was adamant. He believed that his own and

his country's honour was at stake, and that he could not possibly accept any position lower than that of supreme commander. Ike knew, of course, that Giraud's request was impossible. No subordinate general in the expedition could legally accept an order from Giraud, and, moreover, there was not a single Frenchman in the Allied force. On the contrary, noted Ike, 'the enemy, if any, was French'.

All this was 'laboriously explained' to the French general who was 'shaken, disappointed, and after many hours of conference felt it necessary to decline to have any part in the scheme'. If he accepted a subordinate position, he insisted, his countrymen 'would not understand' and his 'honour as a soldier would be tarnished'.

Ike's political advisors were so worried that they suggested placing Giraud in nominal command while Eisenhower reserved for himself 'the actual power of directing operations'. The association of the Giraud name with the Allied course might well, they felt, mean the 'difference between success and disaster'. But Ike would not agree, and the arguments continued, back and forth, until the early hours of 8 November when the French general went to bed. 'Giraud,' he insisted, as a parting shot, 'will be a spectator in this affair.'

In the morning, by which time the invasion was underway, Giraud had had a change of heart. He agreed to participate on the basis that Ike had desired, and was promised in turn that, if he were successful in winning French support, the Allies would deal with him as the 'administrator of the region, pending eventual opportunity for civil authorities to determine the will of the opposition'.

Meanwhile the operational reports of the landings at Casablanca, Oran and Algiers were starting to come in and, by and large, were 'encouraging in tone'. In Algiers, as anticipated, there was 'almost no opposition and the area was quickly occupied'. Ike put this accomplishment chiefly down to the work of Bob Murphy, 'working through General Mast of the French Army, and to the sympathy, even if cloaked in official antagonism, of General Alphonse Pierre Juin [commander of French land forces in North Africa].'

At Oran and Casablanca, on the other hand – and as Mast had predicted – the local forces 'resisted bitterly'. In an attempt to bring an end to the fighting, generals Giraud and Clark flew into Algiers to negotiate with the French authorities. But when Giraud was 'completely ignored', it was a 'terrific blow' to Allied expectations. Ike noted: 'He made a broadcast, announcing assumption of leadership of French North Africa and directing French forces to cease fighting against the Allies, but his speech had no effect whatsoever. I was doubtful that it was even heard by significant numbers.'[3]

16

Party Inhuman

The SBS role in Operation Torch was not confined to ferrying generals to and from enemy shorelines. Roger Courtney's men also took part in marking beaches for landing craft and the attempted destruction of ships in harbour. For the first of those tasks they worked hand in glove with Courtney's old partner on the Rhodes reconnaissance, Lieutenant Commander Nigel Willmott.

After the Rhodes mission, Willmott had continued to press the case for a specialised unit to scout enemy beaches. But nothing came of this until the summer of 1942 when Willmott, newly assigned to the staff of Mountbatten's Combined Operations Headquarters, spoke at a planning conference for Torch in Norfolk House. 'It doesn't matter how many compasses you give them,' said Willmott to the assembled army and navy chiefs. 'They won't find the beaches unless someone guides them in.'

He added, remembering Rhodes: 'Charts are not always right. To fight an offensive war and land on the enemy's beaches, we're bound to need a permanent reconnaissance organisation, with expertly trained officers, and a lot of special gear. In the new amphibious war, something like that is inevitable.'

One or two nodded, but the conversation quickly moved on to other matters. After the conference, Willmott was asked to submit a memorandum on 'navigational requirements' for the Torch landings. He did so, but heard nothing until early September when he received a call from the operation's new staff navigator, Lieutenant Commander R. T. C. Russell, who had just read his memo. Over lunch, Willmott told Russell about Rhodes and the hazards that were not on the Admiralty's charts. 'We got away with it,' he said, 'because the weather was good and we were bloody well trained – but our gear was shocking. It must have used up all our beginner's luck.'

'Can you,' responded Russell, 'put a scheme down on paper? Something for the chief of staff? Shall we say, first thing tomorrow?'

Willmott smiled. 'Well,' he said, 'it makes a change to be rushed.'

The following afternoon, having worked all night on his paper, he was called to a meeting with Captain 'Frothy' Faulkner, chief of staff to Vice Admiral Bertram Ramsay, deputy naval commander for Torch. 'If-if we p-push your idea through,' said Faulkner, stammering slightly, 'ah, could you build a recce team in time?'

That would give him just two months to choose and train a team, and plan its reconnaissance of the five beaches earmarked for the Anglo-American assaults near Oran and Algiers. There would also be an attack on Casablanca, but that was an all-American effort. They were asking him to achieve the impossible, and it was all so last-minute. He could have started months earlier. But even now he was never going to decline the offer. 'I'll need some submarines,' he told Faulkner.

'How many?'

'Two for reconnaissance, at least. And three just before the troops go in, to help my chaps mark the way. It'll be a pretty makeshift outfit, sir.'

'Put up the whole plan,' replied Faulkner. 'If we get it through, you'll have top priority.'

That night, Willmott honed his plans. He would need three Royal Navy navigators and an SBS officer – preferably Roger Courtney – to fly out to Gibraltar with folbots and other special gear. From there, submarines would take them to reconnoitre the North African invasion beaches. He would also train up a larger team of soldiers and sailors, headed by ten officers, to act as 'human buoys' and guide in the Allied landing craft.

Assigning himself as one of the navigators, Willmott chose two more from his colleagues on the Combined Operations staff: Lieutenant Neville McHarg, 'a quiet rubber-faced Cumberland man, not obviously the rugged outdoor sort, but reliable as a rock'; and Lieutenant Frederick Ponsonby, 'a dark-haired exquisite with a penchant for poetry'. For his canoes and military officers, he went to his old collaborator, Roger Courtney, who had recently moved his new unit of SBS from Ardrossan to Tichfield Haven in Hampshire. Having heard what Willmott needed, Courtney said, 'Help yourself. I'm no bloody quartermaster.'

Willmott duly helped himself to ten folbots, five officers and five NCOs. Despite Roger Courtney's special pleading, he was not among them. On receiving the orders forbidding him to go, Courtney responded with a frown, 'Well – that's me. A bloody chair polisher now. Too precious to risk, old boy.'

In his place were assigned his brother Gruff, Dick Livingstone, Jimmy Foot, Lieutenant Basil Eckhard (formerly of the Buffs, Royal East Kent Regiment), who would teach Willmott's men how to canoe, Second Lieutenant P. A. Ayton, Sergeant Stan Weatherall, and corporals N. Thompson, J. Gilmour, A. Salisbury and J. Hutchinson. They were joined at Willmott's temporary base, HMS *Dolphin* at Fort Blockhouse in Portsmouth, by five more naval officers: three navigators – lieutenants Norman Teacher DSO, Donald 'Daddy' Amer and Geoffrey 'Thin Red' Lyne – and two young officers who had volunteered for hazardous service, lieutenants Nick Hastings and George Sinclair. Willmott told them: 'We're going to take part in the biggest invasion in history. Our job will be to make sure that the assaults are made in the right places. First we've got to find out what the beaches are like. There's only one way to do that. We've got to land on them for a good look round. I've done it, and I'm going to teach you how to do it and how to get away.'

He explained how some of them would guide assault craft into the beaches, while others acted as markers, sitting in canoes offshore, with beacons to show the way. 'I'm afraid,' he said, 'it's all rather bad for the nerves. Sitting in a canoe off an enemy beach when you're really tired – as you will be – isn't much fun.'

It was, he added, not a job for everyone. 'If any of you don't feel cut out for it, I shall understand.'

The only comment was from young Nick Hastings, the hand-some and dandyish son of a famous KC. 'And a very fine set of marker buoys they made!' he said, with emphasis.

Willmott laughed. It was, perhaps, with a similar nod to schoolboy humour that his hastily assembled group had been given the code name Party Inhuman.[1]

*

On 23 September 1942, after just ten days of frantic training, Willmott flew out to Gibraltar with McHarg, Teacher and Amer to reconnoitre the landing beaches near Oran and Algiers. The pilots, assault markers and SBS men would follow by ship.

Before leaving, Willmott had been told that only periscope reconnaissance was possible because the naval chief at Gibraltar considered the risk of compromise too great. After they arrived, the decision was reversed and they began practising the drill of launching canoes from submarines and homing once the mission was complete. But just before they were due to leave, the naval planners in London confirmed the original decision. They were not to land. Willmott was furious. 'And what we don't see from the periscopes,' he muttered darkly, 'we'll leave the poor bloody infantry to find out.'

In fact, the beach maps and silhouettes they made were very helpful, as was the revelation that the beach assigned to a motor-ised division was backed by steep cliffs and had no exits for wheeled vehicles or tanks. The plans were changed accordingly.

Once the rest of Party Inhuman had arrived at Gibraltar by sea in mid-October, the training for Torch was stepped up. Runs up the Rock before breakfast were followed by lectures, canoe-building practice and night exercises that could last until 11:00 p.m. They also learned – under the supervision of the SBS men – how to throw grenades, fire tommy guns, fight with their bare hands, and launch canoes from submarines.

Finally on 31 October, eight days before the invasion was due to begin, the Party Inhuman group departed Gibraltar in five submarines. Willmott, Lieutenant Noel Cooper RNVR, Lieutenant Eckhard and Corporal Salisbury of the SBS sailed in HMS *Unrivalled*, skippered by 27-year-old Lieutenant Hugh 'Mossy' Turner RN. Their destinations were the C Beaches, twenty miles east of Algiers. The plan was to drop the markers off in folbots on the night of 7/8 November so that they were in position to begin flashing their torches at midnight. By that time the navigators would have transferred from the submarine to landing craft to lead the assault in to the beaches.

Willmott and Cooper carried out a preliminary folbot reconnaissance on 4 November and found a good anchorage point close to the Bordelaise Rock for the markers, Eckhard and Salisbury, who were launched at 8:15 p.m. on the 7th. Wearing oilskins over their battledress, they struggled through a rising sea and a tidal stream running east to west at two knots to reach the rock at 10:30 p.m. and managed to anchor on the leeward side. At midnight Eckhard began flashing to seaward with his white torch.

Willmott and Cooper, meanwhile, had transferred to separate American landing craft which were both late and out of position. Willmott 'spent a nightmare three-quarters of an hour threading' his vessel 'through a confused swarm of lost boats, hailing and rounding up craft for his sector'. He then set a course inshore, calculating from the North Star, and eventually led the boats with him – a mixed cohort of Rangers and Commandos – on to the right beach, passing Eckhard and Salisbury en route. It was 3:30 a.m., and within minutes Eckhard could hear the sound of tommy-gun fire from the beach and the flashes and loud reports of shore guns exchanging shots with Allied ships.

At 4:00 a.m., their work done and their canoe shipping water,* Eckhard and Salisbury paddled to the shore and grounded in a tricky surf. They found 'troops, wrecked landing craft, three jeeps and an armoured car – facing a six-foot cliff': the consequence

---

* This despite the modification made to the folbots by Willmott in the form of a removeable canopy for the cockpit.

of not letting Willmott's men land for a proper survey. They changed into dry clothes and scrounged rations from the US troops on the beach.

In between sporadic air attacks by German Stuka dive-bombers, the beach was invaded by Arabs on the hunt for food and supplies. Helping themselves to unguarded stores, they carted them up the cliffs. Many were intercepted by a revolver-wielding Willmott who had climbed on to the heights earlier. It was, he mused, a good way of getting supplies up from the beach.

Later he visited a villa on the cliffs and was met by a 'well-fed, prosperous little Frenchman, his brown eyes agitated and his hands a-tremble'. He finally convinced the man that he meant no harm, and was allowed to watch the invasion from the villa's terrace. From there he had a bird's-eye view of the chaos below: the waterline strewn with wrecked landing craft; troops in the wrong place; and, thanks to worsening weather, support waves still to arrive. He watched spellbound as a flight of Junkers Ju-88 torpedo aircraft attacked the Allied ships offshore, with one torpedo striking an American troop transport, the USS *Leedstown*, on its starboard side, the explosion destroying her steering gear and flooding her aft section.[*]

Thank heaven, thought Willmott, the invasion was largely unopposed. If the French had defended the cliffs, it would have been a massacre.[2]

*

Assisting the landings near Oran, 250 miles to the west of Algiers, was Sergeant Stan Weatherall, formerly of 101 Troop, who was on his first operation. Transported in the submarine HMS *Ursula*, Weatherall was part of a team led by Lieutenant Neville McHarg whose job was to guide landing craft into beaches in the Bay of

---

[*] Crippled by this aerial torpedo attack, *Leedstown* was sunk the following day by a U-boat. She lost fifty-nine of her complement of 163.

Arzeu. During the evening of 7 November, Weatherall and his partner, Sub Lieutenant Peter Harris, were launched in a folbot from *Ursula*'s starboard ballast tanks in choppy water and immediately 'shipped a fair amount of water'.

They needed to start bailing out, but as the tool to do so had been 'swilled forward' and Harris could not find it, Weatherall used his boot while his partner paddled and kept them on course. An unexpected hazard was dolphins who headed for them 'like torpedoes' and veered off at the last moment, causing them to ship more water as the canoe bobbed like a cork. They made good headway, nonetheless, and by 9:15 p.m. were in position 200 yards off Z Beach where they dropped the kedge anchor.

Shortly after midnight, they began flashing 'Z' in Morse code (dash-dash, dot-dot) from the infrared transmitter. It was picked up by a landing craft carrying US Rangers who beached on their starboard side at 1:15 a.m., just ten minutes late. 'More assault craft came towards our signal,' remembered Weatherall, 'then veered off left and right to the beach; they were the second and third flights. On land all was quiet for about an hour, when we heard a few shots fired and saw Very lights [pistol flares].'

Having guided the last flight of tank- and jeep-carriers in at 4:15 a.m., and with daylight fast approaching, their job was finished so they paddled up the coast to White Beach. En route were several craft stuck in the shallows. They helped them by carrying their kedge anchors to deeper water. Finally reaching White Beach, they were held up at gunpoint by five US Rangers who asked them if they were a human torpedo. Weatherall noted: 'We were amazed to see such a vast amount of shipping in the bay, when the previous night there were only five canoes along the beach.'[3]

*

The unluckiest Party Inhuman group was led by Lieutenant Geoffrey 'Thin Red' Lyne. Accompanied by two SBS men – Lieutenant Ayton and Corporal Hutchinson – and three naval officers who would act as pilots, Lyne was transported in the S-class submarine HMS *Shakespeare*, skippered by Lieutenant Michael Ainslie RN, to beaches west of Algiers. But Lyne took no part in the invasion because, two nights before the landing, he was on a reconnaissance of the beaches with naval Lieutenant P. D. Thomas when a storm whipped up and their folbot was swept far to the west of the submarine rendezvous and almost swamped. Battered, exhausted and miles from land, they were spotted by a French trawler the following day and, as it approached, they punctured the folbot's air bladders and let it sink, rather than let it fall into enemy hands.

Taken to a naval prison in Algiers and interrogated by French staff officers, they revealed bit by bit their cover story: that they were delivering a message to an agent of the Free French leader Charles de Gaulle, east of Castiglioni, and had eaten it when their capture became inevitable. They were well treated in prison, particularly Lyne who was invited to share the commandant's lavish meals, washed down with wine and brandy.

Noticing one evening that the guards had been issued with weapons, Lyne asked why. 'It is the habit,' said the commandant, 'when a big convoy is passing.'

It was, Lyne knew, the invasion convoy.[4]

He and Thomas were released after Algiers surrendered to the Allies the following day. They were eventually reunited with Willmott, Eckhard and the others, and returned to England, via Gibraltar, in December. As far as Willmott was concerned, the operation had been a great success in that all the markers and pilots – bar Lyne and Thomas – were in position to assist the landings.

Yet they could, and should, have done more: particularly in the realm of pre-invasion beach reconnaissance. That would be, Willmott was convinced, a prerequisite if future amphibious operations were not to end in disaster.[5]

'One of the great episodes of naval history'

Founded in the tenth century by Moorish traders, the Algerian port of Oran had known many foreign rulers: Spaniards, Ottomans and, since 1831, the French. The bulk of its 200,000 residents were European and fiercely resentful of the British since the Royal Navy's ruthless destruction of the French fleet, which had refused to surrender, at the nearby base of Mers-el-Kébir in the summer of 1940. Controlled since then by neutral Vichy France, Oran's bustling harbour – a narrow rectangle, one and a half miles long, lined with quays crammed with barrels of wine and crates of tangerines, and subdivided by four breakwaters – was closely defended by forts and shore batteries that promised destruction to any ship that arrived with hostile intentions.

An attacker's only hope was to come in darkness. Which is why two former US coastguard cutters – HMS *Walney* and *Hartland* – waited until the early hours of 8 November 1942 before making their final approach to the harbour's west-facing entrance. Each ship was carrying 200 men from the US 6th Armored Infantry and a detachment of SBS with folbots and mini torpedoes. Their mission was to storm the harbour and capture or sink the Vichy French warships inside. 'There were believed to be in the harbour,' wrote Lieutenant Eric 'Sally' Lunn of the SBS, 'some destroyers and submarines, and possibly a light cruiser . . . There were also coastal batteries and machine-gun nests. It was however stressed that little or no opposition was anticipated from any of these sources.'[1]

Lunn's detachment was commanded by Harry Holden-White,

recently promoted to captain, who three weeks earlier had been training at Tichfield Haven when he received orders to report to COHQ in London with two officers and eight men for special duty. He arrived the following day – accompanied by, among others, lieutenants Lunn and Colin Pagnam (formerly of the Gordon Highlanders), and Company Sergeant Major Arthur Embelin – and the party was taken from Whitehall to an SOE experimental station near Welwyn Garden City where they were given a demonstration in the use of the same mini torpedoes that Wilson and Brittlebank had carried on their recent ill-fated mission to Crotone. The ones Holden-White and his men were shown, however, were fitted with dummy fuses. They were assured that the mini torpedoes they would collect at Gibraltar would be 'ready for use', and all they needed to do was 'remove the cap from the percussion fuse, the cap and pin from the self-destroying fuse . . . start the motor and release the mine'.[2]

That evening, back in London, Holden-White met the architect and commander of the Oran mission – dubbed Operation Reservist – Captain Frederick 'Fritz' Peters RN, a 53-year-old Canadian-born veteran of the First World War. Having retired from the Royal Navy with a DSO and DSC in 1919, Peters re-enlisted at the start of the Second World War and was commanding an anti-submarine flotilla when he won a bar to his DSC in 1940. He then worked with naval intelligence at the so-called 'School of Spies' in Hertfordshire where he trained, among others, the future traitors Guy Burgess and Kim Philby. 'He had,' recalled Philby, 'faraway naval eyes and a gentle smile of great charm.'[3]

Thin-lipped, with high arching eyebrows and a penchant for slim black cheroots, Peters was just the type of bold and determined – some might say foolhardy – leader required for such a dangerous mission. 'This,' he told a colleague, 'is the opportunity I have been waiting for.'

Others were not so convinced. 'If determined resistance is met from the French navy,' wrote Rear Admiral Andrew C. Bennett, the naval commander of the Oran task force, to Eisenhower, 'which seems to be the general opinion, it is believed that this small force will be wiped out.' Against serious opposition, said Bennett, even 'five times the number of troops would be insufficient'. The plan was 'suicidal and absolutely unsound'.[4]

Yet Peters betrayed no doubts as he explained the role of the SBS to Holden-White: they would remain on the *Walney* and *Hartland* until they were inside Oran harbour, and only then deploy in folbots to destroy any French warships attempting to resist or depart. Holden-White's preference, to maintain the element of surprise, was for the folbotists to go in *before* the defences had been alerted. This, after all, was the SBS modus operandi: arrive silently and, if possible, leave the same way. He immediately telephoned Roger Courtney and voiced his concern. Courtney said leave it with me, and the following morning met Peters and Mountbatten's deputy, Major General Charles Haydon. They accepted Holden-White's reservations and agreed on a new tactic: the five SBS folbots would be dropped by motor launches outside the harbour and go in first.

A couple of days later, Holden-White and his men travelled up to Greenock on the Clyde where *Walney* and *Hartland* were moored. Redesignated as Royal Navy sloops, they both had a crew of ninety-seven and were 250 feet long, capable of seventeen knots, and armed with four guns ranging from 57 mm to five inches. Holden-White joined Peters on *Walney* with six men and three folbots, while Lunn took three men and two folbots onto *Hartland*.

They sailed for Gibraltar in a large convoy on 26 October, and en route Captain Peters discussed the operation. He was, he told the key participants, convinced that any French warships in Oran would fight. But he did not expect the French troops in the town to offer any opposition. As the main objective of the operation was to prevent the French from destroying the port, the role of the American soldiers would be to occupy all tactical positions covering the docks, including the shore batteries. The naval boarding parties, meanwhile, would prevent merchant ships from being scuttled, while the demolition party, led by an SOE officer, took care of any submarine that refused to surrender. They would hold the port, said Peters, until they were relieved by larger US forces converging from beaches to the east and west.

Holden-White and his men were told their targets would be confirmed when they reached Gibraltar. Less welcome was the news from Peters that he was no longer prepared to let them enter the harbour before the sloops. He could not risk *them* giving the game away. So instead they would be dropped off when the sloops were inside the harbour, as originally planned, and to make this possible *Walney*'s shipwright designed a canvas sling that could lower a fully loaded folbot from a davit. 'Using this method,' recalled Holden-White, 'we found that slipping could be accomplished in thirty seconds.'

Try as he might, however, the young SBS officer could not hide his doubts about the mission, particularly the role assigned to Sergeant-Major Arthur Embelin. His job was to help Captain Michael Bolitho, a member of SOE, prevent 'any suitably situated French submarine in the harbour' from submerging by blowing a hole in its side with a 'beehive' explosive charge. To board the submarine they would use a rubber dinghy. Holden-White could not help feeling that 'such a hazardous plan was a waste of both Michael Bolitho and Sergeant-Major Embelin, a superb soldier that I greatly respected'. His misgivings 'contrasted strongly' with the SOE man's 'sunny optimism'. One evening, noticing the look of concern on Holden-White's face, Captain Peters told him: 'Don't look so worried, Harry! It's going to be alright.'[5]

Arriving at Gibraltar in the evening of 6 November, the sloops were loaded with their contingents of US troops while Holden-White and his men took delivery of fourteen mini torpedoes – eight for *Walney* and six for *Hartland* – from a Royal Navy lieutenant who also brought the latest intelligence. This confirmed that there were at least two destroyers in Oran harbour, as well as four armed trawlers. When Peters heard the news, he instructed Holden-White to use his three folbots to target the destroyers and one of the armed trawlers.[6] Lunn and Pagnam, meanwhile, would operate in the inner harbour where four submarines were tied up alongside two floating docks. They would use their mini torpedoes only against warships that had opened fire with medium or heavy guns, switched on their searchlights or were trying to leave the harbour.[7]

A major headache for Holden-White, however, was the fact the torpedoes had been delivered in pieces and without instructions on how to put them together. Five of the fourteen, moreover, had faulty electric motors. 'Luckily,' recalled Holden-White, 'I had Sergeant Major J. Embelin with us, who was a demolition expert, and he was able to assemble them.'[8]

That Embelin had done it correctly was confirmed by the naval lieutenant who, quite by chance, had watched a demonstration in the UK. But that still left them with just nine torpedoes – five on *Walney* and four on *Hartland* – and there was no guarantee they would work.

*

The two sloops left Gibraltar on 7 November and were approaching the east-facing entrance to Oran harbour at 2:55 a.m. on the 8th when the shore battery at Cap Blanc opened fire on HMS *Walney*, the lead ship. Her motor launch (ML) escort immediately began laying a smoke screen. Unfortunately, the ML then collided with *Walney*'s starboard side, damaging one of the three folbots which were hanging from davits, ready to be launched.

Minutes later, *Walney* hit the double boom across the harbour entrance, breaking it 'without difficulty'. This prompted a burst of defensive 37 mm cannon fire from just off the ship's port bow. Fortunately, it passed harmlessly overhead and hit a merchant ship beyond. After thirty seconds this firing stopped. They were now inside the narrow harbour, subdivided by four moles, that extended along the coast for more than a mile. It was, in Holden-White's estimation, 'a deathtrap for a seaborne assault'.

Once opposite the first mole, Du Ravin Blanc, Captain Peters ordered the launching of the folbots. The canoe containing Holden-White and his paddler, Corporal Derek Ellis (formerly of the

Shropshire Light Infantry and 101 Troop), was the first to hit the water. 'Frankly,' wrote the SBS captain, 'I was so bloody glad to be away from it. Soon that feeling turned to guilt as [we] paddled off to find suitable targets for our mini torpedoes. We had not travelled far when there was a huge explosion. We looked back. *Walney* had been hit by shore batteries and was already sinking.'[9]

She had indeed been hit, a shell striking the bridge and killing Peters' French interpreter, Lieutenant Paul Duncan. But it had not stopped the sloop, which steamed on towards its objective at the far end of the harbour, the 200 American soldiers on its mess deck waiting anxiously for the order to disembark.[10]

Meanwhile, Holden-White and Ellis were paddling hard towards their primary target – a destroyer lying alongside the fourth mole, known as the Quai Centrale – at a brisk pace of four to five knots, and using the cover provided by a thin stretch of water between a block of barges and the northern arm of the harbour. 'My mind,' remembered Holden-White, 'was in a turmoil . . . bedevilled by doubt as to the practicability of our making a successful attack on an enemy ship, now that all possibility of doing it secretly appeared lost. Against this, was the impish desire to sink one with something that looked more like a child's toy submarine than a weapon of war.'

Holden-White soon became aware that shells were landing in their vicinity, and 'throwing up great mushrooms of water as they did so'. One or two came uncomfortably close, 'and it felt uneerily like being under a waterfall to look up at their canopies from below'. Oddly he felt no fear, and put this down to the bizarre nature of the situation they were in. He noted: 'None of this was really happening. The harbour was a vast film set, and Ellis and I minor players in an unbelievable drama. Had I died then, I am sure it would have been with the same look of disbelief on my face as that which Gerald Montanaro had noted on the faces of the soldiers killed in France before Dunkirk.'[11]

Hearing French voices from a barge on their port bow, they slowed to barely half a knot to avoid discovery. In this they were successful and, having reached the end of the barges, they moved out of the shadows to try and identify their target. As they did so, a searchlight came on ahead and began to cover an arc from the northern jetty to HMS *Walney* which, by now, had reached a point opposite the mole Quai Centrale. The light caught the bow of the folbot, causing the pair to back-paddle furiously for the cover of the barges. Before they could reach it, 37 mm cannon fire blasted just over their heads.

'It seemed to be coming from a point near the western end of the Quai Centrale,' recalled Holden-White. 'There were also a few shells falling into the sea about twenty yards to the south, and quite a lot of debris (presumably from HMS *Walney*) was falling around us.'

Regaining the shadows, they moored the folbot to the last barge and climbed inside. From there they could see *Walney*'s bridge and surrounding superstructure 'burning furiously' as more shells were fired at it from a French battery on the hill overlooking the eastern end of the harbour. Opposite *Walney*, alongside the northern jetty, an armed French trawler was also on fire.

The pair returned to the folbot. But as there was no sign of their target, and the innermost section of the harbour, the Bassin Gueydom, was 'unapproachable in a canoe owing to the shellfire, small-arms fire and searchlights', Holden-White decided to remain where he was. While he prepared the mini torpedoes for action, he sent Ellis back into the barge to report any warships leaving the Bassin. The corporal carried out his task with 'great coolness', noted Holden-White, 'as small-arms fire was passing about two feet over the top of the barge and he had to have his head over the top in order to observe'.

Five minutes later, Ellis returned to say a submarine was exiting the Bassin. Holden-White edged the folbot forward so that the target was in view. 'In accordance with my orders to attack warships leaving the harbour,' he wrote, 'I fired a Mobile Mine [mini torpedo] at the submarine which was travelling on the surface at three knots. I did not apply enough deflection and I could see from the phosphorescent bubbles sent up by the Mine on the first few yards of its [run] that it was going to pass astern.'

He sent Ellis back into the barge to keep watch while he prepared the second torpedo. Within ten minutes the corporal reappeared with the news that a French destroyer was leaving the inner harbour. Sneaking a look, Holden-White estimated that the warship was moving at 1.5 knots towards the harbour entrance. It was just 200 yards away when he fired the second torpedo, aiming it seventy yards in front of the ship's bows. The torpedo would take, he estimated, about a minute and a half to reach its target. He watched for the explosion but none came.

Instead, the destroyer stopped as its crew scurried about on deck. Corporal Blewitt, who was in the second of the three folbots with Corporal Loasby a short distance away, heard an explosion on the port side of the destroyer, but saw no flash. By now, Holden-White was back in the barge, observing the battle.[12]

Walney looked to be in its death throes. It had taken the worst of its punishment from deck guns on the French sloop *La Surprise*. The first salvo, at a distance of just 300 yards, had destroyed the armour plating on *Walney*'s bridge, killing the helmsman among others. Captain Peters, blinded in his left eye, shouted a rudder instruction, but no one was listening. As *Walney* drifted aimlessly past the French ship, another broadside raked its decks, butchering the defenceless infantrymen. Passing the third mole, a shell exploded in the engine room, depriving the ship of power. Momentum carried it on towards the western end of the harbour as guns on submarines, a shore battery and snipers all took their toll. 'Topside,' read one account, 'the dead were piled three-deep. Below, the deck resembled a charnel house, scarlet with the blood of butchered infantrymen.'

Coming alongside a moored destroyer, survivors on *Walney* flung a grappling iron. But there was no steam to drive the winch, and they never got close enough to board. They were cut down, instead, by the destroyer's deck guns. It was now that the *Walney*'s skipper, Lieutenant Commander Meyrick, and Lieutenant Colonel George F. Marshall of the US 3/6th Armored Infantry were killed.[13] Captain Bolitho and Sergeant-Major Embelin, the sole SBS man still on board, were also among the fatalities, 'killed by machine-gun fire from one of the quays, whilst waiting to disembark from *Walney* and fulfill their mission'.[14]

At 4:15 a.m., *Walney*'s magazine exploded, a shocking sight for Holden-White and Ellis. She then keeled over and sank, taking her dead and wounded with her. Peters was not among them. Shortly before the explosion, he had 'accomplished the berthing of his ship', helping to secure the fore and aft mooring lines with 'utter disregard of his own personal safety'. He then got on a raft with ten other survivors and managed to reach the shore, but soon after was taken prisoner.[15]

Walney's sister ship, *Hartland*, had not fared any better. Following *Walney* into the harbour, she was also pummelled by shell and machine-gun fire, taking three directs hits as she passed through the broken boom. One shell put her engines out of action, but momentum carried her on to her objective on the first mole. En route she was riddled by 'fire from the 5.1 [inch] guns of a destroyer on her port bow and received hits at a range of thirty yards'. By the time she reached the mole, noted 'Sally' Lunn, she was 'burning furiously' and 'out of control'. Efforts were made to secure her bow line, but the rope snapped and she swung out into the harbour with only her stern attached to the mole. 'In this position,' wrote Lunn, it was impossible for the assault troops to make a landing, but some were lowered away in two ship's boats from the starboard side.'

All the while, Lunn, Pagnam and their paddlers – corporals Milne and Bates – took what cover they could from the storm of shrapnel and machine-gun bullets, waiting for the order to launch which never came. It was just as well because one folbot, slung well aft, was 'completely demolished by an early hit on the quarterdeck', while the other survived amidships but 'could not be slipped as it was jammed by wreckage'.

When the order came to abandon ship, the two SBS officers and Bates got on to a Carley life raft with six American soldiers, some of them wounded. They took with them two mini torpedoes with the intention of using them against the French destroyer that had wreaked so much havoc on *Hartland*. But with the whole basin lit up by the fires on *Hartland*, they were spotted from the shore and subjected to 'intense' machine-gun fire which killed three of the Americans. The SBS men leaped overboard, tipping over the raft in the process, and losing both torpedoes. Lunn saw one sink; the other floated and was later recovered by the French.

Striking out for the shore, they turned back when they heard the surviving Americans cry for help. They eventually got them and some other stragglers on to a nearby merchant ship which had lowered a rope ladder. Enticed by cries of '*Ami, ami, venez ici!*', they were promptly taken prisoner. Soon after they were reunited with Corporal Milne who was captured onshore after he had 'immobilised' a French sentry. Searched and disarmed, they were marched through the streets to a civil prison, and later handed over to the military authorities. The locals were 'curious', but only a few were openly hostile.[16]

Also in captivity by this time were Holden-White and his remaining men. He and Ellis paddled their folbot as far as the harbour entrance where they decided to land and link up with advancing Allied soldiers. They were eventually caught by French sentries, 'searched, handcuffed and taken to the Marine Barracks' where they 'remained for two days until the American troops entered the town'.

Of the remaining two folbot crews, one was caught almost immediately when their damaged canoe sank on being launched and they swam ashore. The other got away from *Walney* but was 'unable to make an attack'. Its crew – Blewitt and Loasby – were taken prisoner later that afternoon.[17]

They were the lucky ones. The operation, overall, had been a disaster with horrific casualties. Of the 393 US infantrymen who took part, 189 were killed and 157 wounded. The rest were taken prisoner. The Royal Navy suffered a similar attrition rate with 113 dead and eighty-six wounded, while the US Navy suffered five fatalities and seven wounded. Only the SBS were relatively unscathed, with just one of their eleven men killed, though the rest were captured. Of the 600 or so Allied personnel to take part, therefore, roughly half of them were killed, a death rate that far outstrips the one in six suffered by the British Army on the Somme in 1916, the gold standard for battlefield carnage.

These 300 or so Allied corpses were buried in communal trenches on high ground outside the town, with US engineers having to use jackhammers to break the rock hard ground. Almost thirty bodies could not be identified, and the missing included Lieutenant Colonel Marshall, just 31 years old, who left a wife and two small children.

The Allies had also forfeited two ships, while French losses were a single armed merchantman – set on fire by *Walney* – and an estimated 165 men killed. The failure of Reservist gave the French the opportunity they needed to put the harbour out of action. By the time they surrendered to advancing US troops on 10 November, they had sunk twenty-seven hulks and scuttled three floating dry docks, including the 25,000-ton Grand Dock which blocked the harbour entrance for two months.[18]

In revenge, the Allied navies sank or drove aground a number of French ships that escaped Oran, notably two destroyers and the sloop *La Surprise*, the latter going down with its skipper and fifty men. To obscure the scale of the defeat, moreover, the Allied leaders resorted to a time-honoured tactic: post-facto justification, hyperbolic praise and the award of gallantry medals. Admiral Sir Andrew Cunningham, the Allied naval commander, insisted that the attempt to capture the harbour was 'worthwhile', but foiled 'by the alertness of the French navy'. He added: 'Great achievements in war are seldom brought about without considerable risk to personnel . . . their failure is not in itself proof that the enterprise was faultily conceived or executed'.[19]

Similar language was used in the recommendations for Captain Peters, one of the few survivors, to receive both the British Victoria Cross and the American Distinguished Service Cross.* The citation for the former read:

---

* After the Medal of Honor, the Distinguished Service Cross is the second-highest award that a member of the US Army can be given for extreme gallantry and risk of life in combat.

Captain Peters was in the suicide charge by two little cutters at Oran ... Peters led his force through the boom in the face of point-blank fire from shore batteries, destroyers and a cruiser – a feat which was described as one of the great episodes of naval history. The *Walney* reached the jetty disabled and ablaze, and went down with her colours flying. Blinded in one eye, Captain Peters was the only survivor of the seventeen men on the bridge . . .[20]

The American citation referred to 'extraordinary Heroism in Action' and an 'utter disregard of his own personal safety'. In truth, many of the participants had displayed similar qualities. But as the commander, and the possessor of three other gallantry medals, Peters was singled out for particular attention. Released from captivity, he was given priority air passage home from Gibraltar so that he could make his report in person. His Sunderland flying boat had reached Plymouth Sound when it crashed in thick fog. Badly injured, he was kept afloat by the pilot for more than ninety minutes. But he had died by the time the rescue launch finally appeared. Both gallantry medals were awarded posthumously to his wife.[21]

No fewer than thirty-eight British awards were made for Reservist – an almost unprecedented total, given the relatively small force involved – including one VC, four DSOs, six DSCs, and thirteen DSMs.[22] Three went to SBS men: Harry Holden-White and Eric Lunn got the Military Cross, and Derek Ellis the Military Medal. Lunn's citation read: 'When the ship was hit repeatedly and his own folbot smashed, this officer organised his party to assist in fighting the fires until "abandon ship" was ordered. He later assisted in the rescue of several wounded Americans who were struggling in the water.' Holden-White had recommended his paddler, noting: 'He displayed coolness and performed his duties with quick-wittedness and audacity.'[23]

Once released, most of the SBS men returned to the UK by sea. But Holden-White and Lunn were anxious to report on the performance of the top-secret mini torpedoes, and managed to get a lift with Gruff Courtney, also returning from his recent adventures, in an American B-24 bomber. They landed in Cornwall and were promptly arrested. 'Bloody funny, really,' recalled Holden-White. 'We hadn't got any papers, of course, and wearing these odd clothes, the local police and immigration people surrounded us.'

A brief interrogation and a few telephone calls later, and they were on their way to London under close escort where Holden-White was finally able to report on the mini-torpedo trials. It was only then, he recalled, 'as I explained our efforts to use them, that their range for maximum effect – that is sinking the target – was [found to be] only 50 yards. We had been firing them from 100 to 150 yards, so they were no bloody use from that standpoint.'

At their meeting with Vice Admiral Mountbatten, Holden-White and Lunn were asked if they would agree to be interviewed by the BBC to publicise the first Anglo-American operation of the war. They refused. Holden-White felt strongly that 'to make capital out of such a catastrophe' would be an 'act of betrayal to those who had lost their lives'. When he saw how determined the SBS men were not to cooperate, Mountbatten let the matter drop. Both officers expected to be sacked for defying their chief. But Mountbatten was not a vindictive man and might even have admired their stand.[24]

As recriminations over Reservist flew around Whitehall, Mountbatten's staff did everything they could to absolve themselves of responsibility. 'It should be pointed out once and for all,' minuted Mountbatten's chief of military planning on 17 December 1942, 'that this curious exploit into Oran harbour was entirely run and devised by Allied Force Headquarters. Captain Peters came to this Headquarters and requested the loan of about three Folbotists. These were handed over to him and from that moment until the completion of the operation COHQ played no part whatever.'[25]

Part II

Cockleshell Heroes and
Beachcombers, 1942–4

Blondie

While Roger Courtney's folbotists were performing ever more prodigious feats in the Mediterranean, a new unit was training for arguably the boldest amphibious mission of the war. Its commander was the canoe enthusiast who, along with the other leading lights of Britain's maritime special operations, had approved the creation of Courtney's UK-based SBS in late February 1942: Major Herbert George 'Blondie' Hasler.

Born in 1914, Herbert George Hasler was just 3 years old when his father Arthur, a quartermaster in the Medical Corps, was lost at sea after his troopship had been torpedoed in the Mediterranean. Raised in Southsea on the Solent by his strong-willed mother Annie, young Bert loved both the sea and boating, and would spend many hours playing on the town's shingle beaches and paddling across the lake in a two-seater craft he built at school when he was 12.

At 13, Hasler was sent to Wellington College, the public school famous for preparing boys to become officers in Britain's armed services. He excelled at sports, particularly rugby, cross-country running and swimming. But so mercilessly was he teased in his first term about his name Bert and his Portsmouth accent that he swiftly abandoned both: using instead his second name George and a voice more in tune with his public school contemporaries. Given his love of sailing boats and all things nautical, it was perhaps inevitable that he would choose for his career a seafaring branch of the military. He preferred the Royal Marines to the

Royal Navy for the simple reason that junior officers of the RM were paid more than naval cadets.

He was, noted his biographer, 'a popular but unconventional officer under training and one acknowledged to possess charm, charisma and leadership qualities beyond the norm'. He was, moreover, modest and intelligent, 'with impressive physical strength and powers of endurance'. Not particularly gregarious, he made friends slowly. But once trusted, they were friends for life. It was during his early years in the Marines that his luxuriant moustache and thinning fair hair earned him the nickname 'Blondie'. The name stuck, though he was mostly bald by his mid-twenties, his former golden mane reduced to a monk's tonsure, and an incomplete one at that.

His first posting in 1935 was to the battleship HMS *Queen Elizabeth*, flagship of the Mediterranean Fleet. Two years later he was appointed Fleet Landing Officer for the Mobile Naval Base Defence Organisation, a new unit that contained shore and anti-aircraft guns, searchlights, boom nets and mines to protect ships leaving and returning to port. After the outbreak of war in September 1939, with Hasler now a captain, the unit quickly expanded to include the Royal Marine Fortress Unit (RMFU), whose main task was to protect the Home Fleet's base at Scapa Flow in Orkney. In April 1940, Hasler accompanied the RMFU to Norway where he won praise for his command of two motor landing ships during the Narvik campaign.

Among his impressive feats were the landing of multiple waves of French troops, dodging German bombers and field artillery, and arranging the evacuation of the last Allied troops in his flimsy boats in late May. Yet despite official recognition for his valorous service – in the form of an OBE, the Croix de Guerre and a mention in despatches (the latter for saving a wounded crewman's life after their ship was strafed by a German fighter-bomber) – Hasler was not satisfied. The poor discipline shown by some of his men was, he felt, down to him. 'Was it,' he asked a fellow officer, 'a fault to punish myself for failure of the men under my command when, in practice, it was my lack of leadership?'

Convinced that leading by example was the only way to cajole soldiers, he was determined to push himself to ever greater limits of endurance and skill. To make sure he got the best raw material, he devised 'methods of selection which were to rely heavily on an ability to see through pretence, baloney and even shyness'. In that respect, his powers of intuition were not unlike Roger Courtney's.

There was, moreover, another point of similarity. The modus operandi of the SBS was to accomplish its tasks with as little noise and bloodshed as possible. Hasler's first experience of combat had taught him that he, too, had little time for bloodlust or killing per se. He certainly wanted to 'engage the enemy more closely', but in a manner that would inflict the maximum amount of damage for a minimum cost in lives.[1]

His first move was to write a paper in May 1941 that urged Combined Operations to use canoes and underwater swimmers to attack enemy ships in harbour. Though rejected, the paper was remembered after Italian frogmen had badly damaged two British battleships – *Queen Elizabeth* and *Valiant* – in Alexandria harbour in December 1941, and led directly to Hasler's employment a month later, at the age of 27, at the CODC in his home town of Southsea. His task was to find new ways to attack enemy ships in harbour.

He began working on the boom patrol boat (BPB), a modification of a captured Italian explosive motor boat (the novel weapon that had successfully sunk the cruiser HMS *York* in Suda Bay, Crete, in March 1941), and, at the same time, furthered his interest in folbots by studying their use as a means of guiding BPBs over booms and recovering their jettisoned pilots. His preference, however, was to mount silent attacks on enemy shipping with just canoes. Having agreed on the ideal specifications for a military folbot with Roger Courtney and Gerald Montanaro in early March 1942, Hasler asked the boatbuilder Fred Goatley to design a prototype. Sixteen feet long and twenty-eight and a half inches wide, and equipped with a ridge round the cockpit to secure an innovative waterproof jacket (the forerunner to the modern spraydeck), it would become known as the 'Cockle' Mark II.

Spurred by Montanaro's and Preece's successful limpet-mine attack on the oil tanker in Boulogne harbour in April 1942, Hasler proposed to his bosses a new 'all-Royal Marines unit' to develop new methods of attacking ships in harbour. The idea was warmly received by Mountbatten's chief of staff, Colonel G. E. Wildman-Lushington, himself a Marine, as well as Mountbatten himself, and became reality on 6 July 1942 when the Admiralty authorised Hasler to form the Royal Marine Boom Patrol Detachment (RMBPD), a cover name designed to obscure the unit's true purpose.*

By then Hasler's search for volunteers was well underway. He was looking for 'men eager to engage the enemy who were indifferent to personal safety and free of strong family ties'. If they possessed small-boat skills, that was a bonus. Like Courtney, he did not want 'macho' types, but rather men of quiet determination with adventurous spirits. His first recruit was Lieutenant J. D. ('Jock') Stewart, a Scot from London who had served with him in the RMFU. Bright and physically strong, Stewart became his stores officer. He was soon joined by two young second lieutenants – Jack MacKinnon and Bill Pritchard-Gordon – who were selected from a group of ten officers that Hasler had interviewed at the Royal Marine Small Arms School at Browndown on the Solent in late June.[2]

Born in Oban on the coast of Argyllshire, and raised in the Maryhill district of Glasgow, 20-year-old MacKinnon was the son of a bowling-green keeper and a former hotel chambermaid. For most of his youth he lived with his parents and two younger sisters in a tiny one-bedroom flat on the second floor of a sandstone tenement building. It had a toilet but no bathroom – the family would wash in a tin bath in the kitchen/dining room – and double-bed recesses in both the main rooms. To escape his

---

* Hasler had suggested using the cover name of Royal Marine Harbour Patrol Detachment. It was Mountbatten who altered this to RMBPD.

cramped home, young Jack spent most of his time outdoors, playing football, cycling, hiking and camping in the surrounding countryside. He was a talented athlete, a good swimmer and a keen Boy Scout.

In early 1941, MacKinnon chucked in his job as a clerk at a coal merchants to join up. His father had served in the First World War as a piper in the Argyll & Sutherland Highlanders. But young Jack preferred the Royal Marines and began his training at Exton in East Devon in April. The following January, by then a corporal, he joined HMS *Atherstone*, part of the 15th Destroyer Flotilla at Devonport, and helped to shoot down a German Ju-88 bomber with a Lewis gun during one patrol. Commended by his brigadier, who noted his leadership potential, he was sent for officer training at the Royal Marine Military School at Thurstone in Devon, and passed out top of his class in May 1942.

'He did extremely well in this course,' wrote one of his instructors to Mrs MacKinnon, 'and [I] expect great things of him. I had the honour of being his platoon commander and I thoroughly enjoyed every minute of it. I hope he will write occasionally and let me know how he gets on.'[3]

Standing just five feet seven inches tall, with light brown hair, blue eyes and a pleasant oval face, MacKinnon was not physically imposing. Yet he had done well in both physical and mental tests at Thurlstone, and Hasler must have seen something in his character that convinced him he would thrive in the RMBPD. He was right. A non-smoker who hardly drank alcohol, MacKinnon was high-spirited and sociable, and would play the jazz drums at the unit's parties. He was also athletic, deceptively strong and fearless: his party trick was jumping barefoot from the high Esplanade at Southsea onto the shingle beach.

He was soon a great favourite of officers and men alike. 'A finer man would be impossible to meet,' wrote one of his section to MacKinnon's mother, 'he was loved by all who served under and above him, and I say with all sincerity, a man that everyone was proud of.' Hasler, his commanding officer, described him as 'a very valued member of my unit besides being a close personal friend of mine'.[4]

MacKinnon and Pritchard-Gordon joined Hasler's new unit at Southsea on 4 July and, a couple of days later, were supplemented by two NCOs and four Marines that Hasler had interviewed in Plymouth as potential instructors. By the end of the month the unit had swelled to thirty-five men: a Headquarters Section, a Maintenance Section, and two Boat Sections, each of six two-man canoe teams. The men were housed in two guest houses, the White Heather and Mrs Montague's, with the officers nearby at 9 Spencer Road.[5]

Among the new arrivals was Marine Bill Sparks, a voluble and pugnacious 19-year-old cockney who had been brought up in abject poverty in a tiny two-up, two-down terraced house in London's East End. His earliest memories were of the constant cold and hunger, and vicious fights between his drunken parents, an unemployed former sailor and a factory worker. But despite his tough upbringing, Sparks had a chirpy, upbeat nature. Having left school at 14, he worked as a cobbler until war broke out in 1939. His intention was to follow his father into the Royal Navy; but he was diverted to the Royal Marines by a canny recruiting sergeant who held out the prospect of serving on 'some exotic island, surrounded by beautiful girls in grass skirts'.[6]

Sparks's first eighteen months of active service was as a 4.5-inch gunner on the battlecruiser HMS *Renown*, an eventful period that included escorting convoys, hunting the German battleship *Bismarck*, and clashing with the Italian fleet at the inconclusive battle of Cape Spartivento. But during a spell of sick leave in March 1942, he discovered that his elder brother Benny had been killed when his ship, the light cruiser HMS *Naiad*, was torpedoed off Crete. Raised by their grandparents, Benny was a brilliant footballer and Bill's hero. The news of his death hit his younger brother hard. 'I began hitting the bottle heavily,' he recalled, 'and nothing anyone could say could make me change my mind. And when my leave was over, I remained at home.'

He eventually returned to his unit – persuaded by his father that it was the only way he could 'avenge Benny's death' – and spent a week confined to barracks. One morning, scanning the noticeboard, he saw a 'call for volunteers for specially hazardous service'. Ignoring his father's sage advice not to volunteer 'for anything', he put his name forward. A few days later he was interviewed by a tall young major, prematurely bald but with a 'huge flowing moustache' and blue eyes that 'twinkled'.

'I am Major Hasler,' the officer said softly, before asking a series of questions that made no sense to Sparks.

'Can you swim?'

'Yes, sir.'

'Do you have experience with small boats?'

'No, sir.'

'Are you married?'

'No, sir.'

It was only later that Sparks understood the qualities that Hasler was looking for. He wanted, wrote Sparks, 'unmarried men who possessed a fighting spirit, natural intelligence, resource-fulness and self-reliance. He knew that volunteers like me might end up behind enemy lines, where survival and success would depend equally on intense training and quick wits.'

Convinced that his lack of boating experience would be his undoing, he was surprised and delighted to be on the list of those heading for Southsea. 'I felt,' he remembered, 'ten feet tall. I was going to become a Commando. What I didn't know was that I was to be sent to almost certain death.'[7]

Sparks was assigned to Jack MacKinnon's No. 1 Section and billeted in the White Heather guest house on Worthing Road. It was run by a jolly Welsh lady called Mrs Powell, the wife of a serving Royal Marine, who treated her young guests like family. Just as welcoming was her pretty 15-year-old daughter Heather who was to fall for another of the new arrivals, 20-year-old Marine Bob 'Jock' Ewart, a 'quiet, tall and bony' lad from Glasgow. His other housemates included the Brummie Eric Fisher, a 'very likeable chap who was slightly older than the rest of us'; Yorkshireman David Moffatt, nicknamed 'the Preacher', who 'had a great sense of fun' and became a close friend of Fisher's; and Bill Ellery from Soho, 'a marvellous swimmer, a very good medic and a fine footballer'. Sparks regarded Ellery as 'a generally all-round good man' and they became close pals.

During that first evening at Southsea, they gathered on a stretch of the beach to hear Hasler say a few words of welcome: 'Now, I know you all want to do your bit, but you are by no means in yet, not by a long shot. There are some eliminating exercises to go through, and I'm certain that our numbers will be very much depleted by the end of the day. Training will begin in earnest tomorrow. But for the rest of the evening you can relax and get to know each other.'

Next morning, after a good night's sleep, Sparks felt fit and raring to go. He was shocked, however, when Hasler introduced him and the others to the two-man collapsible canoe. He had been expecting a dinghy, at the very least, not the 'flimsy craft' that Hasler was pointing at.

'Right men, into your swimming trunks,' shouted their senior NCO, Sergeant Sam 'Old Stripey' Wallace. Born in Dublin in 1913, Wallace was an experienced regular who used his keen Irish sense of humour and 'cheerful determination', rather than iron discipline, to inspire his men 'to keep going' when they were exhausted. Tall, dark-haired and tough, he was a man who commanded both 'respect and affection'.

Heeding Wallace's instruction, the men changed in the bell tent on the beach and came out 'ready for the fun to begin'.

They were split into pairs and ordered to try out the canoes. The first group picked up their boat, waded into the shallows and promptly capsized, much to the amusement of their comrades. Hasler watched stony-faced. It turned out that none of the volunteers had experience with small boats. Even Sparks's section commander, Jack MacKinnon (or 'Mac' to his men), was a novice. Sparks recalled:

He was a Glaswegian, broad and athletic, fond of the open air and with a real love of life. He was a top officer, having served in the ranks before earning his commission. He was eager for action against the enemy and just as eager to learn how to cope with these canoes. It was reassuring to see that he was as raw as we were when it came to boats.

When it was Sparks's turn, he said to his partner Eric Fisher, 'Come on. This can't be too difficult.'

They waded into the water, clambered into the canoe and struggled to stay upright. 'Steady! Steady!' shouted Sparks as he felt the craft rolling.

It was too late. Both pitched into the water, Sparks keeping hold of the canoe while Fisher, a non-swimmer, tried to stay afloat. But for his life jacket, noted Sparks, Fisher would have drowned.

From this inauspicious start, things gradually improved. Mac taught Fisher how to swim, and by Hasler the men were shown how to assemble the folbots, until they could do it blindfolded, 'to paddle efficiently, which proved to be far more difficult than it looked', and to navigate at sea, out of sight of land.[8]

They were given lectures about the layout of naval dockyards and how ships are moored, and taught field sketching and note taking, coding and decoding, the use of limpet mines, camouflage and, finally, how to approach a target. But physical fitness was paramount. They raced barefoot along the stony beach – agony for everyone but Jock Ewart who skimmed across the pebbles 'as though he had feet of leather' – built their own assault course under the guidance of their PTI, Sergeant King, and trained in unarmed combat. Sparks particularly enjoyed the latter. 'There was,' he noted, 'a little bit of the wild boy in me, having come from the tough East End of London, but I'd always been active and I thoroughly enjoyed getting into a scrap with someone.'

He came through training unscathed, but not all the recruits were so fortunate. Some got hurt 'quite badly', and those with broken limbs were 'promptly dispatched to hospital and then returned to their units' because, once healed, they were too far behind the others. It was especially heartbreaking for those who had done so well in other aspects of their training.

There were lighter moments. Taught to live off the land, the men became adept at stealing food. 'On one occasion,' recalled Sparks, 'we came across a chicken farm and helped ourselves to a few of the plumpest birds. We made camp by a stream and merrily plucked the chickens, letting the feathers flutter into the stream and drift away. We lit a fire and roasted our mouth-watering booty.' Unfortunately, they were upstream of the chicken farm. Spotting the feathers in the water, the farmer got his gun and went looking for the poachers. He found Sparks and his colleagues polishing off the remains of their meal.

'You chicken thieves!' he roared. 'I ought to shoot you all. I'll blow you off the land.'

'How do you know they're your chickens?' one of the Marines asked.

'Of course they're my chickens.'

'Prove it.'

Unable to do so, he stomped angrily away, prompting the Marines to 'leave his land as soon as lunch was over'.

When no chickens were available, they ate hedgehogs, rats and even worms, and realised that 'things that look repulsive can actually be quite edible'.[9]

19

Operation Frankton

Built in the Regency style of the 1820s, Richmond Terrace in Whitehall was comprised of eight large luxury homes that, unusually for the time, were freestanding and did not face directly onto a street or square. Their famous nineteenth-century residents included the explorer Sir Henry Morton Stanley (No. 2), the ill-fated politician William Huskisson* (No. 3) and the economist Thomas Tooke (No. 7). With the expiry of their leases in the 1920s, however, most were taken into official use and used as an overflow for various government ministries. In 1940, No. 1 became the headquarters for Admiral Keyes' Combined Operations, a stone's throw from its former location in the War Office.

On Friday 18 September 1942, 'Blondie' Hasler was called to a meeting at Richmond Terrace to discuss 'prospective schemes' with Colonel Robert Neville, Mountbatten's chief planning coordinator. Worried that his fledgling unit might soon be absorbed by other more established canoe-borne units like the SBS, Hasler asked to see a list of possible missions because his men, as he put it, were ready for action provided 'it's not a job needing very good navigation or seamanship'. There was, however, nothing suitable and he returned to Southsea disappointed.

Three days later, he was summoned back to Richmond Terrace

---

* As president of the Board of Trade, Huskisson was attending the opening of the Liverpool and Manchester Railway when he was struck and killed by Robert Stephenson's pioneering locomotive *Rocket* on 15 September 1830.

by Lieutenant Colonel Cyril Horton, one of Neville's deputies, who had heard of Hasler's visit and thought he might have something after all. Entering Horton's office, Hasler was handed a document with the heading 'Frankton'. It summarised a major concern for the British government: the use of the port of Bordeaux, sixty miles up the Gironde estuary from the west coast of France, by fast Axis merchant ships who would transport vital military supplies to Japan – including the latest fuses, wireless and radar parts – and return with rubber, wolfram, tin, hides and vegetable oils that were unavailable to the Germans in Europe. Since Germany's invasion of Russia in the summer of 1941, and the closure of the Trans-Siberian rail route, this sea link had become even more vital. At any one time there were as many as ten blockade runners alongside Bordeaux's wharves. Their destruction or interdiction would seriously hamper the Axis war effort.[1]

Various methods had been considered: bombing the port, but as the target area was large it was felt that would result in unacceptable civilian casualties; mining the mouth of the Gironde river, which had been done by the RAF but without any noticeable decrease in sea traffic; and stationing a permanent submarine patrol off the Gironde, which required more vessels than the Royal Navy could spare. That just left an SOE or Commando raid, via a submarine and folbots, which prompted Horton to think of Hasler.[2]

'Is it a mission,' he asked Hasler, 'that your unit could carry out?'

Possibly, said Hasler, but he would need to study the 'Frankton' file before he could give a definite answer. Twenty-four hours later, having worked through the night, he gave Horton and Neville the thumbs up in the form of an outline plan. 'At first examination,' wrote Hasler, in a covering note, 'the Cockle side of the operation appears to have a good chance of success, and it is hoped that RMBPD may be allowed to carry it out.'

Hasler's initial plan involved three folbots and an attacking force of six men. They would be dropped off not more than five miles from the mouth of the Gironde estuary by either a submarine or surface boat, and take four nights to paddle up the river to Bordeaux, lying up each day on the riverbank. During the fourth night, they would attach limpet mines to between ten and twenty cargo vessels at Bordeaux, commencing their withdrawal no later than 2:30 a.m. The limpets would be timed to explode three and a half hours later. Their escape would either be overland or back down the estuary to rendezvous with their pick-up vessel no later than 3:00 a.m. on day eight. As for timing, Hasler estimated that a full spring tide and a new moon would be ideal for an approach in the dark.[3]

Colonel Neville was impressed – it was, he commented later, 'the quickest operational plan on record' – and promised to flesh it out with a study of the natural features of the locality, the probable defences and an accurate prediction of tides and inshore currents. The key figure in this respect was Lieutenant Commander G. P. L'Estrange RNVR, a former Malay rubber planter who was fluent in French and an expert in the topography of France's western coast. It was L'Estrange, noted Hasler, 'who did the bulk of the detailed planning, and personally prepared, with great thoroughness and accuracy, the actual charts, tide tables, etc. used by the attacking force'.[4]

By late October, Hasler and L'Estrange had redrafted the outline plan. It still involved three canoes and six men (including Hasler), but the intention now was to sink a more realistic six to twelve cargo vessels. The attackers would be transported by submarine and dropped nine miles from the Cordouan Lighthouse at the mouth of the Gironde estuary. To take advantage of a flood tide and no moon, the submarine would depart from the Clyde around 25 November and offload the folbots between the nights of 3/4 December and 12/13 December. They would then 'proceed up the Gironde estuary, lying up by day and travelling by night for the full period of the flood tide, reaching an advanced base within ten miles of the objective on the second or third night, and carrying out the attack on the following night'. To return back down the Gironde was no longer considered an option, given the hue and cry that would follow a successful mission. So instead the whole party would 'escape overland through Occupied France to Spain as per special instructions'.[5]

Mountbatten approved the revised plan, but had little expectation that anyone would return safely. With that in mind, he told Hasler that he could not lead the operation: the commander of the RMBPD was too important to lose. Desperate to change Mountbatten's mind, Hasler first approached Neville. 'If they go without me, sir,' said Hasler, 'and don't return, I shall never be able to face the others again.'

He followed this up with a formal appeal to the adjutant general of the Royal Marines in the knowledge that it would be passed on to COHQ. Hasler made four points: it was an 'important' operation with a 'good chance of success', but only Hasler had the 'small-boat seamanship and navigation' skills needed for such a mission; any failure would 'prejudice all future operations'; the commanding officer was duty-bound to go on a new unit's first operation if he wanted to gain his men's respect; and if he was barred from this one, he asked, what type of operation would be permissable for him (after all, had not Major David Stirling accompanied many of the SAS's missions)?

The matter came to a head at a conference to discuss the revised plan for Operation Frankton at Richmond Terrace on 29 October. Reaching the 'Command' paragraph – which stated unequivocally that Major H. G. Hasler OBE, RM would lead the mission – Mountbatten asked: 'But should he, when there is little and, most probably, no chance of returning?'

Hasler's impassioned response was that the plan was his idea; he had trained and selected the men; the canoes were, in large part, his design; and he would not be able to face his men, or continue as their commanding officer, if the mission failed because of his absence. He was determined to lead by example and, moreover, future operations would only benefit from his personal experience.

Of the four other men present, only Neville sided with his fellow Royal Marine. Hasler feared the worst when Mountbatten looked directly at him to give his verdict. But the Chief of Combined Operations surprised everyone by saying: 'Much against my better judgement I am going to let you go.'[6]

Mountbatten had been swayed by Hasler's passion to share his men's fate and, though he might not have admitted it, would have put forward exactly the same arguments himself. In command of a flotilla of destroyers at the start of the war, he had suffered his fair share of accidents and mishaps: after many close shaves, his destroyer *Kelly* was finally sunk by German dive-bombers, with the loss of more than half its crew, off Crete in 1941. Incredibly, though one of the last off the ship, Mountbatten survived to rescue a number of his men who were floundering in the oily waters. For various acts of valour he was awarded two mentions in despatches and a DSO. If there was one thing this flawed but much-loved leader of men understood, it was the responsibility of command.

Hugely relieved, Hasler noted in his diary: '1700 [hrs] – conference . . . to decide if I should be allowed to go. Won after a ding-dong battle.'[7]

Five days later – at a time when its chief focus was on the final stages of Lieutenant General Sir Bernard Montgomery's tide-turning victory over Rommel's Panzerarmee Afrika at the Battle of El Alamein in Egypt* – the British Chiefs of Staff Committee approved the plan for Operation Frankton.[8] Not long after that, Mountbatten doubled the size of the attacking force to a full section of six canoes and twelve men. All that remained, until the date of departure, was to select the men who would go on the mission and continue their training to reflect a long

---

* The huge offensive by Montgomery's 8th Army had begun on 24 October 1942 and by 3 November, the day of the COS meeting, Rommel was close to defeat. A day later General Brooke, Chief of the Imperial General Staff, noted in his diary: 'PM delighted. At 3:30 p.m. he sent for me again to discuss prospect of ringing church bells. I implored him to wait a little longer till we were quite certain that we should have no cause for regretting ringing them.' (Brooke, *War Diaries*, p. 338.) Churchill wrote later: 'It may almost be said, "Before Alamein we never had a victory. After Alamein we never had a defeat."' (Churchill, *The Second World War*, IV, 541.)

approach to the target through enemy-held territory, followed by an overland escape. Much of this was done in Scotland.[9]

*

The men chosen by Hasler for the mission were Lieutenant Jack MacKinnon and the bulk of his No. 1 Section: Sergeant Sam Wallace, corporals Bert Laver and George Sheard, and Marines Jim Conway, Bill Ellery, Bob Ewart, Eric Fisher, Bill Mills, David Moffatt and Bill Sparks.

'Laver,' remembered Sparks, 'was a regular from Barnet, a man of quiet demeanour, round-faced, often keeping himself apart from the evening drink-and-singalongs. He had been present at the sinking of the *Bismarck*.'[10] Born in Birkenhead, Merseyside, the son of a Royal Navy shipwright, 22-year-old Laver was a talented boxer whose one regret having joined the RMBPD was that he was forced to miss his elder brother Jack's wedding. 'I don't mind so much the trip,' he wrote to his brother in mid-November, referring to the final training stint in Scotland, 'but the damned rub is if you're getting married next Sat[urday] your little brother Bert will probably be at the other end of England, and I can't stand for you as best-man Jack, talk about cursed luck.' If Jack had stuck to his original plan of getting married at Christmas, Bert felt certain he would have been there.* 'We're sure to get leave after this trip,' he wrote, 'but it's no good moaning. That won't change it, so you'll have to get me a sub.'[11]

The other corporal, George Sheard, was 'short but tough and often witty, a Devonshire man'. He was also recently married to Renee, a Devonport woman, and the couple were expecting their first child. 'Blondie,' noted Sparks, 'must have thought him invaluable to have included him despite his own rule that only unmarried men could volunteer.'[12]

Of the Marines, Conway was a handsome 20-year-old

---

* Proof that none of the other ranks were told about the mission until they were onboard the submarine HMS *Tuna*.

Stockport lad who 'loved swimming, cycling and his horse'. Before the war he had been a milkman with a horse and cart. 'He would talk to his horse,' recalled Sparks, 'as though it were his best friend and he missed it.' Almost 21, Bill Mills from Kettering was a 'high-spirited lad, stocky, fit, excellent at football and swimming'. Happy to do 'a good turn if needed', he was better-educated than most of his fellow soldiers and had a sweetheart he intended to marry. Sparks 'enjoyed his wit and love of life', and Mills and Ellery became his 'two closest friends in the unit'.[13]

These were the eleven men who, Hasler concluded, 'would best execute the coming mission'.[14]

Their final training exercise was code-named 'Blanket', an attempt to paddle six canoes up the Thames estuary from Margate to Deptford and back unobserved by civilians or military personnel who had been alerted that they were coming. They would cover a total distance of seventy miles and, if challenged, would respond with the password 'Blanket'.[15] It would be the first proper outing for the new and improved Goatley or 'Cockle' Mark II canoe, capable of carrying 480 pounds of equipment and a crew of two. 'It was very much like the original Cockle,' noted Bill Sparks, 'but more robust. Even in the calmest sea, propelling these canoes throughout the night, as we often did, was exhausting. Most of the strain was on the shoulders and arms, and apart from regular arm-strengthening exercises, we had to rest every hour for five minutes to prevent muscles being strained beyond their limits.'[16]

The exercise began at Margate at 8:15 p.m. on 10 November, and finished in the early hours of the 14th. The results were not encouraging. Hasler and Sparks led off in the first canoe, and quickly lost contact with the rest of the party. 'We were not to see them again,' wrote Sparks, 'for the rest of the exercise.' He claimed that, despite close encounters with patrol boats, they got to Deptford and back 'without having been spotted or challenged'.[17]

In fact, all the canoes were challenged at least twice, and only one – Hasler's – got close to Deptford. The rest failed to complete the approach, chiefly because of poor navigation and a lack of stamina. At one point MacKinnon and Jim Conway ran aground on mudflats in fog and, having lost their sense of direction, set off the way they had come. Hasler later described the exercise as a 'complete failure'. At the debrief meeting, recalled Sparks, he was 'in a foul mood, and spared no breath in telling us exactly what he thought of us'. Despite all the training, they had 'let him down' and 'obviously were not ready for operations'.

Sparks and the others were deeply upset as they felt they were. Mountbatten, however, was far from downhearted. 'In that case,' he told Hasler, on hearing the details, 'you must have learned a great deal from your mistakes, and you'll be able to avoid making them again during the operation.'[18]

20

'A magnificent bunch of black-faced villains'

On Monday 30 November 1942, Bob 'Jock' Ewart wrote to his 15-year-old sweetheart from the bowels of the T-class submarine HMS *Tuna*:

Dear Heather – I trust it won't be necessary to have this sent to you but since I don't know the outcome of this little adventure I thought I'd leave this note behind in the care of Norman [Colley]* who will forward it to you should anything unpredictable happen . . . I couldn't help but love you Heather, although you were so young. I will always love you as I know you do me. That alone should [get] me through this but one never knows the turns of fate. One thing I ask of you, Heather, is not to take it too hard. You have yet your life to live. Think of me as a good friend and keep your chin up. Some lucky fellow will find you who has more sense than I had and who can get you what you deserve . . . With your picture in front of me I feel confident that I shall pull through and get back to you some day . . . Thanking you and your mother from the bottom of my heart, at present in your care.

God bless and keep you all.

Yours for ever,

Bob

* Marine Norman Colley, 22, from Pontefract in Yorkshire, was Second Lieutenant MacKinnon's original canoe partner. Replaced by Marine Conway after he broke a bone in his foot playing football barefoot, he was on board HMS *Tuna* as first reserve.

In a separate letter to his parents and two brothers, Ewart explained:

> I volunteered for a certain job, which I trust you will learn about at a later period. I've enjoyed every minute of it and hope that what we have done helps to end the mess we are in and make a decent and better world . . . I have a feeling I'll be like a bad penny, so please don't upset yourself over my safety. My heart will be with you always, you are the best parents one could wish to have. Anyway, Mum, you can always say you had a son in the most senior service and, though I say it myself, 'one of twelve heroes'.[*1]

Hasler and his men had begun their mission earlier that day when *Tuna* left its depot ship in the Clyde estuary and headed for open water. Carefully stowed in *Tuna*'s forward torpedo room were their six collapsed canoes – still packed in their canvas covers – and assorted arms and equipment. Per canoe, this included: three double paddles with elliptical blades; a bailer and sponge; P8 compass and corrector; escape kit; log pads including tide tables; dim reading torch with spare bulbs and batteries; protractors; waterproof watches; camouflage cream and net; eight six-magnet limpet mines; limpet spanners and two placing rods; compact rations for two men for five days; five half-gallon tins of water; a box of Benzedrine tablets; water-sterilising kits; field dressings; bottle of iodine; two morphia syringes; five Hexamine cookers (a tin tripod over a paraffin block); two tins of cough lozenges and laxative pills; and two packets of toilet paper.

To save weight, each man was lightly armed with a Colt .45 automatic pistol, fighting knife and Type 69 hand grenade. Only the officers – Hasler and MacKinnon – were also equipped with a silenced Sten 9 mm submachine gun (weighing just seven

---

* There were in fact thirteen 'heroes' on board: the twelve who would carry out the mission and Marine Colley, the first reserve.

pounds). For personal use, they all had an extra pair of short pants, a rollneck sweater, felt soled boots and socks, woollen gloves, twenty cigarettes and toiletries.[2]

An hour into the voyage, Hasler called a meeting of his men in the twenty-five-feet long forward torpedo room. In amongst the stacked canoes and cargo bags, he had erected a blackboard. Once all the men were assembled, packed into the restricted space like sardines, he turned the board round to reveal a map of the Gironde estuary in France. 'So sorry to disappoint you,' he said, fully aware of the rumours that they were heading for Scandinavia to sink the German battleship *Tirpitz*. 'We're not going to Norway after all. We're going to France.'

His grin faded. 'This is the real thing. The Germans have a fleet of fast, armed ships – blockade runners – operating from the safe harbour of Bordeaux, and running to Japan. These ships are too fast for our submarines to catch. To send in planes to catch them is out of the question because it would have to be high-level bombing and thus liable to be inaccurate; a lot of French people would be killed by our bombs. So Combined Operations has decided to send in someone to blow up these ships. That someone is us.'

As Hasler paused to let his words sink in, Bill Sparks felt only relief. He had assumed the trip to Norway was going to be a 'one-way ticket', as it was such a long way from home, but France 'somehow felt closer, almost on our doorstep'. The major continued: 'The submarine will take five days to reach the point where we'll be put over the side: somewhere in the Bay of Biscay, some ten miles to the south of a headland called Pointe de Grave. Then we're on our own. Passing between the headland and the small island of Cordouan, we'll paddle up the estuary of the Gironde some sixty miles to the port of Bordeaux. And there, we hope, we'll find the blockade runners and sink them.'

The mission, he explained, was code-named Operation Frankton. It would take them 'four days to paddle up the estuary, travelling by night only, lying up during the day, camouflaged on the riverbanks'. Naturally they would have to take care to avoid the locals. One small word in the wrong ear could alert the enemy.

They would travel together for the first night, and then split into two parties of three canoes each. Hasler would command the first group – A Division – made up of his and Sparks's canoe *Catfish*, Laver and Mills's *Crayfish* and Sheard and Moffatt's *Conger*. B Division, under MacKinnon, would consist of his and Conway's *Cuttlefish*, Wallace and Ewart's *Coalfish* and Ellery and Fisher's *Cachalot*. On reaching the target area, A Division would attack the south side of the harbour, while B concentrated on the north.

Hasler then handed out a full set of aerial photographs to each man. The photos showed, in sections, the full course of the river so that the men could choose the best lying-up places. He also gave the men a list of useful French phrases in case they were approached: he was the only one who spoke the language.

'This is just "Blanket" all over again,' said Hasler, hoping to reassure his men but forgetting the mishaps. 'It's going to be tough, but we can do it. Are there any questions?'[3]

Irishman Sam Wallace put his hand up. 'How do we get back, sir?'[4]

'I'm glad you asked that,' said Hasler. 'So here is the bad side of the operation. Because it will take us four days to get to the target area, when the job is complete it will naturally take us four days to get out again. By which time, of course, the balloon will have gone up and the Germans will be searching high and low for us. We can't ask the submarine to wait all that time for us or she may be discovered herself. So, when the job is complete, we will paddle back downriver for about five miles, and there we will scuttle our canoes and make our way across land for the escape.'

Hearing those words, Sparks realised they had been given 'only a one-way ticket' after all.

'There are plans in place,' continued Hasler. 'After the raid, we'll split up and each crew will make its own way across land. We'll all have a bag of escape gear, and use it to travel on foot to a little town called Ruffec. There we need to make contact with someone from the French underground. The Resistance people have been told we're coming, so when we're sure these people are genuine, we're to leave the rest of the escape plans to them.'

After another pause, he said: 'One more thing. Anyone who gets into trouble will be on his own. One man's peril must not jeopardise the operation, and there will be no exceptions to this rule. I realise that this is a bit more than I originally asked of you, so if any man thinks that he is not quite up to it, let him speak up now. I assure you that no one will think any the less of you for it.'[5]

He looked around the room. Some of the men had their heads down, as if concerned. But one by one they looked up and grinned.

Hasler smiled too. 'After all,' he said, 'it's a good deal less dangerous than a bayonet charge.'

Wallace continued the levity: 'If I get captured, I'm going to declare myself neutral, because I'm Irish!'

With everyone committed, Hasler gave some more advice. If approached by a hostile craft, they should take evasive action. If there was no time, adopt a hunkered-down position. If that didn't work, and a craft came alongside, they were to use grenades prior to boarding. But they were never to take offensive action, he insisted, unless compelled to do so. Their first priority was to get through to Bordeaux. If discovered on land, they were to kill silently with a knife and hide the body below the low-water mark.

By now, they had few illusions about what they were being asked to do: it would be hard enough getting to Bordeaux unde-tected; the chances of escape, overland, were diminishingly small. Yet morale, remembered Eric Fisher, could not have been higher: 'We all had tremendous faith in the major and would have followed him anywhere . . . We were going to have a smack at Jerry and he wouldn't know what had hit him. Everyone was in fine shape and rarin' to go.'[6]

With the meeting over, Hasler advised everyone to write their final letters and give them to Norman Colley. He would post them if they did not return. It was now that Bob Ewart penned his two heartfelt letters to Heather and his family. Jack MacKinnon also wrote a short note to his mother:

> You will not hear from me for a number of weeks, so don't on any account worry over the fact you get no letters . . . Remember, dear, look after yourself and Dad, and the children, and I will 'carry on watching crossing the road'. Well cheerio just now, and above all don't worry about me. With lots of love and kisses to you all.
>
> Your loving son, Jacky. xxxxxxxx. xxxxxxxx.[7]

*

Shortly after midday on 6 December, the French coast was sighted through *Tuna*'s periscope and preparations were begun to disembark the canoes that evening. It was not a moment too soon for Hasler and his men. The sea had been typically rough on the journey south through the Bay of Biscay, and most of the Marines were 'dreadfully seasick'. Sparks recalled: 'Our sleeping quarters, among the stores in the forward torpedo room, were not exactly comfortable for those who were ill, and even when the sickness wore off, some of the men were badly hit by bouts of claustrophobia. Unused to life on board a submarine, seasickness was aggravated further by limited sanitary facilities and the foul air that gave us headaches and made us drowsy.'

Told an end to their torment was in sight, Hasler's men were 'itching to get going'. Sparks remembered 'waves of excitement and anticipation' running through the boat.[8] But they were to be disappointed. *Tuna*'s skipper, 30-year-old Lieutenant Commander Dickie Raikes RN, failed to establish their position with 'sufficient certainty' and so postponed the operation for a day. 'This was unfortunate,' noted Raikes, 'as conditions were quite perfect, a nice mist coming down immediately after dark.'[9]

Yet an accurate 'fix' was vital because, as Raikes's deputy explained, 'the RAF had laid a minefield very near where we were planning to disembark the canoes and in any case we could not rely on the RAF's stated position [of the minefield]. The captain and Hasler were obviously most concerned about this.'[10]

The following day, Raikes took *Tuna* north at periscope depth and finally got a fix at 1:45 p.m. There was intense enemy air activity overhead, and at one point they spotted an armed trawler that appeared to be patrolling a line that ran 'nearly through' the 'intended position for disembarking'. As a result, Raikes decided to disembark the canoes closer to the coast than originally planned, and nearer the RAF's 'badly laid mines', much to Hasler's 'evident delight'. The plan now entailed 'coming to full buoyancy four miles off the coast' and 'doing the whole operation in one'.

Tuna surfaced in a flat calm at 7:15 p.m. 'Patrol boat was in sight,' noted Raikes, 'but about four miles away. It was a beastly clear night.'[11]

Calling Hasler up from the wardroom, Raikes mentioned the lack of cover and the presence of the enemy, adding nonchalantly: 'Looks all right for your launching. Do you want to start?'

Hasler took a welcome gulp of fresh air and gazed at the dark French coastline to the east. 'Yes,' he said.

Raikes spoke into the voice-pipe: 'Up canoes.'

Once the order was given, Hasler's men sprung into action. They had already assembled the canoes, inflated the buoyancy bags and packed their equipment in five compartments. They had eaten a final meal and were wearing, over their usual battle-dress trousers and sweater, an olive green and black camouflage waterproof jacket (with Royal Marine and Combined Operations badges sewn on each shoulder) and waders. They also had on a pair of rope-soled plimsolls, a blue woollen cap and mittens, and an uninflated life jacket. Strapped to their waists were a Colt .45 automatic pistol and fighting knife. Their faces were smeared with black camouflage cream.

Given the green light, and supervised by Lieutenant MacKinnon, they began to manoeuvre the canoes up through the torpedo loading hatch and on to the casing. This was a delicate operation as it meant pushing a semi-loaded canoe at an angle of forty-five degrees, and it did not go entirely to plan. The third canoe out, Bill Ellery and Eric Fisher's *Cachalot* (part of MacKinnon's B Division), was snagged on the hatch clamp which tore an eighteen-inch gap in its rubberised canvas side. Called down from the bridge to assess the damage, Hasler knew immediately it was terminal. He turned to Ellery and Fisher. 'I'm afraid you can't go,' he said, grim-faced. 'You must abort your mission and return home with the submarine.'

'Let us try, sir,' pleaded Ellery.

'You'll fill up with water and sink.'

'We can bail out fast enough, sir. And in the morning we'll be able to mend it.'

Hasler was adamant: they were going home. On hearing this, Eric Fisher 'burst into tears'. Ellery was equally devastated, but kept his composure.

Before launching, Hasler said farewell to Raikes. 'Thanks for everything you've done on our behalf, it's time to get along.'

They shook hands. 'The very best of luck to you all,' said Raikes.

'And to you,' replied Hasler. 'I'll be back in March. Will you book a table at the Savoy for lunch on the 1st April?'

'Not bloody likely,' said Raikes, smiling, 'but I'll book one for the 2nd.'

Hasler joined Sparks in *Catfish*, the first canoe to be lifted from the casing into the water using slings and a four-foot steel extension fitted to the four-inch gun. As this was underway, noted Raikes, 'searchlights suddenly started sweeping the sea from Pointe de la Négade and all down the coast, but there was no light opposite us'. He had 'an uncomfortable feeling' that this activity was due to the fact that the submarine had been plotted by a radar station onshore, and the suspicion was 'strengthened by the fact that the [armed] trawler was evidently closing'. Yet he allowed the remaining canoes to be launched.

When all five were in the water, the occupants waved to their two comrades, standing forlornly on the upper casing. Ellery and Fisher responded: 'Good luck!'

It was now 8:20 p.m. and the disembarkation had taken just forty minutes. 'I consider . . . this time was remarkably fast,' reported Raikes, 'and reflects great credit on Lieutenant [Johnny] Bull and his upper deckhands.'

Shortly after, having waved 'au revoir' to, as he put it, 'a magnificent bunch of black-faced villains' with whom it had been 'a real pleasure to work', Raikes ordered *Tuna* to dive and withdraw to the south-west.

Heading for the mouth of the Gironde, Sparks heard 'a slight roar and, turning, saw the black hulk of the submarine sliding away'. They were 'alone'.[12]

'God bless you both'

With *Catfish* leading, the five canoes set off on a north-easterly bearing, intending to pass to the west of the Pointe de la Négade, five miles south of the entrance to the Gironde estuary. The sea was 'oily-calm with a low groundswell'. There was no cloud, but for a slight haze over the land, and it felt bitterly cold.[1]

Away to his right, Sparks could see lights blinking from farmhouses on the shore, a sight that was oddly comforting. The heavily laden canoes, he recalled, 'rode low and the spray of small waves broke over our cockpits, freezing into a frosted coating'. Even so, he was sweating with exertion. He recalled:

> We paddled in silence. All I heard was the breaking of the bow wave and the gentle splashing of paddles. Communication was by hand signals, and the canoes had to remain close enough to see any signals being passed. Occasionally we had to close up, or raft up, and hold on to each other's craft to enable the major to whisper the orders.

After paddling for more than three hours, they could hear the 'vague sound of roaring ahead'. Told to raft up, they were informed by Hasler that this was a tidal race where several currents meet. 'It's going to be pretty rough,' he said, 'but don't worry. Just treat it like rough weather and we'll soon be through it.'

Having tightened their cockpit covers, they set off again. 'Suddenly,' recalled Sparks in *Catfish*, 'we found ourselves tossed about like a cork, as though we were in rapids. We fought desperately to control the canoe with our paddles, finding this far worse than any rough weather we had ever encountered. Four-foot waves, monsters for any canoe, crashed down on us from all directions. I felt sure we would be swamped as we bucked and turned, fighting with all the skills we'd acquired to keep the canoe upright.'[2]

Then, just as quickly as they had entered the race, they were in calm waters again. They had survived, noted Hasler, by manoeuvring the bows 'into the waves' and keeping the cockpit cover 'securely fastened'.[3] Panting with exertion, they looked back to see Laver and Mills appear in *Crayfish*, followed by Sheard and Moffatt in *Conger*. Finally, *Cuttlefish* arrived, crewed by MacKinnon and Conway. But there was no sign of Wallace and Ewart in *Coalfish*.

'We'll go back to look for them,' Hasler told Sparks, and they turned into the surging waters of the race. Sparks blew the whistle round his neck, and mimicked the cry of a seagull. But there was no answering cry, and no sign of wreckage. They had 'vanished into the night'. Sparks recalled a 'leaden feeling of loss – loss of our friends and a third of our force'.

Returning to the others, they continued on their way until they came to a second race, this one more turbulent than the first. Waves as high as five feet broke over *Catfish*, threatening to engulf it. The tiny craft 'pitched and bucked, tossed about like a matchstick'. As before Sparks feared the worst until, without warning, they reached calmer water again. This time only two canoes caught up. *Conger* was missing. They headed back into the torrent a second time, and were soon joined in their search by the other canoes.

Eventually they spotted *Conger* capsized and its crew in the water, their 'blue lips trembling'. Telling Sheard to hold on to the stern of his boat, and Moffatt to grab on to MacKinnon's *Cuttlefish*, Hasler thought it might be possible to bail out the flooded boat. But when Sparks turned it over, he realised it was full of water and impossible to refloat. 'Very well,' said Hasler, 'you'll have to scuttle her.'

Having retrieved some of *Conger*'s limpet mines, which he shared with the other crews, Sparks took out his clasp knife and slashed great gashes in the canoe's sides. Within seconds it had sunk.

Hasler was now faced with an awful dilemma. He had earlier told the men that anyone who got into trouble was on his own. Yet if he followed this rule strictly, and left Sheard and Moffatt to fend for themselves in the freezing water, they were as good as dead. The alternative was to tow them to the nearest beach. But that was likely to be infested with the enemy and might jeopardise the whole operation. It was a no-win situation and Sparks could see that the major was 'tormented'. Eventually he decided on a compromise: to tow the two men as close to the beach as it was safe to go. 'Hang on,' he told them.[4]

With Sheard and Moffatt acting as drag anchors, the going was slow. They passed through a third, less violent, tidal race and eventually approached the mouth of the estuary where the revolving beams from the lighthouse 'had just been switched on at full strength and lit up the scene quite brilliantly for a time'.[5] Sparks felt that at any moment they might be 'sighted and fired upon'. But no shots came. He recalled:

> Now the tide gave us a helping hand, carrying us round the Pointe de Grave and into the Gironde. Only twenty minutes had passed since we had found Sheard and Moffatt – it seemed like hours – and both men were weak with exhaustion and shivering with cold. Time was against us. The tide would soon be turning and we would be swept back into the bay. The major had to make a terrible decision.

Ordering the three canoes to raft up, Hasler told the two men in the water: 'I'm sorry, but this is as close to the beach as we dare go. From here you will have to swim the rest of the way.'[6]

He knew, of course, that in their state they would be extremely lucky to survive. He wrote later: 'The two men in the water were finally left in a position about 1½ miles south east of the

Pointe de Graves . . . From this position the tide should have carried them very close to the mole at Le Verdon, but they were already very cold and unable to swim effectively. Both men were wearing life jackets fully inflated.'[7]

At the time, he said: 'I wish I could take you further, but if we're all caught the operation will be at an end, and none of us want that. Get yourselves ashore, make your escape overland as best you can.'

'It's all right, sir,' replied Sheard. 'We understand.'

Both men reached up to shake hands and wish their comrades luck. Laver responded by handing Sheard an illicit flask of Pusser's rum, provided by the submarine crew. Ignoring the infraction, Hasler said to the men in the water, 'God bless you both.'

Once the men had let go, the three canoes paddled off. 'It was too painful to look back at them,' recalled Sparks. 'Blondie's heart must have been heavy. He knew he was leaving them to their fate. I could hear him sobbing.'[8]

Having wasted so much time in the attempted rescue, Hasler knew it was no longer possible to reach his planned lying-up position on the east bank before it got light. They were also much closer inshore than 'had been intended', and 'the strength of the tide compelled them to pass between the mole at Le Verdon and a line of three or four anchored vessels lying about ¾ mile north-east of it'.[9]

These were the patrol boats they had been warned about. They rafted up, and Hasler issued his orders. They would go through one at a time, using a single paddle and their lowest position, and making as little noise as possible. He and Sparks went first, crouching low, their faces almost touching the cockpit cover. The only sound they made was the dripping of the water from their single-paddle blades. They passed the first boat without incident. But as they reached the second one it began signalling to the shore with a lamp. 'We kept paddling,' recalled Sparks, 'hardly daring to breathe. Then to our horror we saw that there was a jetty ahead which we were going to have to pass, and on it stood a sentry.'

They paddled on, drawing close to the jetty. Rivulets of sweat washed camouflage cream into Sparks's mouth. It tasted bitter. His fear was not for himself, but that the mission would fail. It made him 'more cautious, more careful' in everything he did. He had 'never felt so alive', his senses 'keener, sharper, more acute' than at any time in his life.

They passed the jetty and the third boat, with Sparks expecting to hear gunshots at any moment. His back felt exposed. But the shots never came. Once in the clear, they paused to wait for the others. *Crayfish* appeared 'like a ghost' and Laver gave the thumbs up. More minutes passed with no sign of MacKinnon and Conway in *Cuttlefish*. Eventually they saw a light flash from the second patrol boat, then heard a shout that was answered from the jetty. Sparks tried his seagull call, but there was no response. It was now 6:00 a.m. and, with dawn not far off, they needed to find cover.[10]

With heavy hearts, they headed south and picked up the west bank of the estuary near the Chenal de Talais at 6:30 a.m. The tide was beginning to turn, making paddling more difficult, and Sparks had 'never felt so mentally and physically exhausted'. Their first attempt to land was thwarted by a line of half-submerged stakes that had been placed on an offshore shingle bank, not a defensive position but the 'outer wall of saltings'. It was only as 'daylight was breaking', noted Hasler, that they 'were able to get ashore on a small sandy promontory near the Pointe des Oiseaux'.

Hitting the beach, Hasler jumped out and went to investigate. Minutes later he reappeared and signalled that all was clear. They hauled the remaining two boats out of the water and carried them up to some low scrub above the high-water mark where they were 'concealed as well as possible with the camou-flage nets'. Then they boiled some tea on the Hexamine cooker and ate some of their special compact rations. Their hasty meal over, they climbed under the camouflage net and into their canoes, having first removed the cargo bags so that they could 'lie down, two in each boat, stretched from bow to stern'. Hasler took the first watch.

Before falling asleep, Sparks reflected on the consequences of losing two-thirds of their strike force in one night. It seemed to him, after such a disastrous start, that 'the operation was doomed to failure'.[11]

*

It almost ended a few hours later when some small fishing boats emerged from a nearby creek and anchored just offshore. At the same time a band of local women and children appeared to prepare breakfast for the fishermen. Hasler and his men lay under their camouflage nets 'as the men from the boats came ashore and approached their womenfolk'. They began to chat away 'quite happily' just a few yards from the concealed canoes. 'We silently prayed not to be discovered,' recalled Sparks. 'Then their chattering ceased. All became quiet, and we realised that they had become aware of our presence.'

Hasler knew he had to act. 'I'll try and convince them that we're friends,' he told Sparks. 'All the same keep me covered.'

The major got up, unbuckled his pistol and approached the civilians. Speaking in French, he told them that they were British and 'asked them, as good Frenchmen, not to say anything to anybody'.

The sudden appearance of this strange, tall black-faced apparition, clad in black and green camouflage, alarmed some of the locals who looked 'surprised, suspicious, even frightened'. Some disbelieved his story, saying they must be Germans, but Hasler 'pointed out that in any case it would be better for them to keep silent on the subject'. After a brief discussion among themselves, one of the fishermen told Hasler 'they would say nothing'.

The major returned to his men. 'I think we'll be all right,' he told them. In truth, their only option was to hope for the best. 'We could hardly take them hostage,' noted Sparks, 'and hold them all day; someone was bound to become anxious about them and come looking for them.'

Eventually the locals finished their breakfast and left. But Sparks and the others were fearful that someone – possibly one of the children – might say something. Their prospects, if the Germans caught them, were 'unthinkable'. It was, as a result, an 'unbearably long' day. Sparks and Mills tried to pass the time by recalling their escapades 'ashore in Portsmouth and the fights we had won and lost'. They laughed at the memories, prompting Hasler to comment: 'If we're in trouble, we can always trust you to laugh over it.' Humour, Sparks realised later, was his way 'of coping with the terrible uncertainty'.

At 4:00 p.m. some of the French women returned 'for a further chat', noted Hasler, 'but as we were otherwise undisturbed it seemed as if they had followed our instructions'. Then followed another long wait for the flood tide to begin at 11:30 p.m. At around dusk, Hasler was convinced he could see a line of German soldiers approaching. The men readied their weapons, determined to fight to the finish. But they were soon told to stand down. 'Those enemy soldiers,' said Hasler, 'are nothing but a row of anti-invasion stakes.'

Around 11:00 p.m., with the tide at its lowest ebb, they began to drag the canoes by their painters 'over nearly ¾ mile of sandy mud'. Soaked with sweat, they struggled to launch them across 'outlying sandbanks' and 'small breaking rollers'. Once out into the main shipping channel, however, the going was much easier. They kept a cable's length – or 200 yards or so – from the port or left bank (easily visible by navigation buoys flashing a dim blue light). The weather was 'flat calm, no cloud, visibility good but with haze over both shores'.

They paddled at a fast pace, dipping their paddles into the water 'in an almost robotic fashion'. Freezing cold water seeped into their gloves, numbing fingers, and the sheer exertion of paddling non-stop soon caught up with Sparks who began to flag. Noticing the canoe was not keeping a straight line, Hasler stopped and revived his No. 2 with a Benzedrine tablet, advising the other pair to do the same. The amphetamine soon had the desired effect, with Sparks feeling as if he 'could match any pace the major set us'. Bar the occasional rest, they kept at it for the next six hours and covered twenty-five miles. As dawn approached, they moved closer to the east (or right) bank to find somewhere to lie up just north of Port des Callonges. It was, recalled Hasler, 'extremely cold, so much so that the splashes of salt water were freezing on the cockpit covers. We were fortunate in finding a suitable field at the first attempt, and got the boats in against a thick hedge with the nets over them. There was a farmhouse about 300 yards away, but we were undisturbed during daylight in spite of the arrival of a herd of cows in our field.'

Their plan of movement for the night of 9/10 December was complicated by the fact that there would be three hours of flood tide, followed by six of ebb, and then another three of flood before daybreak. That required an intermediate lying-up place on a feature that Hasler had dubbed the 'Desert Island'. But in order to catch as much tide as possible, he got the men moving while it was still dusk and they were spotted by a French farmer with a dog. 'He came strolling along,' wrote Sparks, 'whistling, unaware of the danger he was in. We were ready to do whatever was necessary had he proved in any way hostile. He virtually walked on top of us.'

Once again, Hasler did the talking. 'We are British Commandos,' he said in French, 'here to do a job. As a good Frenchman, I ask you to say nothing about us to anyone.'

Unable to understand the language, Sparks could only gauge the farmer's expression which moved quickly from surprise to laughter. Hasler grinned in response, and said to his men: 'He wants us to go and have a drink with him.'

'What are we waiting for?' asked Sparks.

Hasler chuckled. 'Sorry, Bill, but not this time.'

'But this man could turn out to be a good ally if we stop and have a drink.'

Hasler was unmoved. Turning back to the farmer, he said in French: 'Thank you, but not today. After the war we will come back and have that drink.'

The farmer shook each of them by the hand. '*Bonne chance!*'

he said. 'I hate the Nazis. Your secret is safe with me.' Then he left with his dog.

As time was short, they got quickly underway but soon had to hide in thick reeds at the water's edge as a motor boat passed by. Hasler became increasingly conscious of the noise they were making as they paddled at cruising speed in a narrow channel between two islands. Their stopping place, 'Desert Island', provided plenty of good cover with its thick reeds and occasional trees. But it was hard to land on its near-vertical banks and finally, after many attempts, they found somewhere they could get ashore and hide the boats.

They set off again at 2:00 a.m. and, crossing the ship's channel, soon found themselves in the narrow passage between Île Verte and the left (or west) bank of the river, home to the famous Margaux vineyards. There was no sign of life, but they made themselves 'as inconspicuous as possible', noted Hasler, 'by using single paddles and keeping right in close to the shores of the island, which are covered with tall reeds'. At 6:30 a.m., approaching the southern end of the same island (a feature known confusingly as Île Cazeau), Hasler began to scout for another place to lie up. He eventually found a small pier, close to the southern tip, and went inland to investigate. Minutes later, he was back with the alarming news that a German anti-aircraft battery was sited just forty yards away. They left in a hurry.

By now, it was 'getting light and to continue any further would be suicide'. So they decided to take their chances on the island, landing where the bank was 'steep, muddy and slippery'. It took a gargantuan effort to haul the boats up the bank, their feet slipping and their clothes caked with mud. With no reeds for cover, they carried the canoes to a patch of long grass in the middle of a field and covered them as best they could with the camouflage nets. 'We were not observed at all in this position,' noted Hasler, 'although a man and a dog came within a hundred yards of us and at one time a herd of cattle came and stood around in a circle looking at us.'

The original plan had been to attack the ships at Bordeaux on the night of 10/11 December. But as they were not yet high enough up the river to allow them to carry out the operation and withdraw while it was still dark, Hasler decided to use the night of the 10th to move to an advanced base, with the attack rescheduled for 11/12 December. They left at 6:45 p.m. under an overcast sky and occasional showers, ideal cover for this penultimate leg of their epic journey. For the first two miles they used double paddles, then switched to single ones as the river narrowed and the port of Bordeaux came into view. Just beyond a pontoon pier opposite Bassens South, they found a small gap in the reeds into which they were able to force the boats. It was 11:00 p.m. on 10 December and, against all odds, they were now in the perfect position to complete their mission. 'We had come so far,' noted Sparks, 'that we had no intention of failing now.'[12]

'We froze, hardly daring to breathe'

'As daylight grew brighter,' recalled Bill Sparks, 'we were able to take stock of our position. We were directly opposite a dock in which, lying alongside the jetty, were two big merchant ships, the *Alabama* and the *Portland*.'

It was the morning of 11 December 1942 and, as was now evident, Hasler and his men had found the perfect hide: 'quite inaccessible and well concealed', yet with an excellent view of the river traffic. Meanwhile just yards in the other direction were houses and the noise of cars and trucks passing along a road. Confident they could not be seen among the tall reeds, they were 'relatively comfortable and able to talk in low whispers and smoke'. For much of the day they slept in their canoes, conserving their strength for the task ahead. All were in good humour, delighted and relieved to have 'penetrated so deep into enemy territory'.[1]

As the light began to fade, they ate a final meal before completing the delicate task of fusing the limpet mines, using a nine-hour setting on the delay to give them enough time to get away. This involved two tasks: breaking the tiny orange glass ampoule that contained the chemical fuse with a thumbscrew, thus allowing acid gradually to 'seep its way into the compartment containing the explosive, and so detonate the mine'; and using pliers to ignite the synthetic fuse, 'a very delicate piece of work that was designed to activate the mine in the case of another mine exploding prematurely, thus ensuring that all the mines exploded together'. They also tested the six-feet long

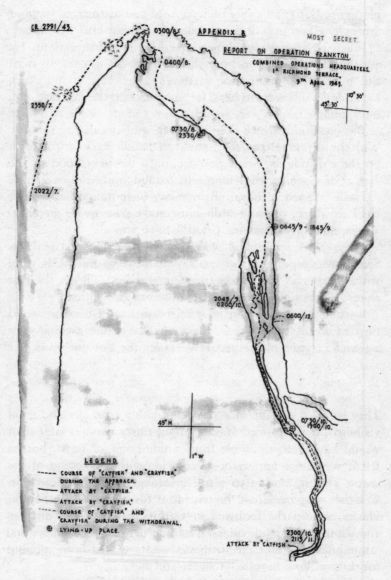

CR 2991/43.

0300/8.

APPENDIX B

MOST SECRET.

REPORT ON OPERATION FRANKTON

COMBINED OPERATIONS HEADQUARTERS.
1A RICHMOND TERRACE.
9TH APRIL 1943.

0400/8.

2350/7.

45° 30'

10° 30'

0730/8.
2330/8.

2022/7.

0645/9 - 1845/9.

2045/9
0200/10.

0600/12.

45° N

1° W

0730/10.
1900/10.

LEGEND

------- COURSE OF "CATFISH" AND "CRAYFISH"
DURING THE APPROACH.

———— ATTACK BY "CATFISH."

———— ATTACK BY "CRAYFISH"

------- COURSE OF "CATFISH" AND
"CRAYFISH" DURING THE WITHDRAWAL.

⊕ LYING-UP PLACE.

2300/10.
2115/11.
ATTACK BY "CATFISH"

The course taken by the canoes *Catfish* and *Crayfish* during
Operation Frankton, December 1942.

placing rods, to make sure they engaged and disengaged without a problem, and put all their escape equipment into two bags.[2]

When all was ready, Hasler issued his final instructions. He and Sparks would 'penetrate the main docks' on the western side of the river and attack whatever targets they found there; Laver and Mills were to head for the docks on the east side and, if no suitable targets were found, return and attack the two ships at Bassens South which they had been studying during the day. With the job completed, they would all 'paddle back downstream on the ebb tide as far as possible, until the next flood or the arrival of morning, then scuttle the canoes and head overland'.

Hasler turned to Laver. 'Remember, Corporal, when the job has been done, you and Mills must make your own way back. We cannot travel together. Good luck to you all.'

They shook hands and wished each other the best of luck. Sparks was especially sorry to say goodbye to Bill Mills who, with Ellery, was his closest friend in the unit. 'I'll get the first round,' Sparks promised, 'when we return to Southsea.'

It would be a belated birthday celebration for Mills who would turn 21 in just four days. Sparks and Laver, meanwhile, were 20- and 22-years-old respectively. Hasler, the 'gov'nor', was 28.[3]

*

They left at 9:15 p.m. in a 'flat calm with a clear sky and good visibility'. It was, noted Hasler, 'about thirty minutes later than would have been desirable from a tide point of view', but he felt it was more important to coincide with the setting of the moon at just after 9:30 p.m. Laver and Mills went first in *Crayfish*, slipping across the river towards the east (right) bank. Hasler and Sparks followed in *Catfish*, paddling out just far enough to find the tide on the west side. 'It was,' recalled Sparks, 'an exhilarating moment; this was what we had been training for during those months of sweat and toil.'

As Hasler and Sparks approached the basin of Bordeaux, they could see a 'good many lights' shining from the jetties, particularly around the lock gates, which prompted them to keep well away from the shore. They inspected possible targets as they 'passed silently by', including various tankers and cargo ships that had been moored in a row. It was, wrote Sparks, 'very thoughtful of the Germans, making our targets so readily accessible'. Having reached two ships rafted together, the larger inner one partially obscured by a German auxiliary naval vessel known as a *Sperrbrecher*,* Hasler decided to turn back and tackle the previous option, a large cargo ship. Thanks to the late start, he wrote, 'it was not possible to examine more than half the length of the target area before the tide began to ebb and it became impossible to proceed any further in silence'.

Pulling alongside the black hull of the cargo ship – which they estimated at 7,000 tons – they were shrouded in darkness. 'We could hear the crew singing,' remembered Sparks.

> I wondered what they'd be singing in a few hours' time. It proved to be an easy target. I attached my magnet-holder to the hull to prevent the tide from carrying us away. The major placed the first mine on the six-foot rod and lowered it into the water, placing the mine on her stern. He detached the rod, having felt the limpet mine clamp itself to the hull. I released my magnetic holder and the tide slowly swept us along, so we could place another amidships and a third on her bows.

They moved on to the *Sperrbrecher* and placed two limpets opposite the engine room. With the tide starting to ebb, they were in the act of turning to go back downstream when they were suddenly bathed in light. 'I looked up,' wrote Sparks, 'and saw the silhouette of a German sentry leaning over the side, shining his torch on us. We froze, hardly daring to breathe.' Split-second thoughts raced through his mind: do we answer if he challenges us? If we ignore him, will he sound the alarm?

---

* Literally a 'Pathfinder' with a reinforced hull that was used to detonate minefields and for anti-aircraft duty. Its displacement was around 8,000 tons.

Aerial photo of Bordeaux harbour overlaid with the track of *Catfish*'s limpet attack.

Fortunately, noted Hasler, they were 'able to get back close to the ship's side and drift along with the tide without making any movment'. The sentry followed them along the deck, shining his torch down at intervals, but was unable to make up his mind what they actually were, thanks to the 'efficiency of the camouflage scheme'. Drifting under the flare of the *Sperrbrecher*'s bows, and finally out of sight, Sparks clamped his magnetic holder to the hull. There they waited for five long minutes while the sentry continued to search the water with his torch. Eventually the light went off and they could hear his 'hobnailed boots clanking away'. He had definitely seen them. But he must have been fooled by their camouflage into believing they were 'nothing more than flotsam'. It had been a very close-run thing.

They resumed their course downstream to two ships beyond their original target: another large merchant ship, on the quayside, and next to it a smaller tanker. With the tide running so strongly that Hasler 'considered it unsafe to get in between the bows of the two ships', which were pointing upstream, he chose instead to attack their sterns. But as they were placing the limpets – two on the bigger ship and one on the tanker – the tide brought the two ships together, trapping the canoe. 'We tried to free ourselves,' recalled Sparks, 'but were caught fast. The canoe began to crack, a muffled sound like pistols firing, as it was squeezed between the giant vessels. I thought that somebody was bound to hear and come looking. If we weren't finally crushed to death, we would certainly be discovered.'

Desperate to save themselves, they heaved against the hulls 'like Samson between the pillars of the temple'. But it was a change in the tide that saved them, the swell parting the ships long enough for them to escape. Once clear, Sparks wiped the sweat from his eyes and knew he was lucky to be alive. Then it dawned on him: they had done it. Despite all the obstacles, they had covered more than seventy nautical miles into the heart of enemy territory and planted eight limpet mines on four ships. He leaned forward and shook hands with Hasler. Their 'job was complete'.

Assisted by the tide and the lighter load (now they had used their limpet mines), they made 'good speed out of the harbour, happy to leave it behind'. Not far from the southern tip of the Île Cazeau, they heard a splashing noise ahead. They stopped and 'sat in anxious silence, listening, peering into the dark', and were astonished to make out the shape of another canoe. It was *Crayfish* with Laver and Mills. They had also heard a noise and stopped, 'waiting to discover what was following them'.

Delighted to be reunited with his chief, Laver explained that he and Mills had gone some distance along the east bank without finding a suitable target. When the ebb tide turned against them, they returned to attack the two ships at Bassens South, as Hasler had instructed, placing five limpets on the larger merchant ship *Alabama* and three on the cargo liner *Portland*. They did not see a single sentry.

'Well done,' said Hasler, adding that for the time being they could continue their escape together, but once on land they would go their separate ways.

They set off with double paddles at full speed, eager to reach the Blaye area of land on the east bank of the estuary before the tide turned. This they managed at around 6:00 a.m., having covered more than twenty-two nautical miles. Only now did Hasler order Laver and Mills to land and sink their canoe, while he and Sparks continued on for another quarter of a mile. 'Then make your way across France as best you can,' he added. 'Good luck to you both.'

They shook hands for a final time. 'Don't forget your promise to buy the first round,' said Mills to Sparks as *Crayfish* moved off into the dark.

Soon after, Hasler and Sparks landed in a deserted spot and, having retrieved their escape equipment, scuttled *Catfish* by slashing its canvas sides and buoyancy bags, and pushing it back into the river to sink. Sparks regretted missing the fireworks he knew would start in an hour or two. 'But,' he wrote, 'I had done my job – both for my country and for my brother, Benny.'[4]

*

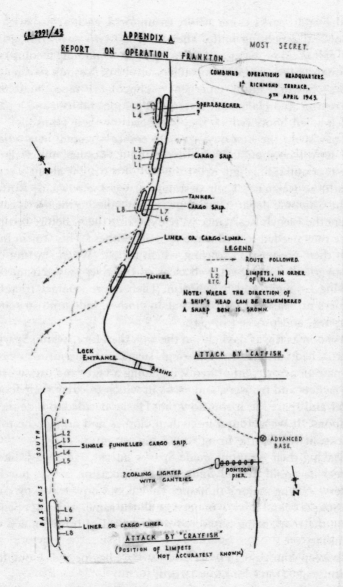

CR 2991/43

APPENDIX A

REPORT ON OPERATION FRANKTON.

COMBINED OPERATIONS HEADQUARTERS.
1A RICHMOND TERRACE,
9TH APRIL 1943.

L5 ——— SPERRBRECHER
L4 ——— ?

L3
L2 ——— CARGO SHIP.
L1

——— TANKER.
L8 ——— L7 ——— CARGO SHIP.
L6

——— LINER OR CARGO-LINER.

LEGEND

· · · · ROUTE FOLLOWED.

L1
L2 } LIMPETS, IN ORDER
ETC. OF PLACING.

——— TANKER.

NOTE: WHERE THE DIRECTION OF
A SHIP'S HEAD CAN BE REMEMBERED
A SHARP BOW IS SHOWN.

LOCK
ENTRANCE

BASINS.

ATTACK BY "CATFISH."

SOUTH

L1
L2
L3 ——— SINGLE FUNNELLED CARGO SHIP.
L4
L5

?COALING LIGHTER
WITH GANTRIES.

PONTOON
PIER.

⊗ ADVANCED
BASE.

BASSENS

L6
L7
L8 ——— LINER OR CARGO-LINER.

ATTACK BY "CRAYFISH"

(POSITION OF LIMPETS
NOT ACCURATELY KNOWN)

Lieutenant Colonel Hasler's diagram of the limpet attacks at Bordeaux by
Catfish and *Crayfish*.

Hasler and Sparks came ashore in uniform, each armed with a pistol and a fighting knife. They also had two days' rations, a half-gallon tin of water and an escape box containing a compass, silk map of France, Horlicks tablets, a tube of Nestlé's sweetened milk, chewing gum, emergency chocolate, tape, matches. Benzedrine and Halazone (water purification) tablets, and a pair of felt-soled boots (which they swapped for their plimsolls).[5]

They spent the first day – 12 December – resting in a wood and set off 'as soon as it was dark, about 1900hrs, and walked across country, finishing up at the end of the night about a mile [south] of Reignac'. Their destination was the town of Ruffec in the Charente department, about eighty miles to the north-east, where the French Resistance were expecting them. Before getting there they needed to find some civilian clothes.[6] This was in line with their pre-mission briefing which stated: 'When starting on the overland escape, get well clear of the river (say ten miles), moving by night and in uniform. Then try to contact friendly farmers or peasants, borrow civilian clothes, hide uniforms and weapons, and proceed by day.'[7]

As soon as it was daylight on the 13th, therefore, he and Sparks approached various farms. Though suspicious, the farmers gave the pair an assortment of items, including a beret and cap, worn-out jackets and trousers, and sacks in which to carry their food, water and spare kit. It was now that Hasler decided to hide their weapons. 'If we're found in civilian clothes and armed,' he told Sparks, 'it will be the firing squad for certain.'

Leaving their weapons made Sparks uneasy. He always liked to feel he could defend himself if the occasion arose. But he understood the major's thinking. They could now travel by day, but Sparks found it 'very unnerving all the same, walking openly along the road, being passed by a great deal of traffic, much of it military'.

To keep him calm, Hasler suggested: 'Imagine we're out for a nice walk. Don't look concerned.'

This was easier said than done. Every time a German military truck passed by, the hairs on the back of Sparks's neck stood up. Hasler, on the other hand, seemed unperturbed. 'He chatted away to me in French,' recalled Sparks, 'gesticulating wildly the way Frenchmen do, while I nodded agreeably or shrugged my shoulders, not having understood a word.'

Asked what Sparks was supposed to do if they were stopped, Hasler responded: 'Say nothing. Pretend you are mute.'

Fortunately, the occasion never arose. The closest they came to discovery was in the village of Saint-Mème-les-Carrières, about halfway to Ruffec, where they were almost knocked over by a squad of German soldiers coming out of a house. Both were badly shaken by the experience and 'indescribably relieved' when the soldiers went on their way. A day later – 17 December – they reached a small hamlet near Saint-Fraigne where, cold, wet and hungry, they tried to get food. But from house after house they were turned away. 'I thought these people were supposed to be on our side,' grumbled Sparks. 'Here we are helping these people out, we've just done a job to help their country, risking our lives, and they don't want to know. Is this all worth it?'

Taking refuge in a barn, they were disturbed by the farmer who told them: 'It is dangerous here. The people who live here do not want you here. It is lucky I saw you or the Boche might come for you. Come with me to my house and I will give you some food.'

Fed on bread and soup, they were told they could spend the night in the farmer's cow shed. They made themselves comfortable in the hay and had barely nodded off when the farmer shook them roughly awake. 'Somebody saw you. The gendarmes are on their way. You need to go now.'

Grabbing their few possessions, they left the shed by a window and ran up a narrow, muddy farm track. It was still raining, so they spent the night sheltering under a hedge. The following day they reached Ruffec and, with no specific instructions, went into a restaurant and ordered soup and drinks. When paying their bill, Hasler slipped the waitress a note explaining who they were. It was a risky moment. But it paid off. 'She sheltered us for 24 hours,' noted Hasler, 'and got in touch with two [Resistance] contacts in Ruffec.'[8]

They were, said one of the contacts later, 'very fortunate'. Had Hasler and Sparks gone into any other restaurant in the town they would have been 'betrayed and captured'.[9] As it was, they were spirited out of Ruffec in the back of a baker's van and led across the nearby Line of Demarcation from Occupied France into the Vichy zone. They remained hidden on a farm until 6 January 1943 when they were taken, by bicycle and train, to Lyons. After lengthy spells in various safe houses – during which time Hasler, much to his regret, was persuaded to trim his flowing, golden moustache because it looked 'too English' – they were moved to Toulouse, Marseilles and finally, in the company of two Allied pilots,* guided across the Pyrenees and into Spain. At times, boiling over with frustration, Sparks would unleash a long list of complaints. Hasler never chastised him. Instead, displaying admirable patience, he waited for the storm to abate and said calmly: 'You feel better now?'

Hasler reached Gibraltar, and safety, on 1 April 1943, almost five months to the day since he and his men had left Holy Loch in Scotland in the submarine *Tuna*. Flown home a day later, he began a lengthy debrief at COHQ. Sparks followed by boat and, once back in London, enjoyed a brief spell of unauthorised leave at his dad's house in Finsbury Park. 'Bill!' yelled his father on opening the door. 'We thought you dead, boy. Oh, Bill, I can't believe it, God, I'm so thankful, so happy to see you.'

It was, Sparks recalled, 'one of the happiest moments of my life'.[10]

---

* One of whom, Flying Officer Werner de Merode, was a 'Belgian prince and a Spitfire pilot who spoke perfect English, having been educated in England'. Sparks considered him 'arrogant and smarmy', and often felt like 'giving him a thump'. (Sparks, p. 122.)

23

'This brilliant little operation'

On 29 April 1943, Vice Admiral Lord Louis Mountbatten forwarded 'Blondie' Hasler's detailed report on Operation Frankton to the Admiralty. He wrote in the 'Most Secret' covering letter:

Of the six canoes, each manned by two Royal Marines, which were launched from HM Submarine TUNA off the mouth of the Gironde river, one was damaged in launching and never left the submarine, two were capsized in tidal races and one lost touch in the mouth of the Gironde.

The remaining two canoes manned respectively by Major Hasler and Marine Sparks and by Corporal A. E. Laver RM, and Marine W. H. Mills, successfully reached their objective, 50 miles up the Gironde river and attached limpets to six ships.

There is good reason to believe that at least three and probably five ships were holed, of which at least three are believed to have been blockade runners.

Of the personnel engaged, Major Hasler and Marine Sparks have successfully regained this country. Lt MacKinnon is believed to be a prisoner of war. Marine Moffatt is known to have been found drowned by the Germans at the entrance to the Gironde river. Nothing is known of the fate of the remainder.

He added: 'This brilliant little operation carried through with great determination and courage is a good example of the successful use of "Limpeteers".'[1]

The full story of Operation Frankton – later immortalised in the 1955 film *Cockleshell Heroes* – and the fate of the other four crews would not be revealed until the end of the war. But snippets of information were available within days of the mission. On 10 December, an intercepted German High Command communiqué stated that, two days earlier, 'a small British sabotage squad was engaged at the mouth of the Gironde and was finished off in combat'. This was later assumed by staff at COHQ in London to refer to at least two of Hasler's crews.

More encouraging news was received by the Naval Intelligence Department (NID) on 21 December in the form of a secret message from an agent in Bordeaux. It read: 'The merchant ships *Dresden* and *Alabama* and three others were damaged by mysterious explosions on December 12th. Two of the ships were at Bassens and three at Bacalan [the port area of northern Bordeaux]. The damage can be repaired.'[2] The message was remarkably accurate. A postwar NID inquiry into the results of Frankton concluded that four ships were 'damaged by explosion' and partially sunk during the morning of 12 December – SS *Alabama*, MS *Tannenfels*, MS *Portland* and MS *Dresden* – with the time of detonation ranging from 7:00 a.m. to 1:05 p.m. A fifth, *Sperrbrecher 5*, was lucky to escape damage when a mine went off in the water, causing the inquiry to assume that 'the explosive charge had dropped off the ship's side and exploded on the riverbed'. The inquiry added: 'All damage was reported as being slight.'[3]

Nothing was known about the fate of the ten 'Cockleshell Heroes' until Major Hasler got word back to Britain in February 1943 that he and Sparks had completed their mission and were still alive. But of the others there was still no definite word, beyond the obvious fact, sent to their families in War Office telegrams at the end of January 1943, that they were 'Missing in Action'. Particularly cut up by the lack of news was Bob Ewart's young sweetheart, Heather Powell. After waving Ewart and the others goodbye the previous November, she had turned to her mother in tears. 'They'll never come back,' she wailed. 'I know they'll never come back.'

Informed by Mrs Ewart that Bob was missing, Heather became ill and was admitted to hospital. She was visited there in April 1943 by Bill Sparks who found her 'weak, unwilling to fight her illness'. It was a 'heartbreaking' sight. She said to him: 'Bobby's not coming back, is he?'

'Of course he is,' replied Sparks, with more conviction than he felt. 'He'll be following me along soon.'

'No,' she said. 'I'm sorry, but he's not coming back.'

Diagnosed with tuberculosis, Heather died – still ignorant of Ewart's fate – in the spring of 1944, a month short of her seventeenth birthday.[4]

Only the Moffatt family received early confirmation that their loved one was not coming back. On 6 April 1943, an official telegram was delivered to Mrs Moffatt at Wheatley Road, Halifax. It stated: 'From information received from a German Casualty List, the body of your son, David Moffatt . . . was washed ashore on 17 December 1942 at Le Bloisenre [sic] and your son was buried on the Ridge of Dunes.' A few days later, Mrs Moffatt opened a second note from Mountbatten himself. 'I cannot give you details of this operation,' wrote the CCO, 'but it will comfort you to know that it was successful. Your son's life was not given in vain. I sympathise deeply and share with you in his loss.'[5]

*

It was not until the end of the war that captured German documents revealed what had happened to Hasler's other men. On 12 January 1944, for example, the German High Command compiled 'for propaganda purposes' a list of Allied servicemen who had been executed for guerilla, Commando and sabotage activities. The fifth entry – 'Sabotage attacks on German ships off Bordeaux' – included a number of falsehoods, but the basic facts were accurate. On 12 December 1942, it stated, 'a number of valuable German ships were badly damaged off Bordeaux by explosives below water-level. Adhesive mines were attached by five British sabotage squads working from canoes'.

It then listed six soldiers – including ranks, dates and place of birth – who had been 'captured a few days later': MacKinnon, Laver, Mills, Wallace, Conway and Ewart. A seventh, Moffatt, 'was found drowned'. The rest, 'amongst them their leader Major Hasler, Marine Sparks and Corporal Sheard, presumably escaped to Spain'. It added:

> The men concerned paddled in their canoes by twos from a submarine up the mouth of the Gironde. They were wearing special olive-grey garments without any military badges. Having carried out the explosions, they sank their craft and tried to make their escape to Spain in civilian clothes with the help of the French civilian population . . .
>
> All those captured were shot in accordance with orders on 23.4.43.[6]

There were errors: Sheard *did not* escape to Spain; the men *were* wearing military badges; and at least some of the executions took place long before 23 April 1943. The 'orders' that the document refers to was in fact a single order: the infamous 'Führer Befehl' or 'Commando Order' of 18 October 1942, issued by Adolf Hitler in response to a number of British Commando raids. 'For a long time,' wrote Hitler, with no hint of irony,

> our enemies have been using methods of warfare contrary to the international agreements of Geneva. Especially brutal and treacherous is the behaviour of the so-called Commandos who, it has been established, are even partially recruited from the ranks of freed criminals in enemy countries. From captured orders it appears that they are ordered not only to chain prisoners but also to kill defenceless prisoners out of hand the moment they believe the latter, as prisoners, impede them in the further pursuit of their objective . . .
>
> For this reason it has already been laid down in a supplement to the Armed Forces report (Routine orders) of 7.10.42 that henceforth Germany will have recourse to the same treatment of

these British sabotage troops and their accomplices, that is to say: they shall be killed without mercy in battle by German troops wherever they are encountered.

I therefore command: from now on all enemies encountered by German troops on so-called Commando expeditions in Europe or Africa whether ostensibly uniformed soldiers or sabotage agents with or without weapons are to be annihilated both in battle and in flight to the last man.[7]

Of course there were no captured orders allowing Commandos to kill 'defenceless prisoners'. That was just a pretext, and a flimsy one at that. In truth, Hitler was so enraged by the increasing number and success of British Commando raids that he issued this order – which allowed the summary execution of any captured Commando, even if he was wearing uniform and unarmed – as a deterrent. It failed in that regard, though it would have lethal consequences for Hasler's men.

*

The first pair to suffer was Sergeant Sam Wallace and Marine Bob 'Jock' Ewart. After *Coalfish* had capsized in the first tidal race, they swam ashore near Pointe de Grave and, cold and exhausted, gave themselves up at 6:00 a.m. on 8 December to a nearby German light anti-aircraft battery, claiming to be ship-wrecked English sailors. It was clear from their uniforms, however – and from sightings of their wrecked canoe and the retrieval of various items of equipment – that they were Commandos on a sabotage mission.

It was also their misfortune to be seen briefly that morning by Admiral Johannes Bachmann, the German flag officer for western France, who was on a tour of inspection. Returning to his headquarters at Nantes on 10 December, Bachmann asked his clerk to find a copy of Hitler's 'Commando Order'. Having read it, Bachmann then contacted his superior at Navy Group West to 'obtain a decision as to whether it was justifiable to shoot the Commando men at once without interrogating first'.*

In fact, Bachmann had already sent a counter-intelligence officer to question Wallace and Ewart in the old fort at Royan. The officer reported that whilst the 'prisoner from Glasgow refused to make any statement, an Irishman had only told them that the two alone were lowered from a submarine which had left England fourteen days before and their task was to sink ships in the Gironde'. The interrogations continued, and one or both gave more details about their unit and its training. But they stuck to their story that they alone had been sent on a mission, and their interrogator seemed to believe them.

Handed over to men from Reinhard Heydrich's SD (Sicherheitsdienst, the intelligence agency of the SS), Wallace and Ewart were informed on 10 December that, in accordance with Hitler's order, they were to be executed. That night they were driven to a wood on the outskirts of Bordeaux, tied to wooden posts in a sandpit, and shot by a firing squad of sixteen navy personnel. 'Two SD men,' recalled the navy officer in charge, 'who had already drawn their pistols, fired several shots into the back of the necks of the victims. The surgeon then established that death had taken place.'[8]

*

The route taken by Corporal Bert Laver and Marine Bill Mills, having parted from Hasler and Sparks near Blaye in the early morning of 12 December, can be partially reconstructed from the testimony of French witnesses. The first sighting was by a young French hunter who found them hiding in a small hut not far from the river. Fortunately, he was sympathetic to their plight and reported their presence to a true 'patriot' who took them

---

* In October 1945, following a lengthy war crimes' investigation, the British Judge Advocate General Office's was of the opinion that 'on the facts before them Admiral Bachmann should be put to trial' for his part in the death of Wallace and Ewart. Bachmann had, in fact, been killed in combat operations on 2 April 1945. (TNA, DEFE 2/218.)

some food. That night, they headed north-east and crossed the main arterial route, now known as the A10, somewhere between Reignac and Saint-Savin. They hid up on the 13th, and set off again after dark, eventually taking refuge in an unoccupied house where they found and consumed some stale bread, cold meat and wine.

During the late afternoon of 14 December, however, they were denounced to the gendarmerie by a French farmer who claimed that 'two British parachutists he had just met on the road in the vicinity of his home had asked him for rest and shelter and that he had directed them into an abandoned house', saying they would be safe there. Instead they were betrayed. Arrested by a gendarme, Laver and Mills (who was one day short of his 21st birthday) were soon handed over to the Feldgendarmerie – the German military police – and later returned to Bordeaux where they were interrogated by the SD. They did their best to confuse their questioners, but eventually admitted most of the detail of Operation Frankton, including the name of Norman Colley as first reserve. They too were shot by firing squad, though the exact date is uncertain.[9]

The circumstances of Lieutenant Jack MacKinnon and Marine James Conway's capture are even more obscure, though there are hints. Two French fishermen saw a single canoe pass them near Fort-Médoc, a little to the north of Île Verte, at 10 p.m. on 8 December. This means MacKinnon and Conway were now ahead of the other two canoes, which did not leave their lying-up point at Pointe des Oiseaux until 11.30 p.m. that evening.

At some point during the evening of 9 December, not far from the junction of the Garonne and Dordogne at Bec d'Ambès, *Cuttlefish* is thought to have been holed by a submerged obstacle. 'They were forced,' stated a German interrogation document, 'to leave the boat as well as the explosives and its entire equipment with the exception of the bag containing money, iron rations and maps.' This information came from Conway; MacKinnon refused to talk.

Swimming ashore, and probably assisted by locals who gave them civilian clothes, they eventually got across the Demarcation Line to La Réole, thirty miles south-east of Bordeaux, on 18 December. But later that day, by which time MacKinnon was suffering from an infected knee, they were stopped and arrested by a gendarme for 'lack of identity documents'. Conway was put in prison and MacKinnon treated at the local hospital. Unfortunately, the German SD got to hear of their arrest and, having lobbied the Ministry of Interior at Vichy, were allowed to take them back to the Occupied Zone on 29 December. 'At about 2300 [hrs] the same evening,' recalled a French gendarme, 'a large detachment of Germans, numbering perhaps fifty, again arrived at the scene and armed with numerous automatic weapons, surrounded the hospital and prison. In the presence of the prosecutor they took over the two Englishmen.'

Even as MacKinnon and Conway were being interrogated in Bordeaux, their families in Britain received two short letters from a M. Galibert, the prosecuting solicitor at La Réole. He wrote to Mrs MacKinnon: 'I expect that you and the whole family are rather well. Seen last week John who was healthy and well. Sincerely yours.' A similar note was sent to Conway's parents.

It was, however, a false dawn. Like Laver and Mills, and possibly at the same time, MacKinnon and Conway were executed by firing squad in early 1943. The lack of definite news was particularly hard for the MacKinnon and Conway families who had been led to believe that their sons were safe. Writing to Mrs MacKinnon after his return to Britain, 'Blondie' Hasler did his best to sound optimistic:

[Jack] is a very valued member of my unit besides being a close personal friend of mine.

I well realise the anxiety which you must be experiencing in the absence of any further definite news of him, and you may rest assured that I will let you know as soon as I hear anything further.

He is the sort of chap you can rely on to look after himself and make the best of any opportunities he gets, so I hope we shall have further news soon.[10]

The final pair of canoeists – Corporal George Sheard and Marine David Moffatt – almost certainly drowned, or succumbed to hypothermia, soon after they were left in the water by the other canoeists in the early hours of 8 December. Only Moffatt's body and the wreckage of the pair's canoe *Conger* were later identified by the Germans, having been found at separate sites on Île de Ré, fifty miles north of the entrance to the Gironde estuary. The Germans assumed, therefore, that Sheard had escaped. But the body of a second 'Englishman' was found even further north, at Les Sables d'Olonne, and this was probably Sheard. Both were buried in unmarked graves.[11]

The years of uncertainty for the families were finally ended in September 1945 when they were informed by the Admiralty that, after extensive investigations, their loved ones were 'missing presumed dead'.

*

Soon after 'Blondie' Hasler and Bill Sparks returned to Britain, Mountbatten recommended them and the missing Corporal Laver and Marine Mills for gallantry awards. 'Hasler's cool, determined and fearless leadership,' wrote Mountbatten, 'was in accordance with the highest traditions of the Royal Marine Corps – and he is strongly recommended for the highest recommendation permissable for a feat of this nature.' He deserved 'a DSO and Brevet Majority* for his action', at the very least, added Mountbatten in a covering note.

Repeating the comments that Hasler had made in his own report, Mountbatten noted that Sparks and Mills 'carried out their work in a cool and efficient manner and showed considerable

---

* Hasler was at the time an acting major.

eagerness to engage the enemy', while Laver 'handled his boat skilfully, and displayed initiative and coolness in making his independent attack'. Only if it was later discovered that Laver and Mills had died should they be given not a medal but a posthumous mention in despatches.[12]

In the event, Hasler and Sparks were awarded the DSO and DSM respectively in the summer of 1943 (though Mountbatten had undoubtedly hoped the major would get the VC). It was the least they deserved for pulling off what was arguably the toughest special forces mission of the war. Just getting to the targets, paddling more than 70 nautical miles by night through enemy territory and evading detection by day, was impressive enough. But then to be able to place the limpet mines on and sink or disable no fewer than five closely guarded merchant ships, before making their escape through Occupied France, Vichy France and eventually over the Pyrenees to Spain, required qualities of endurance, resolution, technical expertise, courage and quick-thinking that few humans possess. *Frankton* was regarded by many at the time and since as tantamount to a suicide mission from which no one was expected to return. That eight of the ten brave participants paid the ultimate price is proof that that cold-blooded calculation was all too accurate.

With typical modesty, Sparks regarded his award as 'a tremendous honour' and was 'immensely proud' to be given it, alongside Hasler, by King George VI at Buckingham Palace. Yet it infuriated him to be told, after the war, that Laver and Mills's DSMs had been downgraded to MiDs because only a VC could be awarded posthumously. 'So give it to them,' he responded. 'The boys did their job. They gave their lives. What more do you want?'

'The Victoria Cross,' insisted his sergeant major, 'can only be given when the deed has been witnessed by a senior officer.'

This conversation, and his belief that the other 'Cockleshell Heroes' deserved to be honoured – particularly Ewart and Wallace who had fooled the Germans into thinking they were acting alone – began Sparks's long quest for some form of official recognition.

It ended, in 1983, with the unveiling of the Operation Frankton Memorial at the Poole Headquarters of the modern SBS. Sparks was slightly disconcerted to see his own name alongside the other nine on the memorial. 'I'm not dead yet,' he told the MP who had campaigned with him. 'It's like looking at your own name on a tombstone.'

'Well,' replied the MP, 'you're not going to live forever and when you are gone, nobody's going to come down and add your name to the list. So I had to put it on.'[13]

24

Coppists

In early December 1942 – as Operation Frankton was nearing its conclusion – Lieutenant Commander Nigel Willmott was called to a meeting at COHQ in London to discuss the lessons learned from the recent landings in French North Africa. Asked about beach reconnaissance, Willmott launched into an impassioned and detailed explanation of why it was important and how it needed to be conducted in the future. He then fielded questions for more than two hours from the senior officers present. The meeting concluded with a unanimous decision to heed all Willmott's warnings and allow him to form a new specialist canoe-borne unit for beach reconnaissance.

'As a result of the experience gained during the North African Operations,' wrote Mountbatten's chief of staff to the Admiralty on 12 December, 'it is clear that if Beach Intelligence requirements for future operations are to be met promptly and efficiently it is necessary that personnel should be trained and equipment provided before the requirement arises.'[1] The Admiralty agreed and Willmott's COPP – Combined Operations Pilotage Parties* – was born.

The task of COPP was as follows: to provide beach intelligence for planning an assault; and to assess the 'suitability of beaches for maintenance and the build-up following the assault'. Wherever

---

* The original name was Combined Operations Beach and Pilotage Reconnaissance Party, but this was shortened to COPP to obscure its true purpose.

possible, therefore, the reconnaissance needed to be carried out as early as it was practical to do so; all findings, however, would need to be confirmed by a final scouting mission. 'In addition to their reconnaissance duties,' noted the COPP mission statement, 'these parties would also be required to act as pilots and markers, and to train additional markers for the actual operation.'

There were two main types of information that a COPP needed to obtain: naval, including sailing directions for landing craft, navigational marks, beach silhouettes, natural landing marks, the location of beach obstructions, the existence of any navigational aids, the general description of the beach, strength of tidal streams and beach gradients; and military, including type of beach, bearing capacity, exits, beach obstructions, enemy defences and navigational marks for troops moving inland.[2]

Developing the Party Inhuman concept, Willmott envisaged ten COPPs, each comprising ten men: a senior officer, or S/COPP, who was a trained naval navigator or hydrographer; a Royal Engineers officer, E/COPP, who was SBS-trained and in charge of gathering military information; a naval assistant, or A/COPP, to the senior officer; a maintenance officer, M/COPP, and spare operational; two seamen ratings as paddlers, leadsmen and coxswains; one seaman rating as a maintenance mate; one electrical artificer or mechanic; one SBS-trained Commando NCO as a paddler/guard to the military officer; and one Royal Engineers draughtsman and spare operational, also SBS-trained.[3]

Many of his original senior officers had served with Party Inhuman: they included Norman Teacher (COPP 3), Neville McHarg (COPP 4), Don Amer (COPP 6), Fred Ponsonby (COPP 8) and Geoff Lyne (COPP 9). Also retained to help train the new Coppists – much to Roger Courtney's annoyance – was Lieutenant Basil Eckhard of the SBS.

The base for the new unit was the Yacht Club on Hayling Island, a nondescript building on an isolated spit of land just a few miles east of Portsmouth (and therefore close to Hasler's HQ at Southsea). It looked, noted one account, 'like the control tower of some small aerodrome', and had been found by one of Willmott's earliest recruits, Lieutenant Geoff Galwey RNVR, 'a slim, wiry, fair-haired youngster' who, despite his earlier discharge from the service with a weak heart, had re-enlisted as a rating and was quickly promoted to petty officer. Tough and ruthless, Galwey became the maintenance officer for Willmott's COPP 1. He was the ideal fixer. To furnish the new base, for example, he took a lorry on a tour of neighbouring barracks. When he found one that was temporarily vacant, he ordered his men inside and they 'stripped it of all they wanted – beds, tables, chairs, mattresses – and staggered out laden'.[4]

The rush was on to form and train two COPP teams by early January 1943 when, according to COHQ, they would be needed in the Mediterranean. As his own COPP 1 was earmarked for training and development, and the senior officer of COPP 2 was employed on special work, Willmott assigned COPPs 3 and 4, under the experienced Teacher and McHarg, to be the first to go on operations. Teacher's deputy was 28-year-old Lieutenant Noel Cooper RNVR, the Party Inhuman officer who had done good work as Willmott's paddler during the Torch landings. Born in Buenos Aires and educated at King's School, Canterbury, Cooper was working in Argentina as a chartered accountant when war broke out. He returned to Britain to serve in the Royal Navy, first as a rating and then an officer, and came to Willmott's notice after he had joined one of the first Royal Marine Commando units (later No. 40 Commando). For demonstrating 'bravery and skill in the hazardous operations in which the Allied forces were landing in North Africa', he was mentioned in despatches.[5]

Joining Cooper in COPP 3 as the military officer was 25-year-old temporary Captain George Burbridge of the Royal Canadian Engineers. Handsome and powerfully built, Burbridge had graduated in engineering from the University of Manitoba before moving to McGill in Montreal for a postgraduate degree. It was there he met his wife Barbara, the two marrying shortly before Burbridge went overseas to join the 4th Field Company in the United Kingdom.[6] Burbridge's opposite number in COPP 4 was

Captain Edward Parsons of the Royal Engineers. Also attached to the teams were two SBS sergeants – Loasby and Milne – and two draughtsmen.[7]

Willmott began his lectures to the new recruits by writing one of his favourite quotes – from the philosopher Bertrand Russell – on the blackboard: 'People would rather die than think. Many of them do.' He wanted his people to be problem-solvers, to think before they acted. In this, he was no different than Courtney and Hasler. Brawn, they knew, was no use without brains.

For want of anything better, the officers of COPPs 3 and 4 were taught to swim in the heavy rubber suits worn by human torpedomen, or 'charioteers' as they were known. 'They were cumbersome,' noted one account, 'designed for wearers who "rode" to their targets and used oxygen containers. They were hardly the thing for tumbling about in surf, or vaulting in and out of canoes.' Nor were they properly waterproof, as water tended to trickle through the wearer's face and wrist seals until their underclothes were thoroughly soaked.

Willmott did his best for the Coppists, procuring night compasses, waterproofed watches and torches, and a device for measuring beach gradients that consisted of a reel with fishing line beaded every ten yards. But both teams were woefully under-equipped, and had been training for less than a fortnight, when they were ordered to report to Havant Station for the first leg of their journey to Algiers on 6 January 1943. They were all wearing khaki battledress but, in the case of the naval officers and ratings, with seamen's caps and shoulder straps. Newly promoted to lieutenant commander, and in overall command, Norman Teacher shook hands with Willmott. 'Goodbye, sir,' he said. 'I'll bet nothing's ready for us.'

'Good luck, Norman,' replied Willmott.[8]

*

Two days later, the two COPP teams sailed from Liverpool on the troopship *Otranto*. 'We still did not know our destination,' recalled Electrical Mechanic Peter Palmer of McHarg's COPP 4, 'but some of our party thought Algiers was a likely one and this proved correct. Most of our time at sea was taken up with lectures, boat drill and PT. The latter was carried out in bare feet and on the boat deck which was set aside for the Queen Alexandra nurse passengers. We were required to perform what seemed to us to be the most ridiculous antics in front of these nurses and these sessions were not at all popular.'⁹

Only recently qualified as an EM, the 21-year-old Palmer had not put himself forward for 'special duty'. Instead he had been asked if he could swim and, having said yes, was told to report to Hayling Island. 'It did not take very long to realise,' he recalled, 'that saying I could swim was virtually the same as volunteering for special service.' After some basic training – including how to escape from a submarine – he and the rest of COPPs 3 and 4 'spent a few days getting our kit & stores together' and the canoes 'assembled to make sure they were OK before everything was packed'.¹⁰

After a five-day voyage – including a typically rough passage across the Bay of Biscay that caused widespread seasickness and living conditions that had to be 'seen to be believed' – *Otranto*'s convoy reached Gibraltar. For Palmer, it seemed odd to see lights twinkling on the North African coast after the strict blackout in Britain. Another five days brought them into Algiers, the location for Eisenhower's Allied Force Headquarters. There the COPP teams transferred to the submarine depot ship HMS *Maidstone* and spent the next week assembling their canoes and sorting out their equipment.¹¹

Despite the urgency of their posting, no one at Algiers seemed to know what to do with the Coppists when they first arrived. Given a tiny shack to house their secret gear, they struggled to keep the local Arabs at a distance. Eventually tiring of this charade, Teacher found a deserted villa across the bay and commandeered it for his men. Supplied by motor launch – with the goods being brought ashore in a dinghy – they spent their time, recalled Palmer, 'building the canoes, organising the stores, doing the inevitable PT and generally preparing for the operations ahead'.[12]

There was still no news of their mission when the CCO, Vice Admiral Lord Louis Mountbatten, arrived briefly in Algiers. Mountbatten had come from the top-level Allied conference at Casablanca on the Atlantic coast of Morocco where Churchill, Roosevelt and their respective chiefs of staff had met to discuss the next phase of Allied strategy *after* the Axis forces had been cleared out of North Africa. The US Joint Chiefs had arrived hoping to suspend operations in the Mediterranean so that Operation Roundup, the cross-Channel invasion of France, could be launched later in the year to assist the Russians. Churchill and his chiefs preferred, by contrast, to attack Sicily next (Operation Husky) and not commit to Roundup until sufficient landing craft were available and, more importantly, German morale and resources had been eroded further. The capture of Sicily would, according to British calculations, safeguard Mediterranean shipping, tie up German troops, provide airfields to bomb targets in occupied Europe, and threaten mainland Italy, possibly driving Hitler's Axis partner out of the war.

What swung the argument in Britain's favour was the support of Roosevelt. The conference ended, therefore, with an Allied commitment to attack Sicily in 1943 around the time of 'the favourable July moon'. The operation would be directed by General Eisenhower, the supreme commander in the Mediterranean, from his headquarters in Algiers. No final decision was made on Roundup beyond a general commitment to launch it when it was thought likely to succeed.[13]

Mountbatten knew, therefore, when he spoke briefly to Teacher and McHarg at Algiers, that their first mission would be a reconnaissance of the beaches of Sicily. But as the news was still top secret, he could only tell them that their wait would soon be over. A week later, Teacher and COPP 3 were ordered to fly to Malta while McHarg and his men remained at Algiers. On Malta, Teacher found two villas on the picturesque north-west coast at Ghajn Tuffieha, overlooking a sandy beach that was ideal for training. There they practised swimming ashore from canoes in the new rubber suits that Willmott had sent from the UK. They were slightly less cumbersome than the 'charioteer' suits; but still leaked. 'Christ,' muttered Teacher, 'I don't think much of these. It's going to be fun if we get waterlogged.' Teacher and his men had been at Ghajn Tuffieha for only a few days when two lorries drew up and a group of naval officers and ratings got out. They were led by a young blond lieutenant who sought out Teacher. 'My name's Smith,' he said cheerily. 'Just flown in with my party from Cairo. I've orders to join you.'[14]

Lieutenant Bob Smith RN was a regular who, the previous summer, had been given command of the Middle East Beach Reconnaissance Party, a new unit initially composed of just seven officers. The training syllabus included 'folbot and collapsible boat work, swimming and beach reconnaissance'. Additional instruction in 'demolition, close fighting and parachuting' had been given by Stirling's SAS. The limitations of Smith's unit were that it had very basic equipment and no experience in homing to submarines. 'The standard of physical training i.e. swimming and paddling is high,' noted a confidential report, 'and the officers are capable of carrying out a rough beach survey and the duties of marker in an assault. But they have not the experience of the UK parties.'[15]

Smith had brought a total of twenty men to Malta – ten officers and ten ratings – to learn what they could from Teacher. They were split into two makeshift COPPs, known as Middle East 1 and Middle East 2. Smith retained command of ME 1, with Glaswegian Lieutenant David Brand RNVR as his deputy. Lieutenant Peter de Kock of the South Africa Naval Forces was put in charge of ME 2. Born in the Cape Province, de Kock was a colourful character who had already received multiple gallantry awards – including a mention in despatches, an MBE and a DSC – for his fearless work on the auxiliary tug HMS *St Angelo*. It came to an end in May 1942 when the *St Angelo* hit a mine and sank three-quarters of a mile off Malta's Grand Harbour. But de Kock survived and, soon after, joined Smith's unit for a new challenge.[16]

Just how difficult that challenge would be was made clear to Lieutenant Commander Teacher when he was summoned to the Lazaretto headquarters of Captain George Phillips RN, the new commander of the 10th Submarine Flotilla, in mid-February 1943. 'We need all three of your teams for the next dark period,' Phillips told him. 'Have you everything ready?'

'As ready as it can be, sir,' replied Teacher.

'It's for Sicily. The Force Commander wants reports of three sectors. They cover a lot of the south coast.'

Phillips went on to explain that each Malta party – COPP 3, ME 1 and ME 2 – would be assigned a submarine and a specific sector to explore: Teacher would cover the western part of Sicily's southern coast, from the mouth of the Belice river eastward to Sciacca; Smith was given the Gulf of Gela; and de Kock the island's southerly cape. McHarg's COPP 4 would also be involved. Sailing separately from Algiers, it would tackle the beaches along the north-west corner of the island, from Trapani near Palermo to Cape Zafferano.* The mission was scheduled for the end of the month, which left precious little time for Teacher to get Smith's men up to speed.[17]

---

* The original plan for Operation Husky, the invasion of Sicily, involved landings across a third of the island's coastline, including much of the south-east and north-west, and the early capture of ports and airfields. The final plan, agreed in early May 1943, was a concentrated beach assault on the south-east of the island, with no immediate capture of ports or airfields.

'The sub will never find us in this!'

HMS *Unbending* surfaced with a roar as her ballast tanks emptied. First up the ladder and on to the bridge was the S-class submarine's skipper, Lieutenant Edward 'Otto' Stanley RN, joined soon after by Norman Teacher in his tight rubber swimming suit. Gazing into the dark starlit night, the pair could see the south coast of Sicily two miles ahead. It 'stretched flatly away on either side in a thin curving strip of sand' that ended on the left in the mouth of the Belice river. Beyond the beach – designated No. 28 – 'rose the dim serrations of mountains against a dark velvet sky'. The sea was flat calm and ideal for folbot operations.

'Captain, sir,' said the first lieutenant through the voice-pipe. 'Permission to open the forehatch?'

'Carry on, Number One.'[1]

It was 8:05 p.m. on 28 February 1943. *Unbending* had left Malta for Sicily a day earlier, and the first evening of the voyage had been devoted to launching the folbot. Now they would do it for real. Teacher's canoe – a 'Cockle' Mark I model, seventeen feet long and thirty inches wide[2] – was brought out of the fore-hatch and on to the casing. Though brand new, it had been condemned by Willmott as 'unseaworthy except in calmest weather' and 'unsuitable' for COPP work in the Mediterranean. He had given the search for a replacement top priority, but it would be too late to help Teacher and his men.

Two ratings held lines at either end of the canoe as it was floated off the trimmed-down casing. Then the paddler, Noel

Cooper, got in the forward seat and Teacher in the back, taking care not to capsize the canoe as it bobbed in the swell. With both men safely aboard, the ratings cast off and the canoe moved away.

Reaching a point just 150 yards off the beach, Cooper threw out a brass kedge anchor to hold the canoe's position while Teacher went over the side. The plan, for this first night at least, was for him to be in the water for no more than two hours. When that time came and went, Cooper started to worry. As extra minutes ticked by, he strained his eyes and ears for any sign of his companion on the beach or in the water. There was nothing. Cooper waited as long as he could. But when fifty minutes had passed, he decided that 'to remain longer was only needlessly compromising his own and the submarine's safety'.

He headed out to sea and eventually made contact with the submarine – more than an hour late – using the infrared lamp. The folbot was recovered and, once the submarine had dived, the debrief began. 'Lieutenant Cooper heard no sounds of fighting on the beach,' reported Lieutenant Commander Stanley. 'It seems most likely that Lieutenant Commander Teacher's suit flooded up and he caught cramp and drifted down the coast with the easterly set [i.e. tidal direction]. It is known that his suit was too small for him and he might easily have torn it slightly, thereby causing flooding, as Captain Burbridge did on a subsequent occasion.'[3]

Despite this unfortunate setback, the survey continued for the next three nights as Burbridge and Cooper took it in turns to go into the water. There were, noted Captain Phillips, no more problems in terms of 'recovering the swimmer or in contacting the submarine' and work on Beach 28 was 'completed on the night of 3rd/4th March'.[4] They moved, for the following night, to another beach, designated No. 30, and once again Burbridge and Cooper did the work. This surprised *Unbending*'s skipper who could not understand why the two increasingly fatigued officers were not prepared to spread the load. 'The only work done by the ratings,' noted Stanley, 'was to clean the firearms taken in the Folbots and to patch holes in the Folbots, as the officers were not willing to employ them as paddlers . . . Had it been possible to employ ratings as paddlers, the work would have been done faster and less strain imposed on the officers.'[5] But for some reason – perhaps because, as Phillips later speculated, they 'wanted to find out the difficulties of the job themselves' before using their ratings – Burbridge and Cooper went out for the fourth night running.[6]

Their canoe was launched at 7:21 p.m. on 4 February and, as agreed, *Unbending* resurfaced and began its homing procedure with the infrared lamp five hours later. But in the interim the sea conditions had worsened from the original calm to a south-easterly wind of force 3 and a swell on the beach. Apart from two brief dives to avoid reconnaissance aircraft, *Unbending* spent the next four hours trying without success to contact the folbot. It then moved to the alternative rendezvous, between eight and twelve miles from the coast, and patrolled it at periscope depth throughout the next day, though the wind was even stronger now and 'conditions for sighting a Folbot poor'. When night fell at 7:20 p.m., Stanley surfaced and continued to signal with the infrared lamp. But there was no sign of the missing men and, at 9:15 p.m., he reluctantly abandoned the search and set a course for Malta.[7]

When Captain Phillips learned what had happened, he deeply regretted the loss of the three officers. Yet he also noted: 'Of five launches carried out, four were entirely successful as far as the homing procedure was concerned. The deterioration in the weather on the last night may have accounted for the failure to make contact with the submarine.'[8]

*

Teacher's outfit was not the only COPP to get into difficulty off Sicily. Bob Smith's Middle East 1 also left Malta on 27 February, in the S-class submarine, *United*, and began its survey of Beach 23 the following night. Smith had taken with him three volunteer reserve officers – lieutenants David Brand and Archie Hart, and Sub Lieutenant Eric Folder – and a single rating. He and Brand went out the first night in perfect conditions and, after a four-hour mission, were safely recovered by the submarine. 'The whole of the first night's operation,' noted *United*'s skipper Lieutenant Roxburgh, 'was carried out without any hitch and to schedule. Lieutenant Smith reported having heard sentries ashore, but that he had no difficulty in working and remaining undetected.'

The same pair were launched in the folbot the following night with the intention of operating inshore for an extra hour. But the pick-up time came and went, and at 2:15 a.m. on the 2nd, with the canoe an hour and a quarter late, *United* picked up two 'sharp explosions' on its ASDIC. This was a 'prearranged signal with the Folbotists to surface the submarine in an emergency and take them onboard'. Yet they 'still showed no signs of appearing', leading Roxburgh to conclude that the sound was possibly a 'coincidence'. He made for the second emergency rendezvous, and searched throughout the 2nd without success. Early on 3 March, Roxburgh withdrew to the southern limit of his patrol area to report the loss of Smith and Brand, the 'probability of Beach 23 being compromised', and his 'intention to proceed to [Beach] 18A with remainder of party'.[9]

Roxburgh feared that the pair had been captured. In fact they were still at large, and part way through one of the great feats of endurance of the war. Their plan had been to map an offshore sandbar, using their sounding gear from the canoe. But the wind whipped up and by midnight was almost at gale force. They struggled for more than two hours to signal the submarine, moving back inshore at one point to check their bearing on a known landmark. Eventually one of Brand's oar blades was snapped by a wave and, with daylight fast approaching, Smith summed up their options. 'The sub will never find us in this! Either we go inshore and give ourselves up, or we bloody well paddle for Malta.'

'I'd rather paddle to hell than go in,' said Brand.

'How far is it?'

'What – Malta? About seventy, what do you say?'

'Look what she's stood up to already.'

'All right,' said Brand. 'Let's have a bash.'

It was the start of an epic voyage. Using the distant cone of Mount Etna as a back-bearing, Smith worked out a course. Then they set off, taking it in turns with the whole paddle while the other man bailed. Hour after hour they struggled through 'boiling waves, great watery hills that slewed this way and that and occasionally caught them abeam'. At one point they spotted an Italian plane overhead and feared it would report them. They plodded wearily on, their muscles screaming with exhaustion. That night the wind died, making their ordeal a little more bearable. But there was still a long way to go.

As dawn rose on 3 March, Smith pointed ahead. 'Look at that!' he croaked. '*Look at that!*'

It was Malta, its low hills rising out of the pale horizon. 'Well – my God!' said Brand. 'Christ – look at that.'

They paddled onwards, and in the early afternoon saw a motor torpedo boat in the distance. Smith got out the tommy gun and fired a burst to attract attention. Then he picked up the Aldis lamp and flashed.

The MTB altered course and came streaking towards them, leaving a great V-shaped bow wave in its wake. Transported back to Sliema Creek, Brand was taken to hospital for treatment to an old hip wound that the ordeal had reopened. Smith, on the other hand, was still game enough to paddle their battered canoe the last half-mile to the submarine base. 'Good God, man!' said Captain Phillips, as he approached the jetty. 'What have you done with the *United*?'[10]

The submarine, as it happened, was still carrying out its mission. Cheered by the news that Smith and Brand had returned to Malta safely, and that Beach 23 was not compromised but still 'unsuitable for further work', Roxburgh decided to move instead to Beach 18A. Aircraft activity and poor weather delayed the operation for a few days, and it finally took place during the night of 8/9 March when Lieutenant Hart and Sub Lieutenant

Folder were launched in the folbot, though there was 'quite a sea running with wind of force 4'. They did not return. Underwater explosions – consistent with the signal underwater explosion charges carried by the Folbot party – were heard at 1:40 a.m. on the 9th. But, apart from that, nothing. By mid-morning, with the wind at force 7 and a heavy swell running from the west, Roxburgh called off the search and withdrew to Malta.[11]

Hart had come unstuck when his swimsuit filled with water. Scrambling ashore to empty it, he ran into barbed wire and was captured by a German sentry. Folder was intercepted the following morning by soldiers in a fishing boat as he tried to paddle out to sea.[12]

*

Working further east from 'Mossy' Turner's HMS *Unrivalled*, Peter de Kock's Middle East 2 party had no more luck than the other Malta COPPs. He and Sub Lieutenant Alfred Crossley, another South African, went to investigate Beaches 13 and 14 during the night of 6/7 March and failed to return. The following night, a Lieutenant Davies went in with Able Seaman James McGuire to look for them and both were captured.

That just left Neville McHarg's COPP 4. Brought from Algiers by HMS *Safari*, McHarg had the task of surveying the north-west coast of Sicily from Trapani to Cape Zafferano. He went out the first two nights with his paddler Lieutenant George Sinclair, another Party Inhuman veteran, but fishing boats and bad weather impeded their progress. Next it was the turn of the military officer, Captain Edward Parsons, and his paddler Leading Seaman Irvine. They were dropped in a nasty swell and did not return. Parsons was caught crawling up the beach by a sentry and Irvine, 'nosing in too close with the canoe, was caught in the alarm that sounded'.

McHarg and Sinclair continued their work as best they could, though by now the Germans on Sicily were thoroughly alive to the presence of Allied submarines. The Coppists gathered as much information as they could from periscope observations, and endured more close calls as *Safari* was lit up one night by shore searchlights and narrowly escaped a chasing E-boat. Eventually they called it a day and returned to Algiers, the only pair of canoeists to return from the mission in a submarine.[13] McHarg and Sinclair were both awarded the DSO for their excellent work; Smith and Brand got DSCs.

*

The first news to reach Nigel Willmott in the UK was a cable from Captain Phillips in Malta. It noted, with regret, that Norman Teacher, Noel Cooper and George Burbridge were all missing from COPP 3. Willmott immediately despatched his base officer, Lieutenant Commander Geoffrey 'Gaffer' Moorhouse, to find out what had happened.[14]

Moorhouse arrived in Malta to more bad news. Of the fifteen canoeists spread across the four COPPs who had taken part in the Sicily reconnaissance, only four had returned: McHarg and Sinclair by submarine; and Smith and Brand by canoe. The other eleven were all missing: either dead or captured.* This was a shocking casualty rate of more than seventy per cent, and unsustainable if it was repeated on future COPP operations. Moorhouse's task, therefore, was to gather all the evidence and make recommendations for the future. On 19 March he wrote to Willmott who, at the same time, was receiving separate reports from Captain Phillips and lieutenants Smith and McHarg.

Willmott reported, in turn, to Mountbatten that the fundamental reason for the loss of Teacher and the other COPP officers was overwork. 'Shortly after arrival at Malta,' wrote Willmott,

---

* Six were captured: Captain Parsons and Leading Seaman Irvine, Lieutenant Hart and Sub Lieutenant Folder, and Lieutenant Davies and Able Seaman McGuire. The remaining five were never seen again and probably drowned: Lieutenant Commander Teacher, Captain Burbridge, Lieutenant Cooper, Lieutenant de Kock and Sub Lieutenant Crossley.

'Teacher had to take a large and almost untrained party from ME under his wing and not only train but equip them as they had nothing at all but three bare canoes – e.g. even no compasses, binoculars etc.' Even Teacher's own canoes – and equipment 'were deficient', admitted Willmott, 'certainly for winter work though perhaps the best that was then available anywhere'. The whole scheme had been regarded in the UK 'as a serious risk'.

Teacher, moreover, had had to plan three separate submarine reconnaissances which 'must have taken up his time and energy completely'. This 'at the cost of training, for which, in any case, there was insufficient time as regards the ME team'. Teacher's loss while away from his canoe may have been due, noted Willmott, 'to his swimsuit becoming waterlogged' as he had complained that it did not fit. As for the other members of COPP 3 – Burbridge and Cooper – their loss was probably down to a lack of 'navigational training' and a 'featureless coast'. Before that 'unfortunate night' they had done 'extremely well'.[15]

Willmott added to his report an appendix of comments by Neville McHarg. They included the observation that the Sicily surveys had been 'carried out in any weather and consequently we all plugged away at it instead of cautiously insisting on calm seas and practically no wind'; that some of the canoeists had put their faith in the infrared transmitter rather than navigation, without realising that the former 'is only a secondary aid'; and that some of the submarines may have been out of position when they lost their canoeists.

A number of additional points were made by Lieutenant Smith who confirmed that 'no homing exercises' were practised with the submarine prior to the mission; that, in 'view of the urgency and scope' of the surveys, every effort was made 'to complete as many beaches as possible during each sortie'; that the 'majority of the Party were relatively untrained in seagoing navigation, thereby not having the self-confidence' to tell the submarine captain 'what they wanted done'; yet Teacher and Smith 'were fully satisfied by the training of all three parties', and Lieutenant de Kock had 'professed himself entirely confident to carry though the job'.[16]

The reason all this mattered is that, despite the losses, Admiral Cunningham was impressed with the work done by Willmott's men* and had already asked for two new COPP teams to be sent to the Mediterranean to complete the Sicily beach surveys before the final plan of invasion was settled. Willmott was reluctant to send them until they had been properly trained and equipped – but he could not disobey a direct order. He gained some solace from the knowledge that the new COPPs – 5 and 6 – would have better swimming suits (specially designed by diving specialists Siebe-Gorman) and improved canoes.

Willmott was convinced that an ill-fitting suit had done for Teacher who, having failed to pick up his canoe, had preferred to swim straight out to sea and drown rather than compromise the mission.

'We'll never know,' said one of his officers.

'Just the same, I'm sure,' responded Willmott. 'I know Norman.'[17]

---

* For example, the report of Beach 28 by COPP 3 – by both periscope observation in daylight and 'swimming by night' – included information on landing craft release positions, currents, beach composition, enemy vigilance, pilotage approach diagrams, water depths and silhouettes. (TNA, WO 252 1199, Beach Intelligence Reports (BIGOT/HUSKY), Sciacca Area, 18 March 1943.)

26

'This, I think, is what you've both been waiting for'

Lieutenant Ralph Stanbury RN felt his breast swell with patriotic pride as the destroyer approached the coast of Malta in early June 1943. From the deck he could see the 'twin towns of Valletta and Sliema, the sun glistening on the sandstone houses which surrounded the narrow creeks and ran down to the harbour entrances'. He was aware of the relentless bombing campaign that the island had been subjected to, and was delighted that this 'battered little bastion of Empire' was to be the base from which he and his men operated.

Four months earlier, having just recovered from a broken leg, Stanbury had been posted to Hayling Island to form COPP 5. A 25-year-old regular naval officer from Somerset, he was serving on the destroyer HMS *Mashona* when war broke out and had vivid memories of the desperate rescue of British troops at the end of the disastrous Norway campaign in 1940:

The towering walls of the fjord reddened by the billows of flame that swept the wooden dwellings of the little village; the dim forms of the two cruisers in the middle of the fjord, where there was room to manoeuvre and limitless depths of water; my own ship – a destroyer – alongside the only jetty which had miraculously escaped the rain of bombs, with six inches of water under the keel, waiting for the men that we were to ferry to the bigger ships. And, finally, the long line of men, trudging wearily down from the end of the Oester valley, the vast walls of the gorge reducing them to a procession of black ants. It was just like a

vision of Dante's *Inferno*, the impression being heightened by the
low roof of smoke, lit with a cherry glow reflected from countless
twisting tongues of flame.

Mashona was bombed and sunk by German aircraft the
following year, with the loss of forty-eight crew. Fortunately for
Stanbury, he had left the ship a few months earlier to take the
navy's long navigation – or 'N' – course at Portsmouth. Having
passed, he served as a navigator on the cruiser HMS *Diomede*
until he broke his leg and returned to the UK to recuperate in
August 1942. He was frustrated by the long period of inactivity
and, once strong and healthy again, he volunteered for special
operations, though there would be many times in the months to
come when he would regret his 'impetuosity'.

With thinning jet-black hair and a luxuriant beard that
'changed in colour from brown near the ears to gold at the
point', Stanbury had listened with mounting excitement as Nigel
Willmott explained to him and two other new senior officers
the vital role that beach reconnaissance would play in the invasion of occupied Europe. Planners would need to know everything
they could about deserted beaches: 'the exact nature and surface
of the beach above and below water, its slope, the feasibility of
any exits off it, or the exact height of any defence works and
obstacles'.

Willmott concluded: 'You are expert at navigation and survey
work, and you will be given any extra instruction and training
that is necessary. You will have under you officers who are
experts in their own particular side of an invasion. Together with
them you will land on the enemy coast and obtain all the information that's needed. Are there any questions?'

Stanbury could not think of any. Now, barely twelve weeks
later, he was about to put his accelerated training into practice
for Operation Husky, the invasion of Sicily. Shocked by the sight
of shattered buildings and wrecked ships in and around the
Grand Harbour, Stanbury was relieved when he and his men
were transported to the same cluster of villas on the Ghajn

Tuffieha headland that COPP 3 had used as its base. Occupying the biggest house, having arrived a week earlier, was Lieutenant 'Daddy' Amer and COPP 6. So Stanbury and his men took over the smaller villa, also covered with a mass of bougainvillea and fronted by a row of pink oleander bushes.

His military officer was 29-year-old Captain Peter T. 'Mat' Matterson RE, a punctilious and conscientious soldier who had been seconded from Courtney's SBS. Matterson was 'always immaculately dressed', recalled Stanbury, 'from the forage-cap perched on his rather round head with its shrewd brown eyes and clipped brown moustache, to his army boots, which he personally polished for at least an hour each night'. Stanbury had never met anyone with better judgement.

Noticing that his boss was a little down at mouth, Matterson asked him what was up. Stanbury explained that, after their arrival, he had spoken to Captain Phillips, commanding the 10th Submarine Flotilla on Malta, who was not keen to lend them one of his boats.

'But why?'

'Well, for one thing,' said Stanbury, 'he has a prodigious number of commitments, such as patrols which have to be carried out. Secondly, he thinks it's too dangerous, both for the boats and more especially for ourselves.'

They went to give the bad news to Stanbury's naval assistant, Sub Lieutenant Douglas 'Duggie' Kent, who was supervising the unpacking of stores. 'A volunteer in the RNVR, expert on Combined Operations,' noted Stanbury,

he could never quite overcome his impetuosity or his resentment at any apparent delay. He was at times embarrassingly frank and outspoken. Although 23 years old . . . he looked no more than eighteen, with his boyish face, rosy cheeks, and round blue eyes. He was as courageous as a lion, and was miserable unless he was in the thick of the fray. Like Mat, he was married, and I rather gathered that an addition to the family was expected shortly.

Having served with the Royal Naval Beach Commandos on the raids at Lofoten, Vågsøy and Boulogne (winning a DSC in the process), Kent was eager for more action and Stanbury's news was hard for him to swallow. He muttered his dissatisfaction.

'We will just have to wait,' said Stanbury. 'Somehow I have a feeling that things may be very much hotter than we expect in the near future.'[1]

*

Stanbury was right. A few days later, he found himself back in Captain Phillips' office at the Lazaretto Submarine Base in Marsamxett harbour, a 'large airy room hung with maps and charts of current patrols and operations'.

'We have been told, Stanbury,' said Phillips, 'to make an examination of the Murro di Porco peninsula.' He walked over to a map of Sicily and pointed to a promontory on the southeast coast, just below Syracuse.

'With what particular end in view, sir?' asked Stanbury.

'I'm afraid they give no details, but the part they are especially interested in is the one and a half miles either side of the lighthouse on the point itself.'

'Are we to land, sir?'

'No. Just make notes – and, I suppose, sketches – of anything you see. Only one of your party will be needed, and I suggest that you go yourself, so as to get acquainted with the area. The water is quite deep within a mile of the shore, so you can get quite close for your inspection.'

Stanbury would be going, added Phillips, with Lieutenant Turner of the *Unrivalled* who had done this sort of thing before. 'He's in the mess now, if you care to go over and discuss things with him.'

Stanbury took his cue, and found Turner – or 'Mossy' as he was known to his friends – in the huge vaulted room, constructed out of giant sandstone blocks, that served as the submarine officers' wardroom at Lazaretto. On entering, Stanbury noticed that the wall to the right of the entrance was the cliff of the creek itself, a clue as to how the base 'had so miraculously survived the blitz of the previous year'. Bombs landing in the water outside, or on the cliff above, would not have 'the slightest effect'. Nor could they disrupt the work at the base – apart from that in progress on the submarines themselves – 'as most of the offices, together with a large number of workshops, were in tunnels and chambers in the cliff itself'.

Stanbury was introduced to Turner, a man of 'medium height, with an athletic figure and very blue eyes'. He had, moreover, 'a mouth that was always smiling out of an extremely artistic-looking beard'. They discussed the coming mission over enormous glasses of gin and lime, served in the bottom half of an old bottle (glasses being at a premium in wartime Malta), and Stanbury found the submariner and his friends to be convivial company and keen to assist. 'They appreciated my difficulties and problems,' noted Stanbury, 'and were always ready and willing to give a helping hand'.

Two days later, Stanbury left on his mission, remaining with Turner on *Unrivalled*'s bridge until they were clear of the breakwater and into open sea. Once through Malta's approach channel, Turner ordered the submarine to dive. A loud klaxon sounded –a 'raucous blare' that Stanbury would come to dread in the months ahead – and *Unrivalled* slipped beneath the waves. 'I suggest,' said Turner, 'we eat now and then surface after dark.'

Stanbury glanced at his watch. It was 7:00 p.m. 'Good show,' he replied. 'I could just do with a bit of supper!'

'Supper!' said Turner, amused. 'We're just going to have break-fast. You see we do all our energetic work on the surface at night. By day we submerge, and everyone takes it easy; in fact, we encourage as much sleep as possible when we're submerged, because it conserves the air if people keep still. So we just convert day into night to suit our routine!'

Breakfast consisted of bacon, beans and coffee, and was eaten in relays as there was not enough room for Stanbury and the four submarine officers to sit together round the mess table. He spent most of the meal trying to prevent a swarm of cockroaches from stealing his bread. 'If for one moment I relaxed my attention,' he recalled, 'I would glance down to see half a dozen of the little beasts having a good feed . . . Disgusting little creatures! The submarine simply swarmed with them, and, as fast as one killed them, more appeared.'

Stanbury slept through the night in one of the wardroom's four tiny bunks, and was woken by Turner at 8:00 a.m., by which time the boat was running submerged up the east coast of Sicily 'with the coastal plateau just visible some eight miles to port'. Supper was on the table.

Having eaten, Stanbury was preparing his sketching material when he was called to the control-room. 'We're about two miles from the coast now,' said the officer of the watch. 'Would you care to take the periscope for a while?'

'Right,' responded Stanbury. 'I suggest we circle slowly about a mile from the shore. I'll sing out anything I see, and you write it down in my notebook. I've got to check bearings so that we don't get inside the fifteen-fathom line.'

He went over to the periscope, cleared the eyepieces, switched to low power, adjusted the focus and checked the depth: twenty-eight feet. 'Up periscope,' he ordered. As the eyepieces came up level with his face, he bent forward and got his first view of Sicily. About a mile away – but appearing to be much closer – was a lighthouse at the eastern end of the Murro di Porco (so called because it resembled a pig's snout) peninsula, below which the land curved round in a wide semicircle, 'forming a large, sheltered bay, with steep cliffs rising sheer out of the water on the northern side'. To the west the coast was lower, but still impracticable for the landing of vehicles.

Just to the north of the lighthouse he spotted something 'squat and sinister': the shield of a coastal gun. Moving the periscope to the left he could see a second and then a third gun, all of them in strong concrete emplacements. Situated where they were, on the top of a narrow peninsula, they commanded the coastline for at least six miles in both directions. Before any troops landed on the beaches four miles south, or at Syracuse two miles to the north, these guns would have to be destroyed. The means became clear when he spotted, at the southern base of the peninsula, a narrow rock beach 'formed by a sudden receding of the cliff'. Behind it there was a clear route up the cliff with clumps of trees and bushes as cover. Concluding that it was 'quite conceivable for a small band of Commandos to land in this place', scale the cliff and knock out the battery, Stanbury dictated the details to the officer standing by.

Apart from a brief scare as a fishing boat passed overhead, Stanbury spent the rest of the day examining the peninsula and sketching it in detail from four different viewpoints. Next day, he asked Turner if he could make a close examination of the landing beaches. He knew where they were because, just before leaving for Malta, Matterson had arranged for him to attend the conference in London 'at which the senior Army officers were being briefed in the plan for the landings'. Having 'seen and mentally noted each beach, with its background', he found they were 'surprisingly easy to identify'. The model of the coastline had been 'uncannily accurate'.

He easily identified, for example, one of the beaches on which the 50th (Tyne Tees) Division was scheduled to land: 'about half a mile long, sandy and gently sloping'. Stanbury noted and sketched every 'pillbox and strongpoint', and the fact that two neighbouring beaches, one of shingle, 'gave easy access to the Syracuse road'. Useful as all this information was, he knew that only a close personal reconnaissance could supply all the answers the attackers would need. But that, as Phillips had made clear, was out of the question.

Once back in Malta, Stanbury's intelligence was airlifted to the Allied Force HQ in Algiers. He was hoping against hope that it might prompt orders for proper beach surveys: not least because Amer and COPP 6 had been allowed to do just that –

working with two 'chariot' crews to survey the beaches of south-east Sicily in early June.* But when no permission for more surveys was forthcoming by late June – little more than a fortnight from the actual invasion – Stanbury and 'Daddy' Amer took matters into their own hands. Riding into Valletta on motorbikes on the day King George VI paid a visit, they were met by Captain Phillips holding a 'pink' secret signal. 'This, I think,' he said, 'is what you've both been waiting for.'

He handed it to Amer, while Stanbury peered over his shoulder. It was an order for the two COPPs to provide urgent information on the invasion beaches before the end of the month. Phillips was to provide any assistance they required. They were to exercise, the signal warned, extreme caution so as not to jeopardise the invasion. The COPP officers looked at each other and smiled. This was it, all right.

Phillips then briefed them on their respective roles: Amer would survey beaches on the south coast, between Licata and Scoglitti, where the American II Corps (part of General Patton's 7th Army) was due to land; while Stanbury would concentrate on the beaches of the south-east coast, between Cape Passero and the Murro di Porco lighthouse, familiar ground from his earlier reconnaissance, and due to be used by the invading spearheads of the British XIII and XXX Corps (part of General Montgomery's 8th Army). If there was a risk of compromise, continued Phillips, they were to use their discretion on whether to land at all. Hearing this, Amer shook his head slightly: clearly, he felt the risk was worth it, as did Stanbury.

'You are to consider the underwater information,' said Phillips, 'as the most important of all, especially as regards bars, rocks, and obstructions. And you're to make yourselves thoroughly

---

* The results were mixed: one 'chariot' (a slow-moving torpedo-like craft operated by two divers sitting astride) sank as soon as it was launched, while the other successfully 'sounded' the approach to a beach on the night of 6/7 June. Two folbot crews also carried out surveys that night: Amer and his E/COPP, Captain D. C. Hunter of the Royal Engineers; and Lieutenant Peter Wild and Leading Seaman Fred Phillips. (TNA, ADM 199/1822 and 1824.)

acquainted with your particular areas, as you'll be in charge of all the marking and piloting during the assault.'

The captain then assigned them their submarines: this time Amer would go in 'Mossy' Turner's *Unrivalled*; while Stanbury went with Lieutenant 'Otto' Stanley of HMS *Unbending* who, since COPP 3's ill-fated beach survey in early March, had won a DSO to add to his earlier DSC for carrying out another clandestine mission and sinking a number of enemy ships. Stanbury was delighted. He had already met the 'good-natured, jovial' Stanley who, though still in his mid-20s, 'was one of the most famous captains in the "trade"'. Stanbury recalled: 'The speed at which he went up and down through the conning-tower hatch was a matter of constant admiration to me, for his ample frame could allow very little, if any, gap!'[2]

'That beach is a deathtrap'

With three large beaches to investigate – numbers 45, 47 and 48 – Ralph Stanbury took two canoe crews in HMS *Unbending*: himself, Captain 'Mat' Matterson, Lieutenant 'Duggie' Kent and Leading Seaman Alfred 'Tommo' Thomas, a Londoner and pre-war ship's steward who had won a DSM while serving on the corvette HMS *Salvia*.* Thomas, 'a pillar of strength and a fund of humour', had passed up a commission to join COPP 5 and Stanbury felt 'extremely lucky to have him'.

They arrived off the east coast of Sicily at dawn on 25 June and spent the rest of the day inspecting the beaches by periscope. The plan was for Stanbury and Kent to land that first night on Beach 45, lying seven miles south-west of the Murro di Porco peninsula, so they spent the final hour of daylight examining its 400-yard length from 'every angle'. Then, having checked and rechecked their timetable, Stanbury struggled into his tight-fitting rubber swimsuit. To prevent water 'seeping inside at the wrists and collar, the rubber at these points had been specially strengthened and toughened', making it 'the very devil to put on'. The hot and fetid atmosphere in the submarine made the job harder still. Once the suit was on, he fastened round his waist a belt containing his revolver, fighting knife, compass 'and the gadgets necessary for taking soundings'.

* Thomas had left HMS *Salvia* by the time she was torpedoed by a German U-boat and sunk with all hands, including one hundred survivors of an earlier submarine attack, on 24 December 1941.

As Stanbury waited for the submarine to surface, the 'thought of landing all alone on a heavily sentried coast' was giving him more than a few qualms. To occupy his mind, therefore, he tried to make a mental list of all the ports of the world he had visited. He was just getting into his stride, and was thinking of one particular place on the east coast of South America where, exactly a year earlier, a 'cool breeze' had 'played gently through the long, dark hair' of his female companion, when he was interrupted by the 'diving stations' klaxon. 'Another moment,' he recalled, 'and we were on the surface. I climbed up the conning-tower ladder on to the bridge. The night appeared pitch-dark after the lighting of the submarine's interior; below me I could hear whispering and movements as "Old Faithful" was brought up from her stowage in the torpedo-compartment and lowered into the water.'[1]

His canoe 'Old Faithful' was a brand-new Mark I model, made by Harris Lebus Ltd, and a vast improvement on the canoe used by COPPs 3 and 4 in March. It had been, noted Willmott, 'well and carefully constructed' and was the first canoe 'in which one can have any confidence, either for operations or for serious training'.[2] As he and Kent lowered themselves into the canoe, Stanbury could hear Stanley wish him 'Good luck' from the conning tower. Matterson added: 'Don't be late!'

Seconds later he was 'automatically paddling towards land', with Kent in stroke behind him. When he looked back, the submarine was gone. He suddenly felt an intense loneliness. Would he ever see the submarine again, he wondered, and what would happen if Kent failed to pick him up after his examination of the beach? His gloomy thoughts were interrupted by Kent's voice. 'I can't see the beach anywhere, Ralph.'

'We'll have to keep our eyes skinned,' he replied. 'It's only 400 yards long, and will hardly show up at all against the background on a dark night like this.'

By now, with the cool night air 'acting like a tonic', Stanbury's anxiety had given way to a 'wild surge of exhilaration'. He had an intense desire to stand up in the canoe and sing, but curbed himself. Instead he swung his paddle with gusto, digging it deep into the water and driving the canoe forward. Rapidly approaching the coast, they could now distinguish the low cliffs and the sound of waves on the shore. Three hundred yards away, they stopped paddling and Stanbury took out his binoculars. He was delighted by what he saw. 'There's our beach,' he said, handing the glasses to Kent, 'directly opposite us. You can also see the northern limit, where the gorge of the Cassibile river emerges, and it appears very dark. We've made it first time.'

'Yes, but look over there,' whispered Kent, pointing to the northern end of the beach where a horn of land jutted out into the sea. Clearly silhouetted on the skyline, halfway along the horn, was a small building that had been invisible from the submarine. As Stanbury looked, 'a door opened, letting out a stream of light, and the sound of men's voices, raised in laughter and song, floated out'. It was obviously a sentry hut and the occupants seemed to be celebrating something. Let's hope they keep going, thought Stanbury, until we finish our job.

Steering south, they stopped a hundred yards from the far end, keeping the canoe end-on to the beach to present as small a silhouette as possible. He looked at his watch: eleven o'clock. Time to go.

Having fastened the gusset on the collar of his swimsuit, he opened the flaps on the canopy of the canoe so he could get his legs out. 'Balance her, Duggie,' he whispered. 'I'm getting out port side. Wait for me at the other end of the beach, where we first came in. I'll swim out and flash my torch for you. OK?'

He eased himself slowly over the side. The slight splash sounded 'alarmingly loud', so keyed up were his senses. 'Cheerio,' said Kent as he backed the canoe away.

Once in the water, Stanbury's courage seemed to desert him. He felt 'utterly lonely and deserted', hemmed in 'by the darkness and terrors that hid in it'. But this fear lasted only for a minute or so. With time moving on, he struck out for the shore, swimming as silently as he could. Reaching the water's edge, he crawled forward on his belly, feeling carefully for mines or tripwires. At a depth of six inches the sandy bottom turned to shingle.

From the beach above him a single pebble rolled down the bank and into the water close to his head. Holding his breath, he drew his revolver and waited. There was no more movement: it must have been an animal. He got to work, taking the stake attached to the reel of stout fishing line on his belt and digging it into the sand near the water's edge. Then, swimming silently away from the beach, he paid out the line. Every ten yards, marked by a bead, he trod water while he took the depth with a thin lead-line. From these two factors – depth and distance – he could work out later exactly how far each type of landing craft would beach from the water's edge.

It took an hour to sound the whole beach. Before leaving, Stanbury was determined to investigate a thick hedge at the back of the beach that he had seen through the periscope. Unwilling to crawl up the snow-white shingle, he made his way up the gorge of the Cassibile river until he was level with the hedge. As he inched towards it, he banged his knee against a rock. 'The pain,' he recalled, 'was excruciating and, to make matters worse, at that moment the door of the sentry hut opened once more, letting out a beam of light that gleamed on the bushes round me. Then the light disappeared and I painfully continued my journey.'

Reaching the hedge, he heard a dog bark 'with staccato suddenness'. His heart was in his mouth, but nothing approached. Once he had all the information he needed, he retraced his steps and re-entered the water. Two hundred yards out, he stopped swimming and used his waterproof torch to flash a code in Morse. He waited, but there was no sign of the canoe. Fearing the worst, he flashed again. Had Duggie lost his bearings? he wondered. It would be easy to do in the inky darkness. 'Then,' he remembered, 'faintly at first, but growing momentarily more clearly defined, the shape of the canoe floated into view, above the level of my eyes as I lay in the water, and having the appearance of being suspended in mid-air. I clambered into my seat – not without difficulty, for I was cold and stiff after my long period of swimming.'

With just over an hour to cover the two miles to their rendezvous, they headed out to sea. It was a gloriously clear night
– with the Milky Way lying 'like a huge white shadow across
the velvet dome of the sky' – and Stanbury paddled at speed to
stave off the chill and the drowsiness that were beginning to
settle on him. Judging they were in position, he paused and
shone his torch, with its narrow-shaded beam, in the direction
the submarine would come from. Then they waited.

After minutes that seemed like hours, they heard a faint
murmur to seaward, growing steadily into the 'muffled beat of
powerful diesel engines'. For a moment it seemed as if the
submarine was about to plough straight past them. So Stanbury
flashed his torch again and the submarine stopped her engines.
They paddled over to her and, within a few seconds, willing
hands had helped them on to the casing. Then Stanbury was
inside the boat, dazed by the light and noise as someone thrust
a cup of cocoa into his hands. He heard the skipper, 'Otto'
Stanley, asking if he had had a pleasant trip. 'Very,' he replied.

He looked up at the clock on the bulkhead and could see that
he had been out, 'under constant exertion', for five hours.
Suddenly he felt exhausted, 'limp and flat – rather like a balloon
from which the air has escaped'.[3]

*

Next day, after sleeping for six hours, Stanbury 'settled down to
the arduous and complicated task of identifying strongpoints
and objects of importance on Beach 45, and "pinpointing" their
positions'. Then they circled underwater to the beach he would
explore that night – No. 47 – long and narrow, and backed by
a steep bank. At its southern end was a large building with two
pillars outside – the Casino d'Avola – that stood on a small,
rocky escarpment. They knew from aerial photos that it was
connected to the main Syracuse highway, a mile or so inland,
but a wide road. There seemed to be a complete absence of
pillboxes and beach defences.

As Matterson was due to mark that particular beach for the assault, Stanbury chose him as his paddler for the landing that night. It passed without serious incident until he realised, swimming back to the canoe, that the torch had sprung a leak and shorted. Unable to flash Morse code, he imitated the sound of a seagull, managing to 'raise a few squawks vaguely similar to one of these birds with a bone in its throat'.

Soon after he heard Matterson's voice ask: 'Feeling sick, old man?'

'I don't do this for pleasure,' Stanbury replied tartly as he hauled himself into the canoe.

'I saw your torch just before it went out,' said Matterson. 'I thought you were having some trouble, so I paddled towards you, and was just on top of you when you made those fantastic noises.'

They paddled out to the rendezvous point where they used Matterson's torch to signal the submarine. Twenty minutes passed, but nothing came. 'Gradually,' wrote Stanbury, 'the dismal truth forced itself into my brain and, as I came to the full realisation of it, the moon climbed slowly over the eastern horizon; with every moment that it rose, our hopes of recovery, already slight, sank. Eighty miles to the south of us lay the nearest friendly shore, Malta; while behind us, at the best, lay the prison camps of Italy.'

Before setting off, Stanbury had one last ace to play. Sitting between his legs was a lantern attached to a twelve-volt battery. It was fitted with a special infrared shade, so Stanbury unclipped the latter and directed the beam, 'like a miniature searchlight', all around him, fully aware that it was as likely to be seen from the shore as from the submarine.

Suddenly they heard a faint murmur to the south, and inshore of their position. It grew momentarily louder but then began to recede into the distance. 'My God!' exclaimed Stanbury. 'It's the submarine. She saw our light all right, but she's overshot us and headed out to sea.'

Dawn was beginning to break as he picked up the torch and

flashed. 'Next moment,' recalled Stanbury, 'we saw the submarine heading straight for us at full speed, her bow wave creaming up and over her snub nose.' They scrambled aboard and were met by Stanley on the conning tower. 'Thank God you're safe,' said the skipper. 'We were on our way back to Malta to break the sad news that we'd lost you, when we saw your lantern.'[4]

*

With one more beach to survey – No. 48 – Stanbury let Kent go ashore after dark on 27 June with Thomas as his paddler. It looked, from their periscope observations, as if there were 'no hazards' and was 'just the sort of beach one would choose for a picnic'.

But no sooner had the canoe launched than the drama started. The submarine was picked up by two radar beams from the shore and, as a result, the shore was swept with searchlights for much of the time that the canoe was away. Even so, *Unbending* evaded detection and successfully recovered Kent and Thomas at the allotted time. Submerged again and heading for Malta, Stanbury spoke to Kent as he changed out of the rubber swimsuit in the wardroom. 'How did everything go?' he asked.

'Pretty grim,' replied Kent. 'That beach is a deathtrap. Look at this swimsuit of yours. It's practically cut to pieces by underwater rocks. I tell you, Ralph, I've never known anything that could look so lovely to the eye and yet be so perfectly foul when examined closely. It really gives me the shudders. It took me half an hour to wade over those rocks and reefs; no landing craft could have got closer than 200 yards to the beach, and the soldiers would be drowned or shot to ribbons before they could land.'

'Thank heavens you found that out. Anything else?'

'Yes,' said Kent. 'Those damned Eyeties haven't the manners of a dog. I shipped a lot of water into your swimsuit clambering over the rocks, and it gave me a bad cramp in my legs and stomach. It's a large flat beach and I could see there was no one around. So I slipped off the swimsuit and was standing just as I was born, massaging my limbs on the water's edge, when the blighters went and turned a searchlight on me!'

Stanbury whistled his astonishment. 'Do you think they spotted you?'

'Good heavens, no. It was the sub they were looking for. But it was certainly somewhat embarrassing.'[5]

*

Within hours of *Unbending*'s return to Malta, COPP 5's complete beach reconnaissance report was on its way to Allied Force HQ in Algiers by aeroplane. The sketches and silhouettes of the beaches followed a day later. Stanbury would like to have taken them in person. But there was more important work at hand, 'planning the guiding of the assault to the beaches'.

Amer and COPP 6 returned the day after Stanbury's party. They, too, brought vital information, though its collection had almost cost Amer his life. During one survey, Amer was swimming a few yards from the water's edge when he was spotted by a sentry who called for a comrade to join him. With Amer 'frozen' in the water, and only his head and shoulders showing, the two Italians could not work out what they were looking at. Was it a seal? They threw stones to get it to move, prompting Amer to act. Slitting open his swimsuit to make it less buoyant, he swam silently away with his nostrils just above water. But the weight of the water in his suit was 'too much', he told Stanbury, and he was on the point of drowning when 'his companion saw his struggles from the canoe and rescued him in the nick of time'.[6]

'Never before had I seen such an armada'

Shortly after dark on 8 July 1943, HMS *Unbending* surfaced and moved to a position a mile off Beach 47 on Sicily's south-east coast where Lieutenant Ralph Stanbury supervised the laying of a special buoy. The buoy was designed to sink to the seabed, where it would be safe from enemy detection or observation. After a delay of twenty-four hours, it would be released by a timer and bob to the surface. Its job was to transmit a radio beam to guide the motor launch which, in turn, would lead in the landing craft at Zero Hour on D-Day, 10 July. A stout cable, moored to the seabed, would keep the buoy in position.

Having laid two more buoys off beaches 44 and 45, a little further to the north, *Unbending* headed for the open sea. As it did so, squadron after squadron of Allied bombers passed overhead. 'In the direction of Syracuse and the coast opposite us,' recalled Stanbury, 'rows of flares were floating down to the earth, while streams of bright-red tracer leapt up to meet them. Then the sky was dotted with the red bursts of ack-ack shells. The sound of the bombs and the ack-ack fire did not reach us for some seconds.'

Watching the fireworks alongside him was the submarine's skipper. 'They're getting it tonight all right,' observed Lieutenant 'Otto' Stanley. 'I suppose this is part of the "softening up" for the invasion.'

But even as the raid ended, Stanbury could see the ominous sign of storm clouds spreading from the north and towering over Sicily, 'oppressive and forbidding'. The wind was rising and 'already the tops of the waves were curling over in foam'.[1]

By morning of the 9th, the weather had not improved. Aware that more than 3,000 warships, supply vessels and landing craft were converging on a hundred miles of Sicily's coast with 160,000 troops, 14,000 vehicles, 600 tanks and 1,800 guns[2] – all part of the largest amphibious operation of the war – Stanbury felt sick to his stomach. He knew that unless the storm abated, a post-ponement of the assault was inevitable. But if anything it got worse. 'Come away from the periscope, Ralph,' urged Captain Matterson at noon. 'You're only torturing yourself, and any amount of looking will not change the weather.'

'I know it,' he replied. 'But it makes me furious that today, of all days, should be rough. We've had lovely weather for weeks, when we haven't specially needed it; now, when it is essential, we get a dose of this appalling sort of stuff.'

At sunset on the 9th, *Unbending* surfaced and headed towards Beach 47 where the first canoe – manned by Matterson and his new paddler Corporal Ronnie Williamson, a Shetlander who was experienced in boat handling and long-distance swimming – would position itself just offshore with a marking light to guide the motor launches and the landing craft. They would then move to Beach 44 and drop off Leading Seaman Thomas's canoe. It seemed to Stanbury, from the level of the conning tower, that the waves were lower than they had been. But he could not be certain.

Turning to Lieutenant Stanley, he asked: 'Has there been any word at all from the convoy?'

'None,' said the skipper. 'Nothing will make them break wire-less silence, as it would betray their position. Are you worried that the operation may have been postponed?'

'Yes, terribly. Supposing we send Mat and Thomas into the beaches and the show is postponed; we'll never be able to regain contact with them or recover them. That means they'll probably be captured as soon as it's light – if they haven't drowned. Then supposing the show is on and they aren't marking their beaches;

how on earth are the landing craft going to find the correct place? The answer is that they won't, and there'll be an unholy mess!'

Moments later, Matterson joined them on the bridge in his camouflaged paddler's suit. 'All ready, Ralph,' he said. 'How long before I depart?'

Nodding towards the white crests of the waves and the clouds of spray flying over the submarine's bows, Stanbury asked: 'Are you honestly considering launching the canoe in that?'

'Yes,' he replied, unperturbed. 'But I'd like you to drop me as close as possible to the beach, because Williamson and I will have our work cut out getting the canoe to move at all in that sea.'

Stanbury looked inquiringly at Stanley, who nodded. 'I'll take the boat in as close as I can,' he said, 'and try to make a lee for you.'

It was nearly 10:00 p.m. and, barring a cancellation, the foremost landing craft would be within ten miles. Stanbury made up his mind. 'All right,' he said, 'we'll be as quick as we can getting the canoe through the open hatch.'

As they crept closer to the shore – two miles, one and a half, one mile – they could see the land, and even the beaches, quite clearly in the moonlight. With the coastline sheltered a little by the Murro di Porco peninsula, the sea was 'indisputably calmer' here, much to Stanbury's relief. Yet, at the same time, he was worried that the submarine might be spotted. 'Don't you think this is near enough, Otto?' he asked the skipper when they were a little over half a mile from the beach. 'It's bright moonlight, and they might see us.'

'You needn't worry,' said Stanley. 'These craft are hard as hell to see in broad daylight, and I'm keeping her end-on to the shore.'

At half a mile, Stanley called a halt and Stanbury descended from the conning tower to the casing. It was, he recalled, 'beastly wet and slippery, and the craft was rolling heavily, beam-on to sea'. Stanbury knew that if a rush of water hit the canoe while it was lying alongside the hull, it would either capsize or be holed. He wracked his brain for a solution, and one came to him. They would launch the canoe from the submarine's snub-nose, which was better protected than the casing, and hope that Matterson and Williamson timed their leap correctly. The ploy worked, but the drama was far from over. The canoe was 'wrenched away', remembered Stanbury, 'by a wild surge of water through the casing, flung high on the crest of a breaker – a fantastic sight silhouetted in the path of the moon, half her length out of water'. It then disappeared in the trough of the wave and, for a moment, Stanbury's heart was in his mouth. But, by some miracle, it 'rose clear on to the crest of the next wave, with the crew paddling for dear life' and then, 'slowly, infinitely slowly', it was 'creeping towards the shore'.

Moving up the coast to launch the second marker-canoe, *Unbending*'s wireless operator searched for the radio beam from the three special buoys. There was nothing, and Stanbury was forced to conclude that the rough weather had broken their moorings. He thanked his lucky stars that he had given sketches and written instructions to the skippers of the three motor launches so they could recognise the beaches without the buoys.

They launched Thomas's canoe off Beach 44 without a problem, and then used the light from flares dropped by the latest wave of bombers to navigate to the correct position, six miles offshore, from where their beacon would guide the invasion convoy. After the bombers came an armada of transport planes towing gliders. 'As they crossed the coast,' recalled Stanbury, 'a wave of anti-aircraft fire rose to meet them. A plane burst into flames and plummeted to earth. But the remainder went inexorably on through a sky pockmarked with a hundred shell bursts.'

At 11:30 p.m. they began to shine the beacon light to the south. As the minutes passed and there was no sign of the convoy, the tension on the conning tower increased. It helped, however, that the sea was getting steadily calmer. Suddenly, close by,

Stanbury heard three shrill blasts on a ship's siren as it put its engines into reverse. Then a destroyer came into view, 'silhouetted against the glow of the fires to the west', followed by the vessels of the convoy, headed by the famous liners carrying the assault troops. Two fast assault ships passed, causing the submarine to roll slightly. They were heading north with Commandos to 'attack and capture the gun-batteries near the lighthouse on the promontory'. It was a mission made possible by his careful observation, and he felt quiet satisfaction as he watched the assault ships speed away.

More ships arrived, including the motor launches who were 'scurrying in and out amongst the great liners like sheepdogs, rounding up the flotillas of landing craft'. Stanbury looked at his watch: it was 2:00 a.m. He had been on his feet for thirty-six hours and was exhausted. In four hours he would have to report to the force commander in the HQ ship *Bulolo*. Now was the time to rest. He climbed down the conning-tower ladder and into the submarine. The second his head touched the bunk he was asleep.

*

Woken by Lieutenant Stanley at 6:00 a.m., Stanbury grabbed his kit and jumped from the submarine into the waiting launch. Out to sea a cruiser was bombarding the shore: after the flash of each broadside, 'huge mushrooms of earth and smoke showed the arrival of the shells on land'. Between the convoy and the shore, a distance of six miles, landing craft 'were hurrying backwards and forwards like water-beetles'. Stanbury recalled:

> Over the land the smoke of battle hung heavily, intermingled with the morning mist. The storm of the previous night had vanished completely, leaving in its place a long undulating swell, on which the hundreds of craft were rhythmically rising and falling. From the promontory to the north, as far as the eye could see, the

ocean was littered with ships – liners, warships, snub-nosed landing craft, oilers, store ships, and repair ships. Never before had I seen such an armada.

Once the launch was secured alongside the *Bulolo*, Stanbury clambered up the ladder and was taken to the bridge where a cluster of senior army and navy officers were watching the invasion. One turned as Stanbury approached – a huge man in a thick blue duffel coat – and Stanbury saluted. It was Rear Admiral Thomas Troubridge RN, the commander of Naval Force A whose responsibility was to land the British XIII Corps. A former skipper of the aircraft carrier *Illustrious* and the holder of the DSO and bar, Troubridge had run Combined Operations at Alexandria for a time and was an enthusiastic supporter of clandestine missions.

'You're Stanbury, aren't you?' asked Troubridge, before turning to the major general by his side. 'This is the officer who sent us those sketches and reports on the beaches. They came in very useful, Stanbury. Thank you.'

'Might I be of any more service, sir?' asked the COPP commander.

'You'd better see the Senior Naval Officer in charge of this sector,' replied Troubridge. 'You'll find him in the *Duchess of Bedford*.'

Stanbury saluted and left. An hour later, eating breakfast in the *Duchess of Bedford*'s saloon, he looked up to see 'Duggie' Kent whose job had been to guide the landing craft to Beach 45. 'Hullo, Ralph,' said Kent, 'I've just got back from the beaches, and I've a colossal hunger on me. Any idea what happens next?'

'No. I'm going to see the Senior Naval Officer again after breakfast. You'd better come with me. How did your show go? Did you manage to find the beach?'

'Oh yes. I had no difficulty, having seen it once already. It's a grand beach – very steep – and the landing craft touched down practically on the water's edge. But you remember the other beach to the north, the one that Tommo is marking?'

Stanbury nodded, his mouth full of bacon and eggs.

'Well, we were never asked to examine that one before the show. I believe they are having a lot of trouble with it now; it's not as good as they thought, by any means. There is a bar a good way out, and some of the craft have stuck on that; perhaps the storm piled it up last night. Anyway, as the smaller craft go in over the top of it, they are heaping up more and more sand. In time they'll form a lagoon there, and won't be able to get anywhere near the beach.'

This was a serious problem, Stanbury realised, as the beaches were needed for resupply until ports could be captured and repaired. After breakfast, they spoke to the SNO who gave them permission to take a small landing craft up the coast in search of an alternative beach. As they headed north, they moved through water strewn with the wreckage of gliders that had been released too early and come down short. Just beyond Thomas's problematic Beach 44, they rounded a headland and discovered a 'short, golden beach'. It seemed deserted, but for the sound of a dog howling at a farmhouse nearby. Examining the water close to the beach, they found it 'deep and free from obstructions or bars'. A quick sweep of the beach – with Kent standing guard with a tommy gun – indicated that it was not too steep for vehicles and exits were available.

Moving further up the coast, Stanbury was delighted to see the 'spiked guns of the battery to the north of the lighthouse' on the Murro di Porco peninsula. The Commando mission – carried out by just under 300 men of the Special Raiding Squadron, formerly 1st SAS – had succeeded, saving countless lives. On the way back, they saw a light on a cliff flashing SOS in Morse. They moved closer to investigate and recognised the maroon berets of the British 1st Airlanding Brigade. Seven men were rescued: six troopers and a lieutenant colonel. 'They were all dripping wet and swearing blasphemously,' recalled Stanbury, 'except the officer, who was simply speechless with fury. I wasn't surprised at his rage when he informed me that he had been training in England for two years, only to be dumped in the ocean a mile from the shore he had come to attack.'*

Returning to the main convoy, they met up with Captain Matterson and Corporal Williamson. The pair had had a tough time. Once in position off Beach 47, they turned on their marking light. But no sooner had they done so than the Italians tried to shoot it out. So, too, did some of the landing craft as they approached the beach, not realising who or what they were. Caught in the crossfire, they were lucky to survive.

Stanbury's last act on 10 July was to check on Thomas and his paddler at Beach 44. There, as Kent had prophesied, the beach was rapidly becoming useless for anything larger than DUKWs – a new amphibious vehicle† – and the smallest landing craft. After narrowly avoiding death at the hands of a German bomb, which exploded twenty yards in front of him, Stanbury found Thomas and told him to paddle his canoe back to the convoy. He and Kent followed in a DUKW.

Next day – 11 July – Kent and Matterson went to have another look at the small beach Stanbury had found, and reported back that it was 'splendid' and they had enlisted some sappers to clear mines and lay special tracking so vehicles could cross the sand. Stanbury joined them with the rest of his party, and later that day they received the first tank landing craft. 'As she came nearer,' wrote Stanbury, 'she half-lowered her ramp in preparation for beaching; then the flat underside of her bows ran gently up the underwater incline. The ramp came down with a rattle of chains, and spanned the water-gap to within a yard of the shore. Within

---

* The 1st Airlanding Brigade's mission was to capture the Ponte Grande bridge at Syracuse. Of the 144 Waco gliders that took off, seventy-eight ditched in the sea after their inexperienced pilots released them too early, two diverted to Malta and Tunisia, ten returned to base and forty-two landed along a twenty-five-mile stretch of the Sicilian coast. The brigade as a whole suffered 313 fatalities, including 225 drowned in ditched gliders. (Buckingham, *Arnhem 1944*, p. 18.)

† Made by General Motors, the DUKW (or 'Duck') was a six-wheel-drive amphibious truck, weighing two and a half tons and capable of carrying a load of 5,000 pounds or twenty-four troops.

two minutes all her vehicles had climbed up the beach and she was off for a fresh load.'

It was the start of a constant stream of traffic over the beach that made up, in large part, for the limitations of the neighbouring Beach 44. Stanbury and his men became 'remarkably bronzed and healthy with the excellent food, the sunshine on our naked bodies, and the pleasant labour of wading into the water to haul out stranded vehicles'. On 13 July, Stanbury and Kent hitched a lift on a lorry into Syracuse, which had been captured on D-Day, and visited Rear Admiral Troubridge in the old pilot's office that was serving as a combined army and navy Headquarters. There they were introduced to Admiral Sir Bertram Ramsay, commanding British naval forces at Sicily, who Stanbury hero-worshipped as the architect of the Dunkirk evacuation.

'What can I do for you, gentlemen?' asked Troubridge.

'Well, sir,' replied Stanbury, 'we feel we've completed our duty for the present invasion and, if there is no urgent need for further beach reconnaissances in Sicily, we would be grateful if we could return to Malta to prepare for the next assault.'

Troubridge agreed that their task was complete, and wished them luck in their next enterprise, as did Ramsay. They saluted and left.

A couple of days later, they loaded their canoes into a landing craft and set off for Malta. As they passed Cape Passero, at the south-eastern tip of Sicily, where the British XXX Corps had landed, Stanbury said a prayer for the souls of two of 'Daddy' Amer's men – Sub Lieutenant Anthony Sayce and Leading Seaman V. F. P. Manning – who had lost their lives there when their canoe was 'swamped by a huge wave as they were shining their beacon light to guide the waves of landing craft to the shore'.* Stanbury realised how lucky his own party had been to come through the invasion 'without a casualty'.[3]

---

* A separate theory is that they were 'struck by a glider that fell short, landing in the sea instead of on the mainland'. (Trenowden, *Stealthily by Night*, Chapter 13.)

Operation Husky was the first true test of Willmott's Coppists, and they came through it with flying colours. 'Much credit,' wrote Admiral of the Fleet Sir Andrew Cunningham in his Sicily despatch, 'is due to the officers and men of the beach reconnaissance parties for their arduous and hazardous effort to obtain details of the beach gradients and sandbars . . . Their casualties in this operation were unfortunately heavy; apart from the natural dislike of such losses, the possibility of capture always gives rise to anxiety on grounds of security.'[4]

Cunningham added in his memoirs: 'We were much indebted to the gallant young men of the Combined Operations Reconnaissance and Pilotage Parties, the "COPPs", who landed and reconnoitred the landing beaches beforehand in folbots sent in from submarines.'[5]

Ralph Stanbury and 'Daddy' Amer, the commanders of COPPs 5 and 6 respectively, were rewarded with the Distinguished Service Cross, as were their deputies 'Duggie' Kent (who now had the DSC and bar) and Peter Wild RN. 'Mat' Matterson of COPP 5 got the Military Cross. Of the ratings, Alfred Thomas got a bar to his Distinguished Service Medal, and two of Amer's party, Leading Seaman Fred Phillips and Able Seaman John Bowden, were given the same decoration.[6]

Willmott was delighted, noting in the COPP Depot's progress report that, having carried out their pre-invasion duties, Parties 5 and 6 then provided 'all the assault markers and also successful pilots for the Sicily landings'. Not content with that, COPP 5 had done 'some subsequent surveying and later ran a newly discovered beach on their own . . . passing in nearly 300 vehicles with one casualty'. It was quite an achievement.[7]

29
X-craft

At the time of her maiden voyage in 1936, the RMS *Queen Mary* was the last word in passenger-ship luxury. Built by the Cunard-White Star Line, the huge three-funnelled, 80,000-ton vessel contained two indoor swimming pools, beauty salons, libraries, children's nurseries and a first-class dining room (the grand salon) that spanned three storeys. She was also extremely fast: her four turbine engines capable of generating speeds in excess of thirty-two knots, enough to win the Blue Riband for the fastest Atlantic crossing.

Requisitioned in 1940 as a troopship, she was painted navy grey – earning her the nickname 'Grey Ghost' – and fitted with anti-aircraft guns. Too fast to be targeted by U-boats, she ranged as far as Sydney in Australia, returning with thousands of ANZAC soldiers. Her most famous wartime voyage, however, began in the Clyde estuary on 5 August 1943 when she slipped her moorings and set sail for Canada. On board was Winston Churchill, his wife and daughter – travelling under the cover names of Colonel, Mrs and Lieutenant Warden – and the British chiefs of staff and their senior planners. They were part of a 250-strong British party heading to the latest inter-Allied conference – codenamed Quadrant – with Franklin D. Roosevelt and his advisors at Quebec City. 'Prospects of victory in Sicily,' wrote Churchill, 'the Italian situation, and the progress of the war made me feel the need . . . for a new meeting with the president and for another Anglo-American Conference.'

Top of the agenda was the twice-postponed cross-Channel

invasion of occupied Europe, now known as Operation Overlord. For much of the first half of the year, the Allied Inter-Service Staff of COSSAC (the office led by British lieutenant general Sir Freddie Morgan, chief of staff to the Supreme Allied Commander) had been preparing a plan. Its most pressing concern was deciding where to land. There were many options – including the Dutch and Belgian coasts – but COSSAC soon focused on just two, both in northern France: the Pas de Calais or Normandy. The former was closer to Britain, and would be easier to protect from the air. Yet, at the same time, its defences were formidable and its harbours too small to support an invasion. On balance, therefore, Morgan and his advisors recommended the Normandy coast, a location first suggested by Lord Louis Mountbatten. Churchill agreed. 'The defences were not so strong as in the Pas de Calais,' he noted. 'The seas and beaches were on the whole suitable, and were to some extent sheltered from the westerly gales by the Cotentin peninsula. The hinterland favoured the rapid deployment of large forces, and was sufficiently remote from the main strength of the enemy.' Nearby, moreover, was the major port of Cherbourg which 'could be isolated and captured early in the operation'.[1]

The voyage to Canada was the first time that Churchill had been briefed in detail on the whole invasion plan, particularly its innovative use of two artificial 'Mulberry' harbours – an idea originally mooted by Churchill himself a year earlier – to land troops, vehicles and supplies once the initial beachheads had been secured. He was delighted with what he heard, declaring the whole project 'majestic'. Now it was just a question of agreeing the finer details with the Americans and finding the 'best answers to the many technical problems'.

This was achieved at Quebec where, during a series of plenary sessions from 19–24 August, Roosevelt and his military chiefs approved Operation Overlord as 'the primary United States–British ground and air effort against the Axis in Europe' with a target date of 1 May 1944. Once strong Allied forces had been established in France, 'operations designed to strike at the heart of Germany and to destroy her military forces' would be under-taken. In the meantime, Allied forces would land in southern Italy (operations Baytown and Avalanche) to drive that country out of the war and 'establish airfields near Rome, and if possible further north'. That would help to tie up German troops who could not be diverted to Normandy.

The plan at this stage was to land Allied troops at three sepa-rate beach locations on the Normandy coast: two British (later code-named Gold and Juno)* and one American (Omaha). Churchill felt, however, that this initial assault was too small and that 'every effort should be made' to increase it by at least twenty-five per cent (which would have meant four divisions landing on the first day instead of three). 'This would mean,' he wrote, 'finding more landing craft. There were still nine months to go, and much could be done in that time. The beaches selected were good, and it would be better if at the same time a landing were to be made on the inside beaches of the Contentin penin-sula.' His mantra, which he kept repeating, was that 'the initial lodgement must be strong'.[2]

While the debate over the number of assault troops would continue, what was not in doubt was that Nigel Willmott's Coppists would have a vital role to play in the naval component of Overlord, code-named Operation Neptune: not only by providing vital details about the topography of the beaches and their defences; but also by acting as markers and pilots for the landing craft. Both tasks presented Willmott with a unique problem. Normal COPP methods – tried and tested in the Mediterranean – were not possible in northern Europe where tidal conditions, steeply shelving coastlines and minefields made it impossible for normal submarines and two-man canoes to deliver swimmers and markers close to a beach. A separate method of insertion was required: either by motor launch or,

---

* The British beaches were named after fish: Gold(fish), Jelly(fish) and, later, Sword(fish). Jelly was changed to Juno – the ancient Roman goddess and sister of Jupiter – because Winston Churchill felt the original name was inap-propriate for a beach on which so many men might die.

even better, some form of small underwater craft that could pass over the minefields safely and allow periscope observation.[3]

The solution was to use an X-craft, a midget submarine designed by Lieutenant Commander Cromwell Varley, a retired naval officer, to assault enemy ships in harbour. Varley's prototype, X-3, was launched in March 1942. Weighing thirty tons, and measuring fifty feet (but with an internal living space of just thirty-five feet, about half the length of a cricket pitch), the X-craft was designed for a crew of three: a skipper, a first lieutenant and an engineer, or engine room artificer (ERA). The control room was at the front, and contained the steering and depth controls, the periscope and 'various navigational items'. Next came the escape compartment, known as the 'W and D' (wet and dry), which allowed a member of the crew to leave and re-enter the submarine in diving gear, 'for the purpose of cutting nets or placing explosive charges'. To the rear was the battery driven motor and diesel engine, giving submerged and surface speeds of 4.5 knots and 6.5 knots respectively. The main difference from a normal submarine was the absence of torpedo tubes. Instead, housed on either side of the pressure hull, were two crescent-shaped explosive charges, each containing two tons of amatol and a time-clock. They would be placed beneath the hull of a target.

The first six operational X-craft – numbered 5 to 10 – were delivered by the Vickers-Armstrong shipyards in Barrow-on-Furness between the end of 1942 and January 1943. Despite teething problems, they had completed their sea trials by April.[4] The skipper of *X10* was 25-year-old Lieutenant Ken Hudspeth from Hobart, Tasmania. A teacher, like his father, Hudspeth was a 'modest, intelligent, responsible man' who had joined the Royal Australian Naval Volunteer Reserve (RANVR) as a sub lieutenant when war broke out. After serving for two years on North Atlantic convoy escort duty, he answered an Admiralty call for volunteers for special and hazardous service. They had to be 'below 24 years of age on selection, unmarried, be good swimmers and of strong and enduring physique'. Though already 24 when he applied, Hudspeth was selected and sent to the Isle of Bute in Scotland for specialist training.[5]

The first mission assigned to Hudspeth and his five fellow X-craft commanders was Operation Source, the attempt to sink the German battleship *Tirpitz* and two other capital ships, *Scharnhorst* and *Lutzow*, anchored behind elaborate defences in or near the Kåfjord in northern Norway. Towed by conventional submarines, the six set off from Scotland at two-hour intervals on 11 September, but only four – *X5*, *X6*, *X7* and Hudspeth's *X10* – covered the full 1,200 miles to their drop-off point near Sørøya Island at the entrance to the Kåfjord. Of the remaining two, *X9* dropped its tow and was never seen again, and *X8* was scuttled after one of its explosive charges caused irreparable damage.

Assigned to attack the *Scharnhorst* – which, as it happened, had left its moorings for gunnery practice the day the X-craft arrived – *X10* got beyond the defensive minefield and was just a few miles from the entrance to the Kåfjord, deep within a network of fjords, when multiple equipment failures gave Hudspeth no option but to abort. He rendezvoused with his towing submarine, but *X10* could not survive a second ocean journey in bad weather and was scuttled en route. Hudspeth arrived back in Scotland to hear that at least two of the other X-craft – *X6* and *X7* – had successfully dropped their explosive charges beneath *Tirpitz*, badly damaging the huge warship. *X5* might also have completed its mission, but as it later sank with all hands there was no one to tell the tale. Two crew from *X7* also lost their lives when it foundered. The remaining crew members of *X6* and *X7* were captured. Both skippers – lieutenants Godfrey Place* and Donald Cameron – survived and were awarded the Victoria Cross for carrying out a 'cool and determined attack' and 'with complete disregard for danger'. Hudspeth was given a DSC.[6] His citation read:

---

* Place had been serving on HMS *Urge* when it torpedoed the Italian battleship *Vittorio Veneto* in December 1941, making him one of the only submariners to have taken part in two successful attacks on Italian capital ships in World War II.

For outstanding courage whilst in command of HM Submarine
X10 during Operation Source in September 1943. This submarine
penetrated Alten Fjord on 22 September 1943 to within four
miles of where Tirpitz was lying ... [Because of the vessel's
defects] Hudspeth had to come to the correct but bitter decision
to withdraw when so near his goal. The successful double passage
of the approaches to Alten Fjord required determination and skill
of a high order.[7]

Winston Churchill, who had long feared the havoc that *Tirpitz*
might cause to the Arctic convoys, was delighted by the news
that the battleship 'had been disabled by the audacious and
heroic attack of our midget submarines'. He wrote to Anthony
Eden, the foreign secretary: 'The resumption of the convoy question is practically sealed in a favourable sense.'[8]

*

Even before the start of the *Tirpitz* mission, Nigel Willmott had
attended meetings in London in late August 1943 – at both
COHQ and General Morgan's COSSAC headquarters in Norfolk
House – to discuss the use of X-craft by Coppists for beach
reconnaissance for Overlord. Willmott was in favour, as was
Mountbatten when he returned from the Quadrant Conference
in early September. An X-craft could pass safely through minefields, allow close beach reconnaissance with both its periscope
by day and a swimmer by night, and was hard to spot by either
radar or the human eye.

Morgan's staff was also in agreement, but thought it might be
better to train X-craft submariners in beach reconnaissance techniques rather than Coppists to operate from X-craft. Determined
not to be sidelined, Willmott pointed out that, according to discussions he had had with 'the officer lately in charge of X-craft',
COPP teams 'could be sufficiently trained' to use the midget subs
in under two months, whereas it would take considerably longer
to teach COPP techniques to submariners.[9] The matter was finally

settled on 17 September at a high-level meeting at Norfolk House attended by, among others, Morgan, Mountbatten* and Rear Admiral Claude Barry, Flag Officer, Submarines. They agreed to provide up to four of the six new X-craft – numbered X20 to X25 – to assist Nigel Willmott's COPP units in their work. The first two would be available by mid-December, and two more a month later. A second meeting at Norfolk House, on 21 October, confirmed that a minimum of three X-craft would be needed for Willmott's 'vital' work, and that 'no other form of craft – surface or submarine – is suitable'.[10]

With the project green-lit, Willmott assigned his own COPP 1 and Lieutenant Geoffrey 'Thin Red' Lyne's COPP 9 to train with X-craft in Scotland. COPP 1 would go up in late October, and hope to be operational by New Year's Day, 1944. Lyne's men would follow on 1 December and finish a month after COPP 1.[11] X-craft, explained one of Willmott's men, 'had no room for passengers, so certain Coppists were sent to HMS Varbel in Loch Striven for two months' training as X-craft crew members and to evolve, with X-craft specialists, reconnaissance techniques.'[12]

Willmott's involvement was a compromise. It had been almost a year since he had taken part in Operation Torch, and he was desperate to help with the beach reconnaissance for Overlord; but he was also, as the head of the COPP Depot, too important to lose, not least because he had 'Bigot' security clearance to see all secret documents relating to the Normandy landings. He was allowed to train on X-craft, and even accompany one on a mission, but he could not leave the midget submarine. The close beach reconnaissance would have to be done by others. It was fortunate, then, that two of the more recent soldier recruits to COPP 1 would prove to be so adept in this role.

The first was 24-year-old Major Logan 'Scottie' Scott-Bowden of the Royal Engineers. The only son of a former army officer

---

* This was one of Mountbatten's last acts as Chief of Combined Operations, as he had recently been appointed Supreme Allied Commander, South East Asia (SACSEA), and would leave by plane for India on 2 October 1943. He was replaced as CCO by Brigadier Bob Laycock.

and Herefordshire magistrate, Scott-Bowden was educated at Malvern College and the Royal Military Academy, Woolwich, where he was renowned as a swimmer and an athlete. Commissioned as a second lieutenant in 1939, Scott-Bowden was wounded in action in Norway with No. 2 Independent Company, an irregular unit formed of volunteers from the 53rd (Welsh) Division to which he was then attached. After lengthy spells as a liaison officer in Canada and the United States, he opted for more hazardous duty and was appointed COPP 1's military officer – replacing the unwell Basil Eckhard – in May 1943. 'I was new to it all,' recalled Scott-Bowden, 'and underwent intense training, including doing a month's recruits' course at the Commando Depot at Achnacarry. Other courses included navigation at HMS *Dryad*, air photography with the Royal Air Force and various Combined Operations indoctrinations.'[13]

A young man with a brusque manner and 'a powerful will which was occasionally to clash with Willmott's', Scott-Bowden cut an awkward figure with his 'massive shoulders, ruddy complexion, bristling ginger moustache, and short legs'. With a perfect build for swimming, he hated walking and canoeing – on exercises he would grumble, 'God – this is murder in this mechanical age' – and got more than his fair share of both as Willmott mixed traditional COPP training with X-craft work in Scotland.[14] He recalled: 'Willmott . . . ensured that we remained superbly fit, swimming naked at dawn even when there was a skim of ice on the little bay near the head of the loch fed with fresh water from a freezing burn. We also climbed mountains, canoed and swam miles in our swimsuits in the loch amongst the seals.'[15]

Sharing Scott-Bowden's pain were the other members of COPP 1, including Lieutenant Geoff Galwey (who had been there from the start), Sub Lieutenant Robin Harbud, the fresh-faced 19-year-old 'son of a Covent Garden fruit magnate', and Sergeant Bruce Ogden-Smith, the scion of a family that for 200 years had made fishing tackle for the wealthy. With his upmarket background and private education, Ogden-Smith might easily have got a commission. Indeed, having joined a Territorial battalion of the

East Surreys, he was selected for officer training. But with his heart not in it, he wrote rude words on an intelligence test and was rejected. Instead he was recruited by his elder brother Colin into the Small Scale Raiding Force (SSRF) – another Combined Operations unit with a maritime capability – and together they took part in the successful SSRF/Commando raid on Sark in late 1942, returning with one prisoner and valuable intelligence.* He later joined Courtney's SBS and was seconded to COPP 1. A year older than Bowden-Smith, with whom he would share most of his daring exploits, and married to the welfare supervisor of a factory in Wales, he was 'a square peg who had luckily found a square hole'.[16]

Welcoming Willmott and his men to Loch Striven was Lieutenant Ken Hudspeth, recently returned from *X10*'s aborted mission to Norway to sink the *Scharnhorst*. Hoping to be sent on another offensive operation 'the sooner the better', Hudspeth and his crew were delighted to hear they would commission the first of the new X-craft, *X20*. Less welcome, recalled Hudspeth, was their assignment: to initiate the 'strangers' of COPP 1 'into the mysteries of small submarine operation, and to take them on exercise expeditions to test the practicability of using our craft in the English Channel'.[17]

These exercises began in mid-December, by which time *X20* had been delivered to HMS *Dolphin*, the submarine base at Portsmouth. They were able to show that three COPP personnel and two X-craft officers 'can be carried and can work and maintain the craft for a maximum period of a week' (i.e. five days off the enemy coast); that the X-craft could 'bottom in 16 to 18 feet of water and make a close and careful study of the shore military defences etc. if the periscope remains unfogged'; that pilotage marks 'can be studied', pilotage directions written, and 'a certain amount of sketching done'; and that swimmers could

---

* Also on the raid was a young Danish-born SSRF officer, Anders Lassen, who would win a posthumous VC in Italy in 1945 while serving with the Special Boat Squadron.

make a maximum of four sorties for both naval and military purposes 'with little chance of detection'.[18]

All being well, Willmott told a meeting at COHQ, the first survey of the Normandy beaches would take place in the January 'dark period', which started around the 17th. Despite the cramped conditions and lack of drying facilities, Willmott regarded the use of X-craft and swimmers as the 'surest and safest method of undertaking reconnaissance without detection in view of the guarded nature of the enemy coast'. X-craft could, moreover, 'operate on the enemy's coast even if a sea patrol was operating'. This 'could not be done in surface craft'.[19]

Operation KJH

Shortly before Christmas 1943, Nigel Willmott and 'Scottie' Scott-Bowden were summoned to a meeting at COHQ in London. The scientists, they were told, had anxieties about the beach-bearing capacity of the Normandy beaches for the passage of heavy-wheeled vehicles and guns, particularly in the British and Canadian sectors – Gold and Juno respectively – 'where in Roman times the coastline and port had been more than a kilometre further out'. Sea erosion had covered with sand what were suspected to be ancient peat bogs. 'Where there is peat,' explained the staff officer, 'there is usually clay which if insufficiently covered by sand is dangerous. Everything except infantry will sink into it.'

In an attempt to find out, the RAF had dropped bombs 'in a selected suspect area' off Normandy, and repeated the pattern of bombs in a place with 'similar geological conditions' on the Brancaster beaches in Norfolk. Air photographs of the craters at both were taken, in an attempt to identify similarities, but the results had been inconclusive. What was needed now, they were told, was a COPP mission to collect beach samples which could then be analysed.

'Can't it wait for the "dark period" in January when we're scheduled to go anyway, sir?' asked Willmott.

'No,' said the staff officer. 'It has to be before then. The Combined Chiefs in Washington have been demanding from COSSAC a firm estimate of the amount of beach trackway required for the invasion. But because of the scientists' uncertainties,

COSSAC hasn't been able to give a firm reply. It's suddenly become urgent because the United States will have to change its vital production priorities to meet a worst-case scenario. If it doesn't do that soon, such requirements won't be ready in time for the invasion.'

The two COPP men nodded. 'How long do we have?' queried Willmott.

'Not long. We've pencilled in 31 December for the mission: it should be dark enough and, with luck, the sentries will be busy celebrating New Year's Eve. But first we need you to do a preliminary test at Brancaster, sailing out at night in a tank landing craft. If you pull that off without being seen, the Normandy trip is on.'

Forty-eight hours later, Scott-Bowden and his fellow swimmer Bruce Ogden-Smith sailed out of King's Lynn and headed north. Once in position off the beach at Brancaster, they were dropped into the water, each man wearing 'a large bandolier with a dozen ten-in[ch] tubes with phosphorescent numbers on their caps'. Also attached to the belt was an eighteen-inch auger that had been designed by Major Sir Malcolm Campbell* for a land speed trial on sand in the 1930s. With an almost noiseless spring mechanism, it could be 'pushed fully into the sand and given one half-turn', so that when it was pulled up it produced a ten-inch core sample for each tube.

Helped by a low mist, they swam ashore and then crawled in a 'W' pattern to cover as much of the beach as possible. Each time they took a sample, they recorded its position on underwater writing tablets strapped to their wrists, and at the same time, remembered Scott-Bowden, they 'located all the sentries without being detected'. One of those sentries was Professor J. D. Bernal, the chief scientific officer to the CCO, who had raised the issue of the peat bogs in the first place, and did not believe that the

---

* The holder at various times of the world speed record on land and water, Campbell made three of his land speed records at Pendine Sands in Carmarthen Bay. He set his final land speed record at the Bonneville Salt Flats in Utah on 3 September 1935, with an average speed of over 301 mph.

Coppists 'could take the samples they required, record accurately from where they had been taken and not get caught doing it'. He was wrong. Scott-Bowden recalled: 'Having gone back to the sea, we then stood up, walked to the shore, shouting to the frozen sentries who converged on our 15 cwt truck at the back of the beach where we displayed our wares in the heavily dimmed headlights.'[1]

They had passed the test and the mission was scheduled for New Year's Eve. The only question now was what form of transport to use. Willmott wanted to go with his two swimmers in Ken Hudspeth's X20. But a last-minute meeting at Fort Blockhouse, Gosport, on 30 December – attended by, among others, Admiral Sir Charles Little, Commander-in-Chief, Portsmouth, Rear Admiral Sir Philip Vian, commanding Naval Force J (due to land troops at Gold and Juno beaches), and Rear Admiral Claude Barry – decided that 'for security reasons it was not intended to use Submarine X20 for reconnaissance if it was found possible for the necessary information to be obtained by any other method'.[2] The method agreed upon was to use two motor gun boats (MGBs) and two small shallow-drafted landing craft, known as LCPs (landing craft, personnel): the MGBs would tow the LCPs across the Channel to the 'vicinity of the French coast' where the latter 'will be slipped to proceed inshore under their own power to carry out the reconnaissance'.[3] Their task was to examine a 'suspect area of beach west of Ver-sur-Mer', in the British Gold sector.

They left Gosport in the afternoon of 31 December. Willmott, Scott-Bowden and Ogden-Smith travelled in one gunboat; Geoff Galwey, the senior officer of the reserve LCP, in another. At around 8:00 p.m., about ten miles off the French coast, they transferred to the LCPs. Then the problems began. First the new radio navigational aid on Willmott's LCP, known as 'QH', failed to get a reliable departure fix, though a 'few vague readings were obtained by stopping the craft from time to time'. Next the weather started to deteriorate, with a south-westerly wind rising from force 3 to low force 4, making 'conditions unpleasant as speed had to be forced to maintain schedule'. It was raining steadily, which reduced visibility, and a 'slightly lumpy cross swell' was coming from the north-west. Lastly, Willmott was informed that the 'only proper anchor' had been lost overboard during the crossing and there was 'no foot-marked sounding pole on board'. He called a 'council of war' to consider aborting the mission, but eventually decided 'to continue, having come so far, to see what could be improvised at least'.

At 10:00 p.m., they finally got a reliable fix and realised they were well to the west of their intended position and still seven miles offshore. They altered course and increased to maximum speed. 'The rain, swell and partially offshore wind were now a help,' noted Willmott, 'from the sound and visibility cover point of view, but time was very short.'

Leaving the reserve landing craft anchored in three fathoms, they moved closer inshore and finally stopped in six and a half feet of water opposite the Ver-sur-Mer lighthouse at around 11:00 p.m. They were 400 yards from the beach. Both swimmers were by now green with seasickness, but they did not hesitate to go over the side.[4] 'It was,' recalled Scott-Bowden, 'a longer swim than planned as the breakers started well out. We found ourselves being taken rapidly east as the storm was creating a much stronger current or "set" along the beach on the rising tide than anticipated.'

He and Ogden-Smith eventually reached the shore opposite the village of La Rivière where 'fortunately the beach was screened by buildings and trees from the lighthouse beam'. Taking cover in some groynes at the back of the beach, they could hear singing and shouting from the direction of the village, and assumed it was German soldiers 'celebrating as they do the world over'. They headed west on foot, noting as they did so a 'useful concrete ramp' that was blocked at the top by barbed wire and heavy steel obstacles known as 'hedgehogs'. Closer to their target beach, they were forced to throw themselves to the ground every minute or so as the lighthouse beam swept by. It was also exposing their landing craft, which was clearly visible offshore. Fortunately, the

weather worsened, with heavy slanting rain making it harder to
see. Eventually reaching the suspect area, they 'started the examination, taking samples according to the pattern required', but
'leaving out one leg of our "W" as we were already at the back
of the beach'. Scott-Bowden remembered:

> The one who took the sample loaded it into a tube in the other's
> bandolier. We took ten each. Then we found a quite large exposed
> patch of peat standing a foot or so above the sand which had
> stood out clearly on the air photographs. We examined the sand
> all round it which was of substantial depth. It was time to go.

They headed out into the surf and started swimming, but were
'smartly flung back'. They tried a second time with the same
result. The wind was strengthening and their prospects of getting
off the beach did not look good. For their third attempt they
'sat as far out in the surf as possible to work out the wave
pattern', and used the lighthouse beam to help them. Timing it
just right, they got through the surf and swam as hard as they
could to avoid being swept back again. Scott-Bowden was in
the lead. Turning his head, he could not see his partner and
feared he had lost him. Then he saw an arm rise up and heard
a yell. 'I swam back somewhat alarmed,' recalled the major,
'thinking he had either got cramp or his suit had sprung a leak
which would cause loss of buoyancy and make things very difficult. When I got close, he shouted, "Happy New Year!"'
    Scott-Bowden was incensed. 'Swim, you bastard!' he demanded.
'Or we'll be back on the beach.'
    But then he saw the funny side and realised that Ogden-Smith
was right: it was well past midnight. 'Happy New Year to you
too!' he shouted, before swimming off.
    Reaching their rendezvous point, they signalled their arrival
with torches fitted with a directional cone. To keep them waterproof, wrote Scott-Bowden, they had used 'several of those
articles designed for keeping down the population' – condoms
– but which in this case 'were vital for saving life!' It was hard

to keep the torch pointing in exactly the right direction, particularly 'in a rough sea in the dark when one needed to be on the top of the wave to be seen'.[5]

But they were eventually spotted and picked up by the landing craft 'in six feet of water 200 yards from the back of the beach' at 12:47 a.m. Both, noted Willmott, were 'somewhat exhausted from their battle with the surf; the swell was now short and rather confused, sometimes breaking'. Almost an hour was spent finding the second landing craft, which had drifted because the seasick crew had failed to secure their anchor cable, and it was lost again as they headed for the rendezvous with the gunboats at a speed of just six to seven knots in high winds and choppy seas. 'The craft officer was temporarily sick,' reported Willmott, 'and she yawed off course and was lost in the dark. The stern lookout [on Willmott's boat] was at this moment calling relief so loss was not noticed for a minute.'[6]

Luckily, they were both near the meeting point with the gunboats which were sighted soon after, and, with the aid of flares, the whole force was reunited at 8:05 a.m. Transferred to their original gunboat, the two swimmers collapsed in bunks. As they lay there inert and pallid – Scott-Bowden 'quenched of his moustache-bristling fire' – it was hard to imagine that these two men were the first of many thousands 'to land on the invasion beaches of Normandy'.[7]

They finally reached Newhaven in the early afternoon, having diverted from Gosport because of the foul weather. While the sand samples were rushed up to London for analysis, Willmott and Scott-Bowden completed their reports. The former was 'as certain as anything can be' that the operation had not been detected by the enemy. Two augers and a fighting knife had been lost on the beach below the water's edge as the swimmers struggled to get through the surf, but they were 'likely to bury themselves in the sand'. Willmott was particularly appreciative of his swimmers who, in his opinion, 'did a fine job, especially as they both suffered considerably from *mal de mer* [seasickness]'.[8]

Scott-Bowden's report noted that 'whilst ashore, no mud, peat or other soft places were found'. The bed of the beach 'was found to be rock' and, whilst wading in the water, peat was suspected 250 yards out and discovered thirty yards from one beach groyne. Yet 'no sharp difference of level between peat and sand was noticed'. He also confirmed that, because of low tidal levels, it would 'not have been possible to operate from X-craft' that particular night.[9]

These findings were confirmed by the beach samples: they were all sand to a depth of ten inches and no sign of mud or peat beneath. The beaches would easily support the weight of tanks and wheeled vehicles, after all. The crisis was over.

Admiral Little sent Willmott his congratulations. He also told the Allied naval commander for Operation Neptune, Admiral Sir Bertram Ramsay, that the operation had been carried out 'with great skill and resolution'. Little added: 'Good seamanship was displayed and valuable lessons learned for any future similar operation. The wise decision of Lieutenant Commander Willmott to continue after parting company with the MGB, was rewarded with success and important information on the beach appears to have been obtained.'[10]

Ramsay agreed. 'I am,' he told Rear Admiral Vian, 'impressed by the results that have been achieved and request that you will convey to these officers and their crews my congratulations . . . on the resolution and skill with which their tasks were carried out in the face of considerable difficulty and hazard. On these operations depends to a very great extent the final success of operation "Overlord".'[11]

'A very formidable proposition indeed'

'Up periscope!' ordered Lieutenant Commander Nigel Willmott.

Perched on a stool in X20's cramped control room, he pressed his face into the small eyepiece and gasped. 'There's a fleet of fishing boats just ahead!' he exclaimed.[1]

It was just after dawn on 18 January 1944. The midget submarine had left HMS *Dolphin* at Gosport at 10:15 a.m. the previous day with five men on board: Willmott, in overall command and responsible for navigation; Lieutenant Ken Hudspeth, the X20's Australian skipper who 'handled the craft with a cool dexterity born of much usage'; Sub Lieutenant Bruce Enzer, the engineer officer, 'a cheerful, nuggety fellow' from Ulster 'who sprang to his work with the zest of an athlete'; and the two COPP 1 swimmers who had brought back the sand samples from Gold Beach, Major Logan Scott-Bowden and Sergeant Bruce Ogden-Smith. Their mission – Operation Postage Able – was to carry out a thorough periscope and beach reconnaissance of the American landing sector on Normandy that would later be code-named Omaha.[2]

Towed across the Channel by a trawler, the X20 had been cast off at 10:00 p.m. at a point close to the minefield that protected Normandy's Calvados coastline. From there it headed south on the surface at a top speed of 6.5 knots, clearing the minefield at just after midnight. As daylight approached, the submarine dived and continued heading for the coast at an 'economical motor speed' of two knots. 'To reach the destination precisely,' noted Hudspeth, 'at this speed and in the strong cross-tides of the Baie de Seine, was a measure of Willmott's remarkable navigational skill.'[3]

It was shortly after diving that Willmott raised the periscope and saw they were surrounded by 'small French fishing boats under sail, trolling in a glass sea'.[4] They were, recalled Scott-Bowden, who was on duty at the helm adjacent to the periscope, 'all pointing south-west into the wind with their nets out'. Hudspeth advised going under the bow of the nearest boat 'to avoid entanglement', and Willmott agreed. There were, he added, armed German soldiers on each boat.

Sneaking a quick look through the periscope in the hope of identifying their unit, Scott-Bowden saw a German soldier in the boat ahead 'leaning back in the bow with a rifle slung over his shoulder and his greatcoat collar up'. The only clue to his unit was that he was 'contentedly smoking a large cherrywood pipe' of the type popular among Bavarians.

Passing under the little fishing fleet, they got their first general view of the beach they knew was earmarked for the Americans. 'It was nearly high tide,' recalled Bowden-Smith, 'when we beached at periscope depth in about seven or eight feet of water on the left-hand sector of what was to be named "Omaha" beach. Willmott took two bearings to fix our exact position and handed the periscope to me.'[5]

Omaha was made up of a number of adjacent beaches that stretched more than five miles from Pointe de la Percée in the west to the village of Sainte-Honorine-des-Pertes in the east. X20 had bottomed in the western, or left-hand sector, between the villages of Saint-Laurent and Vierville. After resting and eating, they got underway and moved east, at periscope depth, to a point opposite the villages of Les Moulins and Saint-Laurent that straddled one of four main routes – or re-entrants – off Omaha. There they began the first detailed periscope reconnaissance.[6]

Through the surprisingly effective and hard-to-detect periscope – it had the 'thickness of a walking stick' and was raised just a foot above the water – Scott-Bowden took a quick general view and was 'astonished to see hundreds of soldiers at work, and how hard they were working'. He already knew, from briefings at General Sir Bernard Montgomery's 21st Army Group Headquarters at St Paul's School in London, that work on the coastal defences had been accelerated since Generalfeldmarschall Erwin Rommel had recently taken command of Germany's Atlantic Wall. Yet here was the evidence: seen from below the camouflage netting so that every type of gun emplacement under construction was visible. He wrote later:

> Oblique photographs taken by reconnaissance aircraft flying along the beach as low as 50 feet could not always indicate whether an emplacement might be for an anti-tank or machine gun or where the embrasure pointed. Generally, they enfiladed along the beaches and many were totally defiladed from fire from the front. The shoulders of the four main valleys leading [from Omaha] up to the high ridge running along the back of the beach contributed to one of the strongest imaginable defensive layouts. Later from another fixed position we would take cross-bearings on our previous observations to pinpoint them exactly.[7]

Scott-Bowden and Willmott 'changed over regularly and took notes for each other'. They also did regular round-checks in case patrol craft were about. Slowly but surely they built up a detailed picture of Omaha's defences. Most of the earthworks and concrete fortifications were 'situated in the defended localities on top of the ridge which commands the beaches'. A lot of buildings at the back of the beach had been demolished, 'presumably with the object of clearing fields of fire'. Nearly all the houses that remained 'had the appearance of being fortified'.[8]

The first scare came at just before 4:00 p.m. as the 'whip crack of Mauser bullets' was heard through the hull, some hitting the water a long way off, but the occasional one 'reasonably close'. Was someone firing at them? Just to be certain they brought down the periscope and 'gently slithered away'. Yet the firing continued for another ten minutes, leading them to conclude that they were not the target.[9]

At around 4:45 p.m. they bottomed a little further to the east, just beyond the point at which the Les Moulins road comes down to the sea. As it was raining, and the visibility was poor, Willmott told his swimmers to prepare for an early evening reconnaissance. They spent more than an hour struggling into their long johns, sweaters and rubber swimsuits with hood and fitted boots. Then they prepared the rest of their kit: 'webbing belt, Colt .45 automatic, spare magazines, Commando knife, wire cutters, wrist compass, wristwatch, emergency ration, water-proofed directional torch to signal for a recovery and an 18-inch earth auger for testing beach-bearing capacity'.[10] They were also equipped with a bandolier with twelve sample tubes, a brandy flask, a body-sounding lead, a beach-gradient reel and stake, and an underwater writing tablet and Chinagraph pencils.[11]

In addition, they had both taken Benzedrine tablets and were wearing body-belts 'with escape aids, including photographs for identification papers which would be provided by the Resistance in case our recovery failed and if we made our rendezvous with them 12 miles inland'. Aware that some of the Cockleshell Heroes were executed on Hitler's orders, Scott-Bowden had 'insisted that our badges of rank were sewn onto our swimsuits and sweaters so that if caught it could be seen we were not disguising the fact that we were soldiers'. They had been warned by the Intelligence Staff that if captured they would probably be taken to Paris for interrogation.

The X20 surfaced just before 7:00 p.m. and the opening of the hatch was, remembered Scott-Bowden, a moment of 'intense relief from the build-up of air pressure and shortage of oxygen'.[12] Willmott then took the mini submarine closer to the shore on battery power and dropped off Scott-Bowden and Ogden-Smith in nine feet of water, 'about 300 yards from the water's edge and 480 yards from the back of the beach'. With a 'moderate sea' and 'some cloud', conditions were good. The swimmers hoped to come out of the sea 400 yards to the west of the Les

Moulins road, well 'away from buildings and possibly sentries'. But they miscalculated the strength of the westerly tide and instead emerged almost directly opposite the road.[13]

Crawling forward in shallow water, they could see a sentry with a torch at the back of the beach, about 200 yards away. Suddenly the beam was shone in their direction and they froze. Their only hope, they knew, was to keep their heads down and their bodies 'aligned with the beam as the gently rising tide could swing us broadside showing our shapes'. Then another torch beam joined the first, as if requested by the first sentry. With their discovery only a matter of time, Scott-Bowden began to slither backwards as silently as possible, and Ogden-Smith followed. They expected a rifle shot, or a shout of alarm, but none came. So they kept moving backwards and, once they felt it was safe, edged west until they were opposite their intended position: a ribbed line of groynes, piled with sand, that sloped down to the water. The sea was so calm they had no trouble taking samples of sand underwater in their augers.

While crawling up to the back of the beach they noticed a single line of footprints in the sand. Then the beam from another light appeared at the top of the beach, 'probably on the road immediately behind it and about 200 yards to the west'. Again they froze, knowing they were 'at a disadvantage with the sentries, having sand and calm waters as our background'. Having already discovered 'the general character of the beach to be good', Scott-Bowden signalled to his partner to withdraw.[14]

They re-entered the sea at 9:20 p.m. and made the first of two recovery signals. They were eventually picked up half an hour later in sixteen feet of water, having swum almost 600 yards from the beach. Both were cold and exhausted. 'It was,' noted Willmott, 'a creditable effort for them to have swum out so far, which was only necessitated by their early return on a still falling tide.'[15]

With the swimmers safely on board, Willmott took X20 out to sea so that they could start the diesel engines and recharge the batteries. While he and Hudspeth took it in turns to keep

watch on deck, 'precariously and uncomfortably strapped to the
raised air induction tube', and Enzer 'looked after everything
else', Scott-Bowden and Ogden-Smith stripped off, checked and
stored their kit, and cleaned their pistols. Revived by a cup of
hot tea, they wrote up their notes before a well-deserved rest.[16]

*

Early the following morning, 19 January, X20 moved by electric
motor to a position opposite the village of Colleville, in the
eastern sector of Omaha, where it bottomed in six fathoms.
Much of the afternoon was spent observing the beach and the
land beyond, with Willmott and Scott-Bowden taking care not
to leave the periscope up for more than thirty seconds at any
one time to reduce the risk of discovery. Once again they noted
the demolition of buildings at the back of the beach, and the
fact that the ridge beyond provided 'excellent commanding
defence positions covering the beaches'. They also spotted a 'large
chain bucket type excavator' working at the main exit from the
Colleville beach, and assumed that it was supplying sand for
concrete work on a gun emplacement halfway up the ridge, and
more defences on top.[17]

At around 4:00 p.m., with the air in the submarine very poor
and many of the occupants sick from oxygen deprivation, they
withdrew to a position a mile and a half offshore so they could
surface and ventilate the interior. Then they returned to a position close to Colleville to prepare for a second beach
reconnaissance. Scott-Bowden, in particular, had been feeling
'very sick', but recovered a little as he crouched on the casing,
waiting for the signal to enter the water. He and Ogden-Smith
were released in eleven feet of water at 8:20 p.m., giving them
a swim to the beach of around 250 yards.[18]

They came ashore at a quiet stretch of the beach, a little to
the west of the road leading to Colleville where they had seen
the bucket excavator. There was little surf and they began using
their augers over a wide area. When they were halfway up the

beach – a total distance of about 250 yards – they heard voices from the direction of the excavator. The night was still and the noise carried easily. But as the sound was not 'guttural', and possibly French, they ignored it and kept working.[19] At the back of the beach, they found a shingle bank 'made mainly of rounded stones about six inches in diameter'. Scott-Bowden recalled: 'We had been particularly asked to check this bank as it might have been difficult for the passage of tanks. It appeared to have been man-made and was above normal water. There was masses of wire immediately behind and a probable minefield. We each took one stone. I lost mine swimming out but Ogden-Smith's was well received.'

While they were still on the beach, they spotted searchlights well inland and, soon after, heard explosions from a bombing raid that had been laid on in the area of the Orne river to divert attention from their mission. Inadvertently, however, the flashes from successive bomb strikes 'lit up the X-craft well out to sea', which was clearly visible to the swimmers on the beach who decided to call it a day.[20]

They re-entered the sea and gave the first recovery signal at 10:00 p.m. As they swam out, they took soundings and, twenty minutes later, were at a depth of eighteen feet. They signalled again but still there no sign of X20. Worried they had crossed in the darkness, they turned back to shore, signalling as they went. It was a nervous moment. Had something happened to the submarine? They knew that if they missed their pick-up, their capture was almost certain. Just as their fears began to take hold, the X-craft appeared and they were hauled on board.[21]

Having repeated the night-time procedure of recharging batteries offshore, X20 was in position off Vierville, at the western end of Omaha, to begin its third periscope observation in the early afternoon of 20 January. It was sitting in just eighteen feet of water, and Lieutenant Hudspeth had shown 'much skill and coolness' in manoeuvring the submarine into position. Among other things, Willmott and Scott-Bowden spotted a sea wall at the back of the beach, in some places nine feet high, that would act as an anti-tank obstacle (though it was not being extended). They also saw more evidence of buildings being demolished to aid fields of defensive fire; some form of 'masonry or concrete anti-tank block' at the main exit from the beach; and troops at work at the top of the ridge, building earthworks and pillboxes. They noted that the slope leading up to the ridge was fairly steep and could only be scaled by tanks in certain places (this did not include the western sector between Les Moulins and Vierville); wheeled vehicles would not get up it anywhere.[22]

Their general comments, relevant to all sectors of Omaha, included the point that the 'ridge provides excellent commanding defence positions covering the beaches' and that the 'slope of the back of the beach or sea wall' would not 'provide any cover from enfilade fire delivered from the high ground'. The concave nature of the slope – 'getting increasingly steep near the top' – allowed defenders on the top of the ridge to have a clear view of the beaches and the ground beyond. They also pointed out that the four valleys 'through which the main routes run inland' from the beach – at Vierville, Les Moulins (Saint-Laurent), Le Ruquet and Colleville – were 'natural defiles' and appeared 'well suited for mining, cratering, road blocking and every other form of obstructing'.[23]

In mid-afternoon, they moved east for a second look at the beach opposite the Les Moulins road. After an hour they heard, once again, the ominous sound of bullets striking the water, as if someone was firing at the periscope which was hastily lowered. 'Had we been detected?' wrote Scott-Bowden. 'We thought not. We were moving very slowly at about half a knot, with the small stick-like periscope exposed, at intervals, about a foot only. As it was not disturbing the water, perhaps it was thought to be a stray mine and was being used as a good aiming mark for target practice.' Fifteen minutes later they withdrew, as more shots rang out. 'Moulins,' noted Willmott wryly, 'seems a cantankerous locality.'

It was, he decided, time to end the mission. He had already gained 'most of the necessary information' and another sortie would have meant delaying until the night of the 21st/22nd to give the swimmers a chance to recover. In any case, with the weather due to worsen, a delay might not have helped.[24] Though he did not mention it, the bullet strikes close to the periscope must also have been a factor. 'There was,' Scott-Bowden wrote later, 'little point in staying around taking an unnecessary risk as, if our presence had been suspected, a search by patrol craft or even aircraft, which might see us in the shallow water, were possibilities. We headed for home.'

As they tied up to HMS *Dolphin*'s jetty in the early evening of Friday 21 January, they were surprised to see, among others, the rear admiral of the submarine base waiting to welcome them back. 'When the rear hatch was opened,' recalled Scott-Bowden, 'setting up a through draught, there was a slight onshore breeze. It was amusing to see the reception committee recoil from the X-craft's four days of accumulated odours.'[25]

*

Next day, while he and Willmott were writing up their reports, Major Scott-Bowden was called to the telephone to speak to Rear Admiral George Creasey, chief of staff to Bertram Ramsay, the naval commander for *Overlord*. 'Are you coming to London this weekend?' asked Creasey.

'No, sir,' replied Scott-Bowden. 'I'm rather busy with paperwork.'

'Oh, I think it would be a good thing if you did. Call in at my office at 2 p.m. tomorrow, Sunday.'

Duly summoned, he caught the train to London that evening and went out for drinks with friends. Next day, still suffering from a hangover, but smartly turned out in his service dress uniform and shiny Sam Browne belt, Scott-Bowden presented himself at Creasey's office in Norfolk House for what he assumed would be a short debrief. Instead Creasey took him straight to a long blacked-out room whose walls were covered with maps concealed by curtains. At the far end, seated on chairs, were ten senior Allied admirals and generals. Having introduced his guest, Creasy drew back a curtain to reveal a small-scale map of the Normandy coastline from the Cherbourg peninsula to east of Le Havre. 'Now Scott-Bowden,' he said, 'describe your recent operation.'

Completely unprepared, the major peered at the map and replied: 'Sir, it's going to be very difficult on this scale.'

Creasy took him to the other end of the long room and exposed a much larger-scale map of Omaha. 'Come on, chaps,' he called to the senior officers, 'bring your chairs down here.'

The delay gave Scott-Bowden a chance to compose himself. Among the admirals – who seemed to have enjoyed a liquid lunch – he recognised Bertram Ramsay and his deputy, Rear Admiral Philip Vian, who would command the Eastern Task Force on D-Day. Also present was Rear Admiral Alan Kirk of the United States Navy whose Western Task Force would land American troops on Omaha. The generals were more subdued, and included Lieutenant General Omar N. Bradley, commanding the US 1st Army, and four of the supreme commander Ike Eisenhower's senior officers: his chiefs of staff, operations, supply and engineers. The last two officers – major generals Nevill Brownjohn and John Inglis – were, like Scott-Bowden, both British sappers and would 'expect a reasonable performance'.

For the next twenty minutes, Scott-Bowden spoke about Operation Postage Able, particularly the role that he and Sergeant Ogden-Smith had played in swimming ashore on successive nights. Then he fielded questions: first from the admirals, who seemed chiefly concerned with offshore sea conditions, an area of expertise that Scott-Bowden struggled with; and then from the generals, queries he naturally found easier to answer. He had good news, in that the surface of all the beaches inspected was 'hard well-compacted sand' and their bearing capacity was 'adequate for all classes of vehicles'. Not so encouraging was his description of the many defences under construction, the ability of the Germans on the ridge to command the beaches below, and the likelihood that the four re-entrants, the easiest routes off Omaha, would be blocked. When the Q&A session was over, only Bradley stayed on to ask more questions. 'One of his principal concerns,' remembered Scott-Bowden,

> was how tanks would move from the beach to the top of the ridge. It was anticipated that the four main re-entrants would be completely blocked for some hours by German demolitions and mines until the United States assault engineers could open them up. There was a diagonal track to the left up which I had seen a pair of Percheron carthorses in tandem pulling a two-wheeled farmcart heavily loaded with rock from an emplacement under construction. He pressed me hard for an opinion on whether tanks could go up this track. I thought that the gradient was suitable but from our periscope view it was impossible to judge the width. Although good for a farmcart, I thought it might be too narrow for a Sherman but light tanks would make it.

After responding to this and other questions, all relating to the problems American troops would face trying to get off Omaha, Scott-Bowden felt compelled to say: 'Sir, I hope you don't mind me saying it, but this beach is a very formidable proposition indeed.'

Bradley put a hand on the young major's shoulder and looked him directly in the eye. 'I know, my boy,' he said softly. 'I know.'

Aware that his comments had not made the American general's job any easier, Scott-Bowden offered to help. 'I don't know if you're aware of this, sir, but, as well as beach reconnaissance, my unit also marks the beaches and pilots in landing craft so they get to the right place on the day of invasion. We did this with some success last year in Sicily and at Salerno. I hope you'll allow us to help you with this on D-Day.'

'Thank you. I'll see what I can arrange. Be sure to give my personal thanks to Sergeant Ogden-Smith.'[26]

*

Soon after Scott-Bowden's conversation with General Bradley, the number of D-Day beachheads was extended from three to five, with a similar increase in the number of divisions due to land. To give more time to produce the extra landing craft, the date of D-Day was put back a month from 1 May to early June. The chief architect of this revised plan was General Sir Bernard Montgomery, commanding the Allied ground forces, who felt that the landings had to be broadened to guarantee success. Backed by Churchill and the supreme commander, Ike Eisenhower, Montgomery added two extra beachheads: Utah, where a second US division would land on the western flank; and Sword, a new British objective on the eastern flank, near the Orne river. 'In a small way,' wrote Scott-Bowden, 'COPP may have assisted in General Bradley's full endorsement of that vital prosposal.'[27]

In his report, Nigel Willmott was generous in his praise of the four men who had accompanied him on one of the most daring and brilliantly executed missions of the war. 'A fine spirit prevailed throughout amongst all hands,' he wrote,

> and in spite of the foul air, super-slum conditions and distasteful sewage system, a strain on the temper, no person was heard to pass strictures upon the habits or antecedents of any other. (At least in one's presence.) . . .
>
> Lieut Hudspeth's grasp of submarine technicalities, coolness and dexterity in handling the craft was of the highest order, and Sub Lieut Enzer's skill and continual cheerful hard work must have been greatly responsible for the success of the expedition in that no major breakdowns and few minor ones occurred.

As for Major Scott-Bowden and Sergeant Ogden-Smith, noted Willmott, their 'fine performance scarcely requires comment from me'.[28]

Hudspeth agreed. 'They were,' he wrote, 'the heroes of the operation and their story deserves fuller telling.'[29]

Willmott's naval superiors were hugely impressed. 'The cool and calculated bravery,' wrote Admiral Little to Bertram Ramsay, 'required to make this sustained and impudent reconnaissance under the very nose of the enemy, and in the extremely unnatural conditions of life in Submarine *X20*, is quite outstanding. The slightest error over the three days of operating off the beaches would have spelt disaster.'[30]

All five men were rewarded 'for their courage and undaunted devotion to duty in a hazardous operation'. Willmott and Hudspeth received bars to their DSCs; Enzer was mentioned in despatches. But the highest honours, quite rightly, were given to the two swimmers. Both received a medal for each of their outstanding exploits: Scott-Bowden a DSO for Postage Able and a Military Cross for KJH; Ogden-Smith a DCM and a Military Medal for the same operations. Willmott also got a mention in despatches for KJH.[31] These two outstanding missions – so vital to the success of D-Day – were Nigel Willmott's last hurrah. Called up from Portsmouth to a meeting with Montgomery's staff at the 21st Army Group's Headquarters at St Paul's School in Hammersmith, he confirmed that the sand *was* hard enough and the offshore gradients *were* suitable at the right tide level. He was expecting orders for the new beachheads to be surveyed, particularly Utah on the shoulder of the Cherbourg peninsula. But Brigadier Edgar 'Bill' Williams, Monty's brilliant 31-year-old chief of intelligence and an Oxford don before the war, was more concerned with how near the mission had come to being discovered. 'Bit of luck, there,' he told Willmott. 'I don't think we ought to press it. We got away without compromising the show – by the look of it. Broadly, now, we know most of what we want to know.'[32]

Williams paused for a moment to polish his thick-rimmed spectacles with a handkerchief. Tall and thin, with a neat tooth-brush moustache, he had served in armoured cars in the desert and was still a major when Montgomery chose him as his chief of intelligence, later crediting him with a tactical innovation – known as 'crumbling'* – that helped to win the Battle of El

* This meant, in effect, 'luring the Germans out of their original positions' so that the Allies could 'smash through a purely Italian front without any difficulty'.

Alamein. 'He saw the enemy picture whole and true,' noted Montgomery. 'He could sift a mass of detailed information and deduce the right answer.'[33]

Trusted implicitly by Montgomery, Williams was unsure whether to authorise more beach reconnaissance for D-Day or not. He tapped the table with his fingertips as he thought. At last he lifted his head. 'I'm against any repeat dose,' he told Willmott. 'As far as my own recommendations go to General Montgomery, anyway.'

A few days later, Willmott handed over the command of COPP 1 to Lieutenant Commander Paul Clark. Willmott had been suffering chronic stomach pains for more than a year and needed a rest. He took advantage of his sick leave to marry his fiancée Prue Wright, a young Leading Wren who had been assigned to the COPP Depot as a driver. The service was at the Holy Trinity Church in Brompton Road on 27 March 1944, and was attended by, among others, Major Roger Courtney MC, Willmott's partner on that first beach reconnaissance of Rhodes three years earlier. Both had come a long way since and, in memory of their joint enterprise, Courtney's wedding gift was a silver-plated Commando knife with the simple inscription: 'Island of Roses, 1941'.[34]

'We all had French identities
in case we were captured'

Lieutenant Jim Booth of COPP 9 was drinking beer in the wardroom of HMS *Dolphin* with George Honour, the skipper of *X23*, when in walked his friend and boss, Geoffrey 'Thin Red' Lyne. Striding up to the pair, Lyne said simply: 'It's the 5th. We leave tomorrow.'[1]

The trio toasted the news. It was Thursday 1 June 1944, and D-Day – the start of Operation Overlord – was scheduled for just four days' time. If everything went to plan, 5,300 ships and 12,000 aircraft would land or drop 150,000 men and 1,500 tanks on or behind Normandy's beaches.[2] Before that could take place, however, the three officers had a vital role to play. Departing in the midget submarine *X23* on 2 June, they would cross the Channel and wait submerged off Sword Beach, the easternmost of the five landing zones, until just before dawn on the 5th when they would surface and begin flashing signals from the submarine and a nearby dinghy, manned by Booth, to guide in the first amphibious tanks and landing craft. Lieutenant Commander Paul Clark and Sub Lieutenant Robin Harbud of COPP 1 would do the same job off Juno Beach in Hudspeth's *X20*. The combined X-craft mission was code-named Gambit.[3]

For security reasons, the Coppists had not been briefed on the overall invasion plan. 'All we knew,' recalled Booth, 'was that there was a point on the map we had to head for and stay there until the landing.'[4] Because of the risk of discovery, and the difficulty of using folbots in the Channel, the two X-craft would act as the only markers on D-Day. Despite Major Scott-Bowden's advice to

General Bradley, the Americans had rejected the use of markers on their beaches as too likely to give the game away. But they were prepared to use some Coppists as pilots for their landing craft and, given their familiarity with Omaha, Scott-Bowden and Sergeant Ogden-Smith had agreed to do that job for the US V Corps. 'For D-Day,' wrote Scott-Bowden, 'we were assigned to Navy Force "O", commanded by Rear Admiral Hall, to assist with pilotage.'[5] Don Amer and the men of COPP 6 would act in the same capacity for the assault troops of the British 3rd Infantry Division at Sword Beach, while Geoff Galwey and COPP 1 did the identical job for the 3rd Canadian Division at Juno. No pilots had been assigned to the US XII Corps heading for Utah.[6]

But it was Booth and his colleagues in the X-craft who had the toughest job. To pull it off required perfect timing, nerves of steel and no small amount of luck. Failure was not an option: their premature discovery, they knew, would jeopardise the whole invasion. It was quite a responsibility for 22-year-old Booth, the Old Etonian son of a retired Leicestershire businessman, who was on his first secret mission. When war broke out, Booth was about to begin his first term of a natural sciences degree at Trinity College, Cambridge. Recovering from a minor operation, he went up late and never, as he put it, 'got into gear'. Instead he gave up his studies after a single term and joined the RNVR as an ordinary seaman.

In 1941, having served on the cruiser HMS *Kenya* as a lookout, he was identified as officer material and sent to train at HMS *Alfred* in Hove. Commissioned as a midshipman, he joined an armed trawler on escort duty up Britain's east coast. 'We saw a lot of action,' he recalled. 'Mainly attacks by German planes. An awful lot of merchant ships were sunk. It was hard picking up survivors, particularly at night. Some [ships] were oilers that caught fire and not many of the crew got off . . . We were hardened to the sights and sounds of war. We all knew, when we were on a ship, that a torpedo could come in any second.'

Promoted to sub lieutenant in 1942, Booth moved to a training job in western Scotland before acting as second in command of an armed trawler that was escorting convoys round the west coast of Africa. In 1943, seeking more adventure, he asked the Admiralty if he could move to a 'more exciting' job. Their response was to send him to HMS *Dolphin* in Portsmouth to train on 'chariots'. He did a lot of diving at Portsmouth with a breathing device known as a Davis Submarine Escape Apparatus* to see if his ears would stand up to the pressure. 'They didn't,' he recalled, 'so they told me I wasn't good enough for the job.' It was just as well because, as he acknowledged later, the chariots were 'hopeless'.

Booth was sent instead to Hayling Island where, having passed the interview with Willmott – satisfying such questions as 'Are you tough enough to swim in freezing water?' – he joined Lyne's COPP 9 as the assistant maintenance officer. It was good timing because, shortly after his arrival, Lyne's party was sent to train with X-craft in Scotland. Not that the boss was particularly happy. According to Booth, Lyne 'didn't really like' being a Coppist because he was a navigator who wanted to work in a battleship. He had come back to COPP after the 'North Africa business' only because Willmott promised it would be for a single operation. The news that he would have to retrain in a midget submarine, therefore, was not well received.

Booth, on the other hand, was desperate to be sent on a mission. But as the assistance maintenance officer he was not operational. This all changed when Lyne's deputy, Sub Lieutenant D. H. Granger, went on his first trip in an X-craft. 'Oh, bloody hell!' he exclaimed. 'I didn't join the navy to go on these bloody things. I want to be on the sea in fresh air. I've had enough.'

There were already signs that Granger was not cut out to be a Coppist. Shortly before travelling north from Hayling Island, he had accidentally shot himself through the foot during revolver practice. He was lucky to escape with a minor flesh wound, but

---

* An early form of aqualung that comprised an oxygen cylinder, a rubber 'lung' worn on the chest and a mouthpiece. Primarily designed as an apparatus for emergency escape by submarine crews, it was also adapted for select diving operations.

the X-craft experience was the final straw. 'If he hadn't resigned,' recalled Booth, 'Lyne was going to sack him anyway. He wasn't appropriate. He didn't have much experience of the sea, whereas I had been on operations since the start of the war.'

Booth became Lyne's new assistant, and the pair quickly knuckled down to some hard training with X23's crew: skipper Lieutenant George Honour, First Officer Jimmy Hodges and mechanic George Vause. Booth got on particularly well with Honour, a dashing 25-year-old Bristolian who, like him, was a member of the RNVR (known as the 'Wavy Navy' because its officers' gold rings of rank were crooked, and not straight like they were for the regulars). In 1942, bored of running stores into Tobruk on a landing craft, Honour volunteered for 'hazardous' service and had been working with X-craft in Scotland ever since. He also – like Willmott – met and married a Wren driver.

Having finished their training at Loch Striven, Lyne's men headed south to join COPP 1 in Portsmouth. Honour's X23 went with them, transported on the back of a lorry, while Booth rode escort on his motorbike. They stayed en route at Booth's family home in Leicestershire, and even stopped at a pub for a pint, leaving the top-secret X-craft in the car park outside. Though covered by a tarpaulin, its shape did not fool one patron who asked Booth, 'What's that? It looks like a submarine?'

'Oh, no,' replied Booth, shaking his head, 'it's nothing like that.'7

*

As darkness fell on Friday 2 June 1944, the midget submarines X20 and X23 left the East Gate in Portsmouth boom and steamed to their rendezvous with the armed trawlers and ML escorts that would take them across the Channel. After struggling to secure their tow bars to the trawlers in the choppy sea, they set off at 11:10 p.m. on the surface 'under main engine at an average speed of three knots to a position halfway across the Channel and sixty miles from the French coast'. There they slipped their tow and continued on the surface, on slightly divergent courses, for another hour. George Honour remembered feeling 'very lonely and thinking that X23 was very, very small' as they drew ever closer to the Normandy coast.

They dived at dawn to avoid observation by enemy planes, and, with 'Thin Red' Lyne navigating, travelled for the whole of Saturday at a depth of thirty feet and a snail's pace of two knots. The only stops were to 'guff through' on three occasions, which meant taking in 'fresh air through the "snortmast" without surfacing' to give the five oxygen-deprived men on board a brief respite. It was a risky manoeuvre. If the induction pipe was swamped, the engines 'would suck the air they breathed inboard and create a dangerous vacuum'. Fortunately, they avoided this calamity and got through the first day without using any of their precious supply of oxygen.

At mealtimes they ate bread and jam, supplemented by chocolate biscuits and sweets, and took it in turns to rest in the two tiny bunks. 'There was no room to move,' recalled Honour, 'and one could not, of course, smoke. All you could do was yarn or sleep fitfully in the increasingly foul atmosphere.' At 11:20 p.m. on the 3rd, as X23 neared the huge web of mines that protected the coast of Normandy, Honour brought her to the surface. Safe channels would be swept through the minefield on D-Day. But as X23 had to go through earlier, and the mines were fixed twelve feet underwater, she did so on the surface with her diesel engine on a running charge, which replenished the batteries but reduced speed.

At 4:00 a.m. on 4 June, with the coast of the Le Havre peninsula a featureless smudge away to the east, X23 dived and paused a few hours on the seabed. Then at 8:30 she was brought up to periscope depth so that Lyne could try to get a fix on his position. 'We were trying to find somewhere we could recognise,' remembered Jim Booth. 'Part of my job was to confirm Lyne's calculations. We had some pictures of the coast to confirm where we were, but that took a long time.'

Eventually recognising churches in villages like Lagrune-sur-Mer, west of the mouth of the Orne river, Lyne took cross bearings and obtained a fix. His dead reckoning had brought him directly opposite his target area: Sword Beach. They remained submerged for the rest of the day, mostly on the bottom, but rising to periscope depth in the late afternoon to obtain further fixes from, among other things, the Ouistreham lighthouse that marked the eastern edge of Sword. At one point, Lyne said to Honour, 'Come and look at this.'

Honour did so and was confronted with the innocuous sight of German soldiers playing football on a beach that could not have been mined.

Confident of their location, they surfaced at 11:15 p.m. to see if there were confirmation that the operation was still on for the following morning in the form of a coded message after the BBC news. But there was no message so they moved to their final marking position: 7,000 yards, or just under four miles, off the eastern edge of Sword. At around the same time, Hudspeth's X20 was arriving at a similar position at Juno. 'At that point,' recalled Booth,

we did the most dangerous thing of all, which was to drop the anchor down. It was my job to do that, and get quickly back inside the submarine. I put my waterproof suit on, came out of a hatch and went across to the bow and got the CQR anchor out of a metal box there and slung it out. We were now trapped in that position and couldn't move. If we'd been seen, we wouldn't have had a hope of getting away.

Their emergency procedure, in the event of being spotted, was to go out as far as they could, sink the X-craft in deep water, and swim ashore. 'We all had French identities,' noted Honour, 'in case we were captured or just drowned. I had the complete disguise outfit of a French taxi driver. That would put the Hun off the scent if he got hold of our bodies, dead or alive. They would never think we were members of one of HM Submarines.' Armed with only their pistols and Commando knives, their instructions were to find the French Resistance and hide until the invasion was over. 'We'd had a short class of unarmed combat,' noted Booth, 'it wasn't very long.' He hoped, of course, it would not come to that.[8]

With the weather worsening – a wind of force 5 and a choppy sea – they listened again to the BBC news at 1:00 a.m. The reception was very faint and they had to switch off the gyro-repeater compass to hear the message: 'Hullo Padfoot, this is Niton. It's pretty in Scarborough.'[9]

'Bloody hell!' said Booth, recognising 'pretty' as the codeword for a twenty-four-hour postponement.* The consequences for those on both X-craft were serious. They would have to spend another day submerged in the same position, using up more oxygen for breathing. Nor did they know how much they had left because there were no dials on the tanks. The solution on X23 was to sleep in rotation. 'It was the right thing to do,' noted Booth, 'as you use less oxygen when you're sleeping. But most of us didn't really get off. We just lay there. My standard position was on the wheel, where I kept my kit.'[10]

After another torturous eighteen-hour stint below the waves, they surfaced at 11:15 p.m. to the 'worst hangover in the world'. It 'enveloped them, and the pain rolled its weight wherever they turned their splitting heads'. Emerging oxygen-starved 'into the clean air always brought nausea and headaches'. It did not help that the sea was still extremely choppy, 'pitching the craft about and making those aloft in the fresh air grab hastily' for a hand-hold. The men below tried to ignore the pain as they listened to the news. Once again, the reception was poor and the gyro-repeater was stopped, never to restart. 'As we were already in our marking position,' wrote Honour, 'this did not prove so serious as it might have done.'

It also allowed them to hear another message for Padfoot, the X-craft call sign, and this time it included the word 'Pomade'. The operation was on for the morning of 6 June.[11]

---

* Ike Eisenhower, the supreme commander, had taken the decision to postpone in the early hours of 4 June after consulting his meteorologists.

33
D-Day

X23 surfaced off Sword Beach at 4:45 a.m. on Tuesday 6 June 1944. It was still dark and, with the first landing craft due in under two hours, the crew's main task was to rig a large white ensign for identification and the signals that would guide in the invasion fleet: a light and a radar beacon on the submarine's mast, and a separate infrared RG lantern on a 'J' type RAF rescue dinghy that would be anchored a short way off to act as a transit mark. Manning the dinghy was the job of Jim Booth and mechanic George Vause. 'It was blowing quite a lot,' recalled Booth,

> and this was when Lyne made the decision not to use the dinghy. He and Clark had decided beforehand that if it was over force 5 it was too risky to unhook the X-craft from its line and anchor in order to take me and Vause to our position. They might not be able to get back. So instead Jimmy Hodges put the main lights on the stern and I put mine on the bow. Because the submarine was moving around so much it was never a proper transit. But it was more lights for the landing craft to see, and better than nothing.

Their lights began flashing seawards at 5:07 a.m. With dawn approaching, it was only a matter of time before they were spotted by the shore defences. Booth stared nervously out to sea, willing the ships to appear. 'But the bombers came first,' he remembered. 'We could see explosions inland. Then the battleships bombarded the beach, their whistling shells going right over the top of us.'

Still there was no sign of the ships and they were getting worried. 'Where are they?' he asked Hodges. 'Where's the invasion?'

Finally, noted Booth, 'the light must have changed because we suddenly saw a huge host of ships coming towards us. Thousands of them. It was incredible. The landing craft came incredibly close to us, including some with DD [amphibious] tanks.'[1]

The approach of the massed ships of the invasion fleet was, for George Honour, a 'frightening sight', though he knew they were on his side. 'One can only imagine,' he wrote, 'what the enemy must have felt, waking up to this awesome spectacle and knowing that they were the targets.' Booth and the others cheered and yelled as the landing craft ploughed past them, a curious sight to the helmeted soldiers as, with most of the submarine underwater, it must have seemed as if they were walking on water.

The landing craft had got this far, in the right place at the right time, thanks to X23's heroics. Taking them in closer was the responsibility of 'Daddy' Amer and the rest of COPP 6. Amer and his deputy Lieutenant Peter Wild were each piloting a squadron of fourteen amphibious tanks of the 13th/18th Hussars into two beaches of Queen sector. Equipped with inflatable canvas skirts and extra clutches attached to two propellors, the DD (duplex drive) Sherman tanks* had been launched 'satisfactorily' from their landing craft at 6:40 a.m. with 5,000 yards to go. This had been reduced from the original 6,000 yards because of the choppy sea. 'Red beach of Queen sector,' noted Peter Wild, 'was clearly recognisable by this time. The light from the X-craft was no longer showing.'[2]

The first mishap was at 7:20 a.m. when the LCTs (landing

---

* Invented by a Hungarian-born engineer called Nicholas Straussler, the DD tank was just one of a number of armoured adaptations that were used on D-Day.

craft, tank) with the support armour overtook Amer's tanks 'on
the port side and stopped ahead, swinging to starboard'. In doing
so they accidentally struck two DD Shermans, sinking one. Amer
moved ahead in his smaller landing craft and, as the smoke
ashore had cleared sufficiently, was able to recognise White Beach
of Queen sector at a distance of 1,000 yards. He stopped and
got one of his Coppists, probably Leading Seaman Fred Phillips,
to check the depth with a sounding pole. It was thirteen feet.
'This information,' he wrote, 'and the bearing of the centre of
the beach, was passed to the CO of A Squadron [13th/18th
Hussars], whose tank passed close on the starboard side.'[3]

A short distance to the east, Wild was able to direct B Squadron
into Red Beach. He and the leading tanks were narrowly missed
by Allied rocket salvoes that fell short and sent up huge geysers
of water and mud. 'Tanks touched down at 0730,' noted Wild,
'in good formation and towards the western end of Red Beach.'
At almost exactly the same time, the majority of A Squadron's
tanks reached White Beach. They were followed in by engineer
tanks and infantry, the former led on to the beach by Captain
Ian Mackenzie RE, Amer's 23-year-old military officer. Born in
Auckland, the grandson of a former New Zealand prime minister,
Mackenzie had travelled to England at the start of the war and
was commissioned soon after. The engineer tanks landed only
five to ten minutes late, he reported, 'about 300 yards from the
back of the beach, within fifteen yards of the exact position.
Underwater obstacles interfered little with this wave at this state
of the tide, as they were clearly visible.'[4]

It was left to Amer to record that when he re-embarked
Mackenzie and his assistant, Sergeant E. A. Gray of the SBS, not
long after the landings, they brought with them 'the two Bren
guns with which they had been firing at houses at the back of
the beach'.[5] Another COPP 6 officer who brought along a Bren
was Lieutenant Don Slater RNVR, 25, from Haverhill in
Cambridgeshire. 'I felt,' he admitted later, 'that my revolver wasn't
quite the thing to attack the enemy with from a landing craft.'
He helped Wild lead in the DD Shermans of B Squadron, and

was confident they were in the right place because he recognised buildings from low-level photographs they had been shown a couple of weeks earlier. As they approached Red Beach, he opened up with the Bren and kept firing until the barrel was so hot he threw it into the sea. 'By that time,' he recalled, 'we were so visible that if there had been any opposition a Bren gun wouldn't have been much defence.'[6]

Lyne on *X23*, meanwhile, had been ordered to report to the command ship of Rear Admiral Arthur Talbot's Force S, HMS *Largs*. 'First we had to pack up all the gear,' recalled Jim Booth, 'and take the anchor up. That was my job, but I couldn't get the bloody thing up. We were all whacked. So Thin said: "Cut the bugger!" He passed me a knife and I cut it.'*[7]

*

A few miles to the west, off Juno beachhead, Lieutenant Commander Paul Clark on *X20* had also dispensed with the marking dinghy, relying instead on 'a shaded light, a tiny radar beacon and a crude mechanical hammer to be picked up by ASDIC'. This latter device, used on something known as a 'bong stick', was operated by Robin Harbud. 'On his heaving perch,' noted one account, 'he was getting a frightful battering from the waves. They broke right over him in a flurry of foam and he would abandon winding to grab wildly for a hold.'

At one point, Harbud missed his grip and was pitched overboard by a wave. He was saved by the skipper Ken Hudspeth who stuck out a foot and Harbud grabbed it. 'Thanks!' he yelled as he scrambled back on to the casing. 'Where in hell are those bloody boats!'

---

* One of the most remarkable pieces of D-Day footage is a thirty-second clip of film, taken from the deck of HMS *Largs* as the tiny *X23* approaches and secures alongside, having completed its mission. Jim Booth is on the casing, struggling to catch the head rope thrown from *Largs*. Soon after, Lyne comes up a rope ladder to enjoy a cigarette on deck, his 'Royal Navy' insignia clearly visible on the shoulder of his waterproof suit.

Eventually, recalled Hudspeth, 'through the murk the first craft appeared and the lines of landing craft surging on the rising sea passed close on either side heading for the beaches, followed by seemingly endless streams of others, with the salvoes from the rocket ships passing overhead'.

Harbud was elated. 'Hurray!' he shouted. 'You bloody little beauties!'

Their job was done. 'We had only to wait,' noted Hudspeth, 'for escort to our trawler waiting offshore, to shackle on the towline, quietly submerge and be comfortably towed through the swept channels to reach *Dolphin* in time for a bath and dinner.'[8]

As the X-craft headed home, Geoff Galwey and two other men from COPP 1 – Petty Officer Briggs and Fireman Apprentice Cecil 'Billy' Fish – were moving in the opposite direction. Desperate to see action, Galwey had managed to wangle a place for himself and the others on a motor launch that was assigned to guide landing craft into Juno beachhead. Galwey had convinced the skipper of the launch that only he could recognise the noise the *X20*'s 'bong stick', or rod sounder (as it was also known), would make on their ASDIC.

He had kept his promise by identifying the staccato pinging as the launch approached the gap in the Calvados rocks, just before dawn. 'There's our marker!' he announced.

Soon they were also receiving the X-craft's radar blips and, eventually, its faint blue light was visible. Having passed the midget, Galwey's launch approached Juno's eastern sector where, because of the rough seas, the decision had been taken not to launch the DD tanks of the Fort Garry Horse, but instead take them right to the beach. This meant the infantry of the 8th Canadian Brigade went in first, opposite Saint-Aubin-sur-Mer, and took heavy casualties. Galwey did his best to help them by spotting targets for Petty Officer Briggs who was manning a two-pounder gun. No sooner had he pointed out a machine-gun nest in the upper floor of a house on the seafront than Briggs fired three shots in rapid succession. The open window 'huffed a gout of smoke and then the whole wall folded slowly inward, like rotten fabric shredding in a wind puff'.

Briggs turned to Galwey. 'Any more, sir?'

Later all three Coppists went ashore and worked for a time as stretcher-bearers before hitching a ride back to the UK on a gunboat.[9]

*

The grimmest scenes of the day were witnessed on Omaha by Major Logan Scott-Bowden and Sergeant Bruce Ogden-Smith, the two Coppists who had scouted the area in January. 'We sailed in [Rear Admiral Hall's] flagship from Weymouth,' wrote Scott-Bowden, 'and stopped briefly before dawn. The very small pilot craft were launched and we went down the scrambling nets to board. I had opted for the right-hand US 29th Division beach pilot boat and Ogden-Smith went with the US 1st Division on the left.'

The major's pilot boat had a crew of three: Dean L. Rockwell, a 'very experienced naval lieutenant' and former professional wrestler from Detroit who was 'doing his fourth assault landing'; a coxswain; and a gunner of 'Mexican extraction' manning a four-barrelled 'pom-pom' anti-aircraft gun. Speeding to the head of the 29th Division's fleet of landing craft, the pilot boat took station in front of eight LCTs which were carrying the thirty-two DD Sherman tanks of the 743rd Tank Battalion scheduled to land first on Omaha's western sector, opposite Vierville. As the LCTs advanced line abreast, the pilot boat took station on its left.

Just before dawn, they noticed a huge armada of 320 US heavy bombers fly overhead. The planes' mission was to pulverise the beach defences. Instead their bombs fell well beyond the ridge line. None hit the beach or its strongly guarded exits. 'That's a fat lot of use,' said Scott-Bowden. 'All it's done is wake 'em up.'

At 5,000 yards out, the distance agreed, Rockwell should have given the signal to launch the tanks. But in such a choppy sea, and a force 5 wind, he was undecided. Looking to his left, Scott-Bowden could see the squadron commander 'in the turret of his tank in the left-hand LCT and by signs made very clear he wished to be taken on in.'

'What do you think?' Rockwell asked Scott-Bowden.

'It is far too rough,' the major replied. 'We should go right in.'

The Coppist's advice would save the lives of many tank crewmen. The thirty-two DD Shermans of the 741st Tank Battalion, supporting the 1st Division attacking Omaha's eastern sector, were not so fortunate. Either Sergeant Ogden-Smith was not asked his opinion or it was ignored, because the tanks were launched as planned, at 5,000 yards, and immediately got into difficulties. 'Some of them went off the ramps successfully,' noted one account, 'and travelled a hundred yards or so before they abruptly vanished below the waves. Some never floated at all.' They had been designed to operate in waves no higher than a foot; off Omaha the swell was up to six feet. Of the twenty-nine tanks launched, only two reached dry land. The others were swamped and thirty-three crewmen drowned. The remaining three tanks failed to disembark, and were later dropped directly on the sand. In this sector, therefore, near the village of Colleville, the assault troops had to face the intense German defensive fire with only five of the thirty-two tanks they had expected.

It was different in the western sector where, thanks to Rockwell and Scott-Bowden, most of the 743rd's DD Shermans reached the beach. 'The LCTs grounded on time,' remembered Scott-Bowden,

and in exactly the right place just short of the beach obstacles full of mines, downed their ramps, and the amphibious tanks emerged still with their canvas flotation gear up which they then had to blow free. Some had difficulty as they were being hit by intense machine-gun fire. Soon they were being knocked out by anti-tank gunfire. Not many tanks survived. From among the obstacles we heaved onboard some tank crew survivors.[10]

By now some of the leading companies of the 116th Infantry were landing in the western sector. But because of the strong tidal set, and the lack of any reliable beach markings, three of the four assault companies were landed much further east than intended. One drifted so far that it came ashore in the 1st Division's eastern sector, intermingled with men from the 16th Infantry who were, themselves, out of position. The 16th's four assault companies were also pushed east, as were subsequent waves, so that the majority came ashore at the Colleville end of the sector. One company was blown so far east it 'had to come back against the wind and tide, and landed ninety minutes late'. All the others were mixed up together, and two stretches of the beach, half a mile long, 'had no infantry at all; other parts had too many'. Men 'found themselves pitched on to the shore in single boatloads, cut off from their officers, faced with defences which were not the ones they had studied in their briefing, under a terrible gunfire which they had never been warned to expect, and with nobody to tell them where they were or what they ought to do'.

With no beach markers, the landing had been a disaster. 'By the time they came within sight of the shore,' noted one Coppist history, 'they were too late and too far off course to pick up their landmarks. In any case these were largely blotted out by smoke . . . The whole assault force on "Omaha" had slipped sideways and it was surging straight for catastrophe.'[11]

Lacking armour support, weighed down by weapons and kit, the mass of disorientated troops in front of Colleville was shot to pieces. Everywhere there were cries: 'I'm hit! I'm hit!' One soldier wrote: 'As soon as we dropped our ramp, an 88 mm [shell] came tearing in, killing almost half our men right there, the officer being the first one . . . I went overboard and headed for the beach. The surf was filled with soldiers trying to get ashore. But the bullets in the surf from the enemy were thick. They were getting killed fast. I reached the obstacles and got behind one to shelter. Just then the landing craft blew up. That got me not caring whether I lived or not. I started to run, through the fire up the beach.'[12]

Another remembered his colleagues moving as if in slow motion. 'Overloaded,' he wrote, 'we didn't have a chance. I was so tired I could hardly drag myself along.' Only nine of the thirty-one men in his platoon survived.[13]

Further west, the under-strength and out of position assault companies of the 116th Infantry were, Scott-Bowden remembered, 'being mown down by the score as they moved in the shallow water'. He added: 'Some made it to the back of the beach. Fire was pouring into the defences but not having much effect. Enemy fire was coming back undiminished. Those who found very slight cover at the back of the beach were killed instantly if they attempted to move.'[14]

For a time there was stalemate as the traumatised survivors from the first wave huddled behind any cover they could find, including the shingle bank at the back of the Colleville beach that Scott-Bowden and Ogden-Smith had identified in January. But from mid-morning a number of heroic actions helped to tip the balance. They included engineers blowing gaps in the shingle bank so that tanks and other vehicles could cross it; anti-aircraft gunners knocking out pillboxes; naval destroyers firing their guns so close inshore their keels scraped on the sandy bottom; and small groups of soldiers inspiring others by their actions. One officer summed up their dilemma: 'Two kinds of people are staying on this beach, the dead and those who are going to die. Now let's get the hell out of here.'[15]

The key moments were witnessed by Scott-Bowden from the pilot boat. 'To the left of where we were, keeping station avoiding incoming craft,

the assault was going better and moving up the ridge; on the right from the place where the sentry had beamed his torch at me five months ago the assault was halted. Destroyers closed in and naval gunfire support started being effective. Even the US battleship *Texas* had closed and was visible broadside-on firing its main armament. Our task was to observe progress and report verbally what we had seen to Admiral Hall. Gradually with immense courage the infantry and engineers, some using man-pack flame-throwers worked along the ridge destroying the rabbit warren of bunkers as the naval gunfire moved along just in front of them. It was a magnificent display of navy and army cooperation. We went back to report; on board they already knew that the battle was being won.[16]

The cost of D-Day was heavy: 10,249 Allied casualties, including 2,700 Britons, 946 Canadians and 6,603 Americans. Of the 4,413 fatalities – an unusually high death rate of almost one in two casualties – 2,499 were American, most of them lost on Omaha Beach where the refusal to use beach markers had proved so costly.[17] Yet despite failing to achieve any of their D-Day objectives – the towns of Carentan, Saint-Lô and Bayeux remained in German hands, and Caen, the major objective, was not captured until 21 July – the landings had gained a foothold in 'Fortress Europe' that was gradually expanded over the coming weeks.

At noon on 6 June, Winston Churchill told the House of Commons that the 'first of a series of landings in force upon the European continent has taken place'. He added: 'So far the commanders who are engaged report that everything is proceeding to plan. And what a plan! This vast operation is undoubtedly the most complicated and difficult that has ever taken place. It involves tides, winds, waves, visibility, both from the air and the sea standpoint, and the combined employment of land, air, and sea forces in the highest degree of intimacy and in contact with conditions which could not and cannot be fully foreseen.'[18]

Though it would not be acknowledged publicly for years to come, Willmott's top-secret Coppists – a combination of naval navigators and pilots, and SBS-trained swimmers (the logical conclusion to that first army/navy foray on the beaches of Rhodes three years earlier) – had played a key role in both the planning and execution of Operation Overlord. They were the first to set foot on the beaches (on New Year's Eve, 1943), and their lonely and dangerous vigil in X-craft from 4–6 June 1944 would ensure that, on the British and Canadian beaches at least, the assault troops landed in the right place at the right time.

'The hazards of the [X-craft] operation,' wrote Admiral Sir Bertram Ramsay, the Allied naval commander for D-Day, 'and the skill and endurance of the officers and men who completed it so successfully are fully appreciated.' They were, he added, to be congratulated 'on their achievement, which so materially assisted the greatest landing of British forces on any enemy coast that has ever taken place in the history of the world'.[19]

Rear Admiral Philip Vian, commanding the British task force at D-Day, wrote in his memoirs: 'The leading ships of Forces S and J were guided to their launching positions by lights displayed by two midget submarines, X23 and X20. The crews of these two little craft had achieved a remarkable feat of endurance. Owing to the postponement of D-Day, they had been forced to lie submerged throughout the long daylight hours of the 5th June, which meant nineteen hours at a stretch during which they breathed the air shut into the boat when they dived at dawn. By the time the assault craft arrived, and their task was completed, they had been submerged for sixty-four of the seventy-six hours which they had been at sea.'[20]

Quite rightly, the bulk of the awards went to the X-craft men: Hudspeth received a second bar to his DSC (the equivalent of three medals), while Paul Clark, Geoffrey Lyne, George Honour and Robin Harbud were given their first. Hudspeth's citation read: 'For gallantry, skill, determination and undaunted devotion to duty whilst commanding HM Submarine X20 during Operation Gambit.' Oddly Jim Booth, who performed the same role as Harbud, and no less dangerous, was only mentioned in despatches, as were 'Daddy' Amer and some of the other Coppists who acted as pilots. The French government made up for the injustice done to Booth when it awarded him its own gallantry medal, the Croix de Guerre. 'It is,' he told me in 2019, 'the only medal I care about.'[21]

Part III
Endgame, 1944–5

34

'Unpopular in high places'

On 12 June 1944, barely a week after D-Day, the Small Operations Group (SOG) was officially formed at Hammenhiel Camp on an island off the north tip of Ceylon (modern Sri Lanka). Its task was 'to pave the way for the liberation of Burma, Siam, Malaya and Singapore' by carrying out deception raids, beach and airstrip reconnaissance, coastal sabotage and the insertion of special agents. To achieve this, it would bring together under one roof, for the first time during the war, the leading exponents of amphibious warfare, including the SBS, COPP, the Sea Reconnaissance Unit (SRU)* and a new Royal Marine Commando unit known as Detachment 385.

It was the brainchild of Lord Louis Mountbatten who, as CCO, had tried in vain to place the SBS and other 'private armies' under a single unified command. This all changed with his appointment as Supreme Allied Commander, South East Asia (SACSEA) in the autumn of 1943. He immediately appointed a Head of Combined Operations to his staff and issued directives to bring together as many irregular units as possible. Even before leaving England he had asked for COPPs and groups of SBS to be sent to India. They were supplemented in the summer of 1944 by Detachment 385, formed from

---

* The brainchild of Lieutenant Commander Bruce Wright of the Royal Canadian Navy, the SRU was made up of four ten-man teams of long-distance swimmers who used paddle-boards to reconnoitre beaches, mark landings and guide in assault boats. Their first mission in February 1945 was to scout enemy territory across the Irrawaddy river.

British-based Royal Marines who had volunteered for 'Hazardous Duties – must be swimmers'.[1]

The first man chosen by Mountbatten to head up the SOG was 'Blondie' Hasler, newly promoted to acting lieutenant colonel, who had arrived in India in December 1943. He designed the organisation of SOG: a headquarters that included Administration & Intelligence, and Planning, Training and Development; and an operational wing of four COPPs (forty-eight men), a Special Reconnaissance Unit (forty men), three groups of SBS (sixty men) and three troops of Detachment 385 (ninety-three men). Hasler is also credited by some authors with choosing Hammenhiel Camp as a base.[2] In fact the man responsible was 28-year-old Lieutenant Geoffrey Hall RN, commanding COPP 7.

'Tall, boyish' and 'pink-complexioned', Hall was serving as navigating officer of a minesweeping flotilla in Scotland when he was ordered to swap jobs with a 'pleasant-looking, dark-haired' lieutenant called Geoffrey Lyne in January 1943. Hall had forgotten that, some time before, he had applied for 'Hazardous Service'. Now that Lyne had had enough of such work, having just returned from his stint with Party Inhuman in the Mediterranean, Hall would have to take his place. He was, he recalled, 'hoisted with my own petard, and though sorry to give up a job in which I had been happy and had had some success, the only course open to me was to obey orders and report to Combined Operations Headquarters in London'.

There he met Willmott, a 'remarkable man' who had just been appointed to set up and command the 'small, highly specialised, clandestine reconnaissance units known as COPPs'. Hall had been selected, said Willmott, as one of the first COPP senior officers to go through the course, and was to report to the Yacht Club on Hayling Island after three weeks' leave. Hall did so, and was part of the training cadre that included Stanbury's COPP 5, Amer's COPP 6 and his own COPP 7. Hall's officers were a mixed bunch. His assistant was Ruari McLean, a voluntary reserve lieutenant from Galloway in Scotland who had won the Croix de Guerre while serving on a Free French mine-laying submarine in 1942. Humorous and affable, McLean became a good friend of Hall's. COPP 7's military officer, Captain Bill Lucas RE, was more of an 'intense and dedicated young man with a slight stammer'. A keen Christian, he was 'fearless, resolute, filled with zeal in a righteous cause and endowed with a nice sense of humour'. The maintenance officer, Norman Jennings, was older than the others, having been a Savile Row tailor in civilian life. 'He had,' recalled Hall, 'a pleasant, easy-going personality, was conscientious and meticulous in his duties and had no heroic ambitions whatsover. His assistant, Midshipman Peter Gimson, was a rotund, genial and rather cheeky youth, with bags of "go". All in all, we made a promising team with a keen and willing spirit.'

Most of their early training was in canoes at night. Hall remembered 'prolonged trips both in harbour and out in the open sea, swimming to beaches, measuring their gradients and testing their varying compositions, and also practising the infrared homing technique'. They made two trips to western Scotland for 'toughening up' and submarine training. During one, after a brief spell of home leave, McLean announced he was getting married. Would Hall, he asked, be his best man? After some hesitation, his boss agreed. He was influenced, he later admitted, by a photo of the bride's sister, Mary Carlisle, who, in his estimation, was 'far more attractive than the bride herself'.

In June 1943, Hall's COPP 7 was ordered to the Mediterranean and the wedding was postponed. But it gave Hall the excuse to start writing to Mary Carlisle, a correspondence that culminated a year later in his proposal of marriage, though they were yet to meet. She responded with a single-word telegram: 'Yes'. By then, Hall and his men were in India, having been reassigned in Egypt. Based at Cocanada, north of Madras (modern Chennai), they were given their first mission in October 1943: to survey the island of Akyab, off the Arakan coast of Burma (now Rakhine state in Myanmar), for a possible amphibious landing. Using canoes from a motor launch, they established that a small islet, guarding the seaward approaches to Akyab, was empty of Japanese, before scouting Akyab itself. On the first night, Hall swam ashore, got caught in his lead line and almost drowned. He was saved by his paddler McLean who noticed his blue torch glowing underwater. 'It was,' recalled Hall, 'a very close shave. Another minute and I would have had it.'

The following night McLean took over the swimming and gradient work, while Lucas went ashore a second time to check the 'defences and exits'. They all returned safely and, two months later, by which time they had been joined at Cocanada by Fred Ponsonby's COPP 8, were informed that Hall and McLean had been awarded the DSC 'for courage and determination in clandestine operations in the Far East'. It was 'fantastic', if unexpected, news and they celebrated in style.

In early 1944, as part of a general move of military headquarters (including Mountbatten's) to Ceylon, Hall was ordered to select a new base on the island for what would become a combined COPP/SBS/Royal Marine Commando establishment. He flew down with Lucas and they eventually found Fort Hammenhiel, built by the Portuguese in the seventeenth century, on a tiny island that was connected to the north-western tip of Ceylon by a narrow causeway. 'Apart from the low causeway, which could be guarded,' wrote Hall, 'it was accessible only by sea, and it seemed a perfect storehouse for all the high-security equipment, arms and explosives which an expanded Commando Training Base would require.' It had plenty of room to build a large camp on the 'flat grassy acres' that were fringed with long white sandy beaches, and the off-lying islets and wide expanse of sheltered water were ideal 'for training and exercises with canoes and swimmers'.[3]

Hall and Ponsonby moved their teams to Hammenhiel in the spring, and were joined there by several more COPPs and two groups of SBS – A and B – that had come out from England. The senior SBS officer was Major Mike Kealy, the man Roger Courtney had left in charge of the original No. 1 SBS (Middle East) when he returned from the Mediterranean in December

1941. Having served for a time under Stirling's SAS, Kealy was back in England by the summer of 1943 and anxious for a new challenge.[4]

According to Gruff Courtney, who in January 1944 was posted with his 'Z' SBS* to Ceylon to work under Force 136 (the local equivalent of the SOE), the formation of the SOG was the culmination of a lengthy campaign by Mountbatten and his senior officers to bring all maritime special operations under the authority of the Royal Marines. When Gruff arrived in Ceylon, he was given an ultimatum: accept Royal Marines authority or move on. He and half of his men chose the latter option and ended up in Australia where they worked for the Services Reconnaissance Department (similar to SOE) as planners, trainers and operatives. Courtney was assigned to the SRD's staff in Melbourne.

Before leaving Ceylon, Gruff sent an 'impassioned memorandum' to Mountbatten, warning that 'it would be a misuse of the unique experience of SBS personnel in small-scale clandestine operations if we were to be put under the control, for operations as well as administration, of Royal Marines less experienced than ourselves'. Morale would 'inevitably suffer'. He got no reply, and many years later tracked down a copy of his memorandum in the National Archives. On it were Mountbatten's initials and the letters 'NA' (no action).[5]

Roger Courtney, meanwhile, was also fighting a rearguard action against the Royal Marines' takeover. Captain E. J. A. 'Sally' Lunn – one of the 'Z' SBS officers who remained on Ceylon and ultimately took over A Group, SBS – wrote later

---

* Formed in March 1943, this special subdivision of No. 2 SBS – just six pairs of canoeists – was sent to the Mediterranean under Gruff Courtney to work with the 8th Submarine Flotilla at Algiers. Its missions included ferrying secret agents, simulating beach reconnaissance (to deceive the enemy) and, in conjunction with the SAS, capturing prisoners and raiding enemy airfields. These joint operations, noted Gruff, 'were not a success' because, metaphorically speaking, 'SAS like to burst in gallantly through the front door, while SBS preferred to slip in at the back through the bathroom window'. (Courtney, *SBS*, pp. 82–3.)

that Roger spent much of the early part of 1944 'making desperate efforts to get himself posted to the Far East to take command of the SBS ... which had gone out under Mike Kealy'. His original plan had been to send Kealy out first, and then take over from him. But it failed, according to Lunn, because 'Roger had made himself very unpopular in high places and as a result found himself shunted into a backwater at home.'[6]

Those in 'high places' were chiefly Mountbatten and his senior staff who were angry that Courtney was not prepared to relinquish the SBS's administrative and operational independence. Their attitude was summed up in a letter from Mountbatten's chief of staff, Major General G. E. Wildman-Lushington, to Brigadier Bob Laycock, CCO, in June 1944. 'As you say,' wrote Wildman-Lushington, 'the Courtney brothers are not very easy to assimilate.' They found a 'less indigestible' officer, noted Gruff, in the form of Mike Kealy.[7]

Gruff believed that the other man working against Courtney was his old collaborator 'Blondie' Hasler. Corresponding years later with the author of a book on special forces, Gruff wrote: 'Your revelations concerning the machinations, eventually successful, of Major Hasler and the Royal Marines to oust my brother from SBS confirm my own researches.' He added in a follow-up letter that Hasler was undoubtedly a key player in these machinations, and that the Royal Marines 'had the ear of Mountbatten, which we definitely did not'. That the SBS retained its independence for so long was because of its 'connection with the submariners' and its 'close alliance with COPP under [Nigel] Willmott'.[8]

The 'backwater' that Roger was sent to by Laycock in early July 1944 was the Commando Basic Training Centre at Achnacarry. Roger had other ideas, however, and wangled a separate appointment as a civil officer with the British Military Administration in ex-Italian Somaliland where he was eventually joined by his 'indomitable' wife Dorrise, a FANY (First Aid Nursing Yeomanry). For trying 'to stand in the path of progress', wrote Gruff, the founder of the SBS was sidelined for the rest of the war.[9]

Back in India, the Coppists were also unhappy at having to bow to Royal Marines' authority. When Geoffrey Hall and his men first got to Hammenhiel, each COPP 'was more or less autonomous and had its own little camp-precinct in the shade of the coconut and toddy palms and close to the beach'. As the temperature increased, they became increasingly informal in their dress, and were often 'attired only in sandals and a native "lungi"'. Their training included jungle warfare and evasion exercises. But the easy atmosphere changed in June 1944 with the formation of the SOG and the arrival of its commandant, 46-year-old Colonel Humphrey Tollemache. First commissioned into the Royal Marines in 1915, Tollemache was a hugely experienced officer who had served in both world wars, most recently as commander of the 3rd Mobile Naval Base Brigade in Ceylon. Yet he knew nothing about special operations, and his appointment was more about diplomacy than expertise.[10]

As a 'patient and tolerant man with a fine sense of humour', Tollemache had the perfect temperament to handle the many strong-minded individuals under his command. They included 'Blondie' Hasler who, if you believe Tollemache, had recommended the colonel's appointment. 'I was happy to be chosen by Blondie to be his commandant,' insisted Tollemache. 'I knew him well, knew his reputation and admired him greatly.' Hasler welcomed Tollemache's arrival, according to Hasler's biographer, because it allowed him to concentrate on what he did best: training, planning and development.

A far more likely explanation is that Hasler *did* want the role of commandant: he had, after all, been given the provisional command earlier in the year. But the powers that be realised a more diplomatic, less forthright boss was required if the diverse elements of the SOG were to work well together. Though recently promoted to lieutenant colonel, Hasler was still just 30 years old and, in the minds of the SBS at least, partly responsible for ending the career of their founder Roger Courtney. So Tollemache was brought in as a safe pair of hands – a lightning rod if you will – and even then not everyone was happy.

With his arrival and the start of the SOG, recalled Geoffrey Hall, 'everything changed'. Gone were the COPPs' autonomous lifestyles, informal attire and camaraderie-based discipline. 'No longer,' wrote Hall, 'did each Navy Party have its commanding officer (with direct access to the C-in-C). Instead the COs were styled "Officer-in-Charge", and reported to the brigadier [Tollemache]. Though this was obviously sensible, it nevertheless caused considerable resentment and not a little friction. I personally felt somewhat humiliated – having myself selected the base and built it into a going concern – at having to revert to a relatively junior status and start paying homage to a "parvenu pongo", however exalted. Nevertheless we settled down eventually, and fairly amicably.'[11]

Tollemache speeded up the process by building an officers' mess and bar. It was quite an 'asset', and helped the officers of the various units to get to know each other. They included the officers of Detachment 385, seven of whom had arrived at Hammenhiel in May 1944 to begin a five-week course under Hasler, while the rest travelled to Ceylon with the main body in June. Before moving on to Hammenhiel, they took initiative and survival tests at a camp near Colombo where about fifty men, or a third of the total, were rejected as unsuitable. 'Many of these men,' noted the 385 Unit History, 'were the "tough guys" who had volunteered because they thought they would be able to wear special badges and fancy coloured hats.' Those who passed were sent to Hammenhiel in late July to begin their specialised instruction, which included 'small-boat handling, general seamanship, navigation, weapon training, swimming and jungle training'. They were also taught 'reconnaissance and siting of airstrips, motor boats and harbour installations, demolitions and incendiarism, open sea work, photo interpretation, ship attack.'[12]

With much to learn, Detachment 385 would not become operational until early 1945 and, in the meantime, the bulk of the SOG's heavy lifting was done by the Coppists and the SBS.

35

Sunbeam

Leros island's Portolago Bay in the Dodecanese is a natural harbour: deep, two miles long and half a mile wide. At the head of the bay is the town of Portolago (or Lakki as it is known today), founded in the 1930s as a model colonial settlement with some of the finest examples of Italian Rational and Fascist architecture, including the covered market and the Casa del Balilla (House of the Fascist Youth). Mussolini himself had a mansion built nearby. The island, like the rest of the Dodecanese, had been ruled by Italy since 1912. But it was only in the 1920s that the bay – a broad gash in Leros's south-east coast – became the Italian navy's main base in the eastern Mediterranean, with port facilities on the southern shore, a double boom across its narrow entrance and several batteries of guns on the high cliffs above.

After its government had surrendered to the Allies on 8 September 1943, the 8,000-strong Italian garrison on Leros – mainly naval troops – swapped sides and were reinforced by 3,500 British troops, including some men from the Special Boat Squadron under Major George Jellicoe, the remnants of Courtney's original No. 1 Special Boat Section, which had recently emerged from SAS control to become a separate unit with its headquarters near Haifa in Palestine. But in mid-November 1943, in one of the most daring amphibious and airborne assaults of the war – code-named Operation Leopard – a numerically inferior German force of under 3,000 men, yet one that benefited from almost total air superiority, retook the island after a vicious five-day battle. More than 8,500 Italian and British troops were taken prisoner, and a further 900 lost their lives. Jellicoe and most of his men escaped at the last minute in a Royal Navy motor launch.[1]

'Leros has fallen,' wrote the commander-in-chief of the Middle East to Winston Churchill on 17 November,

> after a very gallant struggle against overwhelming air attack. It was a near thing between success and failure. Very little was needed to turn the scale in our favour and to bring off a triumph. Instead we have suffered a reverse of which the consequences are only too easy to foresee.

For Churchill, the fall of Leros was a 'bitter blow', the 'first really grievous reverse since Tobruk, 1942'. He blamed General Eisenhower's refusal to provide adequate air cover, a difference of opinion that the British prime minister later characterised as their 'most acute' of the war. Whatever the reason, it resulted in complete German domination of the Aegean as the Royal Navy was forced to evacuate British garrisons on Samos and other islands, losing six destroyers and two submarines in the process, and a further eight warships damaged.[2] Meanwhile Portolago Bay on Leros became the main German naval base in the Dodecanese and it was not until the following summer that Britain felt able to strike back.

Just before midnight on 17 June 1944, the skipper of the Royal Navy's ML 360, a 112-feet-long motor launch built by Fairmile for coastal operations, stopped the craft's two powerful 650 bhp petrol engines a mile and a half from the entrance to Portolago Bay. The signal was given for the six limpeteers on board – all members of the RMBPD's 'Earthworm' Detachment, based at the Raiding Forces Headquarters near Haifa in Palestine – to launch their canoes. This they did from a point just forward of the motor launch's wheelhouse, using three ropes: 'one placed round the canoe a yard from the bows, a second amidships and a third rope a yard from the stern'.[3]

Lowered one at a time 'to avoid confusion and noise', the canoes contained all their equipment except water cans and eight limpet mines. These were handed to the canoe's No. 2, or paddler, once he had climbed down the scramble net and got in. With the No. 1 also on board, the canoe moved a short distance away until the others were loaded. This took about half an hour, and at 12:25 a.m. the three canoes began paddling towards Portolago on a north-easterly course of forty-five degrees. The intention was to reach the island of Leros about a quarter of a mile east of the bay's entrance, so that their final approach would be masked by the coast. 'There was,' noted Lieutenant J. F. Richards, commanding the limpeteers, 'very little wind and the sea was flat calm with only a slight mist.'[4]

Their mission – code-named Sunbeam A – was to sneak into Portolago Bay and sink up to nine enemy ships at anchor: three destroyers, three smaller escort boats and three merchant vessels. The ships were part of a German supply convoy that was returning to Piraeus on the Greek mainland from the island of Rhodes, and had stopped off in Portolago en route. Bad weather had postponed an earlier attack in May. This dark period in June was probably their last opportunity. There was, however, the problem of time. Starting from its forward base on the island of Kastellorizo, just off the coast of Turkey, the motor launch could not get to the drop-off point much before midnight. That left just five hours of darkness for the limpeteers to complete their mission and get away. Aware this was far too tight, Richards 'reorganised his plan' so that on completion the canoes headed for the nearby island of Kalymnos where they would lie up during the day and be rescued the following night.

Despite the obvious dangers – everyone involved knew of the existence of Hitler's notorious 'Commando Order' and their likely execution if captured – there were plenty of volunteers for the mission. No one was keener than Marine Eric Fisher, the No. 2 in the third canoe Shrimp, who was desperate to make up for the disappointment of missing out on Operation Frankton, though the accidental damage to his and Bill Ellery's canoe had probably saved their lives.* On returning to the UK, Fisher, Norman Colley and Bill Sparks had all joined Bill Pritchard-Gordon's No. 2 Section which, on being sent to the Mediterranean, was renamed the 'Earthworm' Detachment. But it was Fisher who got the nod for Sunbeam A. He was partnered in *Shrimp* with Corporal E. W. 'Johnny' Horner. The other crews were Lieutenant Richards and Marine W. S. Stevens in *Shark*, and Sergeant J. M. King – Hasler's former PT instructor – and Marine R. N. Ruff in *Salmon*. They had all 'blacked' their faces and were wearing camouflage 'Anorak Suits'.[5]

Reaching the Leros coast at 12:50 a.m., King told Richards that his canoe was leaking and needed to be bailed out 'at intervals'. But there was no question of King and Ruff aborting: instead the sergeant borrowed Richards' sponge 'to cope with the situation'. The men were now ordered to prime their limpets. When that was done, Richards sent *Shrimp* in first at 1:00 a.m. That was because Horner and Fisher had the furthest distance to cover and arguably the toughest task: sinking three merchant ships that were believed to be moored along the north of the harbour, which meant leaving the shadow of the south-east cliff.[6]

Using split paddles, Horner and Fisher passed the broken boom at the harbour entrance at 1:10 a.m., keeping close to the cliff. Once inside they altered course to cross the harbour and soon spotted two of their targets: the cargo ships MV *Sieglinde*, 'well up on the beach', and the MV *Anita*, 'lying in almost mid-stream'. Approaching *Anita*'s stern, Horner 'clearly saw a group of men' near a deck gun. One of them must have seen the canoe because he issued a challenge that was taken up by two others. Horner and Fisher 'froze motionless' but were unable to prevent their canoe's momentum from taking them 'nearer to their challengers'.

---

* Bill Ellery was the only survivor of Frankton not to serve in Pritchard-Gordon's 'Earthworm' Detachment. Instead he left the RMBPD soon after his return from the mission because, according to one account, he had 'become wayward' and 'could not continue'. It may also be that he was blamed – or blamed himself – for the damage done to his and Fisher's canoe *Cachalot*. (Rees, *Cockleshell Heroes*, p. 188.)

As the voices became more persistent, and Horner could hear men running on a lower deck, he shouted the Italian word 'Patrole', knowing no German.

It was an act of desperation, and both Horner and Fisher expected the Germans to raise the alarm as they headed for the shadow of the northern shore. But no lights were shone and no bullets fired. Scarcely able to believe their luck, they made straight for the harbour entrance and, once outside, chucked their primed limpet mines overboard. They then set a course for Kalymnos. Richards later praised their actions. 'In my briefings,' he wrote, 'all crews were told that whatever happened, they were to take the necessary steps to ensure that the safety of the [other] men, and the operation, were not prejudiced.'

Richards' own canoe *Shark* was the next to enter the harbour. Keeping close to the shadow of the cliff, he and Stevens made their way along the south shore to the naval base where they hoped to find their targets: a destroyer and three smaller escorts. At around 1:40 a.m., with only a short distance to go, they heard a shout from the shore behind them and saw a light. Assuming, correctly, that King and Ruff in *Salmon* had been seen and challenged, they decided to press on and hope for the best.

Failing to spot a destroyer beside the wharf, they kept going and soon located a smaller escort vessel, 'with a gun mounted on a platform in the bows', moored to a buoy. There was no one on deck, but they could hear voices and a dog barking. Coming alongside, Richards steadied the canoe with the magnetic holder while his No. 2, Stevens, placed limpets below the water-line in two positions: fifteen feet from the stern; and a little further forward where Richards judged the engine room to be. Stevens did this by first attaching the limpet to a cleverly designed 'angle piece on the face of his paddle', thus obviating the need for a separate placing rod. To minimise the noise of all the magnets clamping at the same time, it was vital to apply the limpet as gradually as possible.

With both limpets in place, they moved inshore and found

another escort ship, larger than the first, moored between a wreck and a barge. Despite the presence of two sentries on deck – their conversation clearly audible – they were able to attach two more limpet mines. 'In order to pass this craft,' noted Richards, 'I went astern and circled the ship. I then found myself almost alongside [another] escort vessel . . . on which men were talking excitedly. One of the watch-keepers called to a third person to come up on deck, by which time I had started to move slowly away. I am certain that the canoe was not seen.'

Not far away lay yet another small escort ship with a sentry 'plainly' visible. Ignoring his presence, they placed two more limpets: 'one against the engine room, the other fifteen feet from the stern'. Richards had wanted to put the second limpet ahead of the engine room, but the magnetic holder failed in all three positions tried. 'The hull construction here,' he concluded, 'was of non-magnetic alloy.'

With only two limpets left, and time running out, Richards circled back the way he had come, looking for a destroyer. He found one – of the Italian Turbine class, but manned by Germans* – lying against a small jetty. 'I moved in,' he recalled, 'under the bows and manoeuvred to make contact with the magnetic holder. At this point we were urinated upon from above, by a sentry whom we had not seen or heard, and who then moved away.' Ignoring the unexpected shower, Richards got to work. Ideally, he would have placed at least one limpet opposite the engine room. But with up to three sentries keeping watch, and a deck which appeared to be 'very low off the waterline', he did not want to risk moving astern. So Stevens put one limpet twenty-five feet from the bows, and the second ten feet further back.

---

* Following the Italian government's unconditional surrender to the Allies on 8 September 1943, German forces took control of much of Italy and its remaining possessions, including many of the Greek islands. Only a few Italian warships were captured in port and later crewed with Germans. The bulk of the Italian navy escaped to Malta, though one battleship *Roma* was sunk by German planes. Among the 1,600 lives lost was the naval commander-in-chief, Admiral Bergamini.

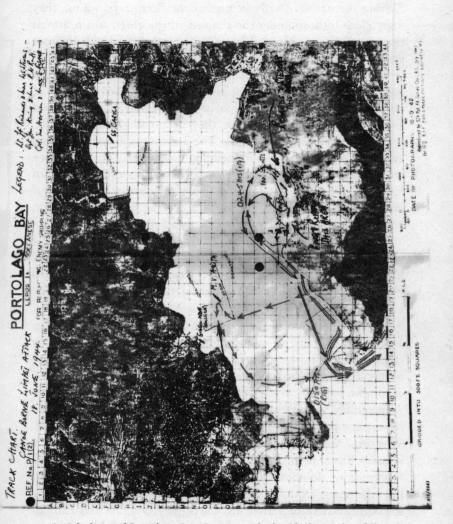

Aerial photo of Portolago Bay, Leros, overlaid with the tracks of the various limpet attacks, Operation Sunbeam, 18 June 1944.

They had accomplished their mission: it was time to leave. Exiting the harbour without further incident at 3:10 a.m., they kept 'close inshore under the shadow of the cliffs, and followed the coastline round for about a mile, and then decided to cut straight across' to Kalymnos.

That just left one canoe: *Salmon*. As Richards suspected, it had indeed been spotted soon after entering the harbour at 1:20 a.m. Challenged by a sentry in a patrol boat, King and Ruff froze. After the third challenge, they back-paddled as far as the boom at the harbour entrance where they moved out into the centre of the channel before heading east again. As before they were hailed from the patrol boat, causing them to pause until King felt it was safe to continue. They finally reached the naval base at 2:15 a.m. and stopped by a derelict barge to 'bail out, since the water in the canoe was around their knees'.

The first of their two destroyer targets was directly ahead: it was, in King's opinion, also of the Italian Turbine class. As several men were talking and smoking at his approach point, King tried from a different angle 'but noticed a sentry standing on a jetty' beside the destroyer. The sentry was soon joined by several more. A final approach from the 'harbour end of the base' was more successful, and three limpets were placed on either side of the ship's stern. With the canoe once again 'half full of water', King wisely decided to leave the bay and make for Kalymnos. It was 2:40 a.m.

Incredibly, despite multiple sightings and challenges, all three canoes got away from Portolago without the alarm being raised. Why no shots were fired, or further investigation made, is a mystery. The sentries probably imagined they were looking at local fishermen or dolphins. Whatever the reason, the canoeists took full advantage. Dodging Greek fishing boats, they all reached the temporary safety of Kalymnos where they beached and camouflaged their canoes in small inlets and found somewhere to hide. From around 4:45 a.m., and continuing for much of the day, they could hear explosions from the direction of Portolago. Richards was convinced that, as well as the noise of the limpets going off,

ABOVE: HMS *Unrivalled* (Mossy Turner), anchoring in an undisclosed naval port.

ABOVE: Lt Hugh 'Mossy' Turner on the casing of HMS *Unrivalled*, Malta, January 1943.

RIGHT: Execution of Sgt Leonard G. Siffleet of M Special Unit by the Japanese at Aitape, New Guinea, on 24 October 1943.

LEFT: Sub Lt Robin Frederick Andrew Harbud RNVR and Sgt E. Cooke unloading their folbot aboard a submarine.

BELOW: Courtney and officers at Hillhead, 1943.

ABOVE: SSRF and SBS visit RMBPD at Eastney to compare canoes, 26 August 1943 (Jumbo Courtney is wearing beret, hands in pockets).

ABOVE: Stan Weatherall (C), Lt Philip Ayton (A), Corporal J. Parkes (B) – latter pair both killed later that month on separate raids – and other members of 2 SBS at Ringway Station after qualifying as parachutists in December 1943.

ABOVE: Major GB Courtney and SBS officers and men (including Sgts F. Preece, J. Gilmour and R. Sidlow, and Capts N. G. Kennard, E. J. A. Lunn, Ft Lt Thompson and Capt A. R. McClair), Hillhead, 1943/44.

LEFT: Major Logan Scott-Bowden.

ABOVE LEFT: Sub Lt K. C. J. Robinson RNVR, of Crosby, Liverpool, a commanding officer in an X-craft at the periscope whilst sailing in Rothesay Bay.

ABOVE: Lt Jim Booth and Lt George Honour aboard X-23 off the D-Day beaches, 6 June 1944.

LEFT: Lt Jim Booth and his sister.

BELOW: Geoffrey Lyne ascends from the X-23 on D-Day.

ABOVE: Method of embarking swimmer alongside canoe as demonstrated by Lt Alex Hughes, Ceylon, c.1944–5.

BELOW AND RIGHT: COPP personnel on a training exercise at Hammenhiel Camp, Ceylon.

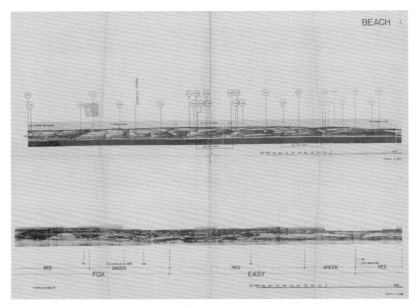

ABOVE: Sketch and photo composite panorama of Omaha Beach with main strongpoints.

BELOW: Beach Obstacle Overprint – Omaha Beach East (Colleville).

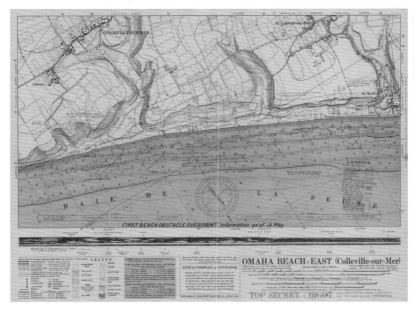

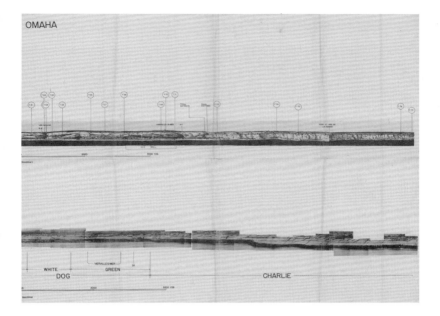

BELOW: Beach Obstacle Overprint – Omaha Beach West (Vierville).

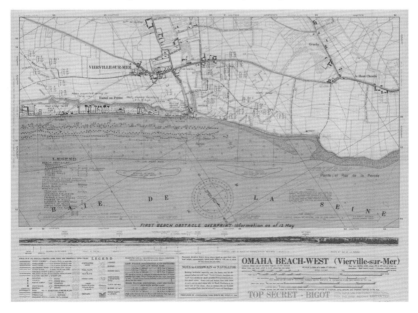

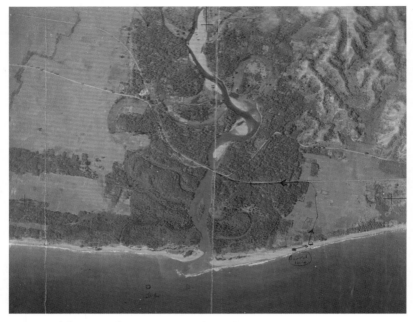

ABOVE: Peudada River Bridge, reconnaissance photo, July 1943.

BELOW: Lt AIex Hughes and COPP 3(1) at Hammenhiel Camp.

they could hear the sound of depth charges as the Germans tried to find the submarine they believed was responsible for the attack.

There were some hairy moments. A fishing vessel discovered Ruff's original hideout on Kalymnos, prompting the limpeteer to threaten the Greek skipper with a pistol. But the Greek 'appeared to be friendly' and was allowed to leave. Later in the day, Richards and Stevens thought they were being fired upon when machine-gun bullets ricocheted over their heads. But they concluded that the bullets were probably a warning to a Greek vessel that had entered a forbidden zone off Kalymnos, and they just happened to be in the line of fire. Wireless contact was made with the motor launch that evening, and by midnight all three canoes had made the rendezvous and were safely on board.[7]

By badly damaging two destroyers and sinking three smaller escort ships, Richards and his men had pulled off one of the most brilliant sabotage missions of the war.* Better still, they had not sustained a single casualty. Bill Pritchard-Gordon, now a captain, was delighted with the result of his detachment's first operation in the Aegean, and singled out three men for special praise: Richards, 'for his excellent leadership and control of this difficult operation'; and King and Ruff 'who showed extreme devotion to duty in pressing home a successful attack against exceptional difficulties'. Richards was duly awarded the DSC, while King and Ruff got the DSM.[8]

Regretting later that he had not put all six men up for awards, Pritchard-Gordon tried to make amends with a recommendation for Horner, Fisher and Stevens in late 1944. The first two, wrote their boss, had shown 'complete disregard for their own safety in a successful attempt to safeguard the operation and the lives of their fellow operators', while Stevens had done 'all that was expected of him and more', as evidenced by the fact that *Shark*

---

* The modern SBS regards Sunbeam as an even 'more successful' mission than Frankton, and in many ways it was (though nowhere near as difficult to pull off). In a single night, three canoes 'effectively neutralised' the enemy's naval forces in the eastern Aegean. (*By Strength and Guile*, p. 27.)

'was never once suspected or challenged even though four sepa-rate ships were attacked during the night, when conditions were far from ideal and the enemy definitely suspicious'.[9]

Unfortunately, while Pritchard-Gordon's superiors agreed that all three had performed creditably – particularly Horner who had 'acted with great coolness, sound judgement and complete disregard for his own safety' – they felt there were 'insufficient grounds' to intervene with the ruling that 'recommendations for awards to personnel serving abroad' had to be made through the commander-in-chief concerned.

Instead of a medal, Eric Fisher would have to be content with a note in his personal file that, during Sunbeam A, he had 'conducted himself with steadfastness and courage of a high order, through the entire action'. For a man who had missed out on Frankton and was, in Norman Colley's words, 'not the toughest but one of the best you could meet', it was a small consolation.[10]

Bridge Over the River Peudada

The northern coast of Sumatra in Indonesia (the former Dutch East Indies) is fringed with sandy beaches and mostly flat for up to two miles inland, 'thence rising from the foothills to the mountainous interior'. It was of particular interest to the Allies in the summer and early autumn of 1944 as the potential site for a large-scale amphibious assault known as Operation Culverin, scheduled for no earlier than 1 March 1945, and to include four Commando units, five infantry divisions and a tank brigade. The loudest cheerleader for the capture of north Sumatra was Winston Churchill. It would, he believed, outflank the Japanese in Burma and make possible an attack on Singapore.[1]

To lay some of the groundwork, therefore, Colonel Tollemache's SOG was tasked with surveying the beaches and disrupting Japanese communications. The first mission was successfully carried out in August 1944 by Geoffrey Hall's COPP 7 (its last operation before its return to the UK in the autumn). The second – the destruction of two bridges – was given to B and C Groups of the SBS. B Group was commanded by Major Douglas Sidders, formerly of the Royal Welch Fusiliers, who had joined Courtney's No. 2 SBS as a lieutenant in April 1942. Apart from his involvement in Operation Forfar Love – an attempt by two pairs of SBS canoeists to scout Dunkirk's east pier that was aborted when they were picked up by a searchlight – he had been starved of action and was eager to do his bit.[2]

Sidders' orders were to destroy the combined road and rail bridge over the Peudada river in north Sumatra. It was a 'single span, with girder truss', 270-feet long (including approaches) and fifteen feet wide, and believed to be 'the sole connection along the coast of Sumatra for all movement between the aerodromes to the west and the towns to the east'. The plan – known as Operation Spratt Baker – was for a submarine to drop four pairs of canoeists offshore. They would then paddle to the mouth of the river, approach the bridge and lay 400 pounds of explosive charges with pencil fuses before making their getaway.[3] It seemed to be a fairly straightforward mission; it proved to be anything but.

Sidders and his eight men – one acting as a reserve – left the north-eastern Ceylon port of Trincomalee in the submarine HMS *Trenchant* in the evening of Tuesday 5 September. His second in command, Lieutenant E. A. W. 'Teddy' Wesley, was a former Gordon Highlander who had joined the SBS as a corporal before being granted an immediate emergency commission in December 1943.[*] The other six men slated for the mission were all NCOs: two sergeants and four corporals.[4]

Five days after leaving Ceylon they reached the coast of north Sumatra and, in failing light, carried out a preliminary periscope reconnaissance of their target. 'From four miles out,' noted Lieutenant Wesley, 'we were able to see the bridge, painted a pale grey and looming very large indeed on the horizon. Then dusk set in and we dived to fifty feet to hold a church service!'[5]

Much to Wesley's surprise, the *Trenchant*'s God-fearing skipper, South African-born Lieutenant Commander Arthur 'Baldy' Hezlet RN,[†] had insisted on a proper observance of the Sabbath. 'It was very strange,' Wesley noted in his diary,

---

[*] Teddy Wesley's third Christian name, Wellesley, hints that he might have been related to Arthur Wellesley, 1st Duke of Wellington, who originally spelled his surname 'Wesley'. Receiving their emergency commissions on the same day as Wesley, 6 December 1943, were George Barnes and Jim Sherwood, two of Courtney's Sannox Bay 'originals'.

[†] Later Vice Admiral Sir Arthur Hezlet. His appointments included Director of the Naval Staff College at Greenwich and Flag Officer Submarines (at the time HMS *Dreadnought*, the first nuclear attack submarine, was launched in 1960).

only four miles from the enemy coast, in the tomb-like silence of the submerged sub, the men gathered together in the cramped space of the Control Room singing hymns to the tune of a mouth-organ. Being RC I didn't attend, but the men seemed to enjoy their singing and I rather envied the simple service. On the second hymn the organist (not an expert) forgot the tune, so the captain had to strike up alone! No sooner was it finished than 'diving stations' were sounded and we surfaced – very thankful for the fresh air as we'd been underneath for fifteen hours and the air was pretty foul.

Next day, having taken evasive action to avoid Japanese planes, *Trenchant* moved to within two and a half miles of the coast so that Sidders and Wesley could carry out a more detailed periscope observation. Wesley was disturbed by what he saw: a 'number of large tents in the trees by the beach, not half a mile from the river mouth', two fires, and 'square shapes that might be huts, pillboxes or watch-shelters on the river mouth'. The bridge itself, sited half a mile upriver beyond a large sandbar, was a 'magnificent girder construction nearly as tall as the trees'. Despite the likelihood that it was being guarded, Sidders decided that the operation was still on. They would 'go in', noted Wesley, 'and make the best of it'. [6]

Trenchant surfaced five miles north of the river mouth at 7:00 p.m. The sea was a flat calm and, once the four canoes had been brought up onto the casing, the submarine began running quietly in towards land. All the while, the eight SBS men – wearing green battledress tunics and trousers, naval gaiters and felt-soled boots – were 'loading pistols and tommy guns, crimping on detonators to fuses, and making all the 101 last-minute adjustments' that such a dangerous operation requires. When that was done, recalled Wesley, 'we sat round the wardroom table and had a last cup of tea while the sweat from our exertions ran down our faces, mingling with the grease paint. The red bulbs cast an eerie light on our features.'

At 8:20 p.m., Hezlet's voice came down the voice-pipe. 'No. 4 Boat Crew to the casing, please.'

That was corporals Watt and Shearston. They climbed through the conning-tower hatch, followed soon after by the No. 3 crew, Sergeant Dawkins and Corporal Wells. Then it was Wesley and Corporal Hickman's turn. As he left, Wesley was encouraged by a friendly 'Good luck' and a pat on the back from unseen hands. Once on the bridge, he filled his lungs 'with the sweet damp air' before picking his way along the casing, and past the remaining canoe, to the bows. There his own canoe – No. 2 Boat – was swung over the casing and lowered into the water. Hickman got into the stern seat and was handed two heavy rucksacks, each holding fifty pounds of explosives. Then Wesley climbed in. 'A whispered "cast off",' he recalled, 'and we were afloat on our own, drifting away from the dark outline of the submarine, with its silhouetted boat party already stooping to lower the next canoe. The night was beautifully calm. The overcast sky pitch-black with the oil-like surface of the sea casting a faint luminosity so that the other canoes appeared like dark shapes floating not on but in a pale ether.'

With all canoes launched by 8:40 p.m., Major Sidders and his paddler Sergeant Thomas 'Toe' Williams led them in an arrowhead formation due south towards the shore. They had two miles to go and the intention was to reach the coast 800 yards east of the river mouth. As he paddled, Wesley had ample time to consider what lay ahead. 'I felt happy, scared, brave and amused, in turn,' he remembered. 'The physical pleasure of being out of the stuffy submarine, together with the conscious enjoyment of paddling a canoe on a warm night, with every dip of the paddle making a million twinkling lights in the dark water, and each canoe leaving a faint, luminous trail, was my first reaction. For a while I just paddled on, contented.'

But then he began to imagine 'machine guns suddenly shattering the stillness as they fired point-blank at us from the beach', and what he would do to survive. He thought of his family, particularly his father who would expect him to 'behave as a man should'. It was the resolve 'not to let him down' that gave Wesley 'a great deal of comfort' and the courage to carry on.

These serious thoughts gave way to levity as he considered how ridiculous they must have seemed: sailing against the Japanese, 'not in a steel tank or battleship, guns and armour as protection, but in a frail canvas-sided folding boat!' It was so ludicrous that he grinned in the darkness.

He was brought back to reality when he checked his compass: they were heading south-east. But why? A few minutes later, Sidders stopped and, thinking he had gone too far, changed course to the south-west, then back to due south. By the time they got near the shore, rising and falling beyond the surf line, they did not know if they were east or west of the river. They paddled in one direction, parallel with the shore, and then back again without seeing the river. At around 10:30 p.m. they came through the surf and stopped on a beach beyond a sandbar. After a brief snoop around, Sidders and Williams reported finding 'a wired-in bunker position and that something was moving around, might be a Jap, might be a cow'. Either way they were in the wrong place so they re-embarked and moved a little further west down the coast where, finally, they spotted the river. Paddling through the surf at the sandbar, Wesley found himself and two of the other canoes in still water.

The fourth canoe – Sidders' and Williams' – appeared soon after, but with only Williams on board. He explained that Sidders, on reaching the sandbar, 'had jumped out of the canoe to do a recce and not moored it'. The swift current had then taken the canoe, leaving Sidders stranded. Wesley went back for him and, with the aid of his night glasses, found Sidders 'wandering up and down the sandspit looking for his canoe'. It was not until just before midnight, and well behind schedule, that the whole party was reunited on a broad beach on the east bank of the river.

Having turned the canoes over and covered them with sand, they set off up the riverbank towards the bridge, but were thwarted by the marshy terrain and the thick, impenetrable undergrowth which came down to the water's edge. Moored a few yards from the shore was a large sampan that, for one mad moment, Sidders considered using as transport. He was dissuaded by Wesley who told him they 'could no more pole a sampan than fly a plane'.

They recovered the canoes and tried paddling up the river, but were foiled by a strong current of at least four knots. At one point a canoe went past Sidders and Williams 'paddling all out and going backwards fast'. So they landed on the west bank and attempted to go that way. But the going was just as tough and, after striking further inland for half a mile, passing a 'large shelter' in which they could hear men breathing, they were stopped by rows of barbed wire. 'The only way to get to the bridge,' reported Sidders, 'which was ½ mile upriver, was to walk well down to westward until clear of the river mouth and thick country and then commence heading south from there until the railway was reached, finally following the line east to bridge.' But as it was almost 2:00 a.m., at which time the moon would rise, Sidders gave the order to return to the canoes and re-embark for the submarine.

He was rapidly losing the confidence of his men who, once back at the beach, stood 'in a foiled angry bunch', arguing in loud tones and suggesting 'wild schemes'. They departed in their canoes at 2:15 a.m. and headed north, signalling to the submarine with a torch when they were a mile out to sea. It picked them up an hour later. They were, recorded Wesley, 'a frustrated, shamefaced bunch! We felt that by our failure we had let the SBS down.'[7]

Their only hope of redemption was if C Group had also failed in its mission that night – destroying the Pente Badja bridge, fifty miles further west, an operation code-named Spratt Able – without alerting the Japanese. They finally got their answer from the other submarine *Terrapin* at 5:50 p.m. on the 12th: 'Unable to land because of surf – believe undetected.'

This was music to B Group's ears. They could try again.

*

The four SBS canoes were relaunched from *Trenchant* into a calm sea at 8:40 p.m. Having persuaded Sidders that his compass was not working, Wesley took the lead and navigated the canoes straight to the mouth of the river, at which point they turned to starboard and landed on a beach a quarter of a mile west, as planned. After a brief moment of farce – with Wesley organising a 'pincer attack' on what turned out to be a 'washed-up log with two thick branches' that he had mistaken for an enemy patrol – they moved a little further up the beach to clear a wooded area and then turned south, cutting their way through a double apron of barbed wire and crossing an empty slit trench.

Beyond lay a dry paddy field and a herd of cattle that followed them as they moved as silently as possible towards the railway line. Reaching it at 11:30 p.m., they took off their heavy packs and rested for a few minutes. They then followed the railway embankment east, prompting dogs to bark as they passed by some dwellings. Wesley was leading as they picked their way over a small bridge. He had just reached the far side when there was a clatter behind him, a long pause, and finally an 'enormous splash'.

It was Corporal Wells, a 'massive fellow', who had not realised he was on a bridge and walked straight off the side. Luckily it was only waist-deep and he quickly rejoined the column, soaking wet but unhurt.

Soon after, at the point where a road joined the railway line from the right, the 'pale grey form' of the bridge came into view. Sidders gave orders to remove packs and advance as a patrol along the gravelly road. There was no sign of sentries through their night glasses, but they could easily have been hidden in the shadows. Leaving his men in a position to cover the bridge, he and Wesley advanced up the middle of the road, tommy guns at the ready, 'trying to look as much like a pair of natives as possible'. They 'reached the ramp unchallenged, crossed the bridge and went fifty yards the other way to make sure'. There was no one about, so they made a quick examination of the bridge's girder structure before rejoining their men.

As they did so, a train approached from the west. 'We crouched down to let it pass,' recalled Wesley. 'It carried no lights but threw out showers of sparks. It was a long, heavily laden train and I prayed that it might be the last ever to cross that bridge.' Once it had gone, they returned to collect their rucksacks and had just got back to the junction of railway and road when they heard a faint crunching sound. Sidders dropped down. The others froze in various positions. Seconds later a Japanese cyclist patrol passed within eight feet of them. There were at least five cyclists, possibly more, and all Sidders could see was the top of their rifles poking over their shoulders. It was, they all knew, a 'close shave'.

They crossed to the eastern end of the bridge – where Sidders had decided to lay the charges – and, with two men acting as sentries, the other six got to work: Wesley and two men were responsible for laying charges on the north (railway) side of the bridge; while Sidders and the remaining pair wired up the south (road) side. Wesley had just started when another train approached, forcing him to crouch down at the base of the girders, barely a yard from the track. He could hear singing in one of the carriages as it passed.

Wesley got up and was in the process of hauling two large Bergen rucksacks, each holding fifty pounds of explosives, onto the girders when dimmed headlights heralded the approach of a vehicle. A 'big American-looking staff car' crawled by and stopped in the village beyond 'where someone seemed to shout orders'. The bridge was clearly an 'unhealthy place' to be so they worked 'feverishly'. Wesley noticed that the 'main girders of the arch and the span met on top of the supporting pillars', making a steel box of around two feet cubed. Into this box he stuffed the contents of both rucksacks, 'fixing a cutting charge of ten pounds onto the lower span just to make sure of the cut'.

As Sidders was working on the opposite pillar, he was approached by Sergeant Williams. 'I've got five of them, sir.'

'Five what?'

'Five natives, sir.'

Lying by the bridge when the second train passed over, Williams had heard noises in some bushes nearby. Going to investigate, he discovered five Indonesians and brought them back at gunpoint. Sidders told him to guard them, having 'first disarmed the only one who carried a lethal weapon, a large and heavy matchet'.

Wesley was the first to finish laying his charges. As he waited for Sidders and his men to do the same, he was shocked at the amount of noise they were making: people 'seemed to stamp about, bang weapons against the girders, drop tools and mutter and curse at each other!' Then a group of locals 'came and started a fire in a three-walled shelter not twenty yards from the far end of the bridge' where they had been working. Every now and again they would pile brushwood onto the fire 'so that the flames leaped up, illuminating the whole scene, throwing the shadow of the girders onto the line of trees beyond'.

At last, Sidders' work was done and they 'pressed the time pencils which were taped onto the instantaneous fuse which linked all the charges'. The delay was set for one and a half hours. It was 2:05 a.m. and time to go.

Taking the five Indonesian captives with them – and using chewing gum and money to keep their goodwill – they retraced their steps to the beach. The trouble started when they tried to get one of the locals into a canoe. Sidders and Wesley had been told at Trincomalee that a prisoner 'would be of the greatest value – particularly a native as they know much more about local defences, disposition of troops and administration than does the average Jap soldier'. They selected a 'young fellow' and led him towards the boats. But as soon as he realised what was happening, he started to shout and struggle violently. Worried the Japanese would hear the commotion, Wesley tried to knock him out: first with his fist; then, when that did not work, by using the butt of his Luger to strike the Indonesian on the top of his head 'with terrific force'.

The captive let out a terrific wail, but was still conscious and struggling as they carried him to the canoe, Wesley's hand over his mouth to stifle the cries. Desperate to escape, he twisted out of their grasp and into the water. Wesley tried to hold him under 'to drown some of the life out of him', but each wave rolled them over and allowed the man to break away, take a breath and yell. At one point he bit deep into Wesley's hand. It was the last straw. Exhausted by the struggle, and unwilling to inflict any more harm on the captive, Wesley let him go and 'patted him on the back – a poor atonement for all that bullying!'

The man crawled up the beach and lay there moaning. He had been yelling, on and off, for more than five minutes and there was a very real chance that any Japanese nearby would have heard him. Wesley was particularly concerned because, en route to the beach, a captive had said 'Nippon' while pointing a little to the west: the site of a possible machine gun a short distance up the coast. He and Hickman got quickly into their canoe, while Sidders and Williams did the same. The other two canoes had been ordered away during the struggle on the beach.

They were just in time. 'No sooner were we afloat,' recorded Wesley, than we saw a torch shining from [a short way to the west], the owner apparently running along the beach towards us. We paddled like mad, expecting a burst of fire at any moment, but once we were through the waves they obviously couldn't see us from the shore, and a Jap machine-gunner would be too well trained to open up on an invisible target.'

They kept up a steady rhythm in silence, 'hoping and praying that the charges wouldn't be discovered'. Wesley kept an eye on his luminous watch and, as the minutes ticked down to 3:35 p.m. – the time of detonation – his heart rate increased. But when the time came and went with no explosion, his heart sank. All the 'danger, work, planning and hopes had come to nothing'. Had they made a mistake or, more likely, were the Japanese able to dismantle the charges before they blew? Such thoughts were swirling through his head as a 'flash like lightning' lit up the sky behind him. He and the others spun their heads to see, at a distance of more than a mile, 'the two ends of the bridge heated to a glowing red by the explosion'. They cheered and, as they did so, 'heard the booming roar' of 400 pounds of high explosives igniting. There was a brief pause, then a 'low continuous rumble like distant thunder'. The bridge had come crashing down.

Elated, they turned back to their course, flashing the pick-up signal as they went. Half an hour later they started to worry. Where was the submarine? Where were the other boats? With dawn fast approaching, they pressed on, hoping to be out of sight of land before it got light. Wesley saw the grim irony of surviving so many close shaves only to miss their rendezvous. He now feared the worst. Would they be machine-gunned from the air, dying happily as they fired back with pistol and tommy gun? Or would a boat come out and ram them? What if they were captured? Would they be shot out of hand or simply tortured?

They kept paddling, not least because the *Trenchant*'s skipper had promised to surface in daylight if he saw them at least four or five miles from the shore. Wesley felt certain they had covered that distance. They had been signalling to seaward for more than ninety minutes and there was no sign of the submarine. Wesley was about to put his white shirt on a paddle and wave it when Corporal Hickman, looking back towards the coast, clearer now as the sky began to brighten, shouted, 'There she is!'

They turned to see the dark shadow of *Trenchant*'s bows and conning tower approaching rapidly from their rear. 'A few seconds joyfully paddling at full speed,' recorded Wesley, 'a scramble up the ballast tanks, and the canoes were being tossed down the open hatch. Five minutes from being sighted we were safely inside, talking our heads off, while the klaxon sounded diving stations.'

It was 5:05 a.m. on 13 September 1944. The long – almost disastrous – delay in their rescue was because the submarine had gone to pick up the first two canoes which were slightly off course. While they were doing this, Sidders' and Wesley's canoes had passed them to the west and gone further out to sea. It was only when the submarine turned and headed away from the coast that it spotted Sidders' signal. Hezlet had already given the order to dive. A few minutes later and it would have been too late.

They carried out a periscope reconnaissance from two miles away at 7:30 a.m. to confirm the bridge's destruction. 'Girder structure seen to be lying twisted in river,' noted Lieutenant Commander Hezlet, 'completely severing road and rail communications.'*

In his report, Sidders praised all ranks for working 'extremely well' and showing throughout 'the usual high standard of courage and self-discipline'. Needless to say, he made no mention of his own shortcomings and singled out just one man: his paddler Sergeant Williams who throughout the operation had 'acted promptly, calmly, fearlessly', and whose decisive action in rounding up the prisoners, even though he was unaware of their nationality, had helped to prevent the alarm being raised. Sidders ignored entirely the vital contribution made by Lieutenant Wesley who, in truth, had led the successful second attempt on the bridge after the major had made such a cock-up of the first. By flagging up Wesley's role, Sidders might have diminished his own. He chose not to do that. The inevitable outcome of this unwillingness to give credit where it was due was the award of just two gallantry medals for Operation Spratt Baker: an MC for Sidders and an MM for Williams. The others were not even mentioned in despatches.†

It is hard to blame Sidders' superiors for this gross injustice. All they had to go on was the official report that Sidders himself had written. Only when extracts of Wesley's contemporaneous diary were published many years later – and quoted extensively

---

* Ten days later, during the same patrol, *Trenchant* sank a large German submarine – *U-859* – near Penang. In stark contrast to Lieutenant Commander Miers' ruthless actions in the Mediterranean, Hezlet surfaced and rescued eleven survivors before the arrival of a Japanese surface patrol forced him to dive and leave the area. (TNA, ADM 199/1865.)

† Wesley was awarded his own Military Cross for gallant and distinguished services during patrols on the Irrawaddy river in February 1945.

in the above account – would a fairer version of events emerge. Many errors were made, particularly by Sidders during the first attempt on the bridge, but the 8-man team eventually pulled off the 'last of a long list of railway sabotage operations carried out by the SBS during World War II' thanks to perseverance and no little luck.[8]

'It's just the sort of operation we've been praying for'

Elizabeth Island – known as Kyunthaya today – is small and lozenge-shaped, covers just thirteen square miles, and guards the entrance to Combermere Bay in what was, in 1944, Burma's Arakan province. That autumn, despite its hilly and jungle-covered terrain, and the fact that it was 200 miles behind enemy lines, the island had been identified by Lieutenant General Sir Philip Christison's XV Indian Corps as a potential base from which the 3rd Commando Brigade could launch nightly raids up the nearby maze of waterways, or *chaungs*, that the Japanese were using to supply their troops in Arakan. If the Commandos were able to cut off this supply line during Christison's Arakan offensive – part of a general advance across the Chindwin river and into central Burma by the whole 14th Army that was scheduled for the end of the monsoon season in December 1944 – it might make the difference between victory and defeat.[1]

To prepare the ground, Lieutenant Fred Ponsonby's COPP 8 was given the job of scouting the island's three main beaches (Operation David): Onchaung in the west, Ondaw in the east, and Kyunthaya in the south. There was also a large *chaung* on the eastern coast that 'meandered up to a small village', and needed to be scouted. Ponsonby – known affectionately as 'Poker-face' – had seven men under his command: three officers and four other ranks. The officers included Ponsonby's assistant, Lieutenant Mike Peacock, a 'quiet, determined youngster' from the volunteer reserve, brave and efficient, who was 'shaping brilliantly' as a Coppist; and his military man, 23-year-old Captain

Alec Colson RE.[2] Educated at Oundle public school, Colson had been called up in 1941 and served his first six months in the ranks. Commissioned in early 1942, he was instructing officer cadets in Newark when he came across the secret debrief of the disastrous Dieppe Raid* which had been circulated to all training establishments. It inspired him to volunteer for the Commandos. But he was diverted instead to 'something better' by his former boss who was working at COHQ.

He was interviewed in May 1943 in London with three other sapper officers, one of whom was Logan Scott-Bowden. 'You've volunteered for hazardous service,' Lieutenant Geoff Moorhouse told them, 'service that will take you an anchor's throw from the enemy's nose. You may find the weather takes the enemy's side. Submarine trips will become as commonplace as bus rides. Casualties are high and the enemy shows no mercy to those he captures. I hope none of you are married. But if you are, or you've got any doubts, just take one step back and the whole thing will be forgotten. No one will think the worse of you.'

As no one moved, they were sent down to Hayling Island to meet the COPP founder, Nigel Willmott, who explained the principles of beach reconnaissance, particularly swimming at night. 'I'd like to do it, sir,' said Colson, 'but I'm a poor swimmer.'

'You needn't worry about that,' replied Willmott. 'When you've got a heavy swimsuit on, the air belt keeps you afloat and there's little difference between a swimming champion and a lame duck.'

Once the shortlist had reduced to two – Colson and Scott-Bowden (with his 'brushed-up moustache' and 'relaxed, confident manner') – there was a final interview with Major Roger Courtney of the SBS back in London. Colson remembered a

---

* The large-scale raid on the northern French port of Dieppe on 19 August 1942 – Operation Jubilee – was intended as a dry run for an invasion of mainland Europe. But of the 4,000 Canadians who landed, 800 were killed and 1,900 captured (including 600 wounded), an unprecedented casualty rate of sixty-seven per cent. A further 466 naval and Commando personnel were lost, as well as one destroyer, thirty-three landing craft, twenty-seven tanks and 105 RAF fighters. German casualties were fewer than 600.

thickset officer with 'a jagged scar from his forehead to his
mouth, strongly suggesting a German sentry's bayonet'. In fact,
Courtney had got the injury by tripping on a step during a
blackout in December 1942, cutting his forehead and breaking
his nose. He told the two sappers that, though under his nominal
command and wearing 'Commando SBS' badges on their shoulders, he would see little of them. Yet he trusted them not to
disgrace the SBS name and added: 'Never let them capture you,
fight to the end.'[3]

Colson took the advice seriously and, after COPP 8's first
couple of missions in South East Asia had been cancelled, he
performed well during Operation Frippery, the survey of north
Sumatra's beaches in August 1944, when he accompanied
Geoffrey Hall on one swim reconnaissance because COPP 7's
military officer, Bill Lucas, was unwell. Operation David was an
opportunity to do a similar job with his own COPP 8. 'It's just
the sort of operation,' declared Mike Peacock, 'we've been praying
for.'

It had, however, one major disadvantage compared to Frippery:
the inability to use submarines because the sea off the Arakan
coast was too shallow. This, in turn, meant no high-powered
periscope to inspect the enemy coast in daylight. But for air
photographs and maps, they would be forced to land blind. To
try to familiarise himself with the terrain, Colson was flown over
the island in a Beaufighter. But he could see little 'except jungle
and paddy', and 'there was no sign of any Japanese'.[4]

COPP 8 left its forward base at Chittagong, East Bengal, in two
Fairmile motor launches in the early hours of 16 October 1944
and headed 400 miles south-east down the Burma coast, reaching
a point off the west coast of Elizabeth Island at 9:30 p.m. Three
canoes were launched one and a half miles off Onchaung beach:
the first was crewed by Ponsonby and his paddler Petty Officer
Bob Gascoigne; the second by Mike Peacock and Leading Seaman
Jim Neil; and the third, converted to take three men, by Colson,
Sergeant Crawford Cumberland and Lance Corporal Duffy (all
soldiers). The conversion was Colson's idea. 'I had had experience

of walking about an enemy beach,' he recalled, 'and [was] convinced I was not of the tough fibre from which solitary spies are made. If the three-man canoe could be made to work satisfactorily I would be able to take Sergeant Cumberland ashore with me and so have company in the darkness.'

Ponsonby led the way, navigating by the luminous dial of his P8 compass. 'Mike and I followed,' recalled Colson,

> one a little to starboard of Freddie's stern and the other a little to port. The sea seemed flat and oily and we paddled on as though we were on a Bank Holiday outing on the Serpentine. The minutes passed and the coastline rose higher and higher in front of us. There was high ground all round Onchaung and the village itself was only a couple of hundred yards behind the beach. The beach was sandy and was divided into two small crescent-shaped coves by a rock knoll which jutted out into the sea. The knoll must have been about sixty feet high and was connected to the land by a narrow neck of land and jungle.

Ponsonby's plan had been to put Peacock, Colson and Cumberland ashore on the western cove, and then proceed himself to the neighbouring eastern cove and 'obtain the underwater gradient' before returning 'to recce the offshore dangers'. But the beach was difficult to identify from close in, and the canoes ended up at the eastern cove. By the time Ponsonby found a passage through some rocks to the correct cove, it was 11:30 p.m. and the mission was well behind schedule. Rafting up, he briefed the two officers. 'We're forty minutes late, I'm afraid,' he said, 'so you will have only an hour and a half ashore. Alec, I think you had better confine your activities to this beach and not worry about the other half. Mike, if you get the gradients on this half of the beach I will paddle round to the other one and work there. Don't bother about anchoring your canoes. I will see to that after you've gone.'

Colson pulled his legs up and swung them over the port side of the canoe. As he dropped into the water, Cumberland and

Duffy leant over to starboard to balance the boat. The water felt cold to Colson on first contact, but was actually quite warm. He and Cumberland started swimming towards the side of the knoll, a hundred yards away. As they got closer, Colson could see the 'waves breaking over the large rocks and sucking back with unpleasant force'. Towering above them was the 'jungle-covered top of the knoll'. Colson's first attempt to land on the rocks was thwarted by the powerful backflow. Next time he managed to hold on and was quickly joined by his sergeant.

'Got your gun ready?' whispered Colson, referring to the Sten sub-machine gun that was slung round Cumberland's neck. 'And for God's sake don't cock it!'

They moved slowly along the rocks, the stones clattering under their feet. Stopping at a large boulder which overlooked the first stretch of sand, Colson said: 'I'm going to move round to the neck of land which joins this knoll. We'll have a look at that track we saw on the air photos.'

Reaching the beach, Colson noticed a beam of light coming from the narrow strip at the base of the knoll. 'See the light?' he whispered. 'I don't like the look of it. I want to move forward until I can see where it is coming from. Get the Sten gun ready and cover me.'

Cumberland nodded. Tugging his revolver free of its holster, Colson crawled forward on his elbows until he could see the source of the light: the open door of a hut, barely forty yards away. Inside he could see shadows on the wall and a mosquito net, and hear the murmur of male voices. It was, he suspected, a sentry post and to go any further would risk discovery. He rejoined Cumberland. 'We won't go this way,' said Colson. 'They're either Japs or native troops. Burmese fishermen don't use mosquito nets. We'll go back to the water and get ashore at the centre of the beach.'

Swimming through the heavy surf, in some places four feet high, they came across an exasperated Mike Peacock. 'This is hopeless,' he told them. 'I can't swim out against this and take soundings at the same time.'

After Colson had explained his own difficulties, Peacock looked at his watch. It was 12:15 a.m. 'We've had three-quarters of an hour already and I don't think we are going to find it very easy to swim out to the canoes.'

Colson agreed. There was little they could do in the remaining forty-five minutes, so they decided to cut their losses and return. But it was extremely hard work as their kapok lifebelts made it almost impossible to dive through the incoming breakers and, time and again, they were thrown back towards the beach 'like pieces of driftwood'.

After fifteen minutes of this, Colson grabbed Peacock and said: 'We'll have to go back the way Cumberland and I came in. If we climb back over the rocks we will be able to swim from beyond the line of breakers.'

They did just that, dropping into the sea on the backwash of a wave and striking out for the canoes. When they thought they had gone far enough, they stopped to shine their torches. Minutes passed and, as they were losing heart, Duffy appeared in the three-man canoe. 'The CO is not back,' he whispered, 'so Neil stayed at anchor.'

Once Colson and Cumberland were on board, they towed Peacock over to his canoe, anchored 200 yards offshore. Ponsonby arrived fifteen minutes later, and together they paddled for forty-five minutes, battling a 2.5-knot cross tide, to make their rendezvous with the motor launch at 2:15 a.m. This first part of the mission had not gone well. But they were all safe and sound and, more importantly, the operation had not been compromised.[5]

*

Having stayed that night at the Commando base at Teknaf in East Bengal – 200 miles up the coast – they set off on their second sortie at 11:00 a.m. on 18 October. Their target this time was Ondaw beach, on Elizabeth Island's east coast. As it was more sheltered and easier to tackle from the 'naval viewpoint', Fred Ponsonby had put Mike Peacock in charge to give him valuable experience. Unfortunately, Peacock was feeling unwell. 'I've got another attack of this stomach trouble,' he told Colson.

Aware that Peacock had had dysentery, Colson asked: 'Do you feel well enough to make the trip?'

'I am going tonight whatever I feel like.'

'It's not worth taking unnecessary risks, Mike,' urged Colson.

'I don't think there is much risk. My temperature is normal.'

'Have you told Freddie?'

'Not yet, and I won't unless I have to.'

Peacock's thinking was that a similar opportunity to lead a sortie might not come again. Colson, meanwhile, had 'every confidence in his ability to do it successfully'. Yet Peacock should have erred on the side of caution, as Sergeant Cumberland did when he told Colson that he was also feeling sick and would prefer not to swim that night. Instead, Petty Officer Bob Gascoigne was slated to accompany Colson. 'I was quite satisfied,' recalled the captain, 'as I knew Gascoigne to be fearless and very easy to get on with.'

The other change from the first sortie was the addition of Lieutenant Geoff Richards, the maintenance officer, who, strictly speaking, was not supposed to be operational. Yet this 'colourful and fearless character' persuaded Ponsonby to let him take part. A former Royal Marine, he had been an inter-services swimming champion at the age of 18. But he left the Marines after a barrack-room altercation left him with a bayonet wound to the back, and for the next decade tried a variety of jobs: fisherman, waiter, chauffeur and policeman. When war broke out, he joined the navy and, after service at Tobruk, volunteered to be a parachutist. Once qualified, recalled Colson, 'he was sent to England to join our unit which used canoes but no parachutes'.

In India the eccentric Richards cut a piratical figure, with his shabby bush-hat, fighting knife and pistol at his waist, and pet monkey on his shoulder. His bushy beard had long been 'the curiosity of the Metropolitan Police Force in the years before the war'. Now he would have the chance to justify his martial appearance on an actual operation.

Arriving off Ondaw beach at 9:00 p.m. on the 18th, the two motor launches anchored while the canoes were prepared. Just before they were launched, Peacock whispered to Colson: 'I took my temperature a little while ago and it was a hundred.'

'Are you going then?' asked an astonished Colson.

'Of course I'm going. I wouldn't miss tonight for anything.'

The three canoes were lowered in a flat calm. They were crewed by Peacock and Neil; Richards and Duffy; and Colson, Gascoigne and Cumberland. It took them half an hour to reach the bay. 'It is just after half past nine,' Peacock told the swimmers, 'and we don't have to be back in the canoes until one o'clock. You can go ashore and I will take the canoes out and anchor them before I swim myself.'

The tasks were as follows: Colson and Gascoigne would carry out the military reconnaissance onshore; Richards would run 'lines of soundings at the western end of the beach'; Peacock would do the same at the centre of the beach where a small outcrop of rock divided the sand into two segments. Colson and Gascoigne got ashore without incident, though the swirling currents were 'surprisingly strong for a sheltered bay'. Colson recalled: 'The noise of the breaking waves made it difficult to hear any other sound. Twenty yards in front was the path which crossed the root of the rocky spit and connected the two halves of the beach. The jungle beyond looked black and impenetrable.'

He told Gascoigne to cover him with the Sten gun while he moved into the jungle, and then follow a few seconds later. The petty officer grunted his acknowledgement – far too loud for Colson's liking – and rattled the Sten's heavy bolt against its metal casing as he readied it to fire. They moved forward in bounds, with Colson checking the edge of the jungle, the bearing capacity of the beach and potential exits for vehicles.

As they were scouting the track leading to the village of Ondaw, Colson saw a light approaching from the beach. They crouched in the bushes and watched as four men 'dressed in white lungis' walked past, one carrying a lantern. At it was already 11:45 p.m., they headed back to the rocky spit and 'started to reconnoitre the other half of the beach'. There they found a narrow branch track which led to the village, and could see occasional glimpses of a fire. Deciding they had seen enough, they re-entered the water and signalled Cumberland to collect them. Minutes later they were in the canoe and paddling to rejoin the other two at anchor. They were the first to return.

Another light signalled and, thinking it was Peacock, Neil set off to collect him. He returned with Richards who transferred to his own canoe. 'How did it go, Geoff?' asked Colson.

'It was as easy as falling off a log,' replied Richards with a grin. 'I had no trouble taking the lines of soundings and only saw one gang of natives.'

It was now 1:00 a.m. – their deadline – but Peacock was still absent. As the minutes dragged by, they began to worry. 'It was easy work tonight,' said Richards. 'I think we ought to start looking for him.'

Colson agreed. He was the only one who knew about Peacock's illness, and feared that might be a factor in his non-appearance. Ordering Cumberland and Gascoigne to remain at anchor, Colson transferred to Neil's canoe and paddled back inshore, followed by Richards and Duffy. 'We ran aground on the right-hand beach where the surf was the least,' recalled Colson. 'Duffy stood guard of the two canoes with his Sten gun, and Geoff, Neil and I started wading in amongst the rocks of the spit. We thought that if Mike had fainted in the water his body would have been washed onto the beach . . . Revolver in hand I waded along the beach to the right. A dog started barking in the huts at the back of the beach. There was nothing in the water so I turned back. The search on the other side of the rocky spit was equally fruit-less.'

As it was now 1:50 a.m., and they had just over an hour to make the rendezvous with the launches, Colson decided to call off the search and rejoin the other canoe. With Richards navi-gating, they paddled for almost an hour until instructed to stop. 'Ahead,' recalled Colson, 'the high coastline of the Burmese mainland lay black and forbidding . . . Neil started to transmit infrared signals on the bearing of the anchored [motor launches]. I scanned the horizon with the infrared receiver.'

But there was no answering signal and, as the time drew closer to 3:00 a.m., they decided to remain where they were for another hour: then, with dawn approaching, they would have no option but to head back to the island and lie up during the day.

While Richards shone his torch in every direction, the others listened anxiously for the sound of engines. They had almost given up hope when they heard the faint throbbing of engines from the direction of Ondaw. Suddenly the MLs appeared, line astern, their guns pointing ominously at the canoes in case they were hostile. At 3:30 a.m. the remaining six Coppists were welcomed back on board the MLs by a visibly upset Ponsonby who had 'spent long hours peering through night glasses and many anxious minutes worrying about the safety of his entire party'. When all seemed lost, their torches had been seen to seaward. But Ponsonby's relief was soured by the news that Peacock was not with them.

In an attempt to explain, Colson mentioned Peacock's high temperature. 'He had made up his mind to go,' he added, 'and thought you might stop him.'

'Well,' responded Ponsonby, 'I suppose it is not much good crying over that now. Tell me exactly what happened tonight.'

Colson and Richards took it in turns, with the latter adding: 'I feel pretty sure that Mike was not alive when we left Ondaw Bay.'

Colson agreed. 'If he fainted in the water, he would have drowned although his suit would have kept his body afloat. His job did not entail leaving the water so it's most unlikely that he's been killed by Japs or natives; anyway, if there had been any trouble Gascoigne and I would have heard it.'[6]

'We're going on a raid'

The sad loss of Mike Peacock notwithstanding, Freddie Ponsonby and his men were keen to finish what they had started. Their hopes were dashed when they received, back at the Commando base at Teknaf, a signal cancelling the rest of Operation David. Bitterly disappointed, the men of COPP 8 began to speculate on the reason.

'Perhaps they feel,' suggested Ponsonby, 'that the loss of Mike had compromised the whole plan and have decided not to risk failure by landing where the enemy expects us.'

'They've probably decided to send the Commando Brigade to another place a thousand miles away,' said Alec Colson, his voice dripping with sarcasm.

In fact, the Commandos were still arriving at Teknaf and, a day later, the Coppists were visited by their deputy commander, Colonel Peter Young. Though just 29 years old, and with a 'tendency to stoutness', Young was a veteran warrior who had taken part in the Lofoten, Vågsøy and Dieppe Raids (winning a DSO for the latter to add to his Military Cross and two bars), and the D-Day landings on Sicily and Normandy. Having asked the Coppists about their two sorties, he wanted to know more about the so-called lookout post. 'What made you think,' he asked Colson, 'that it was something other than an ordinary fisherman's hut?'

Because, said Colson, it had to be camouflaged as it did not appear on any air photos; its position covered both beaches; its light was still on late at night; and its inhabitants were using mosquito nets, and so could not have been locals.

Young seemed satisfied and, having congratulated the Coppists on the information they had gathered, he left.

On 27 October, by which time they were back in Chittagong, Ponsonby received a signal from Young. A smile spread across his face. 'We're going on a raid, Alec,' he said to Colson. 'They hope to get some information about Mike.'

Ponsonby and Colson returned to Teknaf the following day and were briefed on the raid. The plan was for Major 'Jock' Cunningham and thirty men from 42nd (Royal Marine) Commando to land by night at Ondaw, 'thereby avoiding the heavy surf' on the west side of the island, and march the two and a half miles across to Onchaung. They would then sneak up on the lookout post and capture a Japanese soldier. By taking interpreters with them, they hoped to question any locals they came across about Mike Peacock's whereabouts.

The task of disabling the occupants of the lookout post was given to Colson. 'It was agreed,' he recalled, 'that I should crawl close to the open door of the hut and throw in the [quarter-pound stick of] gelignite. Immediately after the explosion three Commandos would rush into the hut and bayonet every man except the one furthest from the door.'

The first mishap was during training. Colson had just tried out a new percussion cap for the gelignite stick, and was about to pick up another, when someone said: 'If anything happens to him on the night, someone else will have to throw the charge.'

'I quite agree,' said Major Cunningham, 'we ought to throw one or two for luck.'

He grabbed the charge, pulled its pin and was about to throw it when there was a premature explosion. He was knocked off balance and, as he fell, he gazed in horror at the 'ragged stump of his right forearm'.

With Cunningham out of action, Colonel Young gave command of the raid to the next senior man, Major Michael Davies. The colonel's 'calmness and directness', remembered Colson, 'were like a sedative to our shocked nerves'.

Before departing, the Coppists and a number of SBS officers

at Teknaf – including Harry Holden-White, and the originals George Barnes and Jim Sherwood – were introduced to Lieutenant General Christison who was on a tour of inspection. He asked them about their recent operations and wished them luck for the future. Colson heard later from Young that Christison had given their raid of Elizabeth Island – code-named Operation Deputy – his blessing.

Accompanied by Colonel Young, the raiding party left Teknaf during the morning of Friday 3 November 1944, in two MLs. By evening, thanks to Ponsonby's faultless navigation, they had reached a point off Ondaw beach and anchored. Young and the raiding party then transferred to a small landing craft that one of the launches had towed behind it. As they neared the black coastline, it seemed to Colson 'a strange way to be entering enemy waters' by comparison with their 'usual clandestine methods'.

The helmsman reduced speed and, soon after, a kedge anchor was dropped from the stern and the bows ran onto the beach with a 'soft sigh'. Davies landed with a splash in a couple of inches of water, and ran forward across the beach to the jungle beyond. He was followed by his men, jumping off the landing craft, one after the other, in two lines 'like ropes being uncoiled from a locker'. When it was Colson's turn, he noticed with satisfaction that Ponsonby had brought them to within a few yards of the rocky spit, the exact spot chosen for the landing. Catching up with Davies, they moved behind the leading Commandos towards the village of Ondaw. But they did not surround the huts quickly enough, because a few shadowy figures were seen escaping inland.

In one hut, built on stilts three feet high, they interrogated an old woman: a lengthy process as one interpreter could only speak English and Burmese, the other Burmese and Arakanese. The old woman claimed, via the interpreters, that there were no Japanese on the island. But when they asked for a guide to Onchaung, she changed her tune. 'She says,' explained the English-speaking interpreter, 'it is not good to go to Onchaung because there are Japanese soldiers there.'

Two fishermen were questioned next. They said there were eight Japanese soldiers at Onchaung, many more at Kyunthaya, but knew nothing about a British naval lieutenant being captured or found drowned. Davies conferred with Young who was waiting at the beach with Ponsonby. The new plan was for Davies to take the whole raiding force to Onchaung – instead of the twenty men originally earmarked – while Young, Ponsonby and a few others remained at Ondaw as a base party. The landing craft, meanwhile, would be anchored 400 yards offshore.

'Three Commandos led the way along the track,' recalled Colson, 'and the guides, interpreters, Davies and myself followed. The track climbed from the village through a tunnel of dark shadowy jungle. In a few yards we came to the limit of my previous reconnaissance and the country from that point to Onchaung beach was as new to me as to anyone else in the raiding force. The jungle came abruptly to an end and the path led into flat paddy fields.'

The guides soon stopped to confer. It was the first of many arbitrary halts, and gave the raiding party the appearance of 'a caterpillar, one part of the column always being stationary'. Not far from Onchaung, the guides left the track to avoid the village and arrive at the far end of the eastern beach. There was a brief scare when some black shapes rushed at the column. They turned out to be wild pigs and, in Colson's opinion, did the Commandos a 'good turn' by putting them on their toes. 'Two hours on enemy territory,' commented Colson, 'without seeing a Jap, combined with the many halts and delays, had made the men weary and overconfident.'

Halting on the edge of the beach, the sound of their movement easily masked by the roar of the surf, Colson and Davies went forward to investigate. To their right lay the full length of the beach 'as it swept in a gentle curve towards the knoll jutting out into the sea'. But it was immediately obvious to Colson that, because the jungle at the edge of the beach was much thicker than at Ondaw, their approach would have to be made along the open stretch of sand.

'Where's the hut?' asked Davies.

'At the base of the knoll on the shoreward side,' said Colson, pointing.

'There don't seem to be any lights tonight.'

'No. It's suspicious. I wonder if some of the natives who escaped from the village have warned the Japs about us.'

Either way, they needed to find out. 'We'll advance along the back of the beach,' said Davies, 'and rely for cover on the shadows cast on the sand by the jungle foliage.'

As he crept along, just behind the leading group, Colson flicked off the safety on his Colt automatic pistol. His only other weapon was the Mills grenade he was supposed to chuck through the doorway of the hut: since Cunningham's accident, the grenade was back in favour.

They were about a hundred yards from the knoll when the jungle to its right erupted in gun flashes and the staccato sound of a light machine gun, probably the excellent Japanese Type 96 Nambu, capable of firing up to 500 rounds a minute from a thirty-round box magazine. It was immediately apparent to Colson that 'the Japs had been waiting for us'.

As the Commandos returned fire with Bren guns, and American tommy guns and M1 Garand semi-automatic rifles, the Japanese responded with blood-curdling yells. 'It was a strange action,' recalled Colson. 'The Commandos were strung out in single file and the Japs were in the jungle on the narrow neck of land joining the knoll to the mainland. Nelson's tactic of crossing the "T" had been repeated, but the Japs were in the favourable position.'

Davies was in a bind. The jungle to the right was too thick for an outflanking movement, and any further advance on the long beach would be suicidal. As he pondered the next move, a Japanese soldier leaped from the jungle just ahead and ran back towards the knoll. A sergeant opened up with his tommy gun and the enemy collapsed on the sand 'with fearful shrieks and moans'. Incredibly he then got back to his feet and staggered towards the water. He was finished off by a Bren-gunner firing from the hip, the bullets tracing 'a dark path of disturbed sand' before overtaking the 'stricken Jap'. His body lay at the water's edge.

Colson felt his shirt being tugged. 'It's time to leave,' said Davies, 'if we're to make our rendezvous with the motor launches. The Japs are thoroughly awake and I can't see any benefit in pressing the assault. Better to live to fight another day.'

The major gave the order to retire, a decision Colson agreed with wholeheartedly. They left the way they had come, with a captain checking their numbers. No one was missing. 'We moved quickly,' noted Colson, 'to prevent the Japs from cutting across country and ambushing us on the track to Ondaw. When we reached the path behind Onchaung we saw the villagers streaming out into the countryside in an effort to escape the scene of battle. The return journey over the paddy fields contrasted with the halting progress behind the two guides.'

Back at Ondaw they found the base party waiting near the beach. They too had seen a Japanese soldier walking along the shore, explained Colonel Young, but he had escaped before they could capture him. Ponsonby signalled to the landing craft and, a few minutes later, it was nosing onto the sand. The surf had got up, however, and, with only half the men on board, the landing craft was forced broadside to the beach by a large wave. Ordered to go astern, the helmsman put the engines into reverse. But he forgot about the kedge anchor, which had been thrown out as they approached the shore, and, as they moved back, the anchor line got tangled in the propellor and cut the engine with a belch of smoke and a splutter. It was a heart-stopping moment. 'The landing craft was helpless,' recalled Colson, 'just outside the breaking waves, and half the force was marooned onshore with an unknown number of angry Japs in the vicinity.'

Fortunately, there were four large paddles for just such an emergency. While the soldiers on board paddled hard to get the craft into deeper water, the skipper stripped off his clothes and dived over the side with a hacksaw. But he struggled to cut through the four turns of rope round the propellor shaft, and kept coming up for air. Meanwhile the Commandos onshore sent anxious messages from a torch flashing Morse code: 'C-o-m-e a-n-d f-e-t-c-h u-s w-h-a-t i-s d-e-l-a-y-i-n-g y-o-u'.

Colson and Ponsonby were in the landing craft. But Young was still on land and his capture would have been a 'serious blow'. It was a huge relief to Colson when the skipper came up for what seemed like 'the twentieth time' and gasped: 'All clear!'

The engine restarted with a roar, and the landing craft moved rapidly back to the beach. This time it remained just off the beach, forcing the other Commandos to wade out to embark. Once the last wet body had been hauled on board, the kedge was taken in and the bows swung to seawards. As they headed for the MLs, a second count took place: this time a Bren-gunner, Corporal Chappel, was missing. Young ordered the skipper of the landing craft to offload most of the men before returning to Ondaw to look for Chappel. He took Colson and Lieutenant Cotton, the intelligence officer, with him. While the landing craft cruised parallel to the beach, Cotton flashed a torch and shouted 'Chappel!' at the top of his voice. There was no response and, after fifteen minutes, they gave up and joined the others in the MLs.

As they headed back to Teknaf, and the adrenalin of the raid began to fade, Ponsonby and Colson felt acute disappointment that they had failed in their twin objectives: to take a prisoner and, more importantly, learn something of Peacock's fate. The Commandos were also distraught at having to leave one of their men in the field: either dead or in the clutches of the Japanese (which might, of course, mean the same thing). On the credit side they claimed to have killed at least ten Japanese in the firefight, though Colson suspected the correct number 'was nearer four'.

The Coppists felt a little better when Colonel Young told Ponsonby that, thanks to his expert navigation, it was the first time he had 'landed at the exact spot selected by the planners'. Hearing that COPP 8 was due to return to the UK, Young offered Colson a job in one of his two army Commandos, 1st and 5th.

But the captain was keen to return to conventional sapper work and declined. Meanwhile the firefight at Onchaung had put paid to the 'plan to sieze Elizabeth Island and use it as an offensive base'. It was, in Colson's words, 'thrown into the incinerator and the flames severed our ties with the island'.[1]

*

David and Deputy were COPP 8's last missions. At their new base at Rajukhal in East Bengal, they handed over their equipment to the reconstituted and newly arrived COPP 3 and set off for the UK on 17 December. By then Colonel Tollemache had recommended Alec Colson, who was at the heart of both operations, for a Military Cross. He had shown 'courage and determination in carrying out hazardous operations against the enemy in Burma in 1944', wrote Tollemache, 'in swimming in dangerous surf conditions in enemy occupied territory on October 16th, and in his efforts to find Lieut Peacock who was missing on October 18th, regardless of risk to himself'. He might have added that Colson did more good work during Operaton Deputy. But higher authorities were less impressed – possibly because Operation David did not pave the way for landings on Elizabeth Island – and Colson had to be content with a mention in despatches, the same award given to lieutenants Ponsonby, Peacock and Richards, Petty Officer Gascoigne, Leading Seaman Neil and Sergeant Cumberland. Colson's consolation, however, was the news that he *had* been awarded an MBE for his part in Operation Frippery.[2]

It would take many more months for Mike Peacock's fate to be revealed. In March 1945, as Lieutenant General William Slim's 14th Army closed in on the Burmese capital of Rangoon, the Japanese emptied the jails of their remaining 600 American and British prisoners. The plan was to march the column of barefoot, emaciated scarecrows back to Siam (modern Thailand). They covered nearly seventy miles in three days and were within striking distance of their destination. But after two days without food and water, and with the sick dropping like flies, the column could go no further. As its survivors lay prone on the ground, waiting for death, they heard a babble of voices. Their Japanese guards were leaving. Soon after, mistaken for the enemy, they were machine-gunned and bombed by a flight of Hurricanes. Fortunately only one man – the senior British officer – was killed. After dark, the others were rescued by British soldiers of the West Yorks who went on half-rations so they could eat. Among the former prisoners, barely alive, was Mike Peacock.

He would later explain how, having dropped off the other swimmers and anchored their canoes off Ondaw beach, he had slipped into the water himself to take soundings. But the exertion, and his sickness, got the better of him and he fainted as he tried to signal his pick-up. When he came to he was drifting out to sea and the others were nowhere in sight. He used all his remaining energy to get back to the beach. It was now 4:00 a.m and time to find somewhere to hide. He headed into the jungle and stayed there all day, tormented by thirst. After dusk he got back in the sea and shone his torch. There was no response.

After another twenty-four hours of torture, he trekked to Ondaw village to ask for food and drink. He was given some. But the villagers' friendliness was an act because, in response to his queries about boats, they led him straight to the sentry hut at Onchaung where he was taken prisoner by three Japanese with levelled bayonets. He was eventually moved, by stages, to Rangoon jail where he was interrogated by two Japanese intelligence officers who assumed, because of the attempted rescue mission, that he was a VIP or an agent. 'Say,' asked one, with an impeccable American accent, 'what did Mountbatten say to you last time you had dinner?'[3]

Peacock was lucky. Of the 140,000 Allied soldiers taken prisoner by the Japanese, more than 30,000 died of starvation, disease and maltreatment (a casualty rate that was seven times greater than those in German or Italian captivity).[4] Most of those captured on secret missions behind enemy lines were executed.

This was the grisly fate of ten survivors* of Operation Rimau, the attempt to sink Japanese ships in Singapore harbour by members of the predominantly Australian Allied Z Special Unit in October 1944. Imprisoned in Singapore's Outram Road jail, they were eventually found guilty of perfidy and espionage, and beheaded with a samurai sword in July 1945, a month before the war ended. According to one of their Korean guards, the men were all young with cropped heads and 'slight beards'. He added: 'For three days before their execution they were given good food, milk and tobacco. They all knew they were going to be executed. When they left their cell to enter the two trucks which were to take them to their execution they appeared in high spirits, laughing and talking and shaking hands with one another.'

The same witness later heard the five Japanese killers 'talking and laughing about the execution, drawing their swords to show how they had struck and then wiping their blades. They teased [Judicial Sergeant Hideo] Nihibara for being so unskilful and requiring two or three shots each time.'[5]

---

* Eight were Australian and two British. The latter were Major Reggie Ingleton (seconded from SOG's Royal Marines Detachment 385) and Able Seaman Walter Falls.

39

'I don't fully believe it has happened'

Lieutenant Alex Hughes was a rarity among COPP senior officers: a naval reservist rather than a regular, he spoke with a regional accent – in his case Scots – and was not averse to talking politics in the mess. Born in the Fife fishing village of Pittenweem, he had criss-crossed the world with the Clan Line of merchant ships before joining the Royal Naval Reserve in 1939. His mature, can-do attitude had impressed Nigel Willmott, as had his willingness to give up his plum appointment as navigator of the escort carrier *Slinger* to command the recommissioned COPP 3 in early 1944.[1]

Though just five feet seven inches tall, Hughes was not the smallest member of his team. That accolade went to his assistant Ian Alcock, also 30, a ginger-haired lieutenant in the RCNVR, who stood just five feet five inches in his stockings. The son of a British naval officer who settled in Canada, Alcock had received his commission in the identical room of the naval base in Esquimalt, British Columbia, that he had been born in twenty-five years earlier. 'It wasn't a nursery now,' recalled Alcock, 'but the office of [Lieutenant Commander] Waugh, RCN.'[2]

Before joining up, Alcock had worked as an apprentice in the merchant navy and as a gold prospector. He told Hughes he owned a mine that brought in hundreds of pounds a week, having discovered it in 1937. Prior to COPP, he worked with landing craft. Hughes considered him an enigma. 'He has courage,' noted his boss, and all the spunk of a small one. Will keep going when bigger and tougher men drop out. He will try anything once – at least. A good man to be with in a tough spot. He is no administrator and doesn't think very much. [He] has few ideas, but once he has . . . will work like hell at it. Drinks like a fish – on leave – repents then does it again. Very popular with the men, particularly his paddler Turner. He couldn't lead a party but he is the ideal member. He is I am sure completely loyal. Work hard, play hard . . . He was once married and divorced. I can see why.[3]

The same age as Alcock, and no taller, was Captain William 'Johnny' Johns RE, the military officer, from south-east London. Like Alec Colson of COPP 8, Johns had served in the ranks as a sapper before receiving an emergency commission in 1942. Since joining COPP 3 in February 1944, he and Hughes had spent most of their 'waking and sleeping hours' together. They were, Hughes noted in his diary, very different characters:

An architect in peacetime, [Johns] has been in the army two years. He is a devout Roman Catholic – all RCs are I think. He has a round face – he is quite short with a feature I nearly always dislike: small black eyes close together . . . I have no doubt that when it suits him he will go behind my back. He did while we were at depot but I found out. He is terribly effusive and fulsome in his thanks to any waiter or mess attendant . . . Pompous and with a great inferiority complex, he almost never gets off his high horse, even with his own men – to their great amusement . . . It has taken some time to convince him that he must do a lot himself. Likes to come down, step into an already stored canoe and push off. That is stupid, of course, and has been stopped. But he is most unsure. He will, even in his most dogmatic moments, appeal to someone else.

The great mystery for Hughes was why Johns had volunteered for maritime special operations in the first place. 'He is,' he wrote, 'just not the type. Despite his claims to a yacht etc. he doesn't know the first thing about seamanship – sailing – or boats. He has no direction sense at night and is consequently scared. He won't leave his canoe more than a few yards out.' But once ashore, Johns was 'an excellent recce officer who had evaded sentries time and again'. He was a good sapper who knew his stuff. Hughes just wished he 'would have the courage to stand by his convictions'.[4]

Another notable member of the team was Leading Seaman Harry Turner, 'a powerful 19-year-old six-footer' from London who, having lied about his age to join up in 1941, had won plaudits for bringing his stricken fishing trawler back to Hull after it was attacked by German planes.[5]

Having arrived at Hammenhiel Camp in early October 1944, Hughes and his men had one priority: to be sent on a mission. A typical entry in Hughes' diary – which he kept in violation of naval regulations – read: 'Tollemache has come back from Kandy but it doesn't look as if there is anything for us. He hasn't sent for any of the Naval Parties so there can't be anything cooking yet. I had hopes but . . .'[6]

COPP 3 finally got its opportunity in late December 1944, a couple of weeks after it had relieved Ponsonby's COPP 8 at Rajukhal in East Bengal. The first job, on New Year's Eve, was for two canoes – crewed by Hughes and Leading Seaman Arthur Ruberry, and Johns and Sergeant Fred Cammidge RE – to scout the beaches of Akyab Island, off the Arakan coast, prior to an amphibious assault (Operation Lightning) a few days later. Having completed this successfully, Hughes and 'Canada' Alcock then led in the first wave of Commandos in landing craft on 3 January 1945. There was no opposition as the Japanese defenders had already evacuated the island, and Hughes got as far as Akyab harbour on the hull of a tank before returning to the beach for evacuation. He and his men were congratulated for their excellent work by the senior naval officers involved.[7]

A few days later, by which time the whole COPP team had moved into the midsection of a wrecked ship in Akyab harbour, Hughes was presented with a more challenging operation: to use explosives to clear wooden stakes from a defended beach on the nearby Myebon peninsula so that assault troops could land. Late on 11 January, three canoes were dropped by ML: Hughes and Ruberry; Alcock and Turner; and Johns and Cammidge. After a back-breaking two-hour paddle against the ebb tide, they grounded their canoes and made their way through soft mud to where the stakes – 'solid teak, twelve inches in diameter, and covered in barnacles' – were situated.

It took them more than an hour to place twenty-five explosive charges, connect them to a Cordtex fuse ring-main, and initiate the six-hour time pencils. 'Working at night in frogmen gear,' recalled Alcock, 'an engineer and I placed explosive charges at the base of each obstacle, then wired each charge to detonate seconds before the assault.' Meanwhile the tide had receded and they had to drag their canoes over 150 yards of mud – 'with a squelch, squelch, squelch, and a suck, suck, suck' – to reach the water. It was a noisy business and Hughes expected searchlights to come on and machine guns to open fire at any moment. Mercifully they did not. They were back at the ML by 1:45 a.m. and, a few hours later, Hughes piloted the assault craft into the beach a short time after the first explosions were heard. Twenty-three stakes had been destroyed, enough to allow the first waves to reach the beach, though under heavy fire. 'The Japs gave us a hot reception with medium MG [machine-gun] fire and mortars,' noted Hughes, 'that awful weapon which arrives alongside with a plop, spitting dirt all over the place.' The landings were a success, thanks to COPP 3, and Mountbatten himself commented favourably on the use of the Coppists in a demolition role. It was also written up in *SEAC*, the South East Asia Command newspaper.[8]

The awards – not confirmed until later in the year – included a Military Cross for Captain Johns. Hughes and most of the others were mentioned in despatches, though the former might have expected at least a DSC. Hughes' generous recommendation for Johns was as follows:

Courage and determination in hazardous operations. In the operation on the Myebon peninsula, Captain Johns was in charge of
the canoes setting explosives on the stakes. The work was done
on mudflats 100 yards from a heavily defended beach occupied
by the enemy. In all two hours were spent on the beach and
throughout he displayed a high degree of courage and initiative,
all the stakes in his section being destroyed. The successful opposed
and unopposed landings could not have been achieved had it not
been for the preliminary operations carried out by the COPP
teams. This act of approaching and exploding the protective stakes
guarding the selected beach on the morning of D-Day and under
the nose of the enemy is strongly commended for recognition.[9]

Hughes confided to his diary: 'The stakes job on Myebon was
a masterpiece of sapper work. [Johns] *is* completely reliable in
his information. Further operations have made him easier to
work with in every way. I still don't like him very much but I
do appreciate him.'[10]

In late January, Hughes' men were relieved on Akyab by COPP
1, under Lieutenant Commander Peter Wild, and returned to
Hammenhiel Camp. They enjoyed a month of rest and relaxation
before their next task: a joint mission with a party of the Royal
Marine Detachment 385, finally operational, to scout the Siamese
island of Phuket – which hugged the neck of land that connected
Siam to the Malayan peninsula – for possible landing places and
potential airfields. 'The purpose here,' recalled Ian Alcock, 'was
to pick the position for a landing designed to slice off the Japanese
forces in Malaya.'[11]

COPP 3's role – code-named Operation Baboon – was for
three teams to land on Phuket's west coast during the night of
8 March, hide the canoes and carry out a full three-day reconnaissance of beaches and an airstrip before returning to the
submarine on 11 March. The teams were as follows: Hughes
and Turner in No. 1 canoe; Alcock and Able Seaman Alan Sowter
in No. 2; and Johns, Cammidge and Flight Lieutenant Norman
Guthrie in No. 3, the converted canoe they had inherited from

COPP 8. Guthrie – a former navigator in a Beaufighter who had been awarded the Distinguished Flying Medal for multiple kills in 1940 and 1941 – was in charge of the airfield reconnaissance.

The seven-man team left Trincomalee on 3 March in HMS *Torbay* – skippered since 1944 by Lieutenant Commander C. P. Norman DSO, DSC – and, having crossed the Bay of Bengal without incident, arrived off the coast of Phuket on the 8th. Peering through the periscope, Hughes noticed that there were groups of tents at 400-yard intervals along their target beach, as well as regular one-man patrols, and so adjusted his plan accordingly. The intention now was to land in a less populated area further to the south, and return to the submarine each morning before it was light.

Torbay surfaced five miles off the coast at 7:30 p.m. and, an hour later, launched the canoes at half that distance. With Hughes' No. 1 canoe in the lead, they moved inshore in the usual 'V' formation. But after just fifteen minutes' paddling, Hughes noticed that Johns' more heavily laden No. 3 canoe had fallen astern, and waited for him to catch up. 'He was in no difficulty,' recalled Hughes, 'and, moreover, this was a fairly common occurrence.'

They resumed paddling at a slower speed, but half an hour later the lead canoes had again lost touch with Johns. After waiting for five minutes, Hughes sent Alcock back to look for No. 3, while he 'paddled backwards and forward at right angles to the approach course'. But it was very dark and he knew that a canoe could easily have passed him 'without being seen'. An hour later, with no sign of either canoe, Hughes and Turner continued on to the shore. At one point, as he crawled up a beach, Hughes was almost discovered by a sentry with a torch. 'I tried to dig myself in,' he recalled, 'but the sand was coarse and hard so I gave up and lay praying. He passed some yards away with torch flashing, but took no interest in the sand outside him.'

Having finished his work, Hughes rejoined Turner and they spent the next hour and a quarter looking for the missing canoes. With no luck, they headed out to sea and were back on *Torbay* by 2:30 a.m. They were relieved to hear that Alcock and Sowter had arrived a few minutes earlier, having completed their own solo reconnaissance. Of Johns, Cammidge and Guthrie, however, there was no sign.

After waiting until the moon was 'dangerously high', the submarine moved out to sea and dived for the day. It was assumed, recalled Hughes, that Johns' party 'had gone ashore and found a good hiding-up place and had stayed there to finish the recce'. Though this was 'not true to form', the alternatives seemed even 'more improbable'. There had been 'no sound of firing and the sea was so calm that the canoe could hardly have capsized with total loss'.

When *Torbay* returned after dark on the 9th, it was 'obvious that something had gone wrong ashore'. There was a 'complete blackout in force', even in the nearby Papra channel which the previous evening had been 'almost floodlit with arc lamps or searchlights'. The submarine also picked up a number of 'unidentified ASDIC transmissions', prompting Norman to cancel that night's landings. He did, however, return to the rendezvous point at 2:00 a.m. on the 10th, in the hope of seeing a signal from No. 3 canoe, but 'no joy'.

That night – the last of the 'dark period' – the remaining canoes completed their beach reconnaissance successfully, though it was obvious that a 'state of alert was in force': all the tents on the beach were still blacked out and patrols were 'more active' than they had been. *Torbay* was at the offshore rendezvous point on the following two nights, 'but nothing was seen'. A final rescue attempt was made on the 18th when both canoes paddled into the alternative 'Escape Point'. Alcock and Sowter lay fifty yards off the beach, while Hughes and Turner paddled its length, just ten yards offshore, before backing off a little. 'From that position,' noted Hughes, 'I could see anyone coming down on to the beach, and I in turn would have been seen by anyone on the lookout for us. There were four tents on the beach and one sentry was seen patrolling the area, very badly, fortunately.'

After waiting an hour, they returned reluctantly to the submarine and set sail for Ceylon. Hughes was now convinced that Johns and the others 'landed and were surprised and captured on that first night'. Otherwise, he was 'certain they would have returned to the submarine on D+1'. The loss of William Johns and Fred Cammidge was 'felt the more' by COPP 3, admitted Hughes, as they were 'two friends as well as shipmates'.[12]

In truth, Hughes had never got on particularly well with Johns and they were not friends. But he was still shaken by his and Cammidge's disappearance. He accepted the loss of men as 'an ever-present possibility', but did not think it could happen to his party. 'Even now,' he noted in his diary, 'I don't fully believe it has happened. With no evidence it is difficult to appreciate. If one sees a man shot and lying there one becomes aware immediately of the tragedy. But when someone just doesn't come back the realisation is slow and painful – because, as in so many things these days, there is no yardstick by which to measure it all . . . I pray that Johnny has been killed – it will save him so much. COPPs are not regarded with favour by our "honourable" foe.'[13]

Despite suffering its first casualties, COPP 3 brought back more very useful beach intelligence. The reward for Hughes, Alcock and Turner – reflecting their performance over the last three operations – were gallantry medals: the officers got the DSC, and Turner a DSM. 'Throughout the whole operation,' wrote Hughes of Alcock, 'he displayed courage and determination to a high degree.' The same 'high degree of bravery' was shown in his previous two missions. As for Turner, he had 'proved himself calm and courageous and carried out his work efficiently, with a complete disregard for personal safety'.[14]

*

It was only after his release from a Siamese prison in Bangkok, later in the year, that Flight Lieutenant Guthrie was able to reveal – via a fellow prisoner – what had happened to the third canoe. Having caught up with the others, they lost contact a second time when they capsized. Though they managed to right the canoe, and Captain Johns got back in, the others were forced to swim alongside 'as it was partially filled with water and could not be manned by all three'.

In desperation, the trio signalled with torches both towards the shore – in the hope of alerting the others – and out to sea. They also shouted. There was no response. Finally, just half an hour before dawn, they reached the shore, utterly exhausted. With time running out, they carried the canoe to the back of the beach and tried to conceal it. But they were spotted doing this by two Siamese civilians who alerted a detachment of Siamese police. In the gunfight that followed, Johns was killed 'immediately' and Cammidge 'shortly afterwards'. Police casualties were one dead and one wounded. In the confusion, Guthrie escaped. But he was captured that evening, two miles away, after villagers reported him to the local militia.

Taken first to the local Siamese naval base, Guthrie was later flown to Bangkok and 'interrogated seven times by a mixed commission of Japs and Siamese'. Fortunately, he stuck to his cover story – that his job was to 'get on the airfield and see what kind of planes were there and how many' – and it was believed.[15]

Given the size of the 1,000-strong Japanese garrison on Phuket, Guthrie was extremely fortunate to be captured by Thais. It saved his life. Some of the men from Royal Marine Detachment 385, who took part in a simultaneous reconnaissance mission on the island, were not so lucky.

'We have by no means lost hope'

The jungle-fringed beach on the west coast of Phuket seemed to Major John Maxwell like something out of a holiday brochure: white sand, swaying palm trees and bright sunshine. He knew, however, that appearances could be deceptive: and that the thirty-mile-long island, famed for its crystal-clear water and spectacular scenery, was crawling with Japanese soldiers and their armed Siamese allies.

He had been viewing the scene through HMS *Thrasher*'s high-powered periscope for some time when he was handed a signal. It was from a sister submarine, HMS *Torbay*, and stated that her COPP 3 canoe team would begin their reconnaissance of the same coast, a little further to the north, that very evening: 8 March 1945. Maxwell was furious. The plan had been for both operations – his own was code-named Copywright – to begin after dark on the 9th. If one team went in early it might jeopardise the other.

Maxwell called a meeting of his officers in the wardroom. His deputy was Major Ian Mackenzie RE, the New Zealander and former member of COPP 6 who had guided engineer tanks in to Sword Beach on D-Day, before personally engaging the German defenders with a Bren gun. Now the senior military Coppist in the Far East, Mackenzie had been seconded to Maxwell's troop of RM Detachment 385 for the duration of the mission. The other officer was Flight Lieutenant Bertie Brown of the RAF whose role was to assess sites for potential airfields on Phuket. Having discussed the news from *Torbay*, they decided not to bring their own mission forward by twenty-four hours. It would mean an earlier rising moon, not enough time to prepare their equipment, stores and personal gear, and the inability to carry out 'close observation of the area at night' from the submarine. *Torbay* was informed accordingly.[1]

Thrasher had left Trincomalee with Maxwell's party – three officers and six other ranks – on 3 March. It was only her second patrol in Far Eastern waters. Fortunately, her skipper, Lieutenant Commander Michael Ainslie DSO, DSC, was one of the navy's most experienced submariners. Two years earlier, then in HMS *Shakespeare*, Ainslie had dropped off members of Willmott's Party Inhuman before the Torch landings. He, too, was of the opinion that Maxwell's mission should not be rushed.

For Maxwell himself, Copywright was the opportunity to show that all the hours of training had been worth it. He had arrived in Ceylon with the other senior officers of Detachment 385 in May 1944, and was eventually given command of No. 1 Troop. The connection with 'Blondie' Hasler, SOG's deputy commander, was not coincidental. They had served together as young Royal Marine officers on the battleship HMS *Queen Elizabeth* in the mid-1930s, and became good friends. Hasler may even have encouraged Maxwell – a resourceful 31-year-old Irishman from Cordruff, County Dublin, who had introduced his friend to the piano and traditional Celtic folk songs – to volunteer for the new clandestine unit. Either way, this was Maxwell's first mission behind enemy lines and he was determined to make a success of it.[2]

His task, over the course of three nights, was to find a site for a new airstrip and assess a beach's suitability – in terms of its underwater gradients and load-bearing capability – for a potential amphibious landing. If, for any reason, the airstrip was a non-starter, he and his men were to return a second time, three days after the first sortie, to find an alternative.[3] Three two-man canoe teams would be used for the first landing: Major Maxwell and Corporal Atkinson; Major Mackenzie and Marine Brownlie;

and Flight Lieutenant Brown and Colour Sergeant Ernest Smith.

The canoes were launched two miles from shore at 8:05 p.m. on 9 March (by which time, of course, two members of COPP 3's canoe teams had been shot dead and another taken prisoner). The weather conditions were 'excellent, almost flat calm, no swell and clear visibility'. An hour's paddling brought them to the correct beach. It was deserted, so they carried the canoes to the fringe of the jungle and camouflaged them. The party now split: Mackenzie, Brown and Smith headed inland to an observation post (OP) on the edge of the open area that had been identified as a possible airfield, taking with them their surveying instruments (including an Abney level), soil-sampling kit and a camera; while Maxwell and the others stayed near the beach to assess its suitability for assault and to guard the canoes.

Mackenzie's group reached their OP just as dawn was breaking on the 10th. They quickly climbed trees from where they were able to photograph the potential airstrip. At 8:00 a.m. they moved to a second OP and did the same. But by now local Siamese were 'wandering all over the area to be covered, making progress extremely slow'. They moved again at 10:00 a.m., and made a wide detour along the coast to reach their third OP. En route they were spotted by three locals but no alarm was raised. They carried on, observing the beach at Bang Thao Bay and taking pictures of two large bunker positions. As they turned back inland towards their third lying-up position, they saw two fifteen-strong Japanese patrols pass between them and the sea. It was a nasty moment, but they avoided detection.

It was not until 5:00 p.m that they arrived at the third OP and took more pictures. They also ventured onto the site of the potential airstrip and took soil samples. Mackenzie quickly realised, however, that the presence of civilians made further work inadvisable in daylight. Once it was dark, they edged round to the southern end of the strip. But yet more Japanese patrols on the road, and the sound of dogs barking from a nearby village, prompted Mackenzie to set off to rejoin the others at the beach.

Any further night reconnaissance was, in his view, 'impossible' and there was nothing to be gained 'by lying-up another day on the strip'.

They met up with Maxwell's team at first light on 11 March. During their absence, explained Maxwell, the canoe party had been spotted by a Siamese man who lived in the bay. But they 'were convinced of his friendliness and merely kept an eye on him'. However, later that day, four fishermen had discovered one of the canoes. What they had done with the information, Maxwell could not say. One obvious danger was that they had reported it to the Thai authorities. But as it was now daylight, there was nothing more to be done beyond the placing of sentries.

A couple of hours later, Maxwell got his answer when a motor launch arrived in the bay with twelve to fifteen armed Siamese police on board. They disembarked and strode across the beach to where Maxwell's party was waiting, armed and ready, in the fringe of jungle. 'Both sides,' remembered Mackenzie, 'opened fire simultaneously.' Recognising their assailants as Siamese and not Japanese, Maxwell ordered his men to cease fire. The Siamese were, he knew, reluctant allies of Japan and still controlled their own security forces. They might, he hoped, be sympathetic if they realised he was an Allied officer. So he grabbed a Union Jack from his kit and advanced down the beach waving it.

At first, the Irishman's unorthodox stratagem seemed to work as the Siamese policemen also ceased fire. But their leader was not interested in negotiation. Instead, approaching Maxwell, he instructed him to strip off his clothes and tell his men to surrender. This prompted a fresh exchange of gunfire, allowing Maxwell to escape, partially dressed, in the confusion. The only casualty was Major Mackenzie who had a minor flesh wound to his head and a bullet through his hand. He could walk, though, and withdrew with the others into the jungle where they patched his wounds as best they could. The policemen did not pursue, and by nightfall the group had made a wide detour through thick undergrowth to the next bay to the north where they spent the night hiding at the back of the beach.

At daybreak on 12 March, they made their way to the southern end of the bay – overlooking the emergency RV position – and waited. Before long an even larger party of Siamese police landed on the beach and opened fire. They shot back but, heavily outnumbered, were forced to withdraw a second time. They now had two wounded: Mackenzie and Colour Sergeant Smith, seriously injured by a bullet to the head. The party split up as it struggled through the jungle, but had reunited by nightfall back at the emergency RV. Sentries were again posted and a watch kept for the reserve canoe team still on *Thrasher*. It failed to appear.*

The party split once more and hid at opposite ends of the bay. 'Jap barges observed moving up and down [the] coast throughout the day,' noted Mackenzie, 'and Thai troops arrived at [the] beach again and spent day searching.' That night, 13 March, they returned to the original escape rendezvous and waited. There was no sign of either a canoe or the submarine and, now that it was D+5, they had no option but to make for the second escape RV point on a peninsula to the north.

Their progress through the thick jungle, in hot and humid conditions, was agonisingly slow. Tormented by thirst and hunger pains, weighed down with two casualties (one serious), they took more than four days to cover a crow's flight distance of just a few miles. En route they saw a large column of Japanese soldiers away to the east, and were spotted in turn by a lone Japanese sentry who quickly disappeared. They simply 'changed direction and carried on'. All the while, Colour Sergeant Smith's condition was deteriorating: he was hallucinating and suffering occasional convulsive fits. They finally reached the second RV beach at 6:00 p.m. on 18 March. Fortunately, it was deserted and, having set up a picket, they kept watch for a rescue party. None came.

---

* Unbeknown to them, the spare canoe – manned by two of Maxwell's men – 'was to have been sent into the emergency RV' from *Thrasher* that night, 12/13 March. But bad weather made this impossible and the chance of escape was lost. (TNA, DEFE 2/95, SOG Narrative of Events.)

At dawn on the 19th, Mackenzie and Brown headed east along the coast to search for native canoes. They returned empty-handed. Major Maxwell made the next attempt, heading south-west towards Laem Son Bay with Corporal Atkinson and Marine Brownlie. They hoped to steal a canoe and use it to return to the original beach where they had buried supplies of tinned food. Reaching the north end of the bay the following afternoon, they spotted a lone canoe and went to investigate. Unfortunately, it had no paddles and, as they were leaving the beach, they were seen by a local. Finding somewhere nearby to lay up for the night, Maxwell considered his next move. He knew that he and the others were too weak to make the journey to the original beach on foot. Their only option, he decided, was to rejoin the others. This became doubly necessary when they realised there was a Japanese camp at the back of the bay.

The trio set off next morning and had covered about half a mile when they encountered a six-man Japanese patrol. They immediately scattered – as arranged – with Maxwell heading south back to the bay. He was captured by the Japanese not long after. Atkinson and Brownlie, meanwhile, had met up again and continued heading north. No other patrols were encountered and they spent most of the day, and the following two, 'resting up'. They finally resumed their march in the afternoon of the 23rd, but were forced inland to avoid yet another Japanese patrol. At 9:00 a.m. on 24 March, they were following a small stream down towards the escape RV when they were seen by a Japanese soldier. They ran through some thick bamboo and emerged onto a track where they encountered another Japanese patrol which immediately opened fire. Marine Brownlie tried to run down the track to the coast and was shot and killed. Corporal Atkinson went back the way he had come, crossing the stream and hiding for the rest of the day in a hollow tree. Having evaded more Japanese soldiers the following day, he rejoined Major Mackenzie and Flight Lieutenant Brown at the escape RV in the early evening.[4]

All three were hollow-eyed and weak from hunger. They exchanged stories. 'Brownlie's done for,' said Atkinson, 'and I think they caught the major.'

Mackenzie explained, in turn, how the delirious and semi-conscious Colour Sergeant Smith had been found by the Japanese in the bower they had built for him while they were away foraging for food. They had been dodging Japanese patrols ever since.

A day later, starving and emaciated, the trio stumbled into a Siamese village in search of food. Taken to the headman, Mackenzie handed over the blood chit they all carried. It read in Siamese: 'This is a British officer. If you help him and treat him well you will be rewarded. British forces will soon be landing to liberate your country and rid it of the hated Japanese conqueror.'

The headman shook his head, though he did then offer food and water. A couple of hours later, a lorry arrived with a Siamese district officer and some soldiers. 'It would be better,' the district officer told Mackenzie, 'if you *not* fall in Japanese hands.'

Mackenzie nodded enthusiastically, and asked for a boat to take them to Rangoon.

'That's not possible,' said the district officer. 'Better you surrender to the Siamese Navy. Japanese, perhaps kill.'[5]

They were taken to the Siamese naval base on Phuket, and then on by seaplane to a jail in Bangkok where Flight Lieutenant Guthrie, the sole survivor of Captain Johns' COPP 3 canoe team, was also being held. There they were interrogated twice by the Siamese who, according to Mackenzie, 'gained no information' beyond the refrain that they would like assistance back to British lines in Burma. A mixed team of Siamese and Japanese interrogators was more persistent. But Mackenzie, like Guthrie before him, stuck to his false cover story: that they were part of a 'special mission to bring off two agents by submarine', but did not even know the agents' identity or what they had been doing. It helped that the Siamese captured their arms and equipment, and they were never seen by the Japanese. The more compromising items – such as the Abney level, soil samples and camera – had been destroyed and buried before they were captured.[6]

Mackenzie claimed later that he was 'treated very well' as a prisoner of the Siamese and 'given plenty of food'. This was because officer prisoners 'were allowed to eat with [civilian] internees and there the food was supplied by the Swiss legation'. While incarcerated, he heard the ominous news that Major Maxwell and Colour Sergeant Smith were 'in the hands of the Japanese'. He also learned that some of the officers who had been in Japanese captivity for some time 'were badly treated and beaten up during interrogation'.[7]

Back at Hammenhiel, Colonel Tollemache and 'Blondie' Hasler were digesting the unpalatable news that nine of the thirteen men sent to Phuket as part of Operations Baboon and Copywright were missing, including two majors, a captain and two flight lieutenants. They were forced to conclude that none of the Copywright party 'were [sic] able to embark in their canoes for the withdrawal'. Had 'they been able to do so, they could hardly have failed to rendezvous with the [submarine] under such favourable conditions'.[8]

It would be many months before the full story was known. Meanwhile, Hasler tried to keep faith that Maxwell would return safe and well. 'By the time you get this,' he wrote to another Marine officer,

> you may have seen that John Maxwell is missing. My best friend, curse it. And me sitting back in the office chair waving goodbye to the brave boys as they go. However, we have by no means lost hope of seeing John again – he is one of the trickiest things ever sent out of Ireland and will make it if anybody could . . .
>
> The outfit is doing quite well on the whole but ye gods it has been hard work for Tolley [i.e. Tollemache] and me.[9]

The first reliable news reached Hammenhiel Camp on 7 August 1945, the day after the dropping of the first atomic bomb on

Hiroshima. It was a signal from higher headquarters, and reported the fate of the six men who had gone on Operation Copywright: Marine Brownlie had been killed in action; Major Mackenzie, Flight Lieutenant Brown and Corporal Atkinson were prisoners of the Siamese; and Major Maxwell and Colour Sergeant Smith (the latter 'seriously injured') were being held by the Japanese.[10]

It later emerged that the news about Maxwell and Smith was hopelessly out of date. They had indeed been held by the Japanese: first in Siam and then in Singapore where they were moved in April 1945 with a British pilot, Flying Officer Tomlinson, whose plane had made a forced landing in the sea off Malacca after a carrier-borne raid on north Sumatra. In Singapore they were interrogated by Captain Ikoda and Lieutenant Kajiki of the Japanese 7th Area Army Intelligence Staff. 'We tried to get information from them,' wrote Ikoda, 'but in vain.'

In mid-July, after eleven Malays and Chinese had been sentenced to death by a Japanese court martial, Ikoda and Kajiki thought this would be 'a good opportunity' to get rid of the British prisoners of war. On 20 July, the day set for the executions, Captain Ikoda drove Maxwell, Smith (partially recovered from his head wound) and Tomlinson to the killing ground on a hill north of Pasir Panjang in the south of the island. After the Malays and Chinese had been executed, Ikoda despatched Tomlinson with his samurai sword before instructing Kajiki 'to behead Major Maxwell and [Colour Sergeant] Smith, showing the way of beheading'.

Ikoda and Kajiki tried to cover up these barbaric murders by claiming that the prisoners had died of illness in hospital. The truth became known only because the pair, in an attempt to save their superiors from blame, wrote a joint confession before they both committed suicide in December 1945. They 'were afraid', noted a British intelligence summary, 'that our investigations would unearth the crime and so bring discredit on their senior officers'.[11]

41

'Where did it go so wrong?'

A month after their return from Phuket, Alex Hughes and Ian Alcock were called to a meeting with the supreme commander, Lord Louis Mountbatten, in his headquarters at Kandy, the ancient royal capital in the hills of central Ceylon. He had moved there from New Delhi in the summer of 1944, preferring Kandy's cooler tropical climate, elegant architecture and relaxed atmosphere to the heat, dust and political turmoil of northern India where the anti-British Quit India movement was making the country increasingly ungovernable. Sited in the spectacular Royal Botanic Gardens, his lavish headquarter tents reminded one visitor of an eighteenth-century Habsburg court. Another was stunned by the 'prodigious number of shiny staff cars' and the many 'sleek, smart and prosperous people' among the 10,000-strong headquarters staff.[1]

For his private residence, Mountbatten had selected the imposing King's Pavilion, a short drive from his headquarters. He would entertain guests there with a thirty-piece orchestra, play golf nearby and race around the island in a brand-new Cadillac escorted by outriders and sirens. 'Kandy,' he wrote, 'is probably the most beautiful spot in the world, and a delightful place in which to work.' Some felt it was too far from the front line in Burma. But Mountbatten – perhaps not surprisingly for an ex-CCO – was always looking for ways to avoid frontal attacks by launching large-scale amphibious and airborne operations well behind enemy lines, and in that sense the proximity of Kandy to Trincomalee, the headquarters of the Royal Navy's Eastern Fleet, made complete sense.

Since taking up his new job, Mountbatten had pressed hard for a number of amphibious operations. First there was Culverin, the assault on north Sumatra (though Churchill was always a more vocal supporter than the supreme commander); then Buccaneer, a landing on the Andaman Islands between Arakan and Sumatra; and, finally, Dracula, an air and seaborne attack on Rangoon. Only Dracula had become a reality after the brilliant land campaign by Lieutenant General Slim's polyglot 14th Army – only one in eight of its soldiers was British – had shattered the Japanese defences in central Burma and recaptured Mandalay and Meiktila in March 1945. In the event, Dracula was a bloodless victory because, shortly before it was launched on 2 May 1945, the Japanese withdrew from Rangoon. Mountbatten acknowledged the debt to Slim's men when he wrote that they 'had really won the battle; for if their rapid advance had not forced Lieutenant General Kimura to evacuate the port, Dracula . . . would have met with severe opposition.'[2]

With Rangoon and most of Burma in Allied hands, Mountbatten's thoughts turned to Malaya and the naval base of Singapore, the loss of which in February 1942, after a lightning Japanese advance down the Malay peninsula, had been the most humiliating British defeat of the war. The invasion of Malaya was planned by Mountbatten's staff in two stages: first a limited operation (code-named Roger) to capture Phuket off the west coast of Siam; followed by a much larger invasion of Malay proper, Operation Zipper. This would enable Singapore to be recovered by the end of 1945.[3]

The failure of the joint reconnaissance of Phuket by COPP 3 and the team from Detachment 385 – and the risk of compromise – had put paid to Operation Roger. That persuaded Mountbatten to strike next at his main objective, Malaya, and was the reason he had called for Hughes and Alcock. He began by asking them about Phuket. Having 'listened grimly' to their account, he explained the real reason for their meeting. 'I realise,' he said, almost apologetically, 'that you're both due a spell of leave. But I urgently need an immediate reconnaissance to be made on the coast of Malaya and, as things stand, there is no one else in Ceylon that I can call on. So will you do the job?'

Having glanced briefly at each other, the two men nodded. 'Yes,' they both said.

There was still a sizeable Japanese garrison in the Malayan peninsula, explained Mountbatten, though it was 'being pushed hard and driven south'. The proposed assault – Zipper – would 'draw a string round the middle of the bag; cut off the Japanese retreating southward from Burma and prevent northern advances and reinforcements from Singapore'. But first they needed COPP 3 to bring back vital information about the landing beaches. 'You'll be thoroughly briefed,' said Mountbatten. 'Good luck.'

That night, Hughes and Alcock had dinner in Kandy with friends of the men lost on Phuket. 'It wasn't a happy party,' remembered Alcock. 'We tried to eat dinner and wound up having too many drinks. Early in the morning we got a transport and drove the 200 miles north to Trincomalee. We slept for a few hours, then started work.'[4]

Their mission – code-named Confidence – was to scout six beaches close to Port Dickson, 200 miles north of Singapore on the west coast of Malaya, during the dark period from 9–14 June. Of those six, they had to identify three beaches that were suitable for landing vehicles and infantry. The work would be done by eight canoeists and four canoes (with two replacements in case of damage). A radio man would remain on board the submarine and guide them back after each sortie. This contingency, it was hoped, would prevent a recurrence of the disaster on Phuket when only four of the thirteen canoeists had returned to their submarines.

The crews chosen were Alex Hughes and Leading Seaman Arthur Ruberry (who had worked well together on the Myebon peninsula); Ian Alcock and Leading Seaman Harry Turner (ditto); Sub Lieutenant Alan Hood and Able Seaman Alan Sowter

(Hughes' partner for Baboon); and Sub Lieutenant Thomas and Sapper Cockram RE. Hood and Cockram were on their first mission.[5] They were needed because the replacements for Johns and Cammidge were not yet fully trained.

Both wartime volunteers, the two sub lieutenants came from very different backgrounds. Thomas was 'a curly-haired Englishman who had been awarded the Distinguished Service Medal' as a rating and had 'an excellent record on corvette duty'. Yet Hughes did not entirely trust him. 'He has a DSM but is really frightened on a job,' noted Hughes in his diary, 'and what is much worse is completely unreliable. He always sees Japs, is challenged by sentries and on the *chaung* op [in Arakan] kept paddling on the wrong side so that the canoe wouldn't go into the beach.'

Hood was '180 pounds, six feet two', and 'a professional Shakespearean actor'. He had joined COPP 3 as deputy commander. But Hughes quickly swapped him with Alcock, the original stores officer, who he felt was more suitable for operations. He regarded Hood, a 34-year-old Cambridge graduate, as 'a great big stolid, slow-thinking, reliable, steady, dashless man'. Hughes noted: 'He keeps very much to himself, taking little or no part in any enjoyment going. Loves walking, reads, spends a lot of time in the garden . . . His knowledge of literature, plays and music is tremendous and liberal. I feel completely uneducated when I talk to him on these subjects.' On military matters Hood was less assured. Yet, for all his flaws, Hughes could not help liking him.

Uncertain how Hood would perform behind enemy lines, Hughes had complete confidence in Alcock. 'I would ask,' he wrote in his diary, 'for no better companion in looking for trouble – or finding it unawares. I am lucky having him.'[6]

*

On 2 June 1945, Hughes and his team pulled up to a Trincomalee jetty in a three-ton truck and began unloading their canoes and special equipment onto a flat-bottomed barge.

'It was 8 o'clock in the morning,' noted Alcock, 'calm and sticky. The wide harbour was glass. A few dead fish rose and fell on the slight swell.'

With the transfer complete, they cast off and motored slowly between the 'steep-banked islands in the harbour' to where the S-class submarine *Seadog* was moored. Its forward torpedo hatch was already open as the crew made room for the Coppists' canoes. Once everything was safely stowed, the *Seadog* set sail for Malaya.[7] 'There are eight of us on this trip,' wrote Hughes in his diary, 'six sleeping and living in a space which measures 8 by 6, including the bunk space, and there is nowhere else . . . We have been on board three days now – God knows what it will be like after another three or so. It will be a relief to go ashore for the job.'

Barely recovered from a broken bone in his foot, Hughes was excited about the new mission, describing it as 'the best yet'. But he would not have been human if recent events had not made him consider the risks. First there was the loss of Johns and Cammidge; then the 'terrific' news that victory in Europe had been declared on 8 May, giving 'heartfelt relief that at least part of it is over'; and, finally, his burgeoning romantic relationship with Joan, an attractive Wren he had met on a night out in Ceylon.[8]

Ian Alcock was also preoccupied. 'The war in the Pacific was going well,' he recalled, 'but I didn't like this operation. Not one bit. The code name was Operation "Confidence". Not a bad name, but my own confidence had been shaken and I was well overdue a leave.'[9] It did not help that they were being transported in a submarine that had no experience of this type of work. The job had initially been given to *Thrasher*, skippered by Mike Ainslie who was 'an old hand at this game'. But when she developed a defective motor, *Seadog* had to step in. Her skipper, Lieutenant Ashley Hobson DSC, was very much a 'new' hand.[10]

After four days, the 'good food' had run out and they were forced to eat iron rations. 'The heat, stickiness and smell,' recalled Alcock, 'began to tell. We were fatigued without any exertion.'

Steaming down the Malacca Straits, the increasingly narrow waterway that separated Malaya from the island of Sumatra, the Coppists began checking their kit and putting the final touches to their swimsuits. Meanwhile Alan Hood kept them entertained by quoting extracts from Shakespeare and Abraham Lincoln's Gettysburg Address, that 'great, clear exposition of the fundamental principles of democracy':

> We cannot dedicate – we cannot consecrate – we cannot hallow – this ground. The brave men, living and dead, who struggled here, have consecrated it, far above our poor power to add or detract . . . It is for us the living, rather, to be dedicated here to the unfinished work which they who have fought here have thus far so nobly advanced. It is rather for us to be here dedicated to the great task remaining before us – that from these honoured dead we take increased devotion to that cause for which they gave the last full measure of devotion – that we here highly resolve that these dead shall not have died in vain – that this nation, under God, shall have a new birth of freedom – and that government of the people, by the people, for the people, shall not perish from the earth.

For Hughes, a member of the left-wing Common Wealth Party – which promoted common ownership of property, morality in politics and vital democracy – these words were particularly moving. He believed fiercely that the great democracies of Britain and the United States needed to change: that big business had to be subordinated to the needs of the individual. But the first step was to defeat the militarists of Japan: and for that great task he was prepared to lay down his life.[11]

In the early hours of 8 June, having just sighted the Aroa Islands on the port bow, they dived to sixty fathoms (360 feet) to negotiate the first of two minefields. It was a tense, nerve-wracking experience. 'No one spoke,' recalled Alcock. 'Every ear listened for the slightest metallic scraping against the pressure hull. Clocks ticked. Slowly. Very slowly. The soft whirr of the electric engines buzzed, slackened, buzzed. [The skipper] raised his head and nodded. We were through at last.'[12]

A day later – having survived a fierce tropical squall of 'ferocious severity' – they were in position off the first of the six beaches. Hobson inched the submarine as close as he dared, and gently brought it up to periscope depth so that Hughes and Alcock could get to work. 'Foot by foot, inch by inch', noted Alcock, 'we examined the shoreline. Our position was touchy. We were a sitting duck for air attack or shore batteries.' He added: 'We fastened a special camera to the periscope and made exposures of the beach area at all hours, morning, afternoon and early evening. Then we made sketches and, as dusk fell, we drew the silhouette and the night landmarks. The drawings, sketches and film would go back to SEAC. Extreme enlargements would show Command precisely what they could expect during the landing.'[13]

They had, during the course of the day, several close shaves with junks and sampans that were passing up and down the coast. One got so close to the submarine that, according to Hughes, 'had the man at the wheel been fully awake he would have seen the periscope slide up and down his side – a tense moment'.[14]

Having surfaced at 7:00 p.m. in inky blackness, the Coppists struggled into their swimming suits. Alcock strapped his .45 automatic pistol in a waterproof holster to his right side, and slung his Commando knife at the back. Then he and Turner 'carefully re-checked the tommy gun' and placed it inside their canoe, along with six hand grenades, three compasses and their 'alto red ray (small radio receiving set)'. Finally, Alcock tested that the shaded blue torch was working, and strapped the underwater writing tablet to his right leg. His other specialist gear included a spring-loaded gun, about four feet long, for testing the firmness of the beach. They were ready.[15]

The four canoes were launched off the casing at 8:00 p.m. Hughes felt that familiar sinking feeling as he led the way into a beach he could not see, bar the occasional flashing of a nervous sentry's torch. An hour and a quarter later – 'by the grace of God and little else' – they reached a narrow spit of sand, just off the beach. They had been 'steering blind with an allowance for a tide the exact strength of which was unknown', and incredibly it had delivered them to the right place. There they split up. 'One canoe [Sub Lieutenant Thomas's] to anchor and remain as a link,' noted Hughes, 'the others . . . to go into the beach and get the information.'

Alcock headed north, Hughes took the centre of the beach, and Hood went south. As he and Ruberry paddled closer in, Hughes took the gradient of the beach with a sounding line, noting the details on his tablet. Then, while Ruberry stayed in the canoe, he swam ashore and crawled up the beach, digging holes and taking samples of sand and mud as he went. Suddenly Hughes noticed a torchlight shining on the water near him, causing him to retreat to seaward a little. As the figure got nearer, Hughes drew his fighting knife 'to deal with him'. Fortunately, the sentry changed direction and headed to the back of the beach. 'I do not think I could have been sighted,' wrote Hughes later, 'as the night was very dark and overcast, and my paddler could not see me at more than ten yards.'

His work done, Hughes got back in his canoe and returned to the sandspit in time for the rendezvous at 10:45 p.m. 'We waited,' recalled Hughes, 'but there was no sign of the others.' The plan was for all three canoe teams to gather information on the spit before meeting up with the link canoe, anchoring a little offshore, at 1:00 a.m. When the others failed to appear, Hughes did the job alone and then left with Ruberry for the second RV. En route they narrowly avoided being mown down by a junk which 'suddenly loomed up out of the darkness', forcing them to do a 'rapid sidestop and lay still'.

They eventually met up with Thomas – having first mistaken the inert canoe for a sampan – and at 1:30 a.m., with time running out, 'and with some heart-burning about the others', both canoes headed out to the pick-up point two miles offshore. They heard later that the submarine had been flashing an infrared signal. They failed to pick this up, presumably because of 'faulty receivers'. Thomas used his 'bong stick' instead, but there was no sign of a conning tower. 'A bit more paddling,' wrote Hughes, 'then we stopped and "bongled" – still no sign. By this time I was feeling very pessimistic and was debating whether it was better to hang on until daylight or go back inshore, destroy the canoes and head inland where we might meet up with a guerilla band. We lit cigarettes and gave another signal – then suddenly that blessed sight – "Seadog"!'

It was 3:15 a.m., forty-five minutes after the latest pick-up time. The submarine hunted around for the others for a couple of hours, 'going in quite close to the beach but nothing was seen'. At dawn they dived and headed for the emergency RV, ten miles offshore. The prearranged signal for this was two grenades at 6:00 a.m. But nothing was heard or seen of the missing canoes. At 10:00 a.m., worried that the mission had been compromised, they headed north for open sea. 'The captain of *Seadog* wasn't very happy sitting around in that enclosed space,' recorded Hughes, 'and I agreed. My orders were to cancel the operation if in any doubt and this I did.'

As for the others, Hughes was forced to conclude that, having failed to make the RVs, they 'went back inshore, destroyed the canoes and made off inland'. He had no doubt that the experienced 'Canada' Alcock and Harry Turner would be able to 'cope with the situation'. But he was 'not quite so sure' about Hood and Sowter.

On the way back to Ceylon, Hughes wracked his brains as to the cause of the missing canoeists and the 'partial failure' of the mission. 'I don't know what happened to them,' he scribbled in his diary. 'Just silence. They didn't home to me off the beach and they didn't home to the [submarine]. Just silence. A black – eerie – depressing silence. Where did it go so wrong? What mistake did they make? What more could I – should I – have done to ensure their safety? Short of not letting anyone but myself go on these jobs, I can't see that we could have taken more precautions?'[16]

42

'We had missed the submarine'

Lieutenant Alcock raised his hand and Leading Seaman Turner stopped paddling. They had reached the correct spot at the north end of the beach. Having anchored the canoe, Alcock slipped over the side and swam to shore. 'I tested the beach,' he recalled, 'took samples of sand and rock, swam back to Turner and slid into the canoe. Using a weighted line, we carefully moved toward shore, taking beach gradients every foot while I recorded the data on my underwater writing pad.'

When this was done – prompting Alcock to conclude that that part of the beach was unsuitable for a landing – they returned to the sandspit. No one was there. Thinking that Hughes might have been delayed, and with more than two hours still in hand before the RV with the link canoe, Alcock decided to return to the north end of the beach to 'double-check' his 'original findings'. This time he found a stretch of beach even further north that *was* usable for an amphibious assault. Pleased they had made the extra effort, Alcock and Turner paddled back to the spit a second time, struggling hard against a northerly set and dodging past a junk heading north.

The spit was empty. At 1:00 a.m., instead of heading towards the link canoe, Alcock made the fatal mistake of paddling south to find Hood and Sowter. He failed. 'I checked my watch,' recalled Alcock. 'Time had run out. We would have to head out independently for the *Seadog*.' They did so, using the infrared receiver and the shaded torch in an attempt to contact the submarine as they went. There was no response. Alcock wrote: 'No sign of the other canoes. Back and forth. Further out, closer in. I forced myself to look at my watch again. We had missed the submarine.'

It was 3:30 a.m. and Alcock had two viable options: keep paddling and hope to reach the ten-mile-offshore emergency RV with the submarine before daylight; or escape with Turner into the Malayan interior. He claimed later that he also considered paddling across the Straits of Malacca to Sumatra, 'still strongly held by the Japanese', and even to Australia, 1,700 miles to the south. 'Our canoe,' he wrote, 'was equipped with a small sail and enough emergency gear to enable us to cross any ocean.' In truth, neither Sumatra nor Australia were realistic, and he chose Malaya – 'a rugged jungle country of 50,000 square miles, about the size of England, ribbed down the centre by a high mountain range and populated by some five million Malays, Chinese and Indians' – because he doubted he could get to the emergency RV in time and, if he tried, there was a good chance he would be spotted by Japanese aircraft flying between Malaya and Sumatra.

In Malaya, on the other hand, he knew from intelligence briefings that he would find a strong guerilla outfit known as the Anti-Japanese Force (AJF), composed mainly of ethnic Chinese Communists, and closely assisted by its civilian counterpart, the Anti-Japanese Civilian Force (AJCF). He had been given an escape map that clearly showed where he could contact these forces in the hinterland of the country. 'We had been told,' he wrote, 'that they would help expedite our escape.'

Having ditched their secret stores and equipment in deep water, Alcock and Turner headed for a point on the shore well to the south of their previous reconnaissance, touching down at just before 5:00 a.m. It was a small cove with grassy banks and a deserted fifty-yard beach. 'Quickly,' recalled Alcock, 'we changed into jungle-green battledress, cut the canoe into pieces and hid all the traces. It hurt but we had to throw the tommy gun overboard too. Its weight would handicap us.'

The kit they did take with them included two automatic pistols and thirty rounds of ammunition; a fighting knife and an escape knife; a prismatic compass; a small army pack with water-sterilising tablets and some concentrated food that would feed a man for seven days; a flask of rum; a small case with a map of Malaya and Sumatra; a Chinese phrasebook; a silk 'blood chit'; and $500 of Malay currency. Turner was wearing rope-soled shoes; Alcock had on parachute boots. The former were more suited to the jungle.

Directly behind the beach was a deep saltwater swamp. As it was getting light, they waded in chest-deep and hid in a tangle of vines and rotting vegetation. They stayed there all day, 'moving only to knock off the long leeches and to protect our faces from the mosquitoes'. At dusk they left the swamp as the skies opened, the rain so heavy it 'actually hurt'. Crossing the coastal road, they jumped a ditch, climbed a fence and found themselves, much to their horror, in the centre of a Japanese army camp. 'There was,' recalled Alcock, 'very little we could do about it but keep moving and we made our way between the huts, looking for the best way to get out. We were lucky during these few minutes as some of the windows were open and we were able to watch the Japanese inside.'

Suddenly some dogs appeared and started barking. They tried to kick them away, but the dogs followed at their heels, yapping and growling. They were saved because the heavy rain had forced even the Japanese sentries into their huts. 'Half-frozen with fear,' noted Alcock, 'we ran, stumbling and tripping, and finally fell into a line of trenches. They were empty, the machine guns unmanned.'

Beyond the trenches there was no fence, just jungle. They welcomed its cloying embrace, astonished that they had made it out of the camp alive. They kept moving until 2:00 a.m., only stopping when they were 'so tired it was impossible to go on'. Worming into a thick patch of undergrowth, they huddled together for warmth as the storm lashed the canopy above. Afraid to light a fire, they ate some food and drank a little rum. Turner grinned. 'They haven't caught us yet.'

'No,' responded Alcock, 'but they had a damn good chance a few miles back.'

Turner nodded. 'If you don't mind me saying so, sir, watch where you're going.'

At dawn, studying the escape map, Alcock could see that the best course would be due east into the forbidden jungle country, where the anti-Japanese forces held sway. They set off after smoking their last two cigarettes, taking a more circuitous course than they would have liked to avoid some plantations being worked by Malays. Towards nightfall they saw their first Chinese. The locals appeared to be 'a rather prosperous lot', whereas Alcock was hoping to come across 'hard-working, poorly clad Chinese'. They kept moving.

Next morning, they were about to move off again when Alcock saw something moving in a nearby tree. It seemed to be a man. There were many more sitting in the branches of other trees and in elephant grass a hundred yards away. 'Don't look,' he said to Turner, 'but they're all around us. Don't move. Keep on talking.'

With agonising slowness, Alcock unhooked a grenade and, keeping it low, pulled the pin but kept his grip on the lever. Then, trying to be casual, he stood up straight. He then nodded to Turner who carefully drew his automatic pistol.

Suddenly, a bandy-legged man dropped from a tree and walked towards them, stopping only to sever a pineapple from its plant. He offered it, smiling.

Alcock responded by handing the man his blood chit, a 'silk Union Jack with writing in ten languages saying I was a British subject and anyone who gave me assistance would be repaid for their trouble'. Fortunately, one of the languages was Javanese, the nationality of the group they had bumped into. 'In a few minutes,' recalled Alcock, 'the whole community was there to look us over – men, women and children. Every family brought something to eat. We were taken to a Javanese bamboo home, and many kinds of fruit, meat, fish and vegetables were spread before us.' They were also offered home-grown tobacco which they rolled into cigarettes using a 1939 copy of the *Straits Times*.

They communicated mostly by sign language until a sergeant from the AJCF appeared. He could speak a little English, and told them that the Japanese were looking for some Europeans who had landed, and were offering ten thousand Singaporean dollars as a reward. Alcock was slightly disappointed. 'Considering the value of their money,' he wrote later, 'I thought . . . we should have been worth more.' The main thing, however, was that they were with friends and safe for the time being.[1]

Late that evening, a Chinese captain in the AJF arrived and said it was much too dangerous for them to stay with the Javanese and they should accompany him back to his base, which was a thirty-mile bicycle ride up the coast road. But first they needed to put on 'native clothes' and blacken their arms, faces and legs. This they did, much to the amusement of the Javanese who were not convinced that Turner's height (six feet one inch) and Alcock's distinctive red hair would fool anyone. The hair was covered by a straw hat.

They set off after midnight, pushing their bicycles for the first seven miles down a trail that led to the coast. From there they cycled north up the road, passing two police stations en route. The Coppists were exhausted, having barely slept since leaving *Seadog*, and at one point Alcock nodded off 'at a curve and ran off the road'. Further on he collided with the back of a bullock cart. Despite these mishaps, they made it safely to the AJF outpost which was sited in a Chinese village. But after speaking to a second captain – immaculately dressed and wearing a cap with three red stars – they were sent on to the main headquarters. 'Two guides went with us,' recalled Alcock, 'and for the rest of the day and all that night we squished through rice fields, skirting rubber plantations and again heading east, inland, through jungle and skirting its edges. Every two or three hours, fresh guides would take over . . . I had lost all track of where I was.'

Finally reaching a small clearing, Alcock was astonished to see 'a familiar figure standing casually beside one of the huts'. It was Sub Lieutenant Alan Hood and, standing next to him, his paddler Able Seaman Alan Sowter. They walked right up to their colleagues who failed to see through their disguise. 'Alan,' said Alcock.

Hood took a step back in surprise. Then realisation dawned and he gave a whoop of delight. He explained that he and Sowter had also looked in vain for the submarine, and had been in the camp for two days. 'They were not,' remembered Alcock, 'in good shape. Crawling jungle sores had opened on Sowter's ankles. The bone was exposed. Hood was running a fever. Turner and I were taken into the jungle. We fell exhausted into leaf huts and slept for fourteen hours.'

Next day, they were forced to watch the gruesome spectacle of a spy being tortured. Trussed hand and foot, he was poked with burning logs in his eyes, mouth, throat, legs and arms until he had confessed all. At that point they cut off his head. 'This might be done with anything,' noted an appalled Alcock, 'a sword, a hoe, an axe.' The Coppists were asked if they wanted to take part. They declined, though they 'were quite willing to shoot a spy if necessary'.

After dark on 21 June, Alcock was taken by Ching Fee, an English-speaking guerilla, to meet a senior AJF officer in a plantation two miles from the camp. 'Six Chinese guerillas were waiting silently for us,' recalled Alcock. 'One came forward, while the others kept me covered. This was the very senior officer. He couldn't speak English but, using Ching Fee as an interpreter, he gave me a thorough questioning. At last he was satisfied. He agreed to try to relay a message back to SEAC.'

It was, explained Alcock, vitally important that SEAC knew they had not been captured, and that their mission, and Operation Zipper more generally, was not compromised. Would the officer help them to gather more information about the potential invasion beaches, asked Alcock? The officer nodded. 'You can go in a sampan with an anti-Japanese fisherman who knows the best beaches on the coast and will be able to take you anywhere you wish to go.'

Hearing this, Alcock wrote out the message for the officer to send to SEAC. It confirmed that the four missing Coppists were 'safe' with the AJF, and added: 'No degree of compromise believed to exist. Due to slight beach defences and assistance available

here by AJF, beach reconnaissance can be continued from here
– if required and approved by you.'

The officer now dismissed his bodyguard and offered Alcock
coffee and something to eat in a house nearby. After the meal,
he came to the point. He was, he said, in charge of 10,000 men.
But he only had enough small arms to equip a few hundred. If
SEAC provided the necessary arms and ammunition, he could
tie down most of the Malayan peninsula, certainly for a distance
of twenty miles along the coast. This might be vital to the success
of Operation Zipper. Alcock was conflicted. It was not his job,
he knew, to form armies. But if he did not cooperate, he doubted
the first message would be sent. So he agreed to write a second
message, requesting an airdrop of small arms and ammunition.

Before departing, Alcock agreed to exchange his .45 automatic
for a Spanish pistol the officer was wearing. 'I feel sure,' wrote
Alcock, 'the swap saved our lives. Later the commander heard
of our difficulties and sent us money and medical aid.' This was
necessary because on 26 June, with a Japanese patrol approaching
the camp, Alcock and the others were taken deeper into the
jungle. After two weeks their clothes were rotting and Hood,
Sowter and Turner were all sporting 'ugly jungle sores and the
bones of their legs were showing; the sores running with foul-
smelling fluid'.

In mid-July, they were moved to a plantation house and given
plenty of fresh food. Their condition rapidly improved and, by
the time they left on 23 July, they were fitter than they had been
since leaving Ceylon, with 'no sign of fever and not a jungle sore
among us'. A day earlier, Alcock had received a reply from SEAC
to his signals. Dated 14 July, it read: 'Your two undated letters
(one with bad spelling) reached us on 4th July . . . You are to
proceed to Negeri Sembilan and wait with Negri A-JF HQ the
arrival of "Reed" through whom you will receive further orders.
In the meantime you are to assist "Reed".'

They set off for Negeri on the 23rd, a difficult and dangerous
journey of thirty miles across swamps and rivers. But the guide
took them the wrong way and abandoned them in the middle of

nowhere. 'We held on until July 28,' recalled Alcock, 'then struck out with a lone guide. We were hopelessly lost for two days. A Japanese patrol was closing in and I knew Sowter could not go on. Finally, we joined a group of six guerillas and they arranged for a Chinese couple to look after Sowter. It was August 6.'

They could not know it, but on that same day, 3,000 miles to the north-east, the USAAF B-29 Superfortress *Enola Gay* dropped the first atomic bomb – 'Little Boy' – on the Japanese city of Hiroshima. Three days later, a second bomb was ignited over Nagasaki. Japan surrendered on the 14th. The Second World War was over.

Alcock did not get the news until 23 August when he stumbled into the camp of the British Paratroop Force 136. Startled soldiers looked up and saw him 'rushing at them naked and bleeding'. It was a wonder he 'wasn't shot'. By then he weighed just eighty-two pounds and was 'delirious with fever, fatigue and relief'. He was taken to see the commander, Lieutenant Colonel Claude Fenner, whose code name was Reed. Fenner explained that his unit had parachuted into Negeri Sembilan three weeks earlier. They were expecting the Coppists. Alcock told him they had been taken in the wrong direction, and begged Fenner to get medical help to Hood, Turner and Sowter – all of whom were too ill to carry on – as quickly as possible. Fenner promised that he would.

Forty-eight hours later, all three were safe in hospital in Seremban. The following morning, the whole party was transferred to the landing ship HMS *Persimmon* for the long voyage back to Ceylon. 'The jungles of Malaya began to slip astern,' remembered Alcock. 'A white ensign was snapping crisply from the halyards. I brushed my hand across my face. It was wet with tears.'[2]

43

'The unusually silent service'

The Small Operations Group in the Far East was disbanded, and Hammenhiel Camp closed, in late October 1945. During the previous sixteen months, the SOG had carried out nineteen independently mounted operations – including beach reconnaissance, attacks on enemy coastlines and missions for clandestine organisations – and 154 small-scale raids on the Arakan coast and along Burma's rivers in support of 'Force Commanders'.[1]

The three SBS groups played a particularly prominent part in the Burma raids, notably during the 14th Army's crossing of the Chindwin and Irrawaddy rivers. 'It is considered,' wrote Colonel Tollemache in his Progress Report of June 1945, 'that praise is due to the [officer commanding] SBS and to the three Group Commanders for the energy and resourcefulness they have shown, throughout the period covered by this report, in their planning and execution of operations, the training of their units, and the overcoming of administrative difficulties.'[2]

Yet SOG total casualties in those 173 operations were remarkably light: three officers and three other ranks killed; three officers and one other rank captured by the Japanese (though only one officer was liberated, the others were executed); three officers and one other rank interned in Siam (all later liberated); three officers and six other ranks missing (two officers and two other ranks, all from COPP 3, joined up with guerilla forces and were liberated); and one officer and one other rank wounded.[3]

The various component parts of the SOG – SBS, COPP, SRU and Royal Marine Detachment 385 – had shown, once again, how effective small, well-trained and highly motivated teams of maritime special operations could be. 'Blondie' Hasler ensured that the doctrine of small-scale raiding and reconnoitring continued after the war when he reported for duty with a cadre of the SOG at the Combined Operations Experimental Establishment at Appledore in north Devon in the autumn of 1945.[4] It was, however, very much a Royal Marines affair. The army SBS and navy COPP would play no future role in Britain's maritime special operations capability.

This cold reality became abundantly clear to the SBS men when they were told, in the wake of their sudden disbandment in late October 1945, that they had to 'fend for themselves' until demobilisation. Moreover, they were 'forbidden by order of the [SEAC] chief of staff to wear the Commando green beret, which was to be worn henceforth only by Royal Marine Commandos'. The order caused 'great resentment', wrote Gruff Courtney, 'as SBS had worn the green beret since 1942, long before Royal Marine Commandos were formed, and it was a tremendous source of pride to individual officers and men'. Most ignored the instruction. One final grievance was the belief that many of the 'recommendations for gallantry awards put forward in 1945 by SBS group commanders for operations in Burma got side-tracked and lost in SOG or SEAC headquarters in the confusion'. It was, noted Gruff Courtney, 'a pity, as the decorations would have been well earned'.[5]

In 1946, Hasler was appointed advisor to the School of Combined Operations Beach and Boat Section (SCOBBS) that was formed out of the nucleus of SOG and based at Fremington, north Devon. He set out his vision for the future of amphibious special forces in a paper entitled 'General Notes on the Use of Special Parties'. There would be, he wrote, a 'requirement for infiltration operations by small parties of uniformed troops' to carry out the following tasks: 'Reconnaissance of enemy-held areas, including beach survey, river crossing'; 'Placing markers and guides for assault landings'; 'Small-scale raids, either with independent objectives or in support of larger operations';

'Deception'; and 'Transporting of experts or agents and of supplies for them'.

Such operations would fall into two categories: Strategic and Tactical. The former would be long-range missions 'required by higher planning staff'; the latter short-range 'required by Force or Unit Commanders'. His intention was for SCOBBS to train small self-contained units of not more than twelve men each to form what he called the Combined Operations Small Raiding Organisation (COSRO). The COSRO parties would operate behind enemy lines or with civilian agents, whereas Royal Marine Commandos would be used for coastal raiding and beachhead operations in bodies no smaller than a troop.

He developed his ideas further in a second paper – 'School of Combined Operations Beach and Boat Section' – that explained SCOBBS' intention to 'train a pool of men who will be available in time of war' to carry out these waterborne operations. They would do so in 'very small boats (such as dories, canoes, inflatable boats etc) and by swimming and wading', and would have to be 'familiar with all types of coast' (including the banks of rivers and lakes) and be able 'to negotiate all forms of natural or artificial coastal obstacle'. Such men would need to be 'not only courageous, but also intelligent and resourceful'.

In October 1947, SCOBBS dropped the word 'School' from its name, combined with the RMBPD and moved to Eastney in Portsmouth to become, a year later, the Small Raids Wing (SRW) of the newly created Amphibious School, Royal Marines. Here were established the Royal Marines Special Boat Sections (at first as the demonstration element of the SRW) in precisely the roles that Hasler had proposed in his two 1946 policy papers. 'With the SBS now taking on the operational roles of, effectively, the RMBPD, COPP, army SBS, SRU, COSRO and SRW,' wrote Hasler's biographer, 'he could leave with the future, as he planned it, secure . . .'[6]

Since 1948, the SBS has undergone various name changes: Special Boat Company in 1951, Special Boat Squadron in 1974, and, after assuming responsibility for maritime counter-terrorism,

Special Boat Service in 1987, the name it still uses today. Also, in 1987, the SBS became – along with the SAS and 14ᵗʰ Intelligence Company – part of UK Special Forces (UKSF). In 1994, recruitment was opened to all three services of the British armed forces as the SBS and SAS began joint UKSF selection. This recognised, among other things, that the two units have around eighty-five per cent task and skill-set commonality. But they also have their own particular attributes and, having passed selection, operators join their respective units (SBS/SAS) to undertake 'specific to task' specialist training. For the SBS this includes boating and diving.

In 2001, operational command of the SBS – formerly delegated to the Commandant General Royal Marines – was retained by the Fleet (Royal Navy). Two years later, to reflect the SBS's independence from the Royal Marines, a new cap badge was issued: a dagger surmounting two blue waves. The motto 'By Strength and Guile' had been altered slightly from 'Not By Strength By Guile' by the then CO in 1998, in recognition of the increasingly kinetic and independent nature of special forces operations.

The SBS today consists of an undisclosed number of operators arranged into various squadrons and sharing the intensely busy operational burden which falls to UKSF.[7] Not only does the modern SBS carry out many of the same roles that its forerunners pioneered in the Second World War, it recruits much the same type of unorthodox, unshowy, but hugely capable problem-solvers that Roger Courtney preferred for his Folbot Troop in 1940. This unbroken historical link is acknowledged by the modern SBS:

Born of the needs of wartime, we are indebted to our bloodline: Commandos, Royal Marines, sailors and soldiers, all of the above and none. Unconventional and irregular, we are misfits who fit in, thinkers who fight and fighters who think. We are the 'man you might find in the supermarket queue' – quiet men with loud secrets to keep. Together we make the impossible possible – if there isn't a way we invent one.

We have minds of our own but a singular spirit: of initiative, invention and bold enterprise . . .

Since 1940, we've rigorously selected the finest soldiers from across Her Majesty's Forces to deliver the most covert and high-risk tasks, at home and abroad.

The ethos of the modern SBS is no different to that of its forefathers in the Second World War. 'We prefer the twilight. Darkness is our friend, stealth our strength, discretion our decisive advantage. We own the night. Like the submarines that first carried us, we are the unusually silent service. The most secret of special forces.'[8]

*

Today's SBS acknowledges that two men played a key role in the founding and development of Britain's maritime special operations capability. 'If Roger Courtney is the father of the Special Boat Service,' it acknowledges, 'Herbert "Blondie" Hasler is the other man.' It adds:

> Throughout [the unit's] tangled bloodline, Hasler's aim – to 'coordinate and develop all forms of stealthy seaborne attack by small parties' – and his emphasis on audacity, tenacity, technology, innovation and tight teamwork shone through. His thinking forms the principles for SBS operators today, whether on land or sea.
>
> If Courtney represents our heart, Hasler is our head; restless, inventive, courageous, never satisfied, always moving forward and armed with a dark sense of humour.
>
> He is our Father of Invention.[9]

In fact, the SBS has – I would contend – a third parent: Nigel Willmott, the founder of COPP. It was Willmott who identified the vital importance of beach reconnaissance for the success of amphibious operations, a principle that still holds good today. It was Willmott who joined Courtney on the Rhodes reconnaissance, the first maritime special operation of the war. And it was Willmott who set in train the daring survey and marking of beaches in the Mediterranean and the Channel that paved the way for the large-scale Allied landings in North Africa, Sicily, mainland Italy and Normandy – arguably the most significant contribution made by naval special forces during the whole conflict. The formation of Willmott's COPPs, acknowledges the modern SBS, was the moment 'we went from being tactical raiders to a strategic strikeforce. The first boots on the ground, the first fins in the sand . . . These small teams took enormous risk, but changed the course of the war.'[10]

If Courtney is synonymous with the SBS's heart, and Hasler its head, maybe Willmott represents its soul: meticulous, indefatigable and self-reliant.

Britain's best general of the Second World War, Field Marshal Viscount Slim, had a low opinion of most special forces. They were, he wrote in *Defeat Into Victory*, his classic account of the Burma campaign, 'expensive, wasteful and unnecessary'. He added: 'There is, however, one kind of special unit which should be retained: that designed to be employed in small parties, usually behind the enemy, on tasks beyond the normal scope of warfare in the field . . . Not costly in manpower, they may, if handled with imaginative ruthlessness, achieve strategic results.'[11]

Slim could have been describing the SOG, and certainly its constituent parts from the SBS and COPP. Gruff Courtney certainly thought so. Both groups, he wrote, 'were small and very specialised, and their retention since the end of 1945 under the mantle of the Royal Marines has, during the Falklands campaign, shown the wisdom of [Slim's] words.' Courtney added: 'Brother Roger and his old friend Nigel Willmott had every reason to be proud of the healthy offspring they fathered on the beaches of Rhodes in March 1941.'[12]

*

What, then, of the achievements of the wartime SBS and its affiliates? Did they justify the cost in blood, treasure and the diversion of resources from other military endeavours? The answer must be a resounding yes. Not all their operations were successful, of course. The costly failures – or partial failures – included the attempted assassination of Rommel in November 1941 (in which the SBS played only a supporting role), the disastrous assault on Oran harbour in November 1942 (ditto), and the aborted missions to Elizabeth Island and Phuket in October 1944 and March 1945 respectively.

But they were vastly outweighed by both the number and impact of the successful missions: the destruction of ships and coastal infrastructure; the rescue of Allied soldiers; the insertion and recovery of secret agents; and, most significantly, the use of Coppists to reconnoitre and mark beaches, and pilot in landing craft for most of the major Allied amphibious landings in North Africa, Europe and the Far East. This last endeavour, alone, saved many thousands of lives. But even the less successful missions had a detrimental effect on the enemy – spreading fear and uncertainty, and diverting troops from other tasks – that made them cost-effective.

Founded in the dark days of 1940 as Britain continued the fight against the Axis powers alone, the SBS was to begin with a small and inexperienced outfit that leaned heavily on its volunteers' raw courage and boyish enthusiasm. Inevitably it made, in its early days, as many mistakes as it enjoyed successes. Yet the psychological impact of its early operations, at a time when Britain's military victories were few and far between, should not be underestimated: both in assuring the British public that its servicemen had the courage and ingenuity to fight back; and in keeping the enemy on the back foot, constantly worrying where and when the next attack from the sea would come.

Moreover, it was quick to learn from its mistakes and gradually became in its many forms – Special Boat Section, 101 Troop, Force X, RMBPD, COPP, Special Boat Squadron, Sea Reconnaissance Unit and Detachment 385 – a highly trained and professional force that was constantly evolving its training, tactics and procedures to suit the challenges it faced. Its operators became, in the process, the pioneers of small team work that is still practised by British special operations units today. Then and now, there's a focus on the collective, not the individual, and a willingness to learn, adapt and develop. 'The battle, after all,' says the modern SBS, 'isn't won or lost on the battlefield. It is won in the barracks. Teamwork and cooperation – these are our force multipliers. And it applies to whoever is on the mission – SBS or otherwise. We are all one team . . . "The strength of the pack is the wolf," said Kipling, "and the strength of the wolf is the pack."'[13]

This principle was very much evident in the close relationship forged between the early SBS and the Submarine Service, one that still exists today. Having developed these bonds of trust, they were able to pull off some of the most spectacular coastal raids in history, none more so than Hasler's Operation Frankton.

What makes these operations so extraordinary is that they were accomplished by a handful of brave and determined men, paddling flimsy canoes, and armed only with knives, pistols and a few sub-machine guns. Transported deep behind enemy lines, they were expected to operate without back-up and the possibility – particularly after the promulgation of Adolf Hitler's controversial 'Commando Order' in 1942 – that if caught they would be executed. Many were. Their willingness to undertake such lonely, uncomfortable and hazardous tasks required courage of the very highest order: not hot-blooded, as are many acts of valour on the battlefield; but cool and calculated. A large number were rewarded with gallantry medals. But others, just as deserving, were not – as is often the way with special forces, when not all acts of courage are witnessed, and where every mission is, in some respects, beyond the call of duty. They took outrageous risks in the belief that the benefits were worth it. The evidence in this book suggests that they were.

Aftermath

'He lived hard and died early'

SPECIAL BOAT SECTION and 101 TROOP

Roger Courtney (MC) never returned to the UK. Resigning his commission in 1948, he moved to Hargeisa in British Somaliland where he worked for the Desert Locust Control. He died of pneumonia a year later, 'supported to the end by his indomitable wife Dorrise', and is buried in a dry watercourse, his grave marked by an old Portuguese cannonball. He was just 46 years old. 'It was with him,' wrote Tug Wilson, 'that just about anything could be tackled. The impossible became downgraded to improbable, then probable, and finally almost a piece of cake.'

His brother Gruff added:

> He was a wild man and should have been an Elizabethan freebooter. He was a tremendous leader of men, with magnetism and cheerful courage, and ambitious only for his SBS and for its reputation. He lived hard and died early . . . following his philosophy of high living and low thinking (his own words). He was no respecter of authority and suffered much frustration from his superiors in rank. Mind you, his outlook is illustrated by the motto composed at his request by a classical don at Oxford University for his beloved SBS: '*Excreta Tauri Astutos Frustrantur* (Bullshit Baffles Brains)', so perhaps his superiors suffered also.[1]

After repatriation from Germany in 1945, **Robert 'Tug' Wilson** (DSO and bar) was appointed adjutant of the University of

Bristol's Senior Training Corps. Bitten by the military bug, he then volunteered for service in Palestine with the 6th Airborne Division, receiving his parachute wings in the process. He remained for a year as the battery commander of an airborne anti-tank regiment, and later fought in Korea with a battery of field artillery. After a stint as the CO of an anti-aircraft regiment, he became the Army Careers Officer for Warwickshire and retired as a lieutenant colonel in 1973. He died in 2002.[2] Of the other Sannox Bay originals, **Jim Sherwood** and **George Barnes** (MM and bar) were commissioned and fought in the Far East with the SBS. Both survived the war.

Tug Wilson's paddler on his final mission, **John Brittlebank** (DCM), was also repatriated in 1945, having served stints in Italian and German POW camps. They met for the last time at Buckingham Palace in 1946 when they were both awarded medals for Crotone. Nine years later, Brittlebank was hit by a car and killed as he was cycling in his native Nottinghamshire.

Gerald Montanaro (DSO) spent the remainder of the war testing experimental craft for the Mobile Flotation Unit. He stayed in the military after the war, rising to the rank of brigadier and retiring in 1965. He died in 1979.

Harry Holden-White (MC) saw out the war in the Far East where he commanded A Group, SBS, and took part in raids behind enemy lines on the Arakan coast of Burma. For this intense and highly dangerous activity, he was mentioned in despatches. After demobilisation, he studied painting at Chelsea School of Art and in Paris. He later married fellow artist Patricia Sanderson and, after the birth of their only child Harriet in 1957, they settled in the Ardèche region of France. 'He loved his time in the SBS and the camaraderie,' remembered Harriet. 'But I don't think he ever really recovered from the war. He wasn't an easy father as he hated noise and would go off for long solitary walks . . . He was a profoundly romantic figure. The last of that generation that had had the privilege to be brought up with wealth, but for whom money was not important.' When Holden-White died, aged eighty-one, in 1998, the SBS sent a representative to his funeral. It was, he said, an honour to be there because the unit was very proud of its former members.[3]

After a stint as commanding officer of the Australian SRD's Group A, **Godfrey 'Gruff' Courtney** (MBE, MC) returned to the UK in 1946 and was seconded to the Foreign Office. He retired as a lieutenant colonel in 1955 and emigrated with his family to Australia where he worked as an export consultant. In 1983 he published *SBS in World War Two*, a history of the unit his brother had founded, and in which he served.[4]

SPECIAL BOAT SQUADRON

George, 2ⁿᵈ Earl Jellicoe (DSO, MC) was among the first Allied soldiers to enter German-occupied Athens at the end of the war. He joined the Foreign Office two years later, serving in Washington and Baghdad before marital difficulties prompted his resignation in 1958. From his seat as a hereditary peer in the House of Lords, he served as a minister in three Tory governments (including First Lord of the Admiralty in Sir Alec Douglas-Home's administration), resigning from front-line politics in 1973. A Fellow of the Royal Society, and president of the Royal Geographical Society and SAS Regimental Association, he was the longest-serving member of the House of Lords when he died in 2007 at the age of 88.

RMBPD

Herbert 'Blondie' Hasler (DSO, OBE, Croix de Guerre) was invalided out of the Royal Marines with a bad back in 1948. He returned to his first love, sailing, and later invented, among other things, a cabin heater, stiff sails, a 'self-tailing' rope winch and the first practical self-steering gear for yachts. He also pioneered the single-handed Transatlantic yacht race, finishing second in the inaugural competition in 1960 to Francis

Chichester's *Gipsy Moth III*. He was a military advisor on the 1955 feature film *Cockleshell Heroes*,* directed by and starring José Ferrer (who played Hasler). Despite his reservations about the film's title and distortion of reality – the limpets, for example, were placed by frogmen – prompting his refusal to attend the royal gala premiere, Hasler became a lifelong friend of Ferrer. 'As to Blondie,' wrote Ferrer, 'I could write a short book on him, for he was an example of what each of us can be if he wants to, and if he sets his standards and ideals high.' At the age of 51, Hasler married Bridget Fisher, a woman half his age, and they had a daughter and a son. They moved to a hill farm in Argyll, Scotland, where Hasler practised organic farming and died of a heart attack in 1987.[5]

After service in the Aegean with the RMBPD's 'Earthworm' Detachment, **Bill Sparks** (DCM) returned to civilian life as a bus driver before a brief stint as a lieutenant in the Malaysian Police Force. Back in London, he worked as a labourer, postman, shoe repairer, milkman, insurance salesman and ice-cream vendor, but eventually resumed bus driving and retired as a garage inspector with respiratory problems in 1986. When his disability allowance was cut in 1988, he auctioned his Distinguished Service Medal which was sold to an anonymous buyer for £31,000. Four years later, Sparks published (with ghostwriter Michael Munn) *The Last of the Cockleshell Heroes*; a second book, *Cockleshell Commando: The Memoir of Bill Sparks*, followed in 2002. Twice married, Sparks had four children (one of whom became a lieutenant in the Royal Marines). He died in 2002.

Norman Colley, the first reserve on Operation Frankton, married in 1945 and left the Marines a year later. He worked for an engineering firm, and later ran a bakery and a sub-post office in South Emshall, West Yorkshire. He died in 2013.[6]

---

* A book of the same name, published in 1956 by Brigadier C. E. Lucas Phillips, sold 250,000 copies.

COPP

Nigel Willmott (DSO, DSC and bar) ended the war on the Admiralty's planning staff. He retired as a captain in 1960, having commanded the sloop HMS *Peacock* for two years and served for a time with MI5. He later moved to Cyprus – having changed his surname by deed poll to Clogstoun-Willmott – and died in 1992, at the age of 81. So secret was the work of Willmott's COPP that it was not revealed until long after the war had ended. 'Even today,' notes the National Army Museum, 'Clogstoun-Willmott and the men of the COPP remain the unsung heroes of the Special Forces.'[7]

After guiding in the amphibious tanks to Omaha Beach on D-Day, **Logan Scott-Bowden** (CBE, DSO, MC and bar) landed in France and took command of 17th Field Company, Royal Engineers, which was busy laying mines to thwart the expected counter-attack of 21st Panzer Division. 'So ended my service with COPP,' wrote Scott-Bowden, 'apart from a threatened Court Martial, for failing to return to the UK, from the new Chief of Combined Operations, Major General Robert Laycock.' Fortunately, Scott-Bowden's new divisional commander was a good friend of Laycock's and disciplinary proceedings were dropped. Scott-Bowden saw out the war with the 17th Field Company, winning a bar to his MC in 1945. He later served in Palestine, Korea, Aden and Northern Ireland (where he formed the Ulster Defence Regiment), and was appointed OBE and CBE. He retired with the rank of major general in 1974. Married with three sons and three daughters, he died in 2014 at the age of 93.[8]

Bruce Ogden-Smith (DCM, MM) should have received his Military Medal for Operation KJH at Buckingham Palace on 6 June 1944. His wife was about to set off from Wales on 5 June when she got a call to say her husband had been unavoidably detained. He was, of course, en route for Omaha Beach with his former swimming partner Scott-Bowden. He returned to Wales after the war and died in 1986. His medals were bought at auction, twenty years later, by Lord Ashcroft.[9]

After returning to Ceylon from Malaya in the summer of 1945, **Alex Hughes** (DSC) married his Wren girlfriend Joan. He stayed on in the navy after the war, working briefly at SCOBBS with 'Blondie' Hasler and retiring with the rank of lieutenant commander in 1959.[10]

Ian 'Canada' Alcock (DSC) was mentioned in despatches for his 'good service' during Operation Confidence. Once recovered from his ordeal with the Communist guerillas in Malaya, he returned to Canada and was briefly assigned to a naval base in Nova Scotia. Retiring from the RCN with the rank of lieutenant commander a year later, he settled in Victoria, British Columbia, and continued his work as a gold prospector. He died at the age of 54 in 1969, leaving a wife and child.[11]

Released from Thai captivity in August 1945, **Ian Mackenzie** studied at the School of Military Survey and was employed in East Africa and by the Ordnance Survey in the UK. His last full military tour was as Chief Survey, Northern Army Group in Germany. He had just taken up a new post as Colonel (Survey) in the Ministry of Defence when he died suddenly in 1968. He left a wife and two daughters.[12]

Ralph Stanbury (DSC) finished the war as the cruiser HMS *Sirius*'s navigating officer. In 1949, he used the pseudonym Ralph Neville (his first two names) to publish *Survey by Starlight*, an evocative memoir of his time with COPP 5. He left the Royal Navy to help train the nascent Nigerian Naval Force in 1957, retiring as a lieutenant commander when Nigeria became a republic six years later. For two decades he ran a beauty salon at Langston Green, Kent, and died in 1998.[13]

Returning to the UK from Ceylon in late 1944, **Geoffrey Hall** (DSC) was given command of the frigate *Bigbury Bay*, then under construction in Aberdeen. He took advantage of the hiatus to meet and marry his fiancée Mary Carlisle, then a Wren officer serving at Portland. He later joined the Naval Hydrographic Service, and took survey vessels to the east and west coasts of Africa, the Seychelles, the mid-Atlantic and the Indian Ocean. For his work in furthering oceanographic exploration, he was awarded the RGS's Cuthbert Peek Award. Promoted rear admiral and appointed Hydrographer of the Navy in 1971, he retired four years later and settled in Lincolnshire with his wife and three children. In 1999, a year after the death of his daughter Virginia, he published his memoir *Sailor's Luck*. He died, aged 88, six years later.[14]

Hall's deputy, **Ruari McLean** (DSC), had a similarly distinguished post-war career. Following his marriage to Mary Carlisle's sister Antonia, he worked as a book designer and, with George Rainbird, founded Rainbird McLean in 1951. The firm's clever packaging of books 'changed the face of illustrated-book publication'. He later founded his own design magazine, *Motif*, and helped to launch the *Observer*'s colour magazine. He became honorary Typographic Advisor to HMSO in 1966, and was awarded the CBE seven years later for redesigning the British passport. The author of numerous books on typographic design – including *Magazine Design*, *How Typography Happens* and *Modern Book Design* – he died in 2006, leaving two sons and a daughter.[15]

Alec Colson (MBE) received a permanent commission in the Royal Engineers in 1945 and retired as a major fifteen years later. He was then ordained in the Church of England, and worked as a vicar in parishes in East Anglia and West Kilburn. He died in 2007.[16] **Geoff Richards**, COPP 8's eccentric stores officer who took part in Operation David, was tragically killed in a fall from a train near Madras in late December 1944. 'He is one of the party we relieved,' noted Alex Hughes, 'a hefty chap with a flaming red beard and a great character . . . He was operational and [it] seems rather hard luck after 18 months service here to be killed in such a manner – on the way home.'[17]

After D-Day, **Geoffrey 'Thin Red' Lyne** (OBE, DSC) left COPP 9 for navigating duties and was mentioned in despatches for mine clearance in the Elbe and Weser rivers during the summer of 1945. He was Queen's Harbour Master at Port Said during the Suez Crisis, and was awarded the OBE. Having left the navy as a commander in 1960, he kept in contact with his former assistant, Jim Booth. 'We got on ever so well,' recalled Booth. 'I knew him right to the end. I'm still in touch with his family.' Married with a son, Lyne died near King's Lynn, Norfolk, in 1982.[18]

At the time of writing, the only living Coppist is **Jim Booth** (Croix de Guerre). After his D-Day adventures on the midget submarine X23, he was posted to the Far East with COPP 9 (then commanded by Lieutenant John Morison). 'In Burma,' recalled Booth, 'we had a rough time. We were caught badly by a group of Japs, but we managed to get away with it. We killed most of them. This was towards the end of the war, as we were driving towards Rangoon.' After the war, Booth married and raised four children. He farmed for a while, but finding it hard to earn a living he trained as a teacher and taught in state schools, returning briefly to farming before retirement. In 2012, he was one of ten surviving Coppists to attend the opening of the granite COPP Memorial on Hayling Island. It was dedicated to their fallen comrades by Lady Mountbatten of Burma, the wife of the late Earl Mountbatten. In 2017, Booth survived a vicious hammer attack at his home in Taunton that left him with a fractured skull; his drug-addict assailant was jailed for attempted murder. Two years later, still not fully recovered, this redoubtable former Coppist returned to Normandy to attend the seventy-fifth D-Day anniversary celebrations. At the time of writing, he was ninety-nine years old and would celebrate his hundredth birthday on 9 July 2021.[19]

Acknowledgements

This book owes its existence to the vision of the late Paddy Ashdown – my dedicatee – who was working on a similar project when he died in 2018. I would particularly like to thank Paddy's widow Jane, Lady Ashdown, for giving me access to and permission to quote from Paddy's unfinished manuscript.

As a former captain in the SBS, and the author of a number of well-received Second World War histories, Paddy was the obvious choice to write the first authorised history of the unit. Following in his footsteps, I was given access to the secret archives of the SBS Association in Poole, Dorset, ably catalogued by Paul E, the Historical Projects Officer. Paul's help with both documents and photographs has been invaluable, and I'm extremely grateful.

I'd also like to thank Will S, CEO of the SBSA, and those members of the SBS past and present who have embraced this project by inviting me to Poole, providing contacts, taking me out on the water, commenting on the manuscript, and generally giving me a unique insight into the methods and ethos of British maritime special operations: 'Jan' K, Russ C, Andy M, Al C, Neil M, Steve C, Shaun P, Sam R and Karl T.

Others who assisted with contacts, books, documents, maps and photos include Harriet O'Grady, daughter of Major Harry Holden-White; Nicky Titchener and Steve Peacock, children of Lieutenant Mike Peacock RNVR; Francis Dickinson, grandson of Lieutenant Commander Edward Tomkinson RN; Robin Walton of the COPP Heroes Memorial Fund and website; Philip Curtis, director of The Map House; Mike Beckett; Robert Lyman; Warwick Woodhouse; Iona McLaren; and James Garvey (whose excellent Master's dissertation on the logistics of the Sicily

campaign was researched and written under my supervision).
Thank you, all.

I'm extremely grateful to Admiral of the Fleet the Lord Boyce,
a former sub-marine commander and Chief of Defence Staff,
and currently the Colonel Commandant of the SBS and Patron
of the SBS Association, for agreeing to write the foreword to
this book. Dr Andy Boyd, also formerly of the Submarine Service,
read the manuscript and set me straight on a number of nautical
matters. It is much appreciated.

At the time of writing, only a few of the original members of
the wartime SBS and its affiliates are still alive. They include Old
Etonian Jim Booth who, as a 22-year-old naval sub lieutenant,
spent forty-eight hours submerged in a midget submarine off
Sword Beach in Normandy, before surfacing to guide in the assault
craft at dawn on D-Day, 6 June 1944. It was a dangerous but
vital mission that saved countless lives, and Booth was kind enough
to share his memories of it with me in 2019. Thank you, Jim.

The book was researched in a number of public archives and
I'm grateful for the help I was given by the staffs of the National
Archives, the National Army Museum, the Imperial War Museum,
and the Liddell Hart Centre for Military Archives.

Lastly, I'm indebted once again to my literary agent Caroline
Michel and publisher Arabella Pike who agreed that I was the
right historian to take this project on; to Arabella's excellent
team at William Collins, notably Katherine Patrick, Jo Thompson,
Iain Hunt, Julian Humphries, Matt Clacher and copy-editor
David Milner; and to my wife Louise, and daughters Nell, Tamar
and Tashie, who have no particular interest in military history,
but accept that I have to earn a living somehow.

Notes

INTRODUCTION

1 G. B. Courtney, *SBS in World War Two* (London: Robert Hale, 1983; repr. 2017), p. 206.
2 Private Papers (PP), Paddy Ashdown Papers, Paddy Ashdown, 'Not by Strength, by Guile: How the SBS changed modern warfare', unpublished manuscript, p. 1.
3 Ibid.

CHAPTER 1

1 Courtney, *SBS in World War Two*, p. 13; John Parker, *SBS: The Inside Story of the Special Boat Service* (London: Headline, 1997; repr. 2004), p. 27; Bernard Fergusson, *The Watery Maze: The Story of Combined Operations* (London: Collins, 1961), pp. 96–7.
2 London, The National Archives (TNA), DEFE 2/740, 'General Summary of Special Boat Section Activities Since Their Formation' by Major R. J. Courtney, 23 November 1943.
3 TNA, WO 218/8, War Diary of No. 8 Commando, 26 September and 17 October 1940.
4 Courtney, *SBS in World War Two*, pp. 13–14.
5 TNA, DEFE 2/842, 'Folbot Canoes, 1940–1943', Director of Combined Operations (Admiral of the Fleet Keyes) to the Admiralty, Ordering Folbots for Inveraray, 14 October 1940; TNA, DEFE 2/740, 'Special Boat Section' by Major R. J. Courtney, 23 November 1943.
6 Poole, Dorset, SBS Association Archives (SBSAA), *By Strength and Guile*, p. 9.

7   Ibid.; SBSAA, Service Records and Documents of Major R. J. A. Courtney.

8   Roger Courtney, *Africa Calling: The True Account of the Author's Strange Workaday Experiences in Kenya, Uganda and the Belgian Congo* (London: George Harrap & Co., 1935), p. 9.

9   Roger Courtney, *Claws of Africa: Experiences of a Professional Big-game Hunter* (London: George G. Harrap, 1934), pp. 11–27, 38–43.

10 Courtney, *Africa Calling*, pp. 9–11; Roger Courtney, *African Argosy* (London: Herbert Jenkins, 1953), pp. 9–13.

11 Courtney, *Africa Argosy*, pp. 11–13.

12 SBSAA, Service Records and Documents of Major R. J. A. Courtney, Undated receipt for purchase of 2-seater sports folbot at Selfridges.

13 Courtney, *Africa Argosy*, pp. 14–17.

14 Ibid., pp. 55, 110–11, 130–1, 171–5.

15 Roger Courtney, *Palestine Policeman: An Account of Eighteen Dramatic Months in the Palestine Police Force during the Great Jew–Arab Troubles* (London: Herbert Jenkins Ltd, 1939), pp. 9–14, 238–9.

16 SBSAA, R. J. A. Courtney's Service Records and Documents.

17 Parker, *SBS*, p. 19.

18 London, Liddell Hart Centre for Military Archives (LHCMA), Papers of Robert Laycock, 1/3, 'Volunteers for Special Service', 9 June 1940.

19 SBSAA, R. J. A. Courtney's Service Records and Documents; LHCMA, Laycock Papers, 1/2, 'Volunteers for Special Service (Officers): London Area', undated.

20 LHCMA, Laycock Papers, 3/9, 8 Commando Officers Seniority Roll.

21 Jock Colville, *The Fringes of Power: 10 Downing Street Diaries 1939–1955* (London: Hodder & Stoughton, 1985), p. 207.

22 London, Imperial War Museum (IWM), James B. B. Sherwood (Oral History), Cat. No. 9783, Reel 1.

CHAPTER 2

1   IWM, Sherwood Oral History, Reel 1.

2   TNA, WO 218/8, War Diary of No. 8 Commando, 25 October 1940; TNA, DEFE 2/842, Ordering Folbots for Inveraray, 14 October 1940.

3   TNA, DEFE 2/842, DCO to Captain G. C. P. Menzies, HMS *Forth*, 27 November 1940; TNA, WO 218/8, War Diary of No. 8 Commando, November 1940.

4   TNA, DEFE 2/842, Major R. J. Courtney to Lord Louis Mountbatten (DCO), 9 March 1942.

5   TNA, DEFE 2/740, 'General Summary of Special Boat Section Activities Since Their Formation' and 'Special Boat Section', both written by Major R. J. Courtney on 23 November 1943.

6   Michael Davie (ed.), *The Diaries of Evelyn Waugh* (London: Weidenfeld & Nicolson, 1976), pp. 487–8.

7   Ibid., p. 488.

8   Ibid., p. 491.

9   Winston Churchill, *The Second World War* (London: Cassell, 1948–54), II, p. 552; TNA, DEFE 2/45, War Diary of the 4th Special Service Battalion, December 1940.

10 Courtney, *SBS*, pp. 30–1.

11 *By Strength and Guile*, p. 10. This is the list of the original twelve members of the Folbot Troop.

12 IWM, Sherwood Oral History, Reels 1 and 2.

13 Courtney, *SBS*, pp. 108–9, 207–8.

14 IWM, Sherwood Oral History, Reel 2.

15 Courtney, *SBS*, p. 133.

16 IWM, Sherwood Oral History, Reel 2.

17 LHCMA, Laycock Papers, 2/5, Administrative Instructions for Landing Exercises PC3 (night of 4/5 January 1941) and PC4 (night of 9/10 January 1941); IWM, Sherwood Oral History, Reel 2.

18 TNA, DEFE 2/842, Brigadier Haydon to the DDCO, 3 January 1942; and DDCO to Brigadier Haydon, 11 January 1941.

CHAPTER 3

1   TNA, WO 218/170, War Diary of No. 8 Commando (B Battalion, Layforce), January 1941; Churchill, *The Second World War*, III, p. 56.

2   *The Diaries of Evelyn Waugh*, p. 493.

3   IWM, Sherwood Oral History, Reel 2.

4   *The Diaries of Evelyn Waugh*, pp. 493–4; TNA, WO 218/170, War Diary of 8 Commando (B Battalion, Layforce), February 1941.

5   IWM, Sherwood Oral History, Reel 2.

6   Ian Trenowden, *Stealthily by Night: The COPPists – Clandestine Beach Reconnaissance in World War II* (Manchester: Crecy, 1995), Introduction: Origin of COPP; Bill Strutton and Michael Pearson, *The Secret Invaders* (London: Hodder & Stoughton, 1958; repr. 1961), p. 15.

7   SBSAA, Service Records and Documents of Lieut. Commander H. N. C. Willmott.

8   Trenowden, *Stealthily by Night*, Chapter Three: Early Beginnings.

9   James Ladd, *Commandos and Rangers of World War II* (London: Macdonald and Jane's, 1978), p. 59.

10 Courtney, *SBS*, pp. 19–20.

11 Ibid., p. 19.

12 IWM, Sherwood Oral History, Reel 2.

13 Trenowden, *Stealthily by Night*, Chapter Three: Early Beginnings; IWM, Sherwood Oral History, Reel 2; Ladd, *Commandos and Rangers*, p. 59.

14 Strutton and Pearson, *The Secret Invaders*, p. 27.

15 LHCMA, Laycock Papers, 3/10, Colonel Laycock to HQ British Troops Egypt on the subject of the 'Folbot Troop, Layforce', 1 May 1941; SBSAA, Service Records and Documents of Major R. J. A. Courtney.

16 TNA, ADM 199/1848, HMS *Triumph* – Report of 2nd Mediterranean War Patrol, 25 March to 5 April 1941.

17 Ralph Neville [Stanbury], *Survey by Starlight: A true story of reconnaissance work in the Mediterranean* (London: Hodder & Stoughton, 1949), pp. 27–8.

18 Trenowden, *Stealthily by Night*, Chapter Three: Early Beginnings; Strutton and Pearson, *The Secret Invaders*, p. 30.

19 Ladd, *Commandos and Rangers*, pp. 58–9.

20 Trenowden, *Stealthily by Night*, Chapter Three: Early Beginnings; Ladd, *Commandos and Rangers*, pp. 59–60; Strutton and Pearson, *The Secret Invaders*, pp. 31-41.

21 HMS *Triumph* – Report of 2nd Mediterranean War Patrol, 25 March to 5 April 1941.

22 'Special Boat Section' by Major R. J. Courtney, 23 November 1943.

23 Strutton and Pearson, *The Secret Invaders*, pp. 44–5.

24 HMS *Triumph* – Report of 2nd Mediterranean War Patrol, 25 March to 5 April 1941.

25 'Special Boat Section' by Major R. J. Courtney, 23 November 1943.

26 HMS *Triumph* – Report of 2nd Mediterranean War Patrol, 25 March to 5 April 1941; TNA, ADM 199/1848, Captain (S), 1st Submarine Flotilla, to Commander-in-Chief, Mediterranean, 17 April 1941.

27 SBSAA, Service Records and Documents of Major R. J. A. Courtney and Lieut. Commander H. N. C. Willmott; unithistories.com/ officers/Army_officers_C02.html [accessed 13 December 2019]

CHAPTER 4

1 LHCMA, Laycock Papers, 5/2, Report on Raid on Bardia by Colonel R. Laycock, 26 April 1941.

2 LHCMA, Laycock Papers, 4/10, HMS *Triumph* Report of Proceedings from 15 to 20 April 1941.

3 Report on Raid on Bardia by Colonel R. Laycock, 26 April 1941.

4 *The Diaries of Evelyn Waugh*, p. 495.

5 Report on Raid on Bardia by Colonel R. Laycock, 26 April 1941.

6 Courtney, *SBS*, p. 30; *By Strength and Guile*, p. 137.

7 TNA, ADM 236/36, HMS *Triumph* – Report of 3rd Mediterranean War Patrol, 24 April to 12 May 1941.

8 William Seymour, *British Special Forces* (London: Sidgwick & Jackson, 1985), pp. 77–82.

9 IWM, Sherwood Oral History, Reel 3.

10 LHCMA, Laycock Papers, 3/10, Colonel Laycock to HQ British Troops Egypt, subject 'Folbot Troop Layforce', 1 May 1941.

11 Private Papers (PP), M. J. Beckett Papers, Letter from G. B. Courtney to Leonard Whittaker, 28 July 1984.

12 LHCMA, Laycock Papers, 3/10, 'Service with the Folbot Section', 16 August 1941, and 'War Establishment of the Folbot Section ME', 26 August 1941.

13 London, National Army Museum (NAM), 9203-218-108, 'The Compleat Folbotist' by Captain Roger Courtney, 21 August 1941.

14 IWM, Sherwood Oral History, Reel 3.

15 TNA, ADM 236/36, HMS *Triumph* – Report of 4th Mediterranean War Patrol, 25 May to 12 June 1941.

16 IWM, Sherwood Oral History, Reel 3.

17 HMS *Triumph* – Report of 4th Mediterranean War Patrol, 25 May to 12 June 1941; IWM, Sherwood Oral History, Reel 3.

18 Courtney, *SBS*, p. 25.

19 TNA, ADM 236/24, HMS *Taku* – Report of 2nd Mediterranean War Patrol, 1–22 June 1941.

20 Courtney, *SBS*, pp. 25–6; HMS *Taku* – Report of 2nd Mediterranean War Patrol, 1–22 June 1941.

21 HMS *Taku* – Report of 2nd Mediterranean War Patrol, 1–22 June 1941.

CHAPTER 5

1   TNA, ADM 199/1922, HMS *Utmost* – Report of 8th Mediterranean War Patrol, 17 June to 3 July 1941; George Simpson, *Periscope View: A Remarkable Memoir of the 10th Submarine Flotilla at Malta 1941–1943* (London: Macmillan, 1972; repr. 2010), p. 110; LHCMA, Laycock Papers, 6/3, Captain Roger Courtney to Colonel R. Laycock, 18 September 1941.

2   Dennis Reeves, *Special Service of a Hazardous Nature* (Warrington: Liverpool Scottish Museum, 2007), pp, 143–6; Simpson, *Periscope View,* pp. 109–10, 128–30; Courtney, *SBS*, p. 32.

3   HMS *Utmost* – Report of 8th Mediterranean War Patrol, 17 June to 3 July 1941.

4   TNA, ADM 236/50, HMS *Urge* – Report of 3rd Mediterranean War Patrol, 23 June to 4 July 1941; Courtney, *SBS*, pp. 32–3.

5   TNA, ADM 199/1922, HMS *Utmost* – Report of 9th Mediterranean War Patrol, 17 July to 3 August 1941.

6   TNA, ADM 199/1922, HMS *Utmost* – Report of 10th Mediterranean War Patrol, 19–31 August 1941 (including 'Report of Special Operation' by Lt R. Wilson); Courtney, *SBS*, p. 34.

7   TNA, ADM 236/36, HMS *Triumph* – Report of 6th Mediterranean War Patrol/Special Operation, 19 August to 2 September 1941.

8   Ibid.

9   *The London Gazette* (Supplement), 9 April 1946; Service records and awards of the seven missing Commandos at commandoveterans.org/raid_sicily_railway_bridge [accessed 9 January 2020]

10 LHCMA, Laycock Papers, 6/3, Captain Roger Courtney to Colonel Laycock, 18 September 1941.

CHAPTER 6

1   TNA, ADM 236/32, HMS *Torbay* – Report of 3rd Mediterranean War Patrol, 28 June to 15 July 1941.

2   Brian Izzard, *Gamp VC: The Wartime Story of Maverick Submarine Commander Anthony Miers* (Yeovil: Haynes, 2009), pp. 6–7, 13, 40–41.

3   HMS *Torbay* – Report of 3rd Mediterranean War Patrol, 28 June to 15 July 1941.

4   Quoted in Izzard, *Gamp VC*, p. 80.

5   HMS *Torbay* – Report of 3rd Mediterranean War Patrol, 28 June to 15 July 1941.

6   George C. Bremner, 'What Corporal George Bremner saw on HMS *Torbay* on July 9, 1941', Letters to the Editor, *Sunday Telegraph*, 26 February 1989.

7   HMS *Torbay* – Report of 3rd Mediterranean War Patrol, 28 June to 15 July 1941.

8 'What Corporal George Bremner saw on HMS *Torbay* on July 9, 1941'.

9 HMS *Torbay* – Report of 3rd Mediterranean War Patrol, 28 June to 15 July 1941.

10 'What Corporal George Bremner saw on HMS *Torbay* on July 9, 1941'.

11 HMS *Torbay* – Report of 3rd Mediterranean War Patrol, 28 June to 15 July 1941.

12 'What Corporal George Bremner saw on HMS *Torbay* on July 9, 1941'.

13 Quoted in Izzard, *Gamp VC*, p. 251. See also Paul Chapman, *Submarine Torbay* (London: Robert Hale, 1989), pp. 65, 164–6.

14 Izzard, *Gamp VC*, pp. 79, 246–8.

15 TNA, ADM 236/32, Captain Raw to Admiral Cunningham, 29 July 1941.

16 TNA, ADM 236/32, Cunningham to the Secretary of the Admiralty, 13 August 1941.

17 'What Corporal George Bremner saw on HMS *Torbay* on July 9, 1941'.

18 Stoker Philip Le Gros, quoted in Izzard, *Gamp VC*, pp. 76–7.

19 TNA, ADM 236/32, HMS *Torbay* – Report of 4th Mediterranean War Patrol, 2–22 August 1941 (including the 'Report of Special Operations'); Izzard, *Gamp VC*, pp. 61–2.

20 Quoted in Izzard, *Gamp VC*, p. 63.

21 'What Corporal George Bremner saw on HMS *Torbay* on July 9, 1941'.

22 HMS *Torbay* – Report of 4th Mediterranean War Patrol, 2–22 August 1941.

23 Quoted in Izzard, *Gamp VC*, p. 81; Chapman, *Submarine Torbay*, p. 71.

24 HMS *Torbay* – Report of 4th Mediterranean War Patrol, 2–22 August 1941.

25 Quoted in Izzard, *Gamp VC*, p. 65.

26 HMS *Torbay* – Report of 4th Mediterranean War Patrol, 2–22 August 1941.

27 commandoveterans.org/GeorgeBremnerSBS [accessed 20 January 2020]

CHAPTER 7

1 LHCMA, Laycock Papers, 6/3, Captain R. J. Courtney to Colonel Laycock, 18 September 1941.

2 TNA, DEFE 2/740, 'General Summary of Special Boat Section Activities Since Their Formation', by Major R. J. Courtney, 23 November 1945.

3 LHCMA, Laycock Papers, 3/16, 'Employment of Special Service Troops in the Middle East' by Colonel Laycock, 16 September 1941.

4 LHCMA, Laycock Papers, 3/16, 'Minutes of a Meeting held on 11 Oct to decide on the Future Organisation of SS Troops in MEF'.

5 Courtney, SBS, p. 40.

6 Eric Newby, A Traveller's Life (London: Collins, 1982), pp. 106–43.

7 TNA, ADM 199/1922, HMS Utmost – Patrol Report for 12th Mediterranean War Patrol, 18 September to 3 October 1941.

8 TNA, ADM 236/37, HMS Truant – Patrol Report for 9th Mediterranean War Patrol, 18 October to 8 November 1941 (including Report of Special Operation, 26–27 October, by Lt R. A. Wilson).

9 Courtney, SBS, pp. 35–6.

CHAPTER 8

1 Quoted in Izzard, Gamp VC, p. 89.

2 TNA, DEFE 2/349, Supplementary Report of Operation 'Flipper' by Lieut. Col. R. E. Laycock; History of the 11th (Scottish) Commando at combinedops.com/Black%20Hackle.htm [accessed 24 January 2020]

3 Michael Asher, Get Rommel: the Secret British Mission to Kill Hitler's Greatest General (London: Weidenfeld & Nicolson, 2004; repr. 2005), pp. 170–1.

4 IWM, Documents 241, Private Papers of Colonel T. B. Langton, Box No. 88/48/1, Biography and T/s draft of Second World War Memoir 'One Among So Many'.

5 TNA, ADM 236/32, HMS *Torbay* – Report of 7th Mediterranean War Patrol, 10–24 November 1941; Chapman, *Submarine Torbay*, pp. 89–90; Asher, *Get Rommel*, pp. 181–8.

6 Supplementary Report of Operation 'Flipper' by Lieut. Col. Laycock; Asher, *Get Rommel*, p. 191.

7 Chapman, *Submarine Torbay*, p. 92; Asher, *Get Rommel*, pp. 192–3.

8 TNA, ADM 236/32, HMS *Talisman* – Report of 4th Mediterranean War Patrol, 10–20 November 1941 (Special Operation in Company with HMS *Torbay*); TNA, DEFE 2/349, Report of Operations 'Flipper' and 'Copper' by Capt. S. Raw, 10 February 1942.

9 Chapman, *Submarine Torbay*, p. 92.

10 Supplementary Report of Operation 'Flipper' by Lieut. Col. Laycock.

11 Report of Operations 'Flipper' and 'Copper' by Capt. S. Raw.

12 Supplementary Report of Operation 'Flipper' by Lieut. Col. Laycock.

CHAPTER 9

1 Supplementary Report of Operation 'Flipper' by Lieut. Col. Laycock.

2 Ibid.; HMS *Torbay* – Report of 7th Mediterranean War Patrol, 10–24 November, 1941.

3 Supplementary Report of Operation 'Flipper' by Lieut. Col. Laycock.

4 Ibid.; Lieutenant Pryor's account of his role in Operations 'Copper' and 'Flipper', at combinedops.com/Black%20Hackle.htm [accessed 24 January 2020].

5 Lieutenant Langton, quoted in Barrie Pitt, *Special Boat Squadron* (London: Century, 1983; repr. 2018), pp. 35–6; HMS *Torbay* – Report of 7th Mediterranean War Patrol, 10–24 November 1941.

6 Supplementary Report of Operation 'Flipper' by Lieut. Col. Laycock.

7   Ferguson, *The Watery Maze*, p. 105.

8   Churchill, *The Second World War*, III, p. 511.

9   TNA, WO 373/100, The Citation for the award of the DCM to Bombardier John Brittlebank, RA, for gallantry on 5 September 1942, by R. E. Laycock, Chief of Combined Operations.

CHAPTER 10

1   LHCMA, Montanaro Papers, Box 1, File 3, Minutes of meeting held at COHQ at 1500 hrs, 25.2.42, to discuss the forming of a Military Special Boat Section.

2   SBSAA, R. J. A. Courtney's Service Records and Documents, Letter from Major Courtney to Brig. Laycock, 12 August 1942.

3   Ewen Southby-Tailyour, *Blondie: A Life of Lieutenant Colonel H. G. Hasler* (London: Leo Cooper, 1998; repr. 2003), pp. 45–6, 49–50.

4   Minutes of meeting held at COHQ at 1500 hrs, 25.2.42, to discuss the forming of a Military Special Boat Section.

5   LHCMA, Montanaro Papers, Box 2, Montanaro Diary, 25 February 1942.

6   James Owen, *Commando: Winning World War II Behind Enemy Lines* (London: Little, Brown, 2012; repr. 2013), pp. 232–3; LHCMA, Montanaro Papers, Box 1, File 3, Report of Recce carried out by det. 101 Special Service Company between Gravelines and Calais on night 12/13 November 1941.

7   LHCMA, Montanaro Papers, Box 1, File 3, Montanaro to Brigadier Haydon, 17 November 1941.

8   LHCMA, Montanaro Papers, Box 1, File 3, Montanaro to Brigadier Haydon, 2 July 1941.

9   Montanaro Diary, 11 November 1941 and 18 February 1942.

10 Montanaro Diary, 25–26 February 1942.

11 TNA, DEFE 2/842, Courtney to Mountbatten, 9 March 1942.

12 Southby-Tailyour, *Blondie*, pp. 52–3.

13 TNA, DEFE 2/740, War Diary of Special Boat Section (Home) for April 1942 and Special Boat Section (Home) War Establishment, 30 March 1942.

14 Special Boat Section Memorandum – Formation to February 1944 by Lieut. Henry S. Quigley, Administrative Officer, at commando veterans.org/2SBS_timeline [accessed 5 February 2020].

15 PP, M. J. Beckett Papers, Stamford Tarlton-Weatherall's Biographical Details, 31 July 1995.

16 IWM, Private Papers of Lieutenant S. Weatherall, Documents 2088, Box No. 76/143/1, Typescript Memoirs, pp. 1–13.

CHAPTER 11

1 LHCMA, Montanaro Papers, Box 1, File 3, Report on Operations against the Enemy in Boulogne Harbour, night 11/12th April 1942 by Captain G. Montanaro; Montanaro Diary, 3, 4, 11 and 12 April 1942.

2 LHCMA, Montanaro Papers, Box 1, File 3, Montanaro to Lieut. General R. P. Pakenham-Walsh, 31 October 1950.

3 Report on Operations against the Enemy in Boulogne Harbour, night 11/12th April 1942 by Captain G. Montanaro; LHCMA, Montanaro Papers, Box 1, File 3, Montanaro to Lieut. General R. P. Pakenham-Walsh, 31 October 1950; Montanaro Diary, 12 April 1942.

4 'Landing Near Boulogne' and 'German Anxiety in Holland', The Times, 23 and 24 April 1942.

5 Montanaro Diary, 12 April 1942.

6 commandoveterans.org/GeraldMontanaro6Commando [accessed 29 December 2020]

7 'General Summary of Special Boat Section Activities Since Their Formation' by Major R. J. Courtney, 23 November 1943; LHCMA, Montanaro Papers, Box 1, File 3, Montanaro to Lieut. General R. P. Pakenham-Walsh, 10 September 1950.

8 Montanaro Diary, 18, 22–24 April 1942.

9 Strutton and Pearson, The Secret Invaders, p. 57.

10 unithistories.com/officers/Army_officers_C02.html [accessed 11 April 2020]; PP, M. J. Beckett Papers, E. J. A. Lunn to Mr Whittaker, 9 August 1973; Courtney, SBS, p. 107.

11 Courtney, SBS, pp. 107–9.

12   Email from Harriet O'Grady (daughter of Harry Holden-White) to the author, 14 September 2021; PP, Harry Holden-White, 'Goodbye to Old Hat', unpublished wartime memoir, Part I, Chapters 1–4.

13   Montanaro Diary, 28–29 April 1942.

14   Richard Branson, *Losing My Virginity* (London: Times Books, 1998), Chapter One: A family that would have killed for each other.

15   Courtney, *SBS*, pp. 109–10; Parker, *SBS*, pp. 77–8.

16   Courtney, *SBS*, p. 110.

17   Weatherall Memoirs, p. 176.

CHAPTER 12

1   TNA, DEFE 2/740, War Diary of Special Boat Section (Home), 25 May 1942.

2   Montanaro Diary, 30 May 1942.

3   Ibid., 15 June 1942.

4   TNA, ADM 236/32, HMS *Torbay* – Report of 8th Mediterranean War Patrol, 9–27 December 1941 (including Report of Folbot Operation by Officer in Charge).

5   Chapman, *Submarine Torbay*, p. 99.

6   Courtney, *SBS*, pp. 36–7.

7   Parker, *SBS*, p. 54.

8   TNA, ADM 358/681, C.-in-C. Mediterranean Fleet to Admiralty, 3 May 1942.

9   Courtney, *SBS*, p. 37.

10   TNA, ADM 199/1826, HMS P42 (*Unbroken*) – Report of 2nd Mediterranean War Patrol, 31 August to 13 September 1942.

11   Report by Captain R. Wilson on operation carried out from HMS/M P42 (*Unbroken*), 5/6 September 1942 in the harbour of Crotone, Italy, in Courtney, *SBS*, Appendix A, pp. 209–16.

12   HMS P42 (*Unbroken*) – Report of 2nd Mediterranean War Patrol, 31 August to 13 September 1942.

13   Captain Simpson to Captain Raw, HMS P42 (*Unbroken*), Patrol Report No. 2, 22 September 1942; TNA, ADM 199/1826, Appendix II to HMS P42 (*Unbroken*) – Report of 2nd Mediterranean War Patrol, 31 August to 13 September 1942.

14 Report by Captain R. Wilson, in Courtney, *SBS*, pp. 215–16.

15 Courtney, *SBS*, pp. 38–9.

16 The Citation for the award of the DCM to Bombardier John Brittlebank, RA, for gallantry on 5 September 1942, by R. E. Laycock.

CHAPTER 13

1 IWM, Sherwood Oral History, Reel 4.

2 Ben Macintyre, *SAS: Rogue Heroes* (London: Penguin, 2016; repr. 2017), pp. 157–62.

3 IWM, Sherwood Oral History, Reel 4.

4 Macintyre, *SAS: Rogue Heroes*, pp. 163–7; IWM, Sherwood Oral History, Reels 4 and 5.

5 Gavin Mortimer, *The SBS in World War II* (Oxford: Osprey, 2013), pp. 11–13; Macintyre, *SAS: Rogue Heroes*, p. 167.

6 Courtney, *SBS*, p. 40.

7 John Lodwick, *The Filibusters: The Story of the Special Boat Service* (London: Methuen & Co., 1947; repr. 2018), p. 38.

8 IWM, Sherwood Oral History, Reel 4.

9 Macintyre, *SAS: Rogue Heroes*, p. 193.

10 Courtney, *SBS*, p. 55.

11 Leroy Thompson, *SAS: Great Britain's Elite Special Air Service* (London: Zenith, 1994), p. 56.

12 Mortimer, *The SBS in World War II*, pp. 207–8.

13 *London Gazette* (Supplement), 4 September 1945, p. 4469.

CHAPTER 14

1 Mark W. Clark, *Calculated Risk: His Personal Story of the War in North Africa and Italy* (London: Harrap, 1951), pp. 71–7.

2 Ibid., pp. 78–80; David M. Key Jr, *Admiral Jerauld Wright: Warrior Among Diplomats* (Manhattan, KS: Sunflower University Press, 2001), pp. 140–1, 151.

3 Courtney, *SBS*, pp. 56–7.

4 Ibid., pp. 57–8.

5   Clark, *Calculated Risk*, pp. 80–1.

6   PP, M. J. Beckett Papers, Talk by Major J. P. Foot to the Dorchester Military Museum, 18 March 1978.

7   Courtney, *SBS*, pp. 58–9; Portsmouth, Royal Navy Submarine Museum (RNSM), A19991/379, Richard Livingstone, 'Mark Clark's Secret Landing', p. 1116.

8   Clark, *Calculated Risk*, pp. 83–4.

9   Ibid., pp. 83–94; Courtney, *SBS*, pp. 59–62; Livingstone, 'Mark Clark's Secret Landing', pp. 1115–19.

10 TNA, DEFE 2/531, Operation Reservist, Major General Mark W. Clark to Vice Admiral Lord Louis Mountbatten, 29 October 1942.

CHAPTER 15

1   TNA, ADM 199/1841, Patrol Reports of HM Submarines *Sceptre*, *Seraph* and *Sinoon*, 1942–1944.

2   Courtney, *SBS*, pp. 63–70; PP, Talk by Major J. P. Foot at the Dorchester Military Museum, 18 March 1978.

3   Dwight D. Eisenhower, *Crusade in Europe* (New York: Doubleday, 1948; repr. 1997), pp. 99–104.

CHAPTER 16

1   Strutton and Pearson, *The Secret Invaders*, pp. 51–8; Trenowden, *Stealthily by Night*, Chapter Six: Party Inhuman.

2   Strutton and Pearson, *The Secret Invaders*, pp. 75–9; Trenowden, *Stealthily by Night*, Chapter Six: Party Inhuman; ADM 199/1821, HMS P45 (*Unrivalled*) – Report of 1st Mediterranean War Patrol, 31 October to 18 November 1942; uboat.net/allies/merchants/ship/2398.html [accessed 24 February 2020].

3   Courtney, *SBS*, pp. 71–2.

4   Strutton and Pearson, *The Secret Invaders*, pp. 67–72.

5   Trenowden, *Stealthily by Night*, Chapter Six: Party Inhuman.

CHAPTER 17

1   TNA, DEFE 2/531, Report on Operation 'Reservist' by Lt E. J. A. Lunn, SBS, 30 November 1942.

2   TNA, DEFE 2/531, Report on Operation 'Reservist' by Captain H. Holden-White, SBS, 17 November 1942.

3   Michael Ashcroft, *Special Forces Heroes* (London: Headline, 2008), p. 78.

4   Rick Atkinson, *An Army at Dawn: The War in North Africa, 1942–1943* (New York: Macmillan USA, 2002; ebook 2003), Chapter Two: Landing.

5   Holden-White, 'Goodbye to Old Hat', Part II, Chapter 2.

6   Report on Operation 'Reservist' by Captain H. Holden-White.

7   Report on Operation 'Reservist' by Lt E. J. A. Lunn.

8   Parker, *SBS*, p. 82.

9   Report on Operation 'Reservist' by Captain H. Holden-White; Parker, *SBS*, pp. 82–3.

10 Atkinson, *An Army at Dawn*, Chapter Two: Landing.

11 Holden-White, 'Goodbye to Old Hat', Part II, Chapter 5.

12 Report on Operation 'Reservist' by Captain H. Holden-White.

13 Atkinson, *An Army at Dawn*, Chapter Two: Landing.

14 Report on Operation 'Reservist' by Captain H. Holden-White; Courtney, *SBS*, p. 74; Holden-White, 'Goodbye to Old Hat', Part II, Chapter 9.

15 Ashcroft, *Special Forces Heroes*, pp. 79–80.

16 Report on Operation 'Reservist' by Lt E. J. A. Lunn; TNA, DEFE 2/531, Report on Operation 'Reservist' by Lt J. C. C. Pagnam.

17 Report on Operation 'Reservist' by Captain H. Holden-White.

18 Atkinson, *An Army at Dawn*, Chapter Two: Landing.

19 Viscount Cunningham, *A Sailor's Odyssey* (London: Hutchinson, 1951), p. 489.

20 *London Gazette*, 14 May 1943.

21 Ashcroft, *Special Forces Heroes*, p. 80.

22 TNA, ADM 1/14319, Awards for Operation 'Reservist'.

23 Report on Operation 'Reservist' by Captain H. Holden-White;

Obituary of Major Eric Lunn, at gallery.commandoveterans.org/
cdoGallery/v/WW2/sbs/obituary+lunnmc628+copy.jpg.html
[accessed 24 April 2020]

24 Parker, *SBS*, pp. 85–6.
25 TNA, DEFE 2/531, Report of Officers taking part in Operation
    'Reservist', 1942.

CHAPTER 18

1 Southby-Tailyour, *Blondie*, pp. 1–38.
2 Ibid., pp. 42–65.
3 Quentin Rees, *Cockleshell Heroes: The Final Witness* (Stroud:
   Amberley, 2010), pp. 162–4.
4 Ibid., pp. 169–71.
5 Southby-Tailyour, *Blondie*, pp. 67–8.
6 William Sparks, *The Last of the Cockleshell Heroes* (London: Leo
   Cooper, 1992), pp. 2–4.
7 Ibid., pp. 6–22.
8 Ibid., pp. 25–9.
9 Ibid., pp. 30–2.

CHAPTER 19

1 Southby-Tailyour, *Blondie*, pp. 70–1, 77–8.
2 TNA, DEFE 2/218, Operation 'Frankton', Minutes of Search
   Committee held at COHQ on 27 July 1942.
3 Southby-Tailyour, *Blondie*, pp. 78–80.
4 Ibid., p. 80; SBSAA, No. 69, Operation 'Frankton', Detailed
   Report by Military Force Commander [Major Hasler], 8 April
   1943.
5 TNA, DEFE 2/218, Operation 'Frankton', Summary of Outline
   Plan, 29 October 1942.
6 Southby-Tailyour, *Blondie*, pp. 82–3.
7 Ibid., p. 83.
8 TNA, DEFE, 2/218, Operation 'Frankton', Extract from the

Minutes of a Meeting of the Chiefs of Staff Committee, 3 November 1942.

9   Southby-Tailyour, *Blondie*, pp. 82–5.

10   Sparks, *The Last of the Cockleshell Heroes*, p. 35.

11   Rees, *Cockleshell Heroes*, p. 184.

12   Sparks, *The Last of the Cockleshell Heroes*, p. 35; Rees, *Cockleshell Heroes*, p. 178.

13   Sparks, *The Last of the Cockleshell Heroes*, p. 35.

14   Ibid., p. 35.

15   Rees, *Cockleshell Heroes*, p. 34.

16   Sparks, *The Last of the Cockleshell Heroes*, p. 33.

17   Ibid., p. 39.

18   Rees, *Cockleshell Heroes*, pp. 34–5; Sparks, *The Last of the Cockleshell Heroes*, p. 40.

CHAPTER 20

1   Quoted in Rees, *Cockleshell Heroes*, pp. 174–5.

2   Ibid., pp. 41–2.

3   Sparks, *The Last of the Cockleshell Heroes*, pp. 45–6.

4   Rees, *Cockleshell Heroes*, pp. 47–8.

5   Sparks, *The Last of the Cockleshell Heroes*, pp. 46–7.

6   Rees, *Cockleshell Heroes*, p. 48.

7   Ibid., p. 168.

8   Sparks, *The Last of the Cockleshell Heroes*, p. 50.

9   TNA, DEFE, 2/218, Operation 'Frankton', Report submitted to the Flag Officer by the Commanding Officer, HMS *Tuna*.

10   Rees, *Cockleshell Heroes*, p. 56.

11   Operation 'Frankton', Report submitted to the Flag Officer by the Commanding Officer, HMS *Tuna*.

12   Sparks, *The Last of the Cockleshell Heroes*, pp. 51–2; Rees, *Cockleshell Heroes*, pp. 63–4; Southby-Tailyour, *Blondie*, pp. 93, 102; Operation 'Frankton', Report submitted to the Flag Officer by the Commanding Officer, HMS *Tuna*.

CHAPTER 21

1 Operation 'Frankton', Detailed Report by Military Force Commander, 8 April 1943.

2 Sparks, *The Last of the Cockleshell Heroes*, pp. 52–3.

3 Operation 'Frankton', Detailed Report by Military Force Commander, 8 April 1943.

4 Sparks, *The Last of the Cockleshell Heroes*, pp. 53–4; Operation 'Frankton', Detailed Report by Military Force Commander, 8 April 1943.

5 Operation 'Frankton', Detailed Report by Military Force Commander, 8 April 1943.

6 Sparks, *The Last of the Cockleshell Heroes*, p. 54.

7 Operation 'Frankton', Detailed Report by Military Force Commander, 8 April 1943.

8 Sparks, *The Last of the Cockleshell Heroes*, pp. 54–5.

9 Operation 'Frankton', Detailed Report by Military Force Commander, 8 April 1943.

10 Sparks, *The Last of the Cockleshell Heroes*, pp. 55–6; Operation 'Frankton', Detailed Report by Military Force Commander, 8 April 1943.

11 Sparks, *The Last of the Cockleshell Heroes*, pp. 56, 59; Operation 'Frankton', Detailed Report by Military Force Commander, 8 April 1943.

12 Sparks, *The Last of the Cockleshell Heroes*, pp. 60–8; Operation 'Frankton', Detailed Report by Military Force Commander, 8 April 1943.

CHAPTER 22

1 Operation 'Frankton', Detailed Report by Military Force Commander, 8 April 1943; Sparks, *The Last of the Cockleshell Heroes*, pp. 68–9.

2 Sparks, *The Last of the Cockleshell Heroes*, pp. 43, 69.

3 Operation 'Frankton', Detailed Report by Military Force

Commander, 8 April 1943; Sparks, *The Last of the Cockleshell Heroes*, p. 69.

4 Operation 'Frankton', Detailed Report by Military Force Commander, 8 April 1943; Sparks, *The Last of the Cockleshell Heroes*, pp. 69–73; Rees, *Cockleshell Heroes*, pp. 83–9.

5 Rees, *Cockleshell Heroes*, p. 61; SBSAA, No. 69, Major Hasler's Post-Operation 'Frankton' Debrief by MI9, April 1943.

6 Major Hasler's Post-Operation 'Frankton' Debrief by MI9, April 1943.

7 TNA, DEFE, 2/218, Operation 'Frankton', 'Alleged War Crimes – Murder of Survivors of Operations against Shipping in Bordeaux on 7 December 1942', Lt Col. Hasler to J.A.G's Branch (War Crimes Section), 1 December 1945.

8 Major Hasler's Post-Operation 'Frankton' Debrief by MI9, April 1943; Sparks, *The Last of the Cockleshell Heroes*, pp. 74–85.

9 Rees, *Cockleshell Heroes*, p.132.

10 Major Hasler's Post-Operation 'Frankton' Debrief by MI9, April 1943; Sparks, *The Last of the Cockleshell Heroes*, pp. 99, 109, 140.

CHAPTER 23

1 SBSAA, No. 69, Operation 'Frankton', Mountbatten to the Secretary of the Admiralty, 29 April 1943.

2 TNA, DEFE, 2/218, Operation 'Frankton', Interim Report by COHQ, 23 February 1943.

3 TNA, DEFE, 2/218, Naval Intelligence Department Inquiry Regarding Results of Operation 'Frankton', 12 July 1946.

4 Rees, *Cockleshell Heroes*, pp. 175–6; Sparks, *The Last of the Cockleshell Heroes*, pp. 143–4.

5 Paddy Ashdown, *A Brilliant Little Operation: The Cockleshell Heroes and the Most Courageous Raid of WW2* (London: Aurum, 2012), pp. 323–4.

6 TNA, DEFE, 2/218, Operation 'Frankton', German High Command's 'Counter-Action to Kharkov Fake Trial', 12 January 1944.

7   NAM, 9203–218–111–1, Typescript translation of the 'Führer Befehl', Hitler's Commando Order of 18 October 1942.

8   Rees, *Cockleshell Heroes*, pp. 93–8.

9   Ibid., pp. 101–6.

10 Ibid., pp. 107–17, 169.

11 Ibid., pp. 117–18.

12 TNA, DEFE 2/218, Operation 'Frankton', Mountbatten to the Secretary of the Admiralty (Honours and Awards Branch), 7 and 13 May 1943.

13 Sparks, *The Last of the Cockleshell Heroes*, pp. 143–6.

CHAPTER 24

1   Strutton and Pearson, *The Secret Invaders*, pp. 80–1.

2   TNA, DEFE 2/971, COPP Organisation 1942–45, Information Required from a Combined Operations Beach and Pilotage Reconnaissance Party (or COPP for short), 31 December 1942.

3   TNA, DEFE 2/1116, COPP Reports and History, War Diary: Outline History of the COPP, 26 November 1943.

4   Strutton and Pearson, *The Secret Invaders*, pp. 81–2.

5   Lieutenant Noel Wilson Cooper RNVR, The King's School, Canterbury's Roll of Honour, hambo.org/kingscanterbury/view_man.php?id=28 [accessed 31 March 2020].

6   veterans.gc.ca/eng/remembrance/memorials/canadian-virtual-war-memorial/detail/2069361 [accessed 31 March 2020].

7   TNA, DEFE 2/971, COPP Organisation 1942–45, Willmott to COHQ, 29 December 1942.

8   Strutton and Pearson, *The Secret Invaders*, pp. 83–7.

9   SBSAA, Serial No. 71, Peter Palmer, 'Algeria & Malta – 1943 – COPPs 3 & 4'.

10 Peter F. Palmer, 'Royal Navy Service from November 1941 to June 1946', coppheroes.org/individuals/palmer-p.htm [accessed 13 September 2019].

11 Palmer, 'Algeria & Malta – 1943 – COPPs 3 & 4'.

12 Ibid.

13 Andrew Roberts, *Masters and Commanders: How Roosevelt, Churchill, Marshall and Alanbrooke Won the War in the West* (London: Allen Lane, 2008), pp. 334–5.

14 Strutton and Pearson, *The Secret Invaders*, p. 94.

15 TNA, DEFE 2/1116, Notes on ME COPPs, 1943.

16 southafricawargraves.org/search/print.php?id=5336 and maltagc70. wordpress.com/tag/hms-st-angelo/ [both accessed 31 March 2020].

17 Strutton and Pearson, *The Secret Invaders*, p. 95.

CHAPTER 25

1   Strutton and Pearson, *The Secret Invaders*, 97; Trenowden, *Stealthily by Night*, Chapter Twelve: Sicily – The First Serious Losses.

2   TNA, DEFE 2/1111, COPP Progress Report No. 1 by Lieut. Commander Willmott, 6 February 1943.

3   TNA, ADM 199/1826, Patrol Report No. 7 of HMS *Unbending* by Lieutenant Stanley, 27 February to 6 March 1943.

4   TNA, ADM 199/1826, Captain Phillips to Vice Admiral Malta, 11 March 1943.

5   Patrol Report No. 7 of HMS *Unbending* by Lieutenant Stanley, 27 February to 6 March 1943.

6   Captain Phillips to Vice Admiral Malta, 11 March 1943.

7   Patrol Report No. 7 of HMS *Unbending* by Lieutenant Stanley, 27 February to 6 March 1943.

8   Captain Phillips to Vice Admiral Malta, 11 March 1943.

9   TNA, ADM 199/1820, Patrol Report No. 11 of HMS *United* by Lieutenant Roxburgh, 27 February to 10 March 1943.

10 Strutton and Pearson, *The Secret Invaders*, pp. 107–13.

11 Patrol Report No. 11 of HMS *United* by Lieutenant Roxburgh, 27 February to 10 March 1943.

12 Strutton and Pearson, *The Secret Invaders*, pp. 113–14.

13 Ibid., pp. 114–15.

14 Ibid., pp. 90–1.

15 TNA, DEFE 2/1116, COPP Reports and History, Willmott to Mountbatten, 29 April 1943.

16 TNA, DEFE 2/1116, COPP Reports and History, Lt Smith to DCO
    (Middle East), 23 March 1943.
17 Strutton and Pearson, *The Secret Invaders*, p. 128.

CHAPTER 26

1   Ralph Neville [Stanbury], *Survey by Starlight: A true story of
    reconnaissance work in the Mediterranean* (London: Hodder &
    Stoughton, 1949), pp. 13–22.
2   Ibid., pp. 24–39.

CHAPTER 27

1   Neville, *Survey by Starlight*, pp. 41–4.
2   TNA, DEFE 2/1111, COPP Progress Report No. 11 by Lieut.
    Commander Willmott, 18 April 1943.
3   Neville, *Survey by Starlight*, pp. 44–52.
4   Ibid., pp. 52–9.
5   Ibid., pp. 59–61.
6   Ibid., pp. 62–3.

CHAPTER 28

1   Neville, *Survey by Starlight*, pp. 64, 68–9.
2   Churchill, *The Second World War*, V, p. 24.
3   Neville, *Survey by Starlight*, pp. 69–91; Trenowden, *Stealthily by
    Night*, Chapter Thirteen: COPP5 and COPP6 in the Mediterranean.
4   John Grehan and Martin Mace (eds), *The War in Italy 1943–1944:
    Despatches from the Front* (Barnsley: Pen & Sword, 2014), p. 36.
5   Cunningham, *A Sailor's Odyssey*, p. 557.
6   TNA, DEFE 2/1111, Honours and Awards for Various COPP
    Personnel 1943–5.
7   TNA, DEFE 2/1111, COPP Progress Report No. 26 by Lieut.
    Commander Willmott, 1 August 1943.

CHAPTER 29

1 Churchill, *The Second World War*, V, pp. 65–6.

2 Ibid., pp. 66–76.

3 Trenowden, *Stealthily by Night*, Chapter Sixteen: Festung Europa.

4 Robert Lyman, *The Real X-Men: The Heroic Story of the Underwater War 1942–1945* (London: Quercus, 2015), pp. 110–15, 138–9.

5 'Occasional Paper 46: Lieutenant Kenneth Robert Hudspeth DSC, RANVR', Naval Historical Society of Australia, at navyhistory.org.au/occasional-paper-46-lieutenant-kenneth-robert-hudspeth-dsc-ranvr/ [accessed 9 April 2020]; Lyman, *The Real X-Men*, p. 151.

6 'Occasional Paper 46: Lieutenant Kenneth Robert Hudspeth DSC, RANVR'; Lyman, *The Real X-Men*, pp. 152–86, 291.

7 'Occasional Paper 46: Lieutenant Kenneth Robert Hudspeth DSC, RANVR'.

8 Churchill, *The Second World War*, V, pp. 233–4.

9 TNA, DEFE 2/1111, COPP Progress Report Nos 29, 30, 32.

10 TNA, DEFE 2/1059, 'Employment of X-craft X20–X25', The Admiral (Submarines) to the Secretary of the Admiralty, 23 October 1943.

11 COPP Progress Report No. 33 (Week ending 18 September 1943).

12 Major General L. Scott-Bowden, 'COPP to Normandy 1943/44 – A Personal Account of Part of the Story', in the *Royal Engineers Journal*, 108/1 (April 1944), 10–18 (p. 14).

13 Scott-Bowden, 'COPP to Normandy 1943/44', p. 14.

14 Strutton and Pearson, *The Secret Invaders*, pp. 142–3.

15 Scott-Bowden, 'COPP to Normandy 1943/44', pp. 14–15.

16 Strutton and Pearson, *The Secret Invaders*, p. 133; David Howarth, *Dawn of D-Day* (London: Companion Book Club, 1959), p. 193; Brian Lett, *The Small Scale Raiding Force* (Barnsley: Pen & Sword, 2013), pp. 31, 106–18.

17 Ken Hudspeth, 'X-craft: X20 in the English Channel', *Naval Historical Review*, September 1944, in navyhistory.org.au/x-craft-x20–in-the-english-channel/ [accessed 9 October 2019].

18 TNA, DEFE 2/1059, 'Capabilities of COPP in X-craft', Willmott to Chief of Combined Operations, 15 December 1943.

19 TNA, DEFE 2/1059, Minutes of Meeting held at COHQ on 4 December 1943 to Discuss the Technique to be Employed in Beach Reconnaissance by COPP in Operation 'Overlord'.

CHAPTER 30

1 Scott-Bowden, 'COPP to Normandy 1943/44', p. 15.
2 TNA, ADM 179/354, Minutes of a Meeting Held at Fort Blockhouse, Gosport, on 30 December 1943.
3 TNA, ADM 179/354, Operation 'KJH', 30 December 1943.
4 TNA, ADM 179/354, Narrative Report on Operation 'KJH' by Lieut. Commander Willmott, 2 January 1944.
5 Scott-Bowden, 'COPP to Normandy 1943/44', p. 16.
6 Narrative Report on Operation 'KJH' by Lieut. Commander Willmott, 2 January 1944.
7 Strutton and Pearson, *The Secret Invaders*, p. 180.
8 Narrative Report on Operation 'KJH' by Lieut. Commander Willmott, 2 January 1944.
9 TNA, ADM 179/354, Condensed Beach Report by Major Scott-Bowden, 2 January 1944.
10 TNA, ADM 179/354, Admiral Little to Admiral Ramsay, 7 January 1944.
11 TNA, ADM 179/354, Admiral Ramsay to Rear Admiral Vian, 17 January 1944.

CHAPTER 31

1 Scott-Bowden, 'COPP to Normandy 1943/44', p. 10.
2 Strutton and Pearson, *The Secret Invaders*, p. 185.
3 TNA, ADM 179/323, COPP 1 Report on Operation 'Postage Able' by Lieut. Commander Willmott, 31 January 1944, Section I: 'Narrative', p. 1; Hudspeth, 'X-craft: *X20* in the English Channel'.
4 Hudspeth, 'X-craft: *X20* in the English Channel'.
5 Scott-Bowden, 'COPP to Normandy 1943/44', pp. 10–11.
6 COPP 1 Report on Operation 'Postage Able', Section I: 'Narrative', p. 3.

7   Scott-Bowden, 'COPP to Normandy 1943/44', pp. 11–12.

8   COPP 1 Report on Operation 'Postage Able', Section V: 'General Military Intelligence', p. 2.

9   COPP 1 Report on Operation 'Postage Able', Section I: 'Narrative', p. 3.

10 Scott-Bowden, 'COPP to Normandy 1943/44', p. 12.

11 COPP 1 Report on Operation 'Postage Able', Section III: 'Swimmers Narrative', p. 1.

12 Scott-Bowden, 'COPP to Normandy 1943/44', p. 12.

13 COPP 1 Report on Operation 'Postage Able', Section I: 'Narrative', pp. 3–4.

14 COPP 1 Report on Operation 'Postage Able', Section III: 'Swimmers Narrative', pp. 1–2; Scott-Bowden, 'COPP to Normandy 1943/44', p. 13; Strutton and Pearson, *The Secret Invaders*, p. 189.

15 COPP 1 Report on Operation 'Postage Able', Section I: 'Narrative', p. 4.

16 Scott-Bowden, 'COPP to Normandy 1943/44', pp. 12–13; COPP 1 Report on Operation 'Postage Able', 'Section I: Narrative', p. 5.

17 COPP 1 Report on Operation 'Postage Able', Section V: 'General Military Intelligence', pp. 2–3.

18 COPP 1 Report on Operation 'Postage Able', Section I: 'Narrative', p. 5.

19 COPP 1 Report on Operation 'Postage Able', Section III: 'Swimmers Narrative', p. 2.

20 Scott-Bowden, 'COPP to Normandy 1943/44', p. 13.

21 COPP 1 Report on Operation 'Postage Able', Section III: 'Swimmers Narrative', p. 2.

22 COPP 1 Report on Operation 'Postage Able', Section I: 'Narrative', p. 6; Section V: 'General Military Intelligence', pp. 2–3; Section V, Appendix A: 'Notes on Periscope Observations', pp. 2–3; Section IV: 'Beach Report', p. 2.

23 COPP 1 Report on Operation 'Postage Able', Section V: 'General Military Intelligence', pp. 2–3.

24 COPP 1 Report on Operation 'Postage Able', Section I: 'Narrative', p. 7.

25 Scott-Bowden, 'COPP to Normandy 1943/44', p. 13; COPP 1 Report on Operation 'Postage Able', Section I: 'Narrative', p. 7.

26 Scott-Bowden, 'COPP to Normandy 1943/44', pp. 13–14; COPP 1 Report on Operation 'Postage Able', Section, Part I: 'Condensed Report', p. 1.

27 Stephen E. Ambrose, *The Supreme Commander: The War Years of Dwight D. Eisenhower* (New York: Random House, 1969; repr. 2012), pp. 336–7; Scott-Bowden, 'COPP to Normandy 1943/44', p. 14.

28 COPP 1 Report on Operation 'Postage Able', Section I: 'Narrative', p. 8.

29 Hudspeth, 'X-craft: X20 in the English Channel'.

30 TNA, ADM 179/323, Admiral Little to Admiral Ramsay, Report on Operation 'Postage Able', 7 February 1944.

31 *London Gazette* (Supplement), 4 April 1944 (p. 1557) and 15 June 1944 (p. 2854)

32 Strutton and Pearson, *The Secret Invaders*, p. 199.

33 Field Marshal Viscount Montgomery of Alamein, *Memoirs of Field Marshal Montgomery* (London: Collins, 1958), Chapter 10: Alamein to Tunis.

34 Strutton and Pearson, *The Secret Invaders*, pp. 199–200.

CHAPTER 32

1 Author interview with Jim Booth, 11 October 2019.

2 Max Hastings, *All Hell Let Loose: The World at War 1939–1945* (London: HarperPress, 2011), p. 533.

3 TNA, ADM 179/475, Operation 'Gambit', Operation Order, 24 May 1944; TNA, ADM 179/475, Report on Operation 'Gambit', 9 June 1944.

4 Author interview with Jim Booth, 11 October 2019.

5 Scott-Bowden, 'COPP to Normandy 1943/44', p. 17.

6 TNA, DEFE 2/1116, Report of Proceedings of COPP 6, Sword Area, Queen Sector, 13 June 1944.

7 Author interview with Jim Booth, 11 October 2019; TNA, DEFE 2/1111, COPP Progress Reports 41 and 42 (weeks ending 14 and 21 November 1943); Howarth, *Dawn of D-Day*, p. 198.

8 ADM 179/475, Reports on Operation 'Gambit' by the Commanding Officers of HM Submarines X20 and X23, 7 and 9 June 1944; Lyman, *The Real X-Men*, pp. 223–4; Strutton and Pearson, *The Secret Invaders*, pp. 204–6; Author interview with Jim Booth, 11 October 2019.

9 TNA, ADM 179/475, Operation 'Gambit' – Operation Order, 24 May 1944.

10 Author interview with Jim Booth, 11 October 2019.

11 Strutton and Pearson, *The Secret Invaders*, p. 209; Report on Operation 'Gambit' by the Commanding Officer of HM Submarine X23, 9 June 1944; Operation 'Gambit' – Operation Order, 24 May 1944.

CHAPTER 33

1 Author interview with Jim Booth, 11 October 2019.

2 TNA, DEFE 2/1116, Operation 'Overlord-Neptune' – Report of Proceedings of COPP 6, Sword Area, Queen Sector, by Lieut. Commander Amer, 13 June 1944, Appendix A: Lt Wild's Report.

3 Operation 'Overlord-Neptune' – Report of Proceedings of COPP 6 by Lieut. Commander Amer.

4 Appendix A: Lt Wild's Report; 'Operation Overlord-Neptune' – Report of Proceedings of COPP 6 by Lieut. Commander Amer: Appendix B: Captain Mackenzie's Report; Obituary of Colonel I. C. C. Mackenzie, the *Royal Engineers Journal*, 83/3 (September 1968), pp. 210–12.

5 Operation Overlord-Neptune – Report of Proceedings of COPP 6 by Lieut. Commander Amer.

6 SBSAA, Serial No. 11, Transcription of interview with Lt Donald G. W. Slater, COPP 6, undated.

7 Author interview with Jim Booth, 11 October 2019.

8 Hudspeth, 'X-craft: X20 in the English Channel'; Strutton and Pearson, *The Secret Invaders*, pp. 210–11.

9 Strutton and Pearson, *The Secret Invaders*, pp. 212–14.

10 Scott-Bowden, 'COPP to Normandy 1943/44', pp. 17–18; Howarth, *Dawn of D-Day*, pp. 141–51.

11 Strutton and Pearson, *The Secret Invaders*, pp. 216–17.

12 Howarth, *Dawn of D-Day*, pp. 150–1.

13 Antony Beevor, *D-Day: The Battle for Normandy* (London: Viking, 2009), p. 95.

14 Scott-Bowden, 'COPP to Normandy 1943/44', p. 18.

15 Howarth, *Dawn of D-Day*, pp. 160–2.

16 Scott-Bowden, 'COPP to Normandy 1943/44', p. 18.

17 'D-Day landings: Operation Overlord in numbers', *Daily Telegraph*, 6 June 2016; dday.org/june-6-1944/.

18 Churchill, *The Second World War*, VI, p. 5.

19 ADM 179/354, Admiral Ramsay to Captain (S), 5th Submarine Flotilla, Portsmouth, 18 June 1944.

20 Sir Philip Vian, *Action this Day: A War Memoir* (London: Frederick Muller, 1960), pp. 137–8.

21 *London Gazette* (Supplement), 14 and 28 November 1944; author interview with Jim Booth, 11 October 2019.

CHAPTER 34

1 Southby-Tailyour, *Blondie*, p. 132; SBSAA, Captain Derek Oakley, *Behind Japanese Lines: The Untold Story of the Royal Marine Detachment 385* (Portsmouth: Privately Published, 1996), p. 7.

2 Southby-Tailyour, *Blondie*, pp. 133–4.

3 Strutton and Pearson, *The Secret Invaders*, p. 223; Geoffrey Hall, *Sailor's Luck: At Sea & Ashore in Peace & War* (Durham: The Memoir Club, 1999), pp. 72–84.

4 specialforcesroh.com/showthread.php?40533–Kealy-Michael-Robert-Bayley [accessed 23 April 2020]; Special Boat Section Memorandum – Formation to February 1944 by Lieut. Henry S. Quigley.

5 Courtney, *SBS*, pp. 143–5.

6 PP, M. J. Beckett Papers, E. J. A. Lunn to Mr Whittaker, 9 August 1973.

7 Courtney, *SBS*, p. 145.

8 PP. M. J. Beckett Papers, Gruff Courtney to Leonard Whittaker, 28 May and 20 June 1984.

9   SBSAA, Service Records and Documents of Major R. J. A. Courtney; Courtney, *SBS*, p. 146.

10 Hall, *Sailor's Luck*, pp. 83–4.

11 Ibid., p. 84.

12 Oakley, *Behind Japanese Lines*, p. 8; SBSAA, Serial No. 63, RM Detachment 385 Diary, Section I.

CHAPTER 35

1   Gavin Mortimer, *The SBS in World War II* (Oxford: Osprey, 2013), pp. 98–104.

2   Churchill, *The Second World War*, V, pp. 196–8.

3   TNA, HS7/26, Appreciation of Operation 'Sunbeam A' by Captain S. Hannah, RM, 20 October 1944.

4   TNA, HS7/26, Report of Operation 'Sunbeam A', 17/18 June 1944, by Lieut. J. F. Richards, RM.

5   TNA, HS7/26, Appreciation of Operation 'Sunbeam A' by Captain W. Pritchard-Gordon, RM.

6   TNA, HS7/26, Report of Operation 'Sunbeam A', 17/18 June 1944, by Lieut. J. F. Richards, RM.

7   TNA, HS7/26, Reports of Operation 'Sunbeam A', 17/18 June 1944, by Lieut. J. F. Richards, Sergeant J. M. King and Corporal E. W. Horner.

8   TNA, HS7/26, Captain Pritchard-Gordon to the Commander, Raiding Forces, MEF, 28 June 1944.

9   Appreciation of Operation 'Sunbeam A' by Captain W. Pritchard-Gordon.

10 TNA, HS7/26, DDOD to Commanding Officer, HMS *Mount Stewart*, 18 May 1945; Rees, *Cockleshell Heroes*, p. 190.

CHAPTER 36

1   TNA, DEFE 2/569, 'Spratt Baker' Operation Order, undated; Philip Ziegler, *Mountbatten* (London: Collins, 1985), p. 261.

2   gallery.commandoveterans.org/cdoGallery/v/WW2/sbs/Capt+dougl as+sidders+MC++2+sbs++jr.jpg.html [accessed 29 April 2020].

3   TNA, DEFE 2/569, Demolition Plan for Peudada Bridge, undated; Courtney, *SBS*, p. 178.

4   commandoveterans.org/EdwardWesleySBS [accessed 1 May 2020]; *London Gazette* (Supplement), 4 January 1944.

5   TNA, DEFE 2/569, Report on Operation 'Spratt Baker', 11–13 September 1944, by Major Sidders.

6   Diary of Lieutenant Wesley, quoted in Courtney, *SBS*, pp. 179–80.

7   Report on Operation 'Spratt Baker', 11–13 September 1944, by Major Sidders; Diary of Lieutenant Wesley, quoted in Courtney, *SBS*, pp. 179–83; Spratt Baker Operation Order, undated.

8   Report on Operation 'Spratt Baker', 11–13 September 1944, by Major Sidders; Diary of Lieutenant Wesley, quoted in Courtney, *SBS*, pp. 183–91; TNA, ADM 199/1865, HMS *Trenchant* – Patrol Report, 5 September to 1 October 1944.

CHAPTER 37

1   IWM, Box No. 98/1/1, Private Papers of Captain A. F. L. Colson MBE, 'Double Handle: The Story of an unsuccessful operation in Burma which took place during October, 1944', pp. 7–8.

2   Strutton and Pearson, *The Secret Invaders*, p. 225.

3   Trenowden, *Stealthily by Night*, Chapter Eighteen: How did one get into COPP?; SBSAA, Service Records and Documents of Major R. J. A. Courtney, Report on Injuries, 13 August 1943.

4   Hall, *Sailor's Luck*, p. 86; Colson, 'Double Handle', pp. 9, 13.

5   IWM, Box No. 98/1/1, Private Papers of Captain A. F. L Colson MBE, 'Operation "David" – Narrative of Events' by Lieutenant Ponsonby; Colson, 'Double Handle', pp. 6, 18–23.

6   'Operation "David" – Narrative of Events' by Lieutenant Ponsonby; Colson, 'Double Handle', pp. 1, 8, 23–31.

CHAPTER 38

1   Colson, 'Double Handle', pp. 31–41.

2   *London Gazette* (Supplement), 20 February 1945 and 22 March 1945; IWM, Box No. 98/1/1, Private Papers of Captain A. F. L. Colson

MBE, 'Recommendation for Award for Operation "David"; unithi stories.com/officers/Army_officers_C02.html [accessed 6 May 2020].

3   Strutton and Pearson, *The Secret Invaders*, pp. 226–35; PP, Mike Peacock Papers, Written Account of His Release from Captivity.

4   forces-war-records.co.uk/prisoners-of-war-of-the-japanese-1939-1945 [accessed 6 May 2020].

5   TNA, HS 1/254, Report on Interrogation of Korean guards by Lieutenant Colonel L. F. G. Pritchard and Major C. H. D. Wild, 14 October 1945; 'Missing Personnel of Clandestine Party from Australia', Lieut. Col. Ritchard to Flag Officer Malaya, 18 October 1945.

CHAPTER 39

1   Trenowden, *Stealthily by Night*, Chapter 26: COPP 3(1) under Alex Hughes.

2   Lieutenant Commander Ian Alcock, 'Lost In Malaya – With A Price On Our Heads', *Edmonton Journal*, Weekend Magazine, 5 January 1963, pp. 2–5.

3   IWM, 93/1/1, Private Papers of Lieutenant Commander A. I. Hughes DSC, Diary: 10 October 1944.

4   Ibid., 7 October 1944.

5   Alcock, 'Lost In Malaya', pp. 2–5.

6   A. I. Hughes Diary: 16 October 1944.

7   Ibid., 5 January 1945.

8   Ibid., 14 January 1945.

9   *London Gazette* (Supplement), 10 July and 23 October 1945; unithistories.com/officers/Army_officers_J01.html [accessed 12 May 2020].

10 A. I. Hughes Diary: January 1944 (Captain Johns).

11 Alcock, 'Lost In Malaya', p. 4.

12 TNA, DEFE 2/95, Report on 'Operation Baboon' by Lieutenant Alexander Hughes, 23 March 1945; Appendix A, 'Report on the Loss of the Military Reconnaissance Party' by Lieutenant Alexander Hughes, 23 March 1945; A. I. Hughes Diary: 9 March 1944.

13 A. I. Hughes Diary: 12 March 1944.

14 TNA, DEFE 2/95, Operational recommendations for Decorations in respect of personnel of COPP 3 by Lieutenant Alexander Hughes, 23 April 1945.

15 TNA, DEFE 2/95, Report on Operation 'Baboon' as told to Major I. C. C. Mackenzie, RE, by Flight Lieutenant N. H. Guthrie, DFM, RAF; Trenowden, *Stealthily by Night*, Appendix 4: Operation 'Baboon' Cover Story.

CHAPTER 40

1   TNA, DEFE 2/95, Report on Operation 'Copywright' by Lieutenant Colonel G. W. Ross, 24 April 1945.

2   unithistories.com/officers/RM_officersM.html [accessed 13 May 2020]; Southby-Tailyour, *Blondie*, p. 154n.

3   TNA, DEFE 2/95, Operation 'Copywright' Outline Plan by Colonel Tollemache, 17 February 1945.

4   TNA, DEFE 2/95, Report on Operation 'Copywright' by Major I. C. C. Mackenzie, undated; Report on Operation 'Copywright' by Corporal R. A. Atkinson, 13 September 1945.

5   Strutton and Pearson, *The Secret Invaders*, pp. 261–3.

6   Report on Operation 'Copywright' by Major I. C. C. Mackenzie, Appendix A: Compromise; TNA, ADM 236/31, HMS *Thrasher*: Report on Operation 'Copywright' by Lieut. Commander M. Ainslie.

7   SBSAA, Serial No. 63, RM Detachment 385 Diary, Operation 'Copywright'.

8   Report on Operation Copywright by Lieutenant Colonel G. W. Ross.

9   Southby-Tailyour, *Blondie*, p. 153.

10 SBSAA, Serial No. 63, RM Detachment 385 Diary, Operation 'Copywright'.

11 SBSAA, Serial No. 45, Copy of Report Extracted from HQ Malaya Command Intelligence Summary: Suicide of Japanese Officers at Rengam.

CHAPTER 41

1   Alcock, 'Lost In Malaya', p. 4; Ziegler, *Mountbatten*, pp. 278–9.

2   Ziegler, *Mountbatten*, pp. 279–80, 291–2.

3   Ibid., pp. 297–8.

4   Alcock, 'Lost In Malaya', p. 4.

5   IWM, 93/1/1, Private Papers of Lieut. Commander A. I. Hughes, Operation 'Confidence' Detailed Plan, 31 May 1945; Report on Operation 'Confidence' by Lieut. Hughes, RNR, 16 June 1945; A. I. Hughes Diary: 4 June 1945.

6   Alcock, 'Lost In Malaya', p. 4; A. I. Hughes Diary: 10 October 1944 and 21 January and April 1945.

7   Alcock, 'Lost In Malaya', pp. 3–4.

8   A. I. Hughes Diary: 8 May and 4 June 1945.

9   Alcock, 'Lost In Malaya', p. 3.

10 A. I. Hughes Diary: 4 June 1945.

11 Ibid., 6 June 1945.

12 Alcock, 'Lost In Malaya', p. 4.

13 TNA, ADM 236/15, HMS *Seadog* – Report of 19th War Patrol by Lt E. A. Hobson, 17 June 1945; Alcock, 'Lost In Malaya', p. 4.

14 A. I. Hughes Diary: 12 June 1945.

15 Alcock, 'Lost In Malaya', p. 4.

16 A. I. Hughes Diary: 12 June 1945; Report on Operation 'Confidence' by Lieut. Hughes, RNR, 16 June 1945.

CHAPTER 42

1   IWM, 93/1/1, Private Papers of Lieut. Commander A. I. Hughes, Report of Personnel of COPP 3 who were unable to contact HMS *Seadog* during Operation 'Confidence' by Lieut. Alcock, 6 November 1945; Alcock, 'Lost In Malaya', pp. 4–5.

2   Report of Personnel of COPP 3 who were unable to contact HMS *Seadog* during Operation 'Confidence' by Lieut. Alcock, 6 November 1945; Ian Alcock, 'Our Jungle Nightmare Ends', *Edmonton Journal*, Weekend Magazine, 12 January 1963, pp. 10, 20, 25, 30.

CHAPTER 43

1 TNA, DEFE 2/780, Record of the Small Operations Group, SEAC, by Lieut. Colonel H. G. Hasler, January 1946.

2 Courtney, *SBS*, p. 204.

3 Record of the Small Operations Group, SEAC, by Lieut. Colonel H. G. Hasler.

4 Southby-Tailyour, *Blondie*, p. 160.

5 Courtney, *SBS*, pp. 204–5.

6 Southby-Tailyour, *Blondie*, pp. 160–76.

7 Email exchange with SBS sources, 29 May 2020.

8 *By Strength and Guile*, pp. 6, 53.

9 Ibid., pp. 27–8.

10 *By Strength and Guile*, pp. 47, 125.

11 Field Marshal Viscount Slim, *Defeat into Victory* (London: Cassell & Company Ltd, 1956), pp. 626–7.

12 Courtney, *SBS*, p. 208.

13 *By Strength and Guile*, p. 85

AFTERMATH

1 Courtney, *SBS*, pp. 14–15, 146.

2 Rex Woods, *Special Commando: The Wartime Adventures of Lt Col Robert Wilson, DSO and Bar* (London: William Kimber & Co. Ltd, 1985), pp. 174–6.

3 Obituary of Major Harry Vere Holden-White, *Daily Telegraph*, 11 January 1999; email to author from Harriet O'Grady (Holden-White's daughter), 14 September 2021.

4 unithistories.com/officers/Army_officers_C02.html [accessed 26 May 2020].

5 Southby-Tailyour, *Blondie*, pp. 175–93; Rees, *Cockleshell Heroes*, pp. 154–7; Ashdown, *A Brilliant Little Operation*, pp. 339–42.

6 thetimes.co.uk/article/norman-colley-x68h9jm6f82 [accessed 27 May 2020].

7 unithistories.com/officers/RN_officersW4.html [accessed 27 May

2020]; nam.ac.uk/explore/nigel-clogstoun-willmott [accessed 27 May 2020].

8   Scott-Bowden, 'COPP to Normandy 1943/44', p. 18.

9   Ashcroft, *Special Forces Heroes*, pp. 125–6.

10 unithistories.com/officers/RNR_officersH.html [accessed 27 May 2020].

11 unithistories.com/officers/RCNVR_officers.html [accessed 27 May 2020]; Alcock, 'Our Jungle Nightmare Ends', p. 10.

12 Obituary of Colonel I. C. C. Mackenzie, the *Royal Engineers Journal*, 83/3 (September 1968), pp. 210–12.

13 unithistories.com/officers/RN_officersS3.html [accessed 27 May 2020].

14 thetimes.co.uk/article/rear-admiral-geoffrey-hall-dw58lz53rpm [accessed 27 May 2020].

15 independent.co.uk/news/obituaries/ruari-mclean-6104296.html [accessed 27 May 2020].

16 unithistories.com/officers/Army_officers_C02.html [accessed 27 May 2020].

17 A. I. Hughes Diary: 29 December 1944.

18 unithistories.com/officers/rn_officersl2.html; author interview with Jim Booth, 11 October 2019.

19 Author interview with Jim Booth, 11 October 2019.

Bibliography

PRIMARY SOURCES, UNPUBLISHED

Liddell Hart Centre for Military Archives (LHCMA), King's College, London
Papers of Major General Sir Robert E. Laycock
Papers of Brigadier Gerald C. S. Montanaro

Imperial War Museum (IWM), London
Private Papers of Captain A. F. L. Colson MBE
Private Papers of Lieutenant Commander A. I. Hughes DSC
Private Papers of Colonel T. B. Langton
James B. Sherwood (Oral History), Reels 1–6
Private Papers of Lieutenant S. Weatherall

National Army Museum (NAM), London
9203-218-108, 'The Compleat Folbotist' by Captain Roger Courtney, 21 August 1941
9203-218-111-1, Typescript translation of the 'Führer Befehl', Hitler's Commando Order of 18 October 1942

Private Papers (PP)
Paddy Ashdown Papers
M. J. Beckett Papers
Harry Holden-White Papers
Mike Peacock Papers

Royal Navy Submarine Museum (RNSM), Portsmouth
A19991/379, Richard Livingstone, 'Mark Clark's Secret Landing'

SBS Association Archives (SBSAA), Poole, Dorset

By Strength and Guile, privately printed handbook

Captain Derek Oakley, *Behind Japanese Lines: The Untold Story of the Royal Marine Detachment 385* (Portsmouth: Privately Published, 1996)

Service Records and Documents of Major R. J. A. Courtney

Service Records and Documents of Lieut Colonel H. G. Hasler

Service Records and Documents Lieut Commander H. N. C. Willmott

Serial No. 11, Transcription of interview with Lt Donald G. W. Slater, COPP 6, undated

Serial No. 45, Copy of Report Extracted from HQ Malaya Command Intelligence Summary: Suicide of Japanese Officers at Rengam

Serial No. 63, R. M. Detachment 385 Diary

Serial No. 69, Operation 'Frankton'

Serial No. 71, Peter Palmer, 'Algeria & Malta – 1943 – COPPs 3 & 4'

The National Archives (TNA), Kew, London

ADM 1/14319, Awards for Operation 'Reservist'

ADM 179/323, Reconnaissance Report on Operation 'Postage Able'

ADM 179/354, Operation 'KJH'

ADM 179/475, Operation 'Gambit'

ADM 199/1820, Patrol Reports of HM Submarines *United* and *Unbeaten*, 1941–1945

ADM 199/1821, Patrol Reports of HM Submarines *Ultor, Union, Undine, Upshot* and *Unrivalled*, 1939–1944

ADM 199/1826, Patrol Reports of HM Submarines *Unbroken* and *Unbending*, 1941–1944

ADM 199/1841, Patrol Reports of HM Submarines *Sceptre, Seraph* and *Sinoon*, 1942–1944

ADM 199/1848, Patrol Reports of HM Submarines *Turbulent, Tempest, Thistle, Triumph* and *Thorn*, 1939–1943

ADM 199/1865, Patrol Reports of HM Submarines *Trenchant*, *Tactician*, and *Taciturn*, 1943–1945

ADM 199/1922, Patrol Reports of HMS *Utmost*, 1941–1945

ADM 236/15, Patrol Reports of HM Submarines *Shalimar* and *Seadog*, 1944–1945

ADM 236/24, Patrol Reports of HMS *Taku*, 1941–1943

ADM 236/26, Patrol Reports of HM Submarines *Talisman* and *Thorn*, 1942.

ADM 236/31, Patrol Reports of HMS *Thrasher*, February–August 1945

ADM 236/32, Patrol Reports of HMS *Torbay*, 1941–1942

ADM 236/36, Patrol Reports of HMS *Triumph*, 1941

ADM 236/37, Patrol Reports of HMS *Truant*, 1940–1942

ADM 236/50, Patrol Reports of HMS *Urge*, 1941–1942

ADM 358/681, Admiralty Casualty Branch: Inquiries into Missing Personnel, 1939–1945

DEFE 2/45, War Diary of the 4th Special Service Battalion, December 1940

DEFE 2/95, Operations 'Baboon' and 'Copywright'

DEFE 2/218, Operation 'Frankton'

DEFE 2/349, Operation 'Flipper'

DEFE 2/531, Operation 'Reservist'

DEFE 2/569, Operations 'Spratt Able' and 'Spratt Baker'

DEFE 2/740, Special Boat Unit: Reports, Diaries etc.

DEFE 2/780, Histories and Accounts of Small Operations Group in South East Asia, 1944–1945

DEFE 2/842, Folbot Canoes, 1940–1943

DEFE 2/971, COPP Organisation, 1942–1945

DEFE 2/1059, X-craft in Combined Operations

DEFE 2/1111, COPP Progress Reports and Honours and Awards

DEFE 2/1116, COPP Reports and History

HS 1/254, Operation 'Hornbill/Rimau'

HS7/26, Operation 'Sunbeam A'

WO 218/8, War Diary of No. 8 Commando, July–November 1940

WO 218/170, War Diary of No. 8 Commando (B Battalion, Layforce), January–March 1941

WO 373/100, Recommendations for Honours and Awards, 1945–1946

PRIMARY SOURCES, PUBLISHED

Published Documents, Diaries, Letters and Memoirs

Chapman, Paul, *Submarine Torbay* (London: Robert Hale, 1989)

Churchill, Winston S., *The Second World War*, 6 vols (London: Cassell, 1948–54)

Clark, Mark W., *Calculated Risk: His Personal Story of the War in North Africa and Italy* (London: Harrap, 1951)

Colville, Jock, *The Fringes of Power: 10 Downing Street Diaries 1939–1955* (London: Hodder & Stoughton, 1985)

Courtney, G. B., *SBS in World War Two* (London: Robert Hale, 1983; repr. 2017)

Courtney, Roger, *Africa Calling: The True Account of the Author's Strange Workaday Experiences in Kenya, Uganda and the Belgian Congo* (London: George Harrap & Co., 1935)

——, *African Argosy* (London: Herbert Jenkins, 1953)

——, *Claws of Africa: Experiences of a Professional Big-game Hunter* (London: George G. Harrap, 1934)

——, *Palestine Policeman: An Account of Eighteen Dramatic Months in the Palestine Police Force during the Great Jew–Arab Troubles* (London: Herbert Jenkins Ltd, 1939)

Cunningham, Viscount, *A Sailor's Odyssey* (London: Hutchinson, 1951)

Danchev, Alex, and Daniel Todman (eds), *War Diaries 1939–1945: Field Marshal Lord Alanbrooke* (London: Weidenfeld, 2001)

Davie, Michael (ed.), *The Diaries of Evelyn Waugh* (London: Weidenfeld & Nicolson, 1976)

Eisenhower, Dwight D., *Crusade in Europe* (New York: Doubleday, 1948; repr. 1997)

Grehan, John, and Martin Mace (eds), *The War in Italy 1943–1944: Despatches from the Front* (Barnsley: Pen & Sword, 2014)

Hall, Geoffrey, *Sailor's Luck: At Sea & Ashore in Peace & War* (Durham: The Memoir Club, 1999)

Kesselring, Albert, *The Memoirs of Field Marshal Kesselring* (London: William Kimber, 1953)

Liddell Hart, B. H. (ed.), *The Rommel Papers* (London: Collins, 1953; repr. 1987)

Montgomery of Alamein, Field Marshal Viscount, *Memoirs of Field Marshal Montgomery* (London: Collins, 1958)

Neville [Stanbury], Ralph, *Survey by Starlight: A true story of reconnaissance work in the Mediterranean* (London: Hodder & Stoughton, 1949)

Newby, Eric, *A Traveller's Life* (London: Collins, 1982)

Reeves, Dennis, *Special Service of a Hazardous Nature* (Warrington: Liverpool Scottish Museum, 2007)

Scott-Bowden, Major General L., 'COPP to Normandy 1943/44 – A Personal Account of Part of the Story', in *The Royal Engineers Journal*, 108/1 (April 1944), 10–18

Simpson, George, *Periscope View: A Remarkable Memoir of the 10th Submarine Flotilla at Malta 1941–1943* (London: Macmillan, 1972; repr. 2010)

Sparks, William, *The Last of the Cockleshell Heroes* (London: Leo Cooper, 1992)

Vian, Sir Philip, *Action this Day: A War Memoir* (London: Frederick Muller, 1960)

Newspapers and Journals
Daily Telegraph
Edmonton Journal
Independent
London Gazette (Supplement)
Royal Engineers Journal
Sunday Telegraph
The Times

SECONDARY SOURCES

Books and Articles

Ambrose, Stephen E., *The Supreme Commander: The War Years of Dwight D. Eisenhower* (New York: Random House, 1969; repr. 2012)

Ashcroft, Michael, *Special Forces Heroes* (London: Headline, 2008)

Ashdown, Paddy, *A Brilliant Little Operation: The Cockleshell Heroes and the Most Courageous Raid of WW2* (London: Aurum, 2012)

Asher, Michael, *Get Rommel: The Secret British Mission to Kill Hitler's Greatest General* (London: Weidenfeld & Nicolson, 2004; repr. 2005)

Atkinson, Rick, *An Army at Dawn: The War in North Africa, 1942–1943* (New York: Macmillan USA, 2002; ebook 2003)

Beevor, Antony, *The Second World War* (London: Weidenfeld & Nicolson, 2012)

Buckingham, William F., *Arnhem 1944: A Reappraisal* (Stroud: Tempus, 2002)

Fergusson, Bernard, *The Watery Maze: The Story of Combined Operations* (London: Collins, 1961)

Hastings, Max, *All Hell Let Loose: The World at War 1939–1945* (London: HarperPress, 2011)

Howarth, David, *Dawn of D-Day* (London: Companion Book Club, 1959)

Izzard, Brian, *Gamp VC: The Wartime Story of Maverick Submarine Commander Anthony Miers* (Yeovil: Haynes, 2009)

Key, David M., Jr, *Admiral Jerauld Wright: Warrior Among Diplomats* (Manhattan, KS: Sunflower University Press, 2001)

Ladd, James D., *Commandos and Rangers of World War II* (London: Macdonald and Jane's, 1978)

——, *SBS: The Invisible Raiders* (London: Arms and Armour, 1983)

Lett, Brian, *The Small Scale Raiding Force* (Barnsley: Pen & Sword, 2013)

Lodwick, John, *The Filibusters: The Story of the Special Boat Service* (London: Methuen & Co., 1947; repr. 2018)

Lyman, Robert, *The Real X-Men: The Heroic Story of the Underwater War 1942–1945* (London: Quercus, 2015)

Macintyre, Ben, *SAS: Rogue Heroes* (London: Penguin, 2016; repr. 2017)

Mortimer, Gavin, *The SBS in World War II* (Oxford: Osprey, 2013)

Owen, James, *Commando: Winning World War II Behind Enemy Lines* (London: Little, Brown, 2012; repr. 2013)

Parker, John, *SBS: The Inside Story of the Special Boat Service* (London: Headline, 1997; repr. 2004)

Pitt, Barrie, *Special Boat Squadron* (London: Century, 1983; repr. 2018)

Rees, Quentin, *Cockleshell Heroes: The Final Witness* (Stroud: Amberley, 2010)

Roberts, Andrew, *Masters and Commanders: How Roosevelt, Churchill, Marshall and Alanbrooke Won the War in the West* (London: Allen Lane, 2008)

Seymour, William, *British Special Forces* (London: Sidgwick & Jackson, 1985)

Southby-Tailyour, Ewen, *Blondie: A Life of Lieutenant Colonel H. G. Hasler* (London: Leo Cooper, 1998; repr. 2003)

Strutton, Bill, and Michael Pearson, *The Secret Invaders* (London: Hodder & Stoughton, 1958; repr. 1961)

Thompson, Leroy, *SAS: Great Britain's Elite Special Air Service* (London: Zenith, 1994)

Trenowden, Ian, *Stealthily by Night: The COPPists – Clandestine Beach Reconnaissance in World War II* (London: Crecy, 1995; ebook 2012)

Websites
combinedops.com/Black%20Hackle.htm [accessed 24 January 2020]
commandoveterans.org/2SBS_timeline [accessed 5 February 2020]
gallery.commandoveterans.org/cdoGallery/v/WW2/sbs/Capt+douglas+sidders+MC++2+sbs++jr.jpg.html [accessed 29 April 2020]
commandoveterans.org/EdwardWesleySBS [accessed 1 May 2020]
commandoveterans.org/raid_sicily_railway_bridge [accessed 9 January 2020]

commandoveterans.org/GeraldMontanaro6Commando [accessed 29 December 2020]

coppheroes.org/individuals/palmer-p.htm [accessed 13 September 2019]

forces-war-records.co.uk/prisoners-of-war-of-the-japanese-1939-1945 [accessed 6 May 2020]

gallery.commandoveterans.org/cdoGallery/v/WW2/sbs/ obituary+lunnmc628+copy.jpg.html [accessed 24 April 2020]

hambo.org.kingscanterbury/view_man.php?id=28 [accessed 31 March 2020]

maltagc70.wordpress.com/tag/hms-st-angelo/ [accessed 31 March 2020]

nam.ac.uk/explore/nigel-clogstoun-willmott [accessed 27 May 2020]

navyhistory.org.au/occasional-paper-46-lieutenant-kenneth-robert-hudspeth-dsc-ranvr/ [accessed 9 April 2020]

navyhistory.org.au/x-craft-x20-in-the-english-channel/ [accessed 9 October 2019]

specialforcesroh.com/showthread.php?40533-Kealy-Michael-Robert-Bayley [accessed 23 April 2020]

southafricawargraves.org/search/print.php?id=5336 [accessed 31 March 2020] uboat.net/allies/merchants/ship/2398.html [accessed 24 February 2020]

unithistories.com/officers/Army_officers_C02.html [accessed 13 December 2019 and 11 April 2020]

unithistories.com/officers/RN_officersW4.html [accessed 27 May 2020]

unithistories.com/officers/RCNVR_officers.html [accessed 27 May 2020]

veterans.gc.ca/eng/remembance/memorials/canadian-virtual-war-memorial/detail/2069361 [accessed 30 June 2020]

Index

Page numbers for Illustrations are in *italics*.